Byron Berline

A Fiddler's Diary

By Byron Berline with Jane Frost

NEW FORUMS

NEW FORUMS PRESS INC.

Published in the United States of America
by New Forums Press, Inc.1018 S. Lewis St.
Stillwater, OK 74074
www.newforums.com

Library of Congress Cataloging-in-Publication Data Pending

This book may be ordered in bulk quantities at discount from New
Forums Press, Inc., P.O. Box 876, Stillwater, OK 74076 [Federal I.D.
No. 73 1123239]. Printed in the United States of America.

ISBN 10: 1-58107-245-7
ISBN 13: 978-1-581072-45-7

Table of Contents

Dedication .... *vi*

Preface .... *vii*

Foreword .... *ix*

Chapter 1 1944 – 1958: Growing up on the Farm
and Learning to play the Fiddle 1

Chapter 2 1958 -1962: High School 15

Chapter 3 1962 – 1963: OU Football and Meeting
the Dillards 25

Chapter 4 1964: A Summer to Remember 35

Chapter 5 1964-1966: College Bands - Newport
Folk Festival 41

Chapter 6 1967: Playing with Bill Monroe 55

Chapter 7 1967-1968: Army Life 69

Journal Entries

1969–Culture Shock - Recording with the Rolling
Stones – Dillard and Clark Expedition 81

1970–Huckleberry Hornpipe – Charting Music
for Charles Manson - Nitty Gritty Dirt Band 95

1971–The Dillard Expedition – Flying Burrito Brothers 106

1972–United Artists Signs Country Gazette – Flying
Burrito Brothers Tour Europe – Traitor in our Midst 123

1973–The Year the Music Died – Clarence White –
Gram Parsons 133

1974–130 Days on the Road with Country Gazette 153

1975–Arnold Schwarzenegger – Sundance –
L.A. Fiddle Band 162

1976–Bluegrass Symphony – Kris Kristofferson –
Vince Gill..172

1977–Dad's Favorites - Mary Kay Place - Elvis 182

1978–Filming "The Rose" with Bett Midler 189

1979–The Palomino - Other Road Stories............................194

1980–Outrageous – You Bet Your Life................................201

1981–Cecil and a Fugue – Tex Williams – Scotland
and Ireland..206

1982–Youllneverplaythevalleyagain – Moonshine 215

1983–Australia – Africa – China – Canada..........................224

1984–Jo El' Sonje – My Last Beer....................................230

1985–Traveling the Globe 235

1986–Stone's Rag – Double Trouble – Cinderella..................241

1987–Dealing in Instruments – Europe – Woody Paul..........245

1988–Kevin Costner - Texas Trail Ride -
Indian Reservation...251

1989–Doo Wah Golf – Walk in the Irish Rain –
South Pacific 256

1990–A New Band Called California 268

1991–A Killer Waltz – Basic Instinct – Christmas
in Connecticut 275

1992–California's Traveler 282

1993–John Hickman Philosophy......................................289

1994–Nickel Creek – Burt Reynolds – Earl Scruggs and
Bill Monroe Recording Together 296

1995–Moving to Guthrie – Chiggers 307

1996–Girdiasis Bug – Byron Berline Band –
Music Hall Opens 316

1997–Bosco and the Tippy Truck – Oklahoma
International Bluegrass Festival - Fiddle Fest....................323

1998–Mae Axton Award 329

1999–Vince Gill and I Induct Each Other Into the
Oklahoma Music Hall of Fame....................................334

2000–Byron Berline Band in Europe – OU National
Champions..338

2001–Cain's Ballroom 341

2002–Byron Berline Band in New York City –
Fiddle Heaven in Italy 343

2003–Western Swing Show 348

2004–A Byrd and a Fish 351

2005–Deadwood – Byron Berline Band in China 354

2006–The Red Diamond Stradivarius 360

2007–Oklahoma Centennial – Getting to Stage 5 365

2008–Record Disks to CDs 369

2009–Earl Scruggs at the Banjo Museum - Texas Shorty 372

2010–Happy Birthday Contest Tune –
Hole in One – Ambassador of Creativity 375

Epilogue 383

Epigraph 384

Index 385

Dedication

Mom and Dad
Byron Berline

Maddison and Haley
Jane Frost

Preface

When Bette and I moved to Guthrie in 1995, I was approached to write a book. The writer was into music and sports, so he thought it would be a fun project for both of us. However, the project never saw the light of day and afterwards I never thought much about it again. At the Oklahoma International Bluegrass Festival in 2010, Jane Frost asked if she could collaborate with me on a book of my adventures and I said yes. I had enjoyed reading Jane's biography of Patsy Montana and knew she would do a good job. So, here we are a couple of years later and a lot of work and jogging of memories. I personally, had never thought about writing down my adventures and memories, but when I would tell some of my old war stories, people would comment, "Why don't you write a book?" Well, here it is finally…enjoy.

Byron Berline

I published *Patsy Montana, The Cowboy's Sweetheart* in 2002. I gave Byron a copy and he liked Patsy's book. Although I have known Byron for 30 years, I never thought about writing his story until visiting in Guthrie, Oklahoma in 2010. Someone asked me about whom I would next be writing and it was then, that I started thinking about writing with Byron. I began pre-research by ordering albums, photographs, magazine and newspaper articles as well as reading numerous, related books. As a bluegrass fan, I was familiar with Byron's music and many of the players. When confident Byron's biography would be an important book, I approached him. He was enthusiastic and we immediately began making plans.

My husband and I had purchased a motor home two years earlier, which was important, because Byron is not retired and if he is not playing somewhere or recording, he is busy with his Doublestop Fiddle Shop. I would need to be in Guthrie while writing the manuscript.

As I am a researcher first, I wanted the book to be well documented. Byron wanted to finally, have written down all the road stories he has told and retold over the years. When he found Bette's journal entries, we were delighted. As a result, *Byron Berline, A Fiddler's Diary* is a chronicle of recording sessions, shows and tours, sprinkled liberally with road stories, prefaced with a description of his life on the family farm, learning to play the fiddle, college life at the University of Oklahoma and his Army life.

Byron is a pleasure to work with and I loved every jam at the fiddle shop, which interrupted our writing sessions. Impromptu concerts were fringe benefits.

As I approached completion of film school and needed to go home to the Ozarks to complete my student film, I knew it would mean missing writing time with Byron. I told him that the only way I could stay in Guthrie and finish the film would be for me to write a new opening and ending to the film and shoot those scenes in Guthrie. As I knew few people in town, I asked if he, John Hickman and the Hunt Brothers would be in it. He and the others quickly agreed. I wrote the new opening and ending and within a few days, we were shooting. We tied up Byron's fiddle shop for an entire afternoon, as well as his time.

I wrapped the film, sent it to my instructor and received my certification.

I told you Byron and I have been friends for a long time. Now you know why.

Jane Frost

Foreword

I am honored to write the foreword for the autobiography of Byron Berline, one of my fiddling heroes! I first met Byron in 1974 when I was 12 years-old when I was lucky enough to have him play guitar for me in the Langley, Oklahoma fiddle contest (competing against his brother!) Later that weekend I got to jam with him at one of the camp sites at the festival, and it was the first time we played the famous fiddle tunes "Sally Goodwin" and "Limerock" together. Being from Seattle, this festival in 1974 was the very first time I was in the South of the United States.

Over the next few years, I got to play often with Byron at festivals and other events. These occasions were some of my most treasured memories as a young fiddler. One of the highlights for me was the very next year in 1975 when we had the 4-fiddle jam set at Bob Baxter's Festival in Los Angeles along with John Hartford and Richard Green. I got to make a recording with Byron later the following year in 1976 with Sam Bush joining us. A true highlight for Byron and I was to re-record "Gold Rush" for the "Heroes" album in 1992 on twin fiddles. We were lucky enough to have Bill Monroe on the session as well.

Byron was able to wear several hats as a professional fiddler, and he was a great role model for me to be around. I have tried to emulate his career in many ways as well. As a teenager I saw close up as to what a natural band leader he was with his groups. He was one of the top session fiddlers in Los Angeles for many years. Byron came out of the fiddle competition scene winning the Weiser, Idaho National Old-Time Fiddler's Contest, so the competition fiddling was something I already had in common with my hero as a teen. He was also very well known in Bluegrass and his transition from old-time fiddling to bluegrass seemed effortless. This specific transition was something I was dealing with too as I was getting into bluegrass as a young teen. Byron was central to the country music scene in California. I admired how he could navigate between all of these things. He even was a guest with orchestras and intersected into that world too. He was a tune writer, wrote some songs, improvised, played the fast and slow stuff equally great. He was everywhere and doing everything, all at the top of the scene. For my eventual career path, he was a great inspiration. My teachers were the legendary Benny Thomasson who really stayed close to the Texas Fiddle genre mostly and the iconic Stephane Grappelli who I performed with and was mentored by, staying in the jazz genre almost exclusively. But Byron's career and the way he was able to take his own style and sound to various musical settings, was the one that I wanted to emulate for my career.

Byron Berline was born July 6, 1944, in Caldwell, Kansas. He remembers fiddling since he was a baby, then starting regular lessons from his dad when he was five. Lue Berline began to take his son to fiddle contests around the area and met misfortune, or fortune depending on how he looked at it, when ten-year-old Byron beat him down in Oklahoma! Byron went on to participate in many contests around the country. In 1953, he met Benny Thomasson in Truth or Consequences, New Mexico, and in 1960 he met more of the great Texas fiddlers at contests in Tatum, New Mexico, and Hale Center, Texas. People like Eck Robertson, Major and Louis Franklin, and Vernon and Norman Solomon had a great impact on young Byron. He went on to win a big contest in Missoula, Montana, in 1964 and the National Old Time Fiddler's Contest in 1965 and 1970 in Weiser, Idaho.

It was when Byron attended the University of Oklahoma in 1962 that he started getting into bluegrass music. The folk boom helped revive bluegrass during this time and one of the younger groups that came on the scene was The Dillards. Byron met them in 1963 and they recorded an album together the next year called Pickin' and Fiddlin'. This is the record that introduced me to Byron's fiddling when I was eleven. Byron met Bill Monroe when he and his dad were playing at the Newport Folk Festival in 1965. After graduating from college in 1967, he played with Monroe for seven months before being drafted into the army. During that time he and Monroe wrote the fiddle tune, "Gold Rush," which was released as a single with "Virginia Darlin" on the flip side. The rest will be in his biography!

The most fun I ever had playing twin fiddles was with Byron. The drive and bounce he creates in the rhythm of his playing makes it so appealing. Byron's bowing is certainly the most powerful anywhere, while keeping a clean and beautiful tone. That, combined with his double stops at quick tempos and his perfect pitch, is quite thrilling to listen to. His own arrangements of fiddle tunes have given them all a new ring. Byron's bright and uplifting personality reflects so much in his music that you just can't help but smile. Enjoy reading about the life and music of one of the great fiddlers in American history!

Mark O'Connor
Musician, Performer, Composer

Byron is one of the greatest musicians I have ever known and one of my dearest friends. He has played and recorded with some of the best musicians in the world.

Byron is very versatile and plays with soul. He projects a feeling with his musicianship, that complemented other musicians he was playing with.

He played the old fiddle tunes...exactly, as they were written.

Douglas Dillard
Musician/Performer/Songwriter

The WE FIVE had a recording session for our new album, "Catch the Wind" in 1970 for Vault Records. Byron played fiddle on the last cut, "Milk Cow Blues" and I still get chills just thinking about it.

Jerry Burgan
Performer

I understand the L.A. culture shock. I went from Topeka, Kansas to the Los Angeles area. Byron Berline has been my hero since high school.

Jim Triggs-Luthier

Many have kind words and raves for Byron Berline. These words are not just compliments; they are facts. His music makes people happy, he plays hot and inspired, has his own style that compliments any song that goes through his strings, and he is a nice guy!

The first time I saw Byron Berline perform was 1965, with The Dillards in Orange County, Calif. I was a teenage banjo picker trying to learn notes from the incredible Doug Dillard and Berline came out with them and played Hamilton County Breakdown, from their new album together. "Oh, my God!" I thought, "That's how real live fiddle playing is! And how a banjo can be used with it!" It was one of the most exciting things I had ever heard. I had heard L.A. bluegrass, but it was not the same. They'd swing the bat, but he knocked it out of the park with every soulful bow stroke. I was at a record store the next day waiting for it to open so I could get that album.

Byron plays at a master's level, with amazing tone and attack. He was the first I heard to play freeform (improvise/ jamming)…and in that magic space that makes notes exciting. I've never heard a bad note from his fiddle…and, even though it seems incongruous…those big hands speeding up and down the delicate fingerboard against the tiny separation of strings make magic music.

If lucky enough to play with Byron, you will play better; he brings out the best abilities of players joining him. Some of my best playing was with Berline. He probably thought I was recording him (the many times I have made it work out to do so) because I just 'needed a fiddle', not knowing I really wanted to hear him play live.

On the 1970 Nitty Gritty Dirt Band "Uncle Charlie and His Dog Teddy," album I hired Byron. I felt like I had a master of the Flatt & Scruggs level, a legend to me before he became one, making my music sound hot. Byron had to go into the studio to overdub, record his fiddle onto the Dirt Band's already cut Randy Lynn Rag, and make it sound like he was playing hot and live with the band.

Flawlessly, with all of the excitement of a live performance, he did it in one take. Byron, I miss playing with you. You are a constant inspiration both as the kind person you are and for you exquisite talents with that fiddle you have made a part of your life...and thankfully, for some recorded moments, it became a part of mine.

John McEuen
Nitty Gritty Dirt Band

All the awards, credits and accolades aside, it can be said of Byron Berline that he is simply a super nice fellow from Oklahoma whose fiddle playing changed the face of American roots music. When I look at all the recordings I have in my collection on which his astounding work made an impact, I have to sit back in wonder. I actually had the privilege of being included on some of those sessions and got to watch things go down with the powerful, effortless and silky technique that is his alone. The Irish musicians call him "Strongbow" for good reason. Some people make the music business worth all the effort. Byron is one of those unique people, and I am blessed to call him friend.

Steve Spurgin
Songwriter/Performer

I have known Byron since the '70s when he lived in the Los Angeles area. Byron and I lived near one another in the San Fernando Valley. There is so much great music history from that era, so many band combinations and Byron was right in the middle of it all. Byron's place was known for great jams, all of which I was a part and we also worked together on recording projects.

The thing that stands out to me is when in 1978 I was recording my " Houndog Ramble" Dobro instrumental album, on which Byron plays fiddle. I did not have a guitar player and asked Byron if he knew of one for the session. On the day of the session, Byron introduced me to a fella that I had not met before, it was Vince Gill. It was not long into the session that I realized this guy was not just a rhythm guitar player and we quickly did some arrangement changes and Vince laid down some really cool guitar breaks. The last time I played with Byron was 2005 at his festival in Guthrie, OK. It was a real treat to sit in with his band. Byron it's been a pleasure to know you and you are still the king of "Sally Goodin."

Your friend and fellow picker,
LeRoy Mack McNees
Musician, Performer

There have been plenty of fine fiddlers in this country in its 200+ years of existence. Thomas Jefferson was said to have been a fiddler, though no contemporary made any comments as to whether he could keep good time, and he made his way in another line of work.

Byron Berline has stood out for me as being among the country's best to ever draw a bow across the strings, and I've heard plenty of fiddlers in my day. I first met Byron in the spring of 1967, when he was a Blue Grass Boy, performing with Bill Monroe during one of Bill's shows I presented in California at UCSB. The rumors I'd heard about his flashy Oklahoma-style fiddle breaks were confirmed, and I could tell that Bill was pleased to have Byron in his band.

Later, Byron moved to Los Angeles and found work in this nation's "entertainment capitol", both with his various bands and in radio, TV, and recording studios. He was quickly recognized as a musical resource, of course by fellow musicians, but also by people normally immune or blase regarding virtuoso musical performance. He was able to work out a balance between his musical and his business skills, making his way through the pitfalls of a life in Hollywood's entertainment industry while remaining a great musician and a decent human being. And that is no easy task!

What immediately became obvious to me was his musical fluidity and inventiveness, his respect for those who had played before him, and his seeming effortlessness as he performed. I could see that perhaps twenty years' practice could give him the command of the finger board, but it seemed that he would have to have lived more than one lifetime to develop that amazing bowing arm he displays, and to me, it was a confirmation of the Eastern philosophical concept of eternal recurrence --- which states that we must live our lives over and over until we get it right. Byron's home was for years an oasis of warmth and musicality in LA, and it was always a pleasure to visit Byron, Bette, and Becca in Van Nuys and to embark on musical adventures. Although I miss his proximity here in California, I know that his friends and family have welcomed him back to Guthrie. Indeed, Byron is a musical treasure for the entire nation, and it's wonderful that he and Jane Frost have written this well-deserved book.

Peter Feldmann
Musician, Performer, Musical Historian

I met Byron just after he recorded "Pickin' and Fiddlin'" with The Dillards. I think that was around 1966? I was very impressed with his fiddle playing, as I'm sure most people were here in L.A. Byron always had a smooth style, applicable to both Swing and Bluegrass. He left a big hole here in Los Angeles when he moved back to Guthrie.

Herb Pedersen
Musician, Performer

I first met Byron Berline in 1967, when I unexpectedly became a temporary member of Bill Monroe's Blue Grass Boys, and was thrown together with Byron for a couple of days before leaving on a west coast tour. I was young, very naive, eager but pretty inexperienced, but Byron showed me nothing but gracious acceptance, patience, and kindness. Even though he was a nationally known fiddle champion and I was just a college kid in over my head he spent time and energy teaching me fiddle tunes and helping me become a better musician and performer. I have never forgotten that generosity of spirit and I think it says a great deal about Byron the man. We know plenty about Byron the musician, but his unselfish helping hand and open spirit meant the world to me, and it speaks volumes about his character.

Ranger Doug
Riders In The Sky

What can you say about someone you've known and played music with for 36 years, except not enough, so here goes!
We played a lot of music together, (135) shows & (40) of 'em

with symphony orchestras! A consummate musician, he happened to be, lucky for me, a quintessential source of inspiration for the idea behind the Bluegrass Band & Symphony Concerts we performed together. Not only was he a great performer, some of our best charts were based on his fiddle melodies, harmony lines & arrangement ideas. He also has a great stage presence, knows to keep things moving and can take a joke, or deliver one! Our "Crabgrass" (band only) gigs were always fun & challenging, forcing us to keep learning new material. Byron is inspiring to play music with, or to hang out with & talk shop (since he runs one, that can cover a lot). Across the fiddle, the bow couldn't ask for a better friend, & across the board, I couldn't either.

Mason Williams
Musician, composer,
writer, performer

Chapter 1

1944 – 1958: Growing up on the Farm and Learning to play the Fiddle

At noon, on September 16, 1893, Henry Berline became one of over 100,000 hopefuls making the Land Rush into Oklahoma Territory. Caldwell, Kansas was one of nine points where the Land Rush began and many traveled long distances as quickly as possible over rough terrain, on a hot and dusty day. Fortunately, Henry Berline Sr. and his wife, Luzetta Wood Berline, only had to cover a short distance of ten miles. They staked their claim and from that day in 1893, their homestead has been the Berline Family Farm. Over 100 years old, it remains in the Berline family today. Seven months after my grandparents made the land run and began homesteading, my dad, Lue George Berline, was born April 11, 1894.

It took about six months to build a sod house out of wild prairie grass sod. They cut strips of sod about a foot wide, four inches thick and then laid them, grass side down, like bricks to make the walls of the "soddy." When dad was old enough, he attended a sod schoolhouse. Sod structures were not very big, but safe from the weather and homesteaders continued building this way until well into the 1900's. There is one original sod house remaining on the Oklahoma prairie, built in 1894, about the time grandfather built his sod house. Preserved by the Oklahoma Historical Society, you can see it at the Sod House Museum in Aline, Oklahoma. The Berlines eventually built a farmhouse and my siblings and I grew up in that home.

Dad's mother came from Illinois and his dad came from Germany, so my dad was the first Berline generation born in this country. My mom, Ann Elizabeth Jackson Berline, came from Kentucky.

Musicians in the Berline family began with dad. Lue Berline began playing the five-string banjo when he was a teenager. In 1912 or 1913, when he was about eighteen or nineteen years old, his dad took him to a dance and told him that if, he wanted to amount to anything, "Play the fiddle." In other words, play the fiddle not the banjo. Dad sent off to Montgomery Ward or Sears and Roebuck and got a fiddle through a mail order catalogue. He learned to play the instrument and read music by taking lessons from an old black man living in Caldwell, Kansas, the nearest town. He also learned from the Watson boys living about three quarters of a mile from the Berline farm. The way you learned back then was through your neighbors and friends…you only rode a horse so far and that was it. There were no radios, record players, or electricity to run them.

After learning to play the banjo and fiddle, dad picked up the guitar. Mom played the piano and often accompanied dad when he entered fiddle contests and played at various social functions. He began entering fiddle contests and winning in 1930, many years before I was born. Sometimes he played up to six barn dances a week after working all day on the farm.

I was very fortunate to come from a musical family.

I grew up with four older siblings, Henry, my oldest brother, born in 1931, then Leonard, my sisters Eleanor and Janice, and then me.

I was born Byron Douglas Berline, July 6, 1944 in Caldwell, Kansas; dad was fifty years old. My first memory is that of having coal oil lamps and candles for lights; we did not yet have electricity on the farm. I vaguely remember that. Music, I remember always hearing music.

The top 40 hits of 1944 reflected the World War II years, especially from Bing Crosby and the Andrew Sisters, Maxine, Patty, and LaVerne. Bing had several hits including "I'll Be Seeing You" and one, perhaps a peak at my future, "San Fernando Valley."

Here is another of my earliest memories and I was probably only about three or four years old. I crawled on the floor under

Mom and Dad, Elizabeth and Lue Berline, taken in the early 1960s.

dad's legs and grabbed the fiddle bow while he played. He sat me between his legs, brought the fiddle around and put it up under my chin then brought the bow around and put it in my hand. Then he played it, as if I was playing the fiddle and I thought that was special. I have done that with kids and they remember it.

Another early memory is that of a man with a wagon and team of horses who lived on our road and he went up and down the road delivering ice for iceboxes. This was before we had electric refrigerators.

Henry and Leonard got into a big car wreck when I was four or five years old. It was a 1930's Ford, our family car and they rolled it. Henry landed on a barbed wire fence and when they got home, all skinned up, dad doused horse liniment all over them. He used Absorbine Senior and he put it on everything. Oh the smell, it just filled the house!

Dad grew up working the farm and was around horses all his life. He never liked them and got tired of taking care of them. When I lived on the farm, we grew wheat and had cattle; purebred registered short horns, chickens, dogs, and cats, but we never had horses. He would not even buy me a pony. Many of my friends had horses and I wanted one, so bad. They even rode them to school. Although it is not important now, at the time it was.

When I was small, my chore was to find and gather the eggs. It scared me to death to have to go into some of those dark places in the barn, like a manger; I imagined a snake in every nest. Although we had cattle, we only had one milk cow and I went out to the barn with Henry or Leonard every morning and night at milking time. When I got a little older, I did the milking and eventually did all the chores on the farm.

Even before I played the fiddle I sang, "Sioux City Sue" or "Fifty Cents," some of the old songs and dad always played for PTA meetings, pie suppers, and square dances.

They remodeled the farmhouse in 1949. I remember that! They put in indoor plumbing! I was five years old and the house was I do not know how old and we got a radio. There was a local station out of Wichita, Kansas we could pick up. We always listened to country music. Mornings we listened to Lester Flatt and Earl Scruggs, then Bob Wills at noon. KITO in Vinita, Oklahoma still plays Bob Wills at noon.

Five is also the age I started playing the fiddle and the first tune I learned was "Mississippi Sawyer." It was the easiest tune dad knew. He evidently did not know "Boil the Cabbage Down" because I never heard him play it. The way he taught...I just watched him play. He played and then would say, "Now you try it." I sat there and really watched his fingers. Okay, he is putting his fingers here and there, then this... I do not think dad really knew how to teach fiddle playing; not many people do, very well. I am laughing. Nevertheless, he showed me how to play and that was okay. Fiddle playing has been a wonderful vocation and has allowed me to do and see things that I would never have imagined. It all began in those early years of training at home and with friends. I

eventually learned to play the fiddle with mother's help and encouragement. Then I learned "Rag Time Annie." That and "Mississippi Sawyer" are both old time fiddle tunes and they are included, as dad taught them to me, in my "Fiddling Thru the Years," songbook. The original publication had a companion cassette tape but technology caught up with me and now it comes with a CD.

After you learn a couple of things by memory you just play

Byron, age 4, Christmas of 1948; one year before learning to play the fiddle. *From the Berline Collection.*

them, you do not think much about it and that is the way kids do things. It is like reciting a poem; it is just there. Once I learned a couple of tunes, when people came to the house, it was, "Okay, come in, you've got to play for everybody." I did not hate it, but I did not want to quit playing outside with the kids.

Bob Berline is my first cousin and his dad Lee, is my dad's brother. Bob gave me my first fiddle, a half size and I still have it. The tailpiece broke and stayed that way for six months although I kept asking dad to fix it. He finally drilled a hole on the end and used some wire to hold it…that wire is still on it. I played that fiddle for maybe a year or two and went right to a full size.

When I started school at age six, Janice was still in grade school, but Henry, Leonard, and Eleanor were already in high school. Janice went with me to the rural school for two years, before she entered high school. The rural school went from first through the eighth grade and then we all went to high school in Caldwell, Kansas.

Where we went to grade school was unusual because there was a school located a little west of our farm and another one to the south. One school was about one and a half miles from our farm and the other about two miles. Every semester we changed and went to the other school and that way it was equal distance for everyone. Depending on which school was closest, kids did not have to go so far to school for an entire school year…just every other semester.

Everyone brought their lunch every day…the school had no cafeteria. They heated the schoolhouse in winter with a coal-burning stove and the kids gathered kindling to start the coal burning. There were horse barns for those who rode horses to school, but by the time I attended not many kids rode horses — someone drove them to school or they rode bicycles and I remember walking to school a few times.

I also remember playing on stage for the very first time when I was seven years old, in 1951 at the Sumner County Fair in Caldwell, Kansas. I knew I had to play, was scared to death and I had to go to the bathroom every ten minutes. There was a pool hall right by the stage and I would run in there. I was on what I thought was a huge stage and the audience paid attention to me. When I began to play, car horns honked, people yelled and I thought, "Hey, this is okay!"

I was also seven years old when I first started fooling around with the guitar.

I went to various fiddle contests with dad and went with him to Frank Mitchell's house in Enid, Oklahoma. Frank was an excellent fiddler and had a great tone when he played. Frank Mitchell was a good friend of dads and they went to a lot of contests together. Cecil Hiatt was another friend of dad's and

Byron, age 7, on the Berline farm.

he was always part of the mix. He sang, played guitar and the bones. He is the one that taught my nephew Barry Patton, Eleanor's son, to play the bones. Cecil and his wife Bernice, had a son Claude, about my age. Their daughter Foy, was about Janice and Eleanor's ages so we all ran around together. Then there was Herb Bulene from South Haven, Kansas. All these players went to contests and played at different places and I always went wherever they played.

We went all over Oklahoma and Kansas, to Texas...even Truth or Consequences, New Mexico, to attend fiddle contests. In April of 1953, when I was eight years old, mom and dad and I went with Frank Mitchell, his wife and son Mike, who was a little older than I was and all six of us rode to New Mexico in Dad's new Buick. Truth or Consequences, New Mexico, which they named for the Ralph Edwards television production, had a big rodeo with fireworks and a fiddle contest. Many well-known fiddlers came to New Mexico to compete and I remember this being the first time I saw Eck Robertson on stage. Benny Thomasson was also there. Dad and Frank Mitchell got into the finals of the fiddle contest, but Frank McGraw won it, although we never could figure out why because he was not near the caliber of fiddler as were the other players.

When Eck Robertson played, the judges disqualified him. They had a time limit of maybe three or four minutes and were very strict about it. Eck came out and started playing "Sally Goodin'" and you cannot play that tune in three, four, or five minutes. He was in the middle of it, really going to town, when they blew the whistle. You are supposed to stop when the time limit is up, but Eck just kept playing. They blew the whistle again and he just kept playing. Finally, two men got on stage, picked him up, and carried him off.

We went to Clarksville, Arkansas one time, but we did not travel all that much, except around Oklahoma and Kansas. Most fiddle contests are in June and July and with a farm to run, especially at harvest time, dad was always busy and could not get away. In fact, Dad ran the combine until he was seventy-two years old.

I remember riding in the car with dad, having the Grand Ole Opry on the radio, going to Caldwell on Fridays to pick up my brothers and sisters. They were in high school and lived in town during the school week then came home to the farm on weekends. This was quite common for rural families. During the week it was just dad, mom and me, so it was exciting when we picked them up for the weekend or a long holiday.

The first fiddling contest I entered was in Blackwell, Oklahoma in 1954 when I was 10 years old. I knew two tunes and that is all that was required to enter. Dad entered it too and I beat him. He acted as if he was upset...which he was not.

Larry Strueble a violinist about four years older than I was, lived in Caldwell and we sometimes played against each other in contests. He and Frank Mitchell were both there the day I won by beating dad.

Leonard played the fiddle and entered some contests and although Henry, Eleanor and Janice all played music, they were not interested in playing the fiddle. I was dad's last hope of having another fiddler in the family. I knew he was proud, even though I beat him the first time out. Then we went to Deer Creek, Oklahoma where Dad and I entered the fiddling contest. I won, beating him again.

He told a newspaper reporter, "I was so proud I could of bust, but there was an old timer or two in the contest who looked down their noses at the kid – and they're still doin' it."

In addition to contests, there were school programs and talent shows that provided ample opportunities for me to play.

Then television came along and we got a TV set in 1952 or 1953. There were a lot of country music shows on TV. The Ed Sullivan Show began airing on television in 1947 and it had country music acts. Arthur Godfrey began his show in 1950 and the Ozark Jubilee began telecasting in 1955 out of Springfield, Missouri. We watched Tennessee Ernie Ford when his show aired a year later in 1956 and the Porter Wagoner show when it began in 1961. We also went to live, Grand Ole Opry type shows in Enid, Oklahoma. They always had Grand Ole Opry stars on these shows and I remember seeing Kitty Wells, Benny Martin's brother and Dale Potter.

All the Berlines played something...well, except Henry; he never played a musical instrument although he did try to play the fiddle one time, from what I hear. Dad played the old fiddle tune, "Pop Goes the Weasel." He played the song up to the part where it goes, "POP, goes the weasel." Then he took the bow and fiddle, up over his head or maybe behind his back and played the "POP" part of the song. When Henry was about twelve years old, he tried to do that, just like dad, but he lost his balance, fell on the couch, and broke the bow. That ended his musical instrument playing days and from then on, he just played the radio and record player.

Leonard joined the armed forces in the early 1950's and they stationed him in Tokyo, Japan during the Korean War. When he came home, he took off for Arizona, not bothering to tell anybody

The Berline family on the farm in Oklahoma. front row l to r: my sister Janice, I'm the little fellow in the middle, and my sister Eleanor. back row l to r: My brother Leonard, Grandpa Jesse Jackson, my dad Lue Berline, my mom Elizabeth Jackson Berline, and my brother Henry.

where in Arizona...he just left. We finally talked to a friend of his and found out where he was.

An exciting event for me was playing for Pistol Pete's ninety-fifth birthday party at his home in Perkins, Oklahoma, about twenty-five miles from Guthrie. Pete was born Frank Eaton in 1860 and most people who live around here know who he is. For those unfamiliar with Oklahoma history and this colorful character of the old west, I want to add just a little more about him, then you will understand what a big deal this was to an Oklahoma boy of eleven.

Frank was born in Connecticut, but his family moved to Kansas when Frank was eight years old. His father was a veteran of the Civil War's Union Army and he had a dispute with some men who had been Confederates and had ridden with Quantrill's Raiders. These men murdered Mr. Eaton in cold blood, right in front of Frank.

A friend of the family encouraged him to avenge his father's death and taught Frank how to use a gun. At the age of only fifteen, they nicknamed Frank Eaton "Pistol Pete" and he carried that moniker until his death in 1958 at the age of ninety-seven. He earned the name for his handling of guns and shooting abilities even though he was quite young and his left eye, crossed. Pete went to Fort Gibson, Oklahoma where he competed against cavalry sharp shooters. Upon beating every one of them, his reputation was immediately born in Oklahoma Territory.

He became the youngest commissioned U.S. Marshal. He served under Judge Isaac Parker, known as the "hanging" judge in Fort Smith, Arkansas. Pete's U.S. Marshall's duties included everything from southern Kansas to northern Texas, the heart of which was Oklahoma.

When Pete was twenty-nine years old, he participated in the Oklahoma Land Rush of 1889, settling near Perkins where he served as Sheriff. Pistol Pete served in law enforcement until late in his life. He eventually killed five of the six men responsible for his father's death; someone beat him to the sixth. Pistol Pete was a living legend...the real thing. His image of the old west and its way of life became a strong symbol to Oklahomans as well as those of other western states. Pistol Pete is the mascot of OSU (Oklahoma State University) and the Wyoming Cowboys.

Pete and dad were good friends. Dad used to play music with some other friends out at the 101 Ranch and Pete was always there. Pistol Pete said to dad, "I want your boy to come play at my birthday party." Pete was 95 and I was eleven. What a thrill.

Rollie Goodnight was another legend from Oklahoma. He lived in Guthrie and was the Sheriff and U.S. Marshal. Rollie Goodnight and Pistol Pete were buddies and rode together a lot. Rollie's dad remarked that his son would die with his boots on so every time Rollie got in a scrape, he removed his boots and said, "Just in case I get hit." He did not, however die with his boots on and it is amazing he lived as long as he did. People in Oklahoma and Kansas did not read about the old west, they lived it.

When I was about twelve years old, mom, dad, my brother Leonard and I, went to Tonkawa, Oklahoma to a talent contest. First prize was an opportunity to be on TV, Channel five in Oklahoma City. I won and thought that was just great! We all drove down to Oklahoma City and I was on the TV show. I do not know what show it was…I just do not remember.

I was in a lot of little contests here and there, most of them gave ribbons and things like that to the winners, but once in awhile there was money. Waukita, Oklahoma gave five or ten dollars for third and second place and maybe twenty-five dollars for first.

From sixth or seventh grade and up through high school, Frank Mitchell cut record disks, fiddle only and I listened to those a lot. He was a great fiddle player and I played those disks until the grooves wore out, taking the needle off and then putting it back on again until I learned to play what he was doing.

I listened to Frank's disks, the radio and to dad, entered fiddle contests, and performed wherever, whenever I could. Mom accompanied me on the piano or Leonard played the guitar.

I remember trying to learn to play "Black Mountain Rag," but with little success. Beverly, my sister in law, gave me a 33 1/3-rpm record, and it only had two songs on it, one of which was Black Mountain Rag. No matter how much I worked at it, I never could play it as it sounded on that record.

I met Buster Jenkins, aka Frank Kinard, from Ottawa, Kansas, in 1958 when I was thirteen years old when Mom and dad took me to a fiddle contest in Burlingame, Kansas. Frank Kinard was in the fiddle contest. He also played banjo and during contest breaks Jack Theobald, Kenny Plumber and Frank Kinard, all three from Kansas, played together. They played a bluegrass set, with Frank playing banjo and that was the first live bluegrass I ever heard. They introduced bluegrass in Kansas. It knocked me out! I loved it. Then Frank got out his fiddle and they played Black Mountain Rag.

Back stage after the contest, I asked him, "Can you show me how to play Black Mountain Rag?"

"First thing you have to do," he began, "is retune your fiddle." Then he showed me how to do that and I could play the tune immediately. That is the key to playing that tune...you have to retune your fiddle.

Dad was fascinated with anything that had to do with new technology. He bought a record disk-recording machine made by Wilcox Gay. He put blank disks on the turntable and when you wanted to record something, you just lowered the arm and a stylus cut the music into groves on the blank...just like a regular record. Dad recorded everything we did and no one was immune...he recorded mom playing the piano, Leonard on his trombone, me on the fiddle, Janice on the trombone, Eleanor on the piano...he was always recording somebody. I still have that machine...I wonder if it still works.

Chapter 2
1958-1962: High School

I entered my first year of high school in the fall of 1958 and stayed in town with another freshman, Jim Harris and his family. We gave the Harris's money for room and board and paid out of state tuition because our farm was over the state line, in Oklahoma. Tuition was $90 a year for each of us; Henry, Leonard, Eleanor, Janice and me, to go to high school in Caldwell, Kansas. They had an enrollment of one hundred fifty students... the whole high school.

We could have gone to Deer Creek High School, in an even smaller town, where they had eight-man football. All our friends attended Caldwell High School; at ten miles away, it was the closest town and it was home to us.

The two social organizations of the high school, Kays for boys and Kayetts for girls, had various fund-raiser events and one was a talent show. The Kays had a monthly meeting in the auditorium and for entertainment; they made the freshmen boys do a skit or whatever we could do.

I played a little piano, some boogie-woogie, so Jim Harris and I worked up a deal where I played the piano and he did the Don Knotts thing of acting real nervous. We picked up the idea from Don Knotts on TV's Andy Griffith Show.

"Are you nervous?" Andy asked.

"NOPE!" Don quickly replied.

The upperclassmen went nuts over our comedy routine! They

made so much noise it disturbed the other classes and teachers had to reprimand them, telling them to quiet down. The principal eventually had to shut down the meeting. It was weird... here we were freshman and all the upper classmen thought we were just great.

After that, everyone was after me to play the piano even though I kept saying, "I am not a piano player!" It was funny however, I do remember teaching my grade school teacher, Dee Aldridge, how to play the piano. Dee is a great person.

We had all kinds of musical instruments at home and I dabbled with most of them, such as guitar, fiddle, and piano.

Dad liked to play records and each morning before we got up, he put a record on the player and that was our daily wake-up call. We never knew if it would be fiddling, banjo, or what, but we knew there would some kind of music playing. Dad liked bluegrass, western swing, country; he liked it all.

I bought one of his birthday presents at a record store in Wichita and as dad was a banjo player, I knew he liked banjo music so I bought a Flatt and Scruggs record and he played it a lot.

We all played the piano and band instruments. Eleanor played the drum, Janice the trombone...Leonard played trombone and I thought I would play trombone too, because trombones were already in the house. When I got to high school the band director looked at me, saw how big I was and noted I was a freshman who did not know how to play any of the band instruments. I told him I would be playing the trombone.

He said, "No, you're gonna play the sousaphone."

"Why's that?" I asked.

He said, "You can play the trombone if you want to start off with fourth and fifth graders... taking lessons with them. Well... you can do that or you can start out right in the high school band if you play the sousaphone."

"Oh, I'll do that!" I said. He talked me into it.

Dad did not want me to play football fearing I might get my fingers hurt, but I wanted to play football so bad! Mom finally talked him into signing the release so I could play. Mom and dad never missed a game in which I played or a fiddle contest I entered and it did not matter where it was held...they were always there. That was great and this continued even when I went to college; they went to every track meet and football game, no matter where it was.

Al Williamson was my high school coach for football and track and I loved that man...he was just great, a neat person. Long after I was out of school and playing music, we occasionally got together and he told me the following story after dad passed away.

When I was a freshman in high school and first went out for football, dad paid a visit to coach Williamson. Dad was a big, strong man and rather imposing. Coach said he did not know who dad was and really did not know me as I had attended a country school and was new to Caldwell High School.

Coach Williamson said dad entered his office and said in a gruff voice, "You the football coach?"

Then dad said, "My boy wants to play football and I guess I'm gonna let him, but if he gets his fingers hurt in any way I'm gonna come in here and kick your ass!"

"He did that?" I said.

"Yes he did." The coach replied. "And every time you went on the field to play I prayed you didn't get your fingers hurt."

I had never played organized football before, just on the playground. In high school I made the freshman football team and played in the marching band with that big sousaphone. Several of us on the football team did this. We marched on the field at half time then ran three blocks to the school, put our instruments away, took off the band uniforms, put on football uniforms, ran back to the playing field, hoping to play a minute or two at the end of the game and we did this at every home game. We got to play depending on how far ahead our team was in the game. You know how they do.

The next year, as a sophomore, I grew a little bigger, a little stronger and I made first string, but varsity football meant I would not be marching with the band during half time. The band instructor did not like it, but he understood and I still played at various functions, although I did not march in the band during football season.

I went out for track and made the team. I threw the javelin in high school, which is very lucky for me because only five states in the country had javelin throwing in high school and Kansas happened to be one of them.

Tom Puma, from another little town in Kansas, was on their high school track team and our schools competed against each other. Tom did not throw the javelin, but although he was not very big, boy could he throw the discus and shot. He had the most incredible snap. I never beat him in the discus and barely beat him in shot put.

I participated in football, basketball, and track...the only three sports offered. I would like to have played baseball, but the high school did not have it.

I played tackle in football until my senior year when I became an end. I knew I was not going to be big enough to play tackle in college.

I played center in basketball, because I was one of the taller players.

When I was sixteen, mom, dad, and I made a second trip to New Mexico. Carl Hazlewood, a very good Texas-style fiddle player lived there and he put on a contest. Carl's fiddle student,

Mom, Dad and I in our living room at the farm in the 1960s.

Garland Gainer, was a big, rancher type whose fingers were huge...much bigger than mine and he played a good fiddle. Garland, Carl Hazelwood and the other Texas fiddlers had a different style than what I played. Their playing, more improvised, embellished and kind of "swingy," defined the Texas Swing style of fiddle playing.

Exposed to those players for a few days, their style of playing just kind of sunk in. This is why fiddle contests were so important, because we found new ways of playing the old tunes, ways to embellish them so that we could be a little better fiddle player than were our competitors.

Vernon and Norman Solomon and Eck Robertson, from Texas, showed up for the contest...Eck seemed to make it to all the contests. Known as the "Sally Goodin'" king, Robertson recorded the tune for RCA in 1922...one of the first fiddle players ever to record. Louis Franklin is Major Franklin's nephew, both very good Texas fiddlers and Major was one of dad's favorites. Getting to hang around those players was quite a musical eye opener. Dad taped a lot of the sessions and when we went home, we listened to them many times.

With all that listening...the style just sunk in and I started playing that way. I remember mom noticed the difference and said, "What is it? You're playing differently."

Texas Swing just started coming out and it was for the better, I think. I am laughing.

I was seventeen when we went to Hale Center, Texas and we went there a couple of years before I went to college, but never after that. The Hale Center contest was home to the "A" Texas fiddlers and meeting and playing with them was invaluable.

All the hotshot Texas fiddlers attended, such as Louis and Major Franklin, Benny Thomasson, Vern and Norman Solomon, Eck Robertson and Texas Shorty, aka James Chancellor. James is a year older than I am and we played against each other in contests. There were certainly a lot of other good fiddlers, but those were the biggies and they really impressed me with their playing. After the contests, at the jam sessions, they got with it and really cut loose.

There were not however, very many young fiddlers. Louis Franklin's son, Larry, was younger than I was, Randy Elmore was one of the younger ones and I remember the young Solomon brothers, Rickie and Mike...I think they were younger.

Dad played for dances but I did that very little, except for the 101 Ranch. By this time, square dance callers began using records, instead of live musicians. I remember the first time I tried to play for a square dance...I played "Rag Time Annie" and I got tired so I started to quit, but oh, my, no. I guess a fiddler's arm would fall off before dancers would ever let him stop playing.

I tried to find all the fiddle records I could, but mainly those by Tommy Jackson. These were square dance records without the calls and he just played straight fiddle tunes. I learned everything I could from those records then I got two Howdy Forrester albums, on the MGM label, and learned all of those tunes.

George Downing, a couple of years older than I am, played guitar and he worked at a filling station in Caldwell, where we jammed. He still lives in Caldwell and continues to play for dances. George and I entered a talent contest at a fair, during my senior year in high school and I remember this one girl in my class got so upset when we won.

I dated a little, but not much because I was too bashful. I had a date to the prom, but I never got serious about any of the girls. I never even drank beer until I was out of high school.

After home games, the school had dances down in the old gym. The shy, bashful boys, like me, stood in a line on one side of the gym and the shy, bashful girls stood in a line against the opposite wall. We were scared to death to ask a girl to dance...I would not do that.

One by one, my brothers and sisters graduated from high school and left home. Henry was married and raising a family, Leonard was married, Eleanor went to nurses training in Winfield, Kansas and after Janice finished high school she was going to get married, but she went to beauty college in Enid, Oklahoma instead. Eventually, I was the only one living at home with mom and dad and we continued going to fiddle contests.

We went to a contest at St. Joseph, Missouri when I was a senior. Another contest I won was at Joyland Park in Wichita, Kansas. That was the first year KFDI radio held the contest and was the first big event for Mike Oatman. Mike was a DJ at KFDI and at one time, he was part owner of GEB (Great Empire

Broadcasting) in Wichita, Kansas. Mike Oatman is in the Country Music Disc Jockey Hall of Fame.

We went to contests in Konawa and Mangum, Oklahoma and many of the Texas fiddlers showed up at those contests.

All through high school, I kept active in sports as well as music. My senior year, as a defensive end, I made the most tackles, over sixty, for the Caldwell team. If memory serves me, I threw the javelin about 200 feet and that is quite good, especially for someone in high school.

Roger Rains, a fullback, and I both made All State in football and as a result, colleges and universities heavily recruited both of us. They called us at home, sent literature about their school's athletic program, and offered us several scholarships. Letters of invitation came from Washburn University at Topeka, Pittsburg State in Kansas, the University of Kansas at Lawrence, Emporia State in Kansas, Wichita State in Kansas, OSU in Stillwater, Oklahoma and the University of Oklahoma at Norman.

I even got a telegram delivered to the high school, from Jack Mitchell, football coach at the University of Kansas. I had never before received a telegram.

WESTERN UNION
LAWRENCE, KANSAS
DEC 4, 1961
BYRON BERLINE
CALDWELL HIGH SCHOOL
CALDWELL, KANSAS
CONGRATULATIONS ON YOUR ALL STATE SELECTION, PREPARATION FOR THE BLUEBONNET BOWL WILL PREVENT OUR VISITING WITH YOU IMMEDEATELY HOWEVER WE ARE VERY HAPPY FOR YOU AND WILL BE LOOKING FORWARD TO VISITING WITH YOU FOLLOWING THE BOWL GAME
JACK MITCHELL FOOTBALL COACH UNIVERSITY OF KANSAS

I knew OSU was already high on my list but Roger Rains had decided to go to the University of Oklahoma in Norman. His girlfriend, also from Caldwell, was already there. OSU (Oklahoma State University) in Stillwater wanted me and that is where I thought I wanted to go. My brother Leonard, Janice's husband, Nick and some of my friends went there and actually, OSU was the first school to show interest in me. They showed special interest in track, because I threw the javelin and as a result, the OSU track coach really wanted me to enroll which I thought that was great.

All through my senior year of high school, coaches showed up to recruit me, but when it came time to visit OSU's campus, I was rather disappointed. They invited mom, dad, and me to come see where I would be going to school and I really looked forward to it. They put me with an OSU football player, to show me around the campus. He was a freshman end and I was an end at the time, but he was the most boring dude I ever met. He just sort of stood around and stared into space. I also did not care for the living arrangements at OSU because they did not have athletic dorms, which meant their athletes stayed in different dorms all over campus. It was a terribly disappointing experience because, for a number of reasons, I really wanted to go to OSU.

Shortly thereafter, I received an invitation to visit the Oklahoma University campus in Norman. Rudy Feldman was my recruiting coach and when he called, he said, "Put your fiddle in the car when you come."

I was a little dumbfounded and asked, "What for?"

"Just bring it." He said. Then he followed up our phone conversation with the following letter:

THE UNIVERSITY OF OKLAHOMA
NORMAN · OKLAHOMA
January 25, 1962

Mr. Byron Berline
F.F.D. #2
Caldwell, KS

Dear Byron:

I enjoyed talking with you on the phone recently and hope that perhaps I will have an opportunity to see you again before your visit on 17 February.

Congratulations on the fine job you did in your schoolwork. I hope your basketball team continues to win.

We are all looking forward to having you and your family visit us. I was serious when I asked that you bring your fiddle down with you. I spoke to some of the boys that play instruments in the dormitory and they said they would enjoy getting together with you and playing a few tunes.

Please give my regards to your parents.

Sincerely,
Rudy Feldman
Assistant Football Coach

We toured the campus, attended an OU ball game and afterwards, I and other recruits went to the locker room and met all the team players.

Leon Cross is the athlete OU paired with me. He eventually became an All American guard and he loved country music. He took me to their training room and explained that they played Hank Thompson on the loud speakers when they taped ankles, etc. and they did play Hank Thompson's "Oklahoma Hills."

I said, "Man, this is great!"

Then they took me to see Washington House, the athletic dorm located right across from the stadium; they told me to bring my fiddle.

When we walked in, some of the football players had guitars and they said, "Get out your fiddle. We're gonna jam." Monty Deer was a quarterback, Mike McClellan a running back and two or three other players...I just do not remember who all was there.

I thought, "This is too cool!"

We jammed for about an hour and they said, "Now, you have to come here."

I said, "I think you're right."

I had more fun! You would think it would have been the opposite because OSU is a more agricultural school with a more country type of atmosphere.

OU's full athletic scholarship accepted, including their wanting participation in both football and track, was great...just what I wanted to do. Bud Wilkinson being coach at OU did not hurt any because he was such a gentleman. Some of the other OU coaches were not.

I graduated from Caldwell, Kansas High School in the spring of 1962 and there were 33 in my graduating class. Our Fiftieth Class Reunion was in 2012 and it does not seem possible.

That summer we read about the National Fiddle contest in Weiser, Idaho and I wanted to go...the third week in June at harvest time. Dad was sixty-eight and I was shy a few weeks of my eighteenth birthday. Henry was almost thirty years old and after all those years, dad finally thought Henry could manage the combine. Believing the farm could get along without him, we headed for Weiser and that was the first time we took a real long trip.

The contest had three divisions, junior, open, and senior. I did not want to be in the junior division so I fibbed about already being eighteen and signed up for the open division. Dad entered the senior division.

Eck Robertson kept by the new time limit rules and won the National Old Time Fiddle Championship in 1962.

Dad played back up on the banjo and I placed sixth that first year, playing more of a Texas style of fiddle tunes while the other contestants played jigs and reels. I learned a lot about the kind of playing required in the contest and met so many new fiddle players. We had a good time; I learned a lot and knew I would come back.

Chapter 3
1962 — 1963: OU Football and Meeting the Dillards

I entered the University of Oklahoma in the fall of 1962 without declaring a major because I did not know what I wanted to do.

Freshmen were not eligible to play varsity football although they checked us out to see what we could or could not do. We worked out with the team, put in all the practices, but played only two freshman games against OSU and Tulsa.

Bud Wilkinson was a great person and what you saw is what you got, but Bob Ward was another one of THOSE coaches. Off the field he was one of the nicest people you ever met, but the second he walked through the gate he turned into a different animal, wild eyed and frothing at the mouth. He just went nuts! Every football player hated to be around him at practice and he always picked on someone; making an example of them…he almost tortured players.

Bob Ward coached tackles and ends and as I was an end, he was my coach. One day we gathered at a corner of the practice field to go through the "iron gates," exercise. We ran the gates, hit a dummy, drove it back five yards or whatever and if you raised-up you got your head knocked off.

We went down in our stance, the signal called; we ran through the exercise and stopped. Coach Ward yells, "Berline! Don't you know your right from your left?"

"Yes sir." I said.

He jumped me. "Now don't get smart." He continued. "You hit with your left shoulder."

"Right shoulder," I told him. I knew I did it correctly, but did not say anything more.

"Get down in your stance." He shouted.

With everybody standing around watching, I got down into my stance. I knew he was looking for something...anything wrong. He tried to find something so he could really berate me.

He looked at me for a minute and then said in a sour, mocking voice, "You play the violin, don't ya? If you don't do this right I'm gonna' stomp your fingers."

"You try it." I thought.

The guy next to me, Ronnie Frost, a left-hander, leaned over and in a low voice said, "I did it...I hit with my left shoulder."

"Oh, thanks." I said.

Coach Ward saw several of us go through the gates at the same time, saw somebody hit with their left shoulder and thought I was that person.

It did not take long before the word got out to the rest of the players. "I hear Coach Ward is going to stomp your fingers."

I said, "Well, he didn't, but he threatened to."

Ed McQuarter was a huge tackle and one of the few black players on the OU team. One-day coach Ward said to the team, "Now I want you to throw a forearm this time when you block."

We just stood with our hands on our hips. Ward walked up to big ole McQuarter and said, "I want you to throw a fore arm like this..." Wham! He hit him right in the nose and blood went everywhere.

I thought, "Ed McQuarter could kill you with one blow, you idiot!"

Ed just turned around and walked into the training room.

It just made me so mad that Coach Ward did that! He did not last much longer after this incident...thank goodness.

When receiving my scholarship, Bud Wilkinson said that in addition to football, I could play basketball or track; it was up to me to choose. He wanted me to play football first then it was open to play any sport I wanted. I thought that was strange because of not being that great of a basketball player. I was okay, but not that good.

I broke my thumb playing football that first year and consequently, could not play the fiddle for six weeks. I told dad, "Well, I broke my thumb." Dad just kind of reacted like, "Well, what are you gonna do?" It was the thumb on the right hand, thank goodness. A fiddler really uses the fingers on the left hand. If you play football long enough, it is inevitable you will break something. That injury started me thinking a little bit and after it healed up I went to track, bypassing football altogether.

In the early 1960's there were very few good javelin throwers in Oklahoma. Throwing the javelin in high school put me in a position to get on the OU track team. They wanted me, knowing I was good, even in high school.

At the Freshman Big 8 track meet in the spring of 1963, I won the javelin event.

Bill Carrol, OU track coach said, "Next year, why don't you skip football and just come out for track?"

I thought, "This is a good idea."

Going through spring football workouts and practice, at one point I got up as high as the third team, but remained an end, only weighing about 185 pounds. Ralph Neely, the biggest tackle we had, weighed about two hundred forty five or two hundred fifty pounds and stood six foot six. He was big, but nothing like the three hundred twenty pound players that universities have today.

Bud Wilkinson ran the first string offense and one day at practice, said he needed somebody to play defensive tackle.

We stood on the sidelines and I said, "Well, I played tackle in high school."

"Get in there." He said.

I just had one of those days and spent most of the time in the backfield making tackles...for losses. After practice, Coach Wilkinson said, "You like that position, don't you?"

I love defense and just going after the ball.

From about fifth string end he immediately moved me up to third string tackle, ahead of seniors who were not very happy about it. I was there... about a week. I moved back to being an end...knowing I was not "hoss," enough to play tackle. I was big, but not big enough to play against those real big players, especially Ralph Neely. One time I played across from him, got down in my stance and he looked like an elephant. Ralph eventually became a professional football player for the Dallas Cowboys.

I softly said, "Ralph, go easy," and he did.

It takes a while to catch on to college football because it is so different from high school. In the early 1960's players went back and forth between defense and offense. Today you usually play one or the other which would have been great because I loved defense.

At the end of each season, the university required every athlete to review their progress in whatever sport they played and I had to talk to coach Bud Wilkinson who was also the athletic director. I also needed to talk to him about my desire to drop football and just participate in track. I was scared to death, afraid he would blow up or something.

At the performance review, he said he thought I was doing well in football and said to keep working at it, blah, blah, blah. He finished and as it came time for me to leave. I said, "There's something I want to say."

"What's that?" He asked.

"You know I went out for track this spring and would like to concentrate on that." I told him,

"Have you talked to coach Carrol about this?" He asked.

"It was his idea." I replied.

Bud said, "I told you when you came to OU, you could play whatever sport you wanted and I'll keep my word. If this is what you want to do, it's okay with me."

That is all there was to it.

Playing football and track would be impossible today because you can no longer participate in two sports, you must commit to a specific sport.

When I made the change to concentrate solely on track, the university newspaper published an article about it. In the accompanying photo, I wore a cowboy hat, had a football in one hand and a fiddle in the other. A reference to that article came back a couple of years later, from a female student.

I made it through my first year at OU and looked forward to the fall of 1963 and being on the track team.

The summer of 1963, mom, dad, and I went back to Weiser, Idaho a second time and I entered the National Old Time Fiddle

Contest. Different events surrounded the fiddle contest including the jams and all of this lasted four days.

Lloyd Wanzer and Bill Yohee were locals and always attended the Weiser contest. I borrowed Bill Yohee's guitar player, Bill Durham, Buddy Durham's cousin. Bill was a very good flat picker and rhythm guitar player and using him to back me up in the contest was okay because Bill Yohee was out of the contest by that time. Bill Durham did a good job playing for me... it worked out great. I won second place, about six hundred dollars in prize money and a trophy. Lloyd Wanzer from Caldwell, Idaho, not Kansas, won first place. I moved up from sixth place in 1962 to second place in 1963 and looked forward to the Idaho contest in 1964.

In the fall of 1963, my sophomore year at OU, I decided to major in physical education thinking I might coach. I did not want a degree in music; I wanted to play music and knew I no longer wanted to live on the farm in Caldwell.

The press had quite a time with the football-fiddle thing. I guess it was unusual, but I was surprised how far-reaching the story went. I received a copy of the following letter:

NATIONAL BROADCASTING COMPANY, INC.
30 Rockefeller Plaza, New York, N.Y, 10020
Circle 7-8300
September 6, 1963

Mr. R. W. Barnard
703 South Main Street
Caldwell, Kansas

Dear Mr. Barnard;

I would be very interested in talking to Mr. Berline if he is ever in New York and available for a "Tonight Show" appearance.

Have him call me when he gets in the city — the telephone number is CI 7-8300, Ext. 2336.

Thanks so much for calling,

Sincerely,
Ken Joffe

I have no idea how this came about and I did not make it to New York City. I have done a few things since then...wonder if the "Tonight Show" invitation is still open?

During my sophomore year at OU, I had more time to play music. College football keeps you busy with a lot of meetings, practices, workouts, there is a big playbook to memorize as well as regular studies...all very time consuming. Track freed up more time.

Folk music was very popular on campus and they had hootenannies and coffee houses featuring mainly folk music with just a little bluegrass here and there, by artists such as Peter, Paul and Mary, the Kingston Trio, Pete Seeger and Joan Baez. Every Friday at four o'clock, the student union had a hootenanny called, "Friday at Four." I went to one and without having to spend so much time with football...tried out for the next show. They put me with a ten or twelve piece folk group and said, "Okay, you all can play Friday, November 22, at four o'clock."

I went to class, studied and worked out with the track team, but I did not play music with anyone because most of the players were just learning or anyway, just not at my level of playing. I did spend a lot of time at the student union where other musicians hung out, which is where I met Bill Caswell, a student my age from Bartlesville. Bill played guitar and banjo quite well and followed whatever I did so we began jamming. Bill had musician friends living in Bartlesville who came to Norman to jam. That is how I met Royce Campbell, an exceptional flat pick guitar player. Then I met Tim and Joe Coulter, OU students who played bass, guitar, and banjo. They had a group called the Cripple Creek Trio or something like that, mainly playing folk tinged with bluegrass.

Oklahoma City broadcasted a Hootenanny TV show and I decided I wanted to be on it. They put the four of us together, the Coulter brothers, Bill Caswell, and me. Norman, Oklahoma is in Cleveland County, so we called ourselves the Cleveland County Ramblers and I suppose we were. We worked up two tunes, "Cripple Creek" and "Lonesome Road Blues."

They booked Buffy Sainte-Marie, a Native American famous for her hit songs "Until It's Time for You to go" and "Universal Soldier." They also booked the Kimberlys, two sisters who married two brothers and they were very good playing a sort of folk-country style and a few years later they recorded an album with Waylon Jennings. Steve Brainard, whose dad owned the Buddhi club in Oklahoma City, was also on the show and someone named Mason Williams a graduate of Oklahoma City High School.

The first time I met Mason we hit it off just great and I remember him saying, "Hey, you want to see my 51 Chevy?"

We went out to the parking lot and sure enough, he had a 1951 Chevy. It was not even that old, maybe about twelve years. We still laugh about that...Mason and I have been good friends ever since.

The Cleveland County Ramblers did the show, had a lot of fun and for the next couple of years we played sorority and fraternity parties, OU functions...we played everywhere we could.

November 22 arrived and I looked forward to doing the "Friday at Four" show. That morning I picked up a campus newspaper and noted a group called the Dillards, was to perform. I thought, "Oh, great...another little folksy group." You know the type...can't pick their noses."

That afternoon everything changed when we learned of the assassination of President John F. Kennedy in Dallas, Texas. I went to the student union and discovered they decided to go ahead with plans for the Friday at Four Show.

I did my part with the big folk group and as the first group to go on, when we finished I put my fiddle away then Bill Caswell and I stood by the stage to watch the rest of the show. Four musicians, wearing buckskin shirts, began carrying instruments on stage and I remember thinking, "Well, they look impressive."

Pop Brainard ran the Buddhi club at ninth and Hudson in Oklahoma City and it was a very popular place to go. The Buddhi brought in big folk artists like Joan Baez, Peter Yarrow, Eric Darling, Judy Collins, the Smothers Brothers, Pete Seeger, Tom Paxton, Baxter Taylor and I remember Hoyt Axton played there.

Pop booked the Dillards for his club and they came to the "Friday at Four" show on the OU campus at Norman to help promote their two-week appearance at the Buddhi club in Oklahoma City. Pop's girlfriend attended the show and heard me play. She stood near the stage, by Bill and me. Next to me was one of the players in the Dillards group.

She said to him, while pointing at me, "You should get him to play some fiddle with you all."

When I met Doug Dillard, he looked at me and asked, "Can you play old time fiddle?"

I said, "That's all I play. I don't play anything else."

"Well, I want to hear you play." He said. "When we get through you come back to the dressing room and bring your fiddle. I want to play one with you."

I had not heard them play yet, but said, "Okay."

Bill Caswell and I went out front and sat down with the audience as the emcee introduced the Dillards. When they began to play my mouth dropped open and I almost said out loud, "Oh, my God. Just listen to that! Jiminy Christmas, these guys are amazing!" I never before heard live bluegrass, like that!

They finished their set and I could not get backstage quickly enough. Student unions have many little rooms up and down the hallways and I checked every one of them, but could not find the Dillards. Finally I saw them emerging from one of the rooms. They were all, out of costume, dressed, carrying their instruments, and preparing to leave.

I reached them and said, "I'm sorry I missed you."

Doug Dillard said, "Wait just a minute. I want to hear him play his fiddle." Then to me he said, "Get out your fiddle." Then he got his banjo.

"Just play one." He told me.

I knew they only played real fast and "Hamilton County Breakdown" was the only fast tune I knew. I learned it from a Tommy Jackson record, so I thought, "Well, I'll just play that one."

I started playing and Doug, on banjo, fell right into it. The others began unloading their instruments. Mitch Jayne took the cover off of his bass, Rodney Dillard got out his guitar, and Dean Webb pulled out his mandolin. We sat there and jammed for an hour or more playing one tune after another and I just floated up to the ceiling. Never before had I played with anybody like that. It was like, "This is unbelievable!"

They said, "Man, you've got to come down to the club tonight and play with us!"

Bill Caswell and I followed the Dillards to Oklahoma City.

We jammed and ran through some things and I got to play on stage with them at the Buddhi club.

That weekend and the following week, I spent a lot of time with the Dillards. The next Thursday was Thanksgiving and I knew they were going to be at the Buddhi the following week. When I went home to the farm for Thanksgiving, I told dad I wanted to take the tape recorder back to school with me. This was not a little portable cassette recorder. It was a big reel-to-reel recorder. New technology still fascinated dad.

I said, "I want to tape something you are not going to believe."

I took the recorder to the Buddhi and Don Tetter, a noted guitar repairman from Oklahoma City, helped me connect the tape recorder to the live feed of the PA system. Once plugged in-line I recorded all the shows we played and got quality recordings without any other noise.

The Dillards stayed at the Heartbreak Hotel, a little bedroom type place on the second story above the club. We jammed for a couple of hours, one tune after the next and I recorded some thirty songs. I still have that original tape recording.

That night the Dillards asked me to record the "Pickin' N' Fiddlin'" album with them and my thought was…"Halleluiah!"

What luck, meeting the Dillards who actually had the means to get a record deal…and they kept their word.

For me, Friday, November 22, 1963 was memorable in different ways and that day will always stand out in my mind. I received one of the biggest breaks of my career and will always be thankful to the Dillards for giving me that opportunity.

On Thursday, February 27, 1964 the Cleveland County Ramblers, played for the opening performance of an OU variety show called the "Sooner Scandals." Friday night we played again and did two shows on Saturday. Our photo and a write-up came out in The Oklahoma Daily, the University of Oklahoma newspaper.

Gomer Jones, assistant coach, took over when Bud Wilkinson left OU to run for the U.S. Senate. Bud and his opponent, Fred Harris, both asked me to play for their fundraisers, which I did. I evidently did not do as well for Bud as I did for Fred, because Fred won.

I received the following letter dated March 22, 1964, on Bud Wilkinson for U.S. Senate Club stationery.

Bud Wilkinson for U.S. Senate Club
STATE HEADQUARTERS
16 Northwest 5th Street, Oklahoma City
March 22, 1964

Dear Byron:

I want you to know how much I appreciated the contribution of the Cleveland County Ramblers to our headquarters official opening. The success of the party was due in large part to the music and the fine spirit of your group.

Mary joins me in thanking you for your music.

Sincerely,
Bud Wilkinson

Mr. Byron Berline
Jefferson House
University of Oklahoma
Norman, Oklahoma

It disappointed me when Bud Wilkinson lost because I knew him and thought a lot of him as a coach, but Fred Harris won the election and he came around to me again later on.

In the spring of 1964, my high school friend and fellow track enthusiast, Tom Puma and I once again competed against each other, this time at the collegiate level. Tom represented KU and I competed for OU. Tom tried to throw the discus and shot put, but at the collegiate level, the discus and shot put are bigger, heavier and so was I. Finally, I thought I could beat him in the discus and shot put, but Tom started throwing the javelin and I never did beat him! It just made me so mad!

I am laughing. I often think of Tom and wonder where he is…I would like to see him again.

I finished my sophomore year at OU with fond memories and a bright look to the future.

Chapter 4
1964: A Summer to Remember

In June of 1964, mom, dad, and I went to Missoula, Montana for their National Fiddler's Contest and I remember that people had many tape recorders going at all the contests. At Weiser, Idaho I met Phil and Vivien Williams out of Seattle, Washington. They had a reel-to-reel tape recorder and taped everything. They went to all the big contests and were at Missoula in 1964. The jam they taped occurred in the bar of the Palace Hotel the night before the final round of the contest and several jam sessions went on at the same time in the same general area. I remember Texas Shorty and I played "Bill Cheatham." Gene Mead, a great guitar player was there too.

The Williams' went home after the contest, took the best of all the musicians and then they included them on the "Jam Sessions" album, releasing it on their Voyager label. The following is from the liner notes for that cut: "Almost everyone in the room was drunk – except the fiddlers, who take turns out doing each other in elaborate variations of this tune."

It was definitely a hot jam session. Those jam sessions were so much fun and at the finals the following night, I won...1964 Missoula, Montana National Fiddle Champion! We made the long 1400-mile trip home from Montana, mom, dad, that trophy and me.

In just a couple of weeks, we left again, this time for Weiser, Idaho, and another 1400 miles to the National Old Time Fiddle Contest. I came into the contest with the new Missoula win and the year before, having won Second at Weiser, so I felt good going into the 1964 contest.

These fiddle contests all run on about the same rules. For the first round, each fiddler plays a hoedown, a waltz and one tune of choice. That makes a total of three tunes you must play and each round you must play three more without repeating any tunes. Judges eliminate some of the contestants after each round and these rounds continue over four days until the night of the finals the total number of fiddlers has been whittled down to only the best players.

Once again, I did not have a guitar player to back me up. The year before, I borrowed Bill Yohee's guitar player, Bill Durham and it worked out just great. Bill Durham was there again, for the first round and I asked him to back me up. I also picked up a banjo player named Brooks Otis from California. I will never forget...it was the morning round of competition when I got on stage and began playing "Tom and Jerry," which is a standard contest tune. Bill Durham began playing off chords and offbeat.

"Oh, No!" I thought.

He was sober...I knew he was not drunk. He played that way on all three songs of the first round and when I looked at him, he kept his head down, refusing to look at me. Everyone in the audience knew what was going on and after the round ended, a local, Duane Youngblood, said, "I knew that was going to happen...I overheard them talking."

As it turned out, Bill Durham, a bricklayer, worked for Bill Yohee and Yohee put Durham up to the stunt...Durham felt he had to because Yohee was his boss.

I thought, "Well, isn't this nice?" I was naïve.

I did not use Durham again, but by that time, my score was way down, making me maybe fourth or fifth in the contest. I was so glad Dad won the Senior Division, Lue Berline Old Time National Fiddle Champion.

Here is something interesting about Brooks Otis, who played banjo back up. Otis said, handing me a tape, "Here's a group you ought to listen to. They are really good."

Otis recorded the Kentucky Colonels, mostly live stuff, on his nice Sony, reel-to-reel machine and that tape eventually came out on Rounder records. He gave me a copy of the tape and that was my introduction to Clarence and Roland White, Scotty Stoneman and Roger Bush. Those musicians came into my life a few years later.

The Dillards came through with their offer to play on their Pickin' N' Fiddlin' album and after coming home from Weiser, I caught a flight out of Oklahoma City. The Dillards flew me to L.A. on the Fourth of July, 1964 and two days later, while in the studio, I turned twenty.

When the Dillards hit L.A., they hit it big, signing an Electra recording contract, the Andy Griffith TV show as The Darlins family and several other things…it was like a dream come true for them. Some reviews however, indicated they were not as traditional as they let on to be, but the Dillards, from Salem, deep in the Missouri Ozarks, were about as traditional as you could get and they wanted to prove it to their critics. That is why they wanted to cut the fiddle album, not the only reason, but it was one of them.

Other than fiddle contests, I had hardly ever been out of the state of Oklahoma and had never been in a recording studio. I was nineteen years old flying on a major airline to California to make a record with the Dillards…this was a very big deal! When I arrived, the Dillards were in the studio mixing their "Live Almost" album, recorded live at the Mecca Club where they were still playing some bookings. They wanted to finish mixing this album before starting the "Pickin' N' Fiddlin'" album.

Doug Dillard and Dean Webb lived in a house in Topanga Canyon, west of L.A. on highway 101. It is a beautiful area with mountains, lots of hills and the big canyon. I stayed with Doug and Dean and remember going to their house after the recording session in order to get ready for their gig at the Mecca. There were many winding roads going up to their house in the hills. I rode out there with Doug in his little ole Volvo that looked like a 1948 Ford and the tires were completely bald. The "Mecca" was sixty miles away in Orange County so we drove back down the winding roads to get on the Interstate. Doug had all these girlfriends around him and after we played the gig he invited them all back to the house. He decided to…just have a party. We drove back to Topanga Canyon and all those girls showed up.

Before long, Doug took one of the girls off into the bedroom and that was that. We did not see him anymore, which left me to sit with this other gal…it was late and she wanted to go home. As it got closer to daylight, she really insisted she had to leave. I pounded on the bedroom door and said, "Doug, this girl needs to be getting home."

"Here, you take her." He said as he opened the door and handed me his car keys. I told him I did not know where to go, but he insisted she would tell me. Never having been to California, it was a maze to me. I asked how to get her home and she said, "You get on the 101 then take "5" and go through Hollywood, etc. I managed to get there by following her directions and dropped her off at 7 am. I asked how to get back to Doug's house and she repeated the directions in reverse. Did I mention that it was morning rush hour?

To make a long story short, I had Doug's phone number but not his address. I finally stopped and tried to call him but he would not answer. I kept stopping, asking directions, and trying to get Doug to answer his phone. When I finally got to Topango Canyon, all those little winding roads and all the driveways looked alike. I must have gone into ten places thinking, "No, this doesn't look right." It was noon before I finally made it back… five hours and when I finally found the house, I could have killed Doug. I told him, "Don't you ever put me in that situation again!"

We cut the entire Pickin' N' Fiddlin' album in just two days with no over-dubs in one eight-hour session and one six-hour session. They only had three tracks, but we did not even use them, we just sat around in a circle and played into a single track. They later came out with multi-track recording on big wide tape with twenty-four up to sixty-four tracks. Tape recording remained the norm for many years.

We cut Hamilton County Breakdown and Crazy Creek, both of which I learned from Tommy Jackson records. Then Tom and Jerry, Fisher's Hornpipe, Durang's Hornpipe, Twinkle, Twinkle, Paddy On The Turnpike, Black Mountain Rag, Jazz Bow Rag, Apple Blossom, Cotton Patch Rag, Wagoner, Wild John, Drunken

Billy Goat, Soppin' The Gravy and Sally Johnson, all traditional tunes I learned from dad or other Texas fiddle players.

Chris Hillman came into the studio and I met him for the first time. It was interesting meeting him. He hung around Dean Webb...anything to learn more about the mandolin. Shortly after our meeting in 1964, Chris played bass with Jim McGuinn, David Crosby and Gene Clark in a group called "Beefeaters." The Dillards' producer, Jim Dickson, also managed "Beefeaters" and he worked for World Pacific Studios, located on West Third Street in Hollywood, as a producer and talent scout. Dickson had "Beefeaters" record a Bob Dylan tune, "Mr. Tambourine Man." They changed the name of the group to the "Byrds" and Chris Hillman, the bluegrass mandolin player, became the band's bass player.

Eddie Tickner managed the Dillards and Jim Dickson, the producer, picked up the Dillards right off the bat and got them a record deal. Jim turned out to be the one who also produced the Flying Burrito Brothers, the Byrds, and later on, Country Gazette. It was one big family of music people.

Music historian, Ralph Rinzler, wrote the liner notes for the "Pickin' N' Fiddlin'" album. Ralph was a folklorist, historian, writer and as a musician, played banjo, mandolin and guitar. He got to know Doc Watson and helped him promote his music. Ralph then interviewed Bill Monroe and the resulting article, published in "Sing Out" magazine, named Bill Monroe the "Father of bluegrass music." Ralph became Bill Monroe's manager and booking agent and because of Ralph Rinzler's involvement, Bill Monroe's career blossomed as well as that of Doc Watson.

In 1963 Ralph left performing with the Greenbrier Boys and at Alan Lomax's request, began doing fieldwork for the Newport, Rhode Island Folk Festival. Fieldwork means he traveled all over the country searching out traditional music and musicians to play it.

Ralph's knowledge of music, his desire to preserve the best traditionalists and his connection with the Newport Folk Festival, gave me an opportunity that opened my eyes and ears to some of the greatest artists in the country. I am grateful and feel quite lucky to have known him.

After we finished recording I stayed with Doug Dillard and Dean Webb for about two weeks, traveling and playing with them. I remember going to Petaluma, California to the Sonoma-Marin Fair.

Doug, Dean, and I went to the Troubadour one night where a big thirteen piece folk group was performing, called "The Men" and to be honest, we got a little bored.

Doug had a girlfriend working at the Troubadour and she gave him a pitcher of beer. He tried to pour it into a mug… completely missed the mug and poured beer all over his pants.

We decided to leave. We got in the car and headed down to Ledbetters. Doug took his pants off in the car and held them out the window to dry as we traveled. When we got to Ledbetter's, we all got out of the car and Doug still had his pants in his hand. The person at the door said, "Put your pants on Doug and come on in!" Guess he knew Doug pretty well.

It was great! I had a ball. I flew back to Oklahoma taking some great memories with me. The summer of 1964 was exciting and I had the time of my life!

Chapter 5
1964-1966: College Bands - Newport Folk Festival

I entered my junior year at OU in the fall of 1964 and began meeting more musicians. Bill Caswell introduced me to Glen Mowery, a good rhythm guitar player and singer. Glen and Royce Campbell were buddies. Charlie Clark and his 15-year-old son Mike, played banjo and they were into bluegrass music. Walter Hawkins played guitar and while I lived in Jefferson House, the athletic dorm, sometimes we got together there and jammed.

I started forming a new group called the "Blue Stem Boys." My roommate, a sprinter named Frank Deramus, did not play an instrument but he sang a lot of songs. We made him a wash-tub bass and got him started playing. The Blue Stem Boys had Bill Caswell on guitar, Gary Price on banjo, Frank Deramus on washtub bass and me on fiddle.

Garrets House of Furniture sponsored a TV show on Friday evenings on Oklahoma City's KOCO-TV, called "Oklahoma Jamboree." Bill Snow, Sonny Woodring, Wiley Walker, and Gene Sullivan starred in the show. Wiley and Gene had a morning radio show back in the early 1950's so were already famous in Oklahoma. Wiley Walker played fiddle, Gene Sullivan played guitar and they wrote "When My Blue Moon Turns to Gold Again" and "Live and Let Live." They played music and did some comedy things. Gene, the comedian, did songs like "Please Pass the Biscuits" and "Sleepin' at the Foot of the Bed." They really were great entertainers and very popular.

The Blue Stem Boys loaded our instruments into the car and drove to Garrets House of Furniture in Oklahoma City. The clerks in the store were the performers on the TV show...including Bill Snow, Sonny Woodring, and Wiley Walker. We told them we wanted to try out for their television show and asked if that would be possible.

They asked, "Well, what do you do?"

We said, "Well, a little bluegrass."

"Let's hear ya." Bill Snow said.

So we went outside, unloaded our instruments and auditioned right there in the furniture store with all those people as our audience.

Snow said, "Okay, you can be on our show starting Friday."

"That's great!" I told him. "What do we need to do?"

He told us to work up two songs and that is just what we did.

I knew doing a television show we would need to be a little more professional so I told Frank he needed something better than a washtub bass. I said, "Let's look in the newspaper and see if we can find you an upright bass." We looked in the Oklahoma City paper and found a bass for 75 bucks and we could not believe it because a Kay bass today would run $1500 minimum.

We hauled that bass up to our little dorm room in Jefferson House and it filled up the whole room. Frank did not know how to tune it so I tuned it up and showed him a few chords. He learned exactly what we had to do for the Oklahoma Jamboree. We did this for about two weeks and by about the third week Ed Shelton, a banjo player from Dallas, Texas had moved to town. Walter Hawkins brought him over to Charlie Clark's place one weekend and upon meeting him and hearing him play, I remember thinking, "Gosh, he is really good...very professional.

I said, "Hey, you want to do some playing?"

"Yeah!" he said.

We let Gary Price go.

Ed was a lot of fun and he drank beer, as we all did in those days. (I finally discovered beer...could girls be far behind?) The Blue Stem Boys rehearsed at Ed's house, worked up some stuff and we had a lot of fun.

I said, "We've got a TV show, you know?"

Ed said, "Yeah, I've seen you on TV."

The following Friday when we showed up for the Oklahoma Jamboree, Frank Deramus had worked up two more songs he could play on the bass. We walked into the studio and Bill Snow greeted us with, "We just fired the house band. You guys are it."

Poor ole Frank heard that and went, "What am I gonna to do?"

Frank learned two songs a week for the show, but as the house band, we had to back up some of the Grand Ole Opry stars and other artists performing on the show as well as our two songs each week.

I just told him to smile. "The audience can't really hear the bass anyway. Just act like you're having a good time."

He finally got to where he could play a little more, but boy was he in a panic. It worked out okay.

The TV show was on Friday nights at six or seven PM and then, at nine o'clock, they asked us to play at the Westerner Ballroom where we played until about one o'clock in the morning. We also played at the Westerner on Saturday. They did not pay us for the TV show; it was just for exposure and that was a good thing. For Friday and Saturday nights at the Westerner, we got fifty bucks each, twenty on Friday and thirty on Saturday... not bad for college kids in the mid 1960s. We liked that. This went on for quite a while and then I began wanting to do something else. Bill and Sonny asked our band to do a regular weekly TV show in Amarillo, Texas, but I told them I could not do that; it was time to move on to something new.

I saw Alan Munde, from Norman, around campus. He was maybe a year or two younger than I was and just learning to play the banjo. One time on the way to a jam session I stopped at a music store, Alan was there and I asked him if he wanted to jam with us at Ed Shelton's house. I told him that Ed was a good banjo player. Alan went with us and it changed his life. He heard Ed play then Ed started showing Alan a lot of stuff and Alan just started getting real good, real quick. It was rather amazing.

The band, no longer doing the "Oklahoma Jamboree," began playing on a TV show called Walker House of Lights. It was the same band, but with a few different players in it. It had Ed

Shelton, Bob Wood who later had a big music store in Del City, Oklahoma, and me.

After that, we formed a band with Alan Munde, Walter Hawkins, and Albert Brown. The band got a TV show on a UHF channel with Jack Beasley at KLPR in Oklahoma City. It was a live show on Tuesday nights and we had a great time playing a lot more bluegrass. We played the TV show for several weeks in addition to other places.

Ed Shelton had played with the Stone Mountain Boys while living in Dallas. He worked for the National Cash Register Co. and when they transferred him to Oklahoma City, he stayed in touch with the band. We kept the road hot going back and forth to Dallas to play with them or some of them would come to Norman to play. This is when I met Mitchell Land, Tootie Williams and all of the Stone Mountain band members. They showed me a lot about bluegrass music, really got me playing more bluegrass and learning more about it. Later on, I ended up producing one of the Stone Mountain Boys albums. Royce Campbell continued to come around, so we had a lot of good jam sessions.

In 1965, we had a Grand Ole Opry type show to do in Wichita, Kansas. Hap Peebles produced these shows in the Wichita area and he booked Pee Wee King and Sheb Wooley on this one.

We had Ed Shelton, Mitchell Land, Royce Campbell, and me; Glen Mowery met us in Wichita. We went to Ed's house on Friday, jammed all afternoon and all night...we never went to bed. The next morning we loaded up and drove out to the farm in Caldwell, had dinner with Mom and Dad then went on to the show in Wichita and were exhausted when we got there.

Mitchell Land's wife, a large woman, took some kind of diet pills and Mitchell said, "I've got some of these diet pills we could take and probably keep us awake." He said, "Try this," as he handed each one of us a little brown diet pill. I had never taken a pill in my life, and then we stopped to get a six-pack of beer to chase them down.

We were flying and ready to play. We got on stage and played every tune 90 miles an hour. We played good that night, but awfully fast. When it was over, we got in my car, a stick shift Chevrolet Corvair. Ed Shelton and Mitchell Land rode with me as we headed back to Oklahoma City. We had been up for two days but still buzzing from the diet pill. We cut back through Belle Plain, Kansas before getting on the interstate and as we came around a big curve at midnight, in the bright, full moonlight, I saw a Shetland pony in the middle of the highway. I stopped the car, got out, all six foot three of me, but instead of trying to get the pony out of the way…I got on him. In fact, we all took a ride…out in the middle of nowhere. We wore white shirts and in the moonlight, anyone could have seen us. After the rodeo, we got on I-35 and everything was fine. Ed sat in the backseat playing his banjo and Mitchell sat in the front seat playing his mandolin. It sounded so good. They just picked their butts off and we were really having a good time.

After a while Ed said, "I'm getting a little tired, would you mind if I closed my eyes back here?

I told him, "Go ahead, no problem." Mitchell was in front with me.

We went a little farther down the Interstate and Mitchell said, "Byron, I'm really getting sleepy."

"No problem," I said. "I'm going to light up a cigar…I've got it. I'm fine."

We all woke up at the same time, down in a tall weeded, Johnson grass and sunflower median, somewhere around Guthrie. Sunflowers hitting the top of the car woke us up. As we drove through the weeds, the bumper hit the sunflower stalks and the heads banged down on the hood and roof. When we woke up all we saw were sunflowers.

I was barely going, maybe ten miles an hour in high gear… chucka, chucka, chucka. I could just as easily have been going sixty miles an hour, but when I fell asleep, my foot slipped off the gas so we were barely moving. I had no idea where we were, but I never stopped… just put it in second gear, eased it back up through the tall weeds and onto the pavement.

A truck had stopped on the highway and the driver had a light shining down in the median, probably wondering what we were doing.

We did not stop and we sure did not go back to sleep. It scared us to death. We had a guardian angel that night and I will never forget it. As there are now culverts and drop offs along that highway, today it might have been a different story.

GMC produced Corvairs between 1960 and 1969 and Ralph Nader brought up safety issues regarding the Corvair, in his 1965 book, "Unsafe at Any Speed." I guess some of that would depend on the driver.

During the spring semester, in March of 1965, the Dillards Pickin' N' Fiddlin' album came out. That was really the beginning of my professional career and I was still a college student. Producers read liner notes to see which musicians are on a record. From that album, I would receive many studio and other jobs. The album cover looked good to me, "The Dillards, with Byron Berline, Fiddle; "Pickin' And Fiddlin.'"

I completed my junior year at OU and in June of 1965, mom, dad, and I headed back to Weiser, Idaho to the National Old Time Fiddle Contest. After recalling the disaster of the previous summer, I took the best guitar player I knew, Royce Campbell, to back me up.

I remember meeting Sammy Bush at the fiddle contest. He was thirteen years old and ended up winning the Weiser Junior Division three times. The jam sessions were lots of fun, Bill Yohee entered the contest, but I relished in the win that year, 1965 National Old Time Fiddle Champion. I came home with prize money, that big trophy and many good memories.

Ralph Rinzler, writer of the Dillards' "Pickin' and Fiddlin'" album liner notes, knew that dad and I played fiddle. Ralph was involved in the selection of talent for the Newport Folk Festival and he decided he wanted some fiddlers so he invited dad and me to perform, along with Eck Robertson, Arthur Smith, and Tex Logan, a fiddler and friend of Bill Monroe's. Mom, dad, and I drove 1656 miles to Rhode Island and they paid our expenses out there and decent money to perform. It was a blast and absolutely, unbelievable! I had never met any of the big acts. I heard them on radio, TV and of course, records, but never actually met any of them…except the Dillards. Peter, Paul, and Mary were there, Bob Dylan, Joan Baez, Bill Monroe, Sam and Kirk McGee, Charles River Valley Boys and Everett D. Lilly. I met and jammed some with Mike Seeger who is Pete's brother and Bob Siggins, the banjo player with the Charles River Valley Boys. Jim Rooney was there, as was Cousin Emmy, an older act and she played banjo. I knew of Bill Keith who played with Bill Monroe and knew he played old fiddle tunes like "Sailor's Hornpipe" and "Devil's dream." Bill Keith was one of the first well known for recording fiddle tunes on the banjo. These are all bluegrass people. I also knew Bill Monroe would be there and I wanted to meet him.

Tex Logan and I began to jam at the house where all the entertainers stayed. He began teaching me one of his tunes, "Down in the Bluegrass." I learned it and a few years later Country Gazette recorded it. I started meeting all these new players and Tex said, "I'll introduce you to Bill Monroe." We continued playing and Bill Monroe showed up and listened to us jam. He came over and said in that unmistakable, high, soft voice, "Why don't you play with me on my show...you and Tex?" I played fiddle with Bill Monroe and his Bluegrass Boys, Bill on mandolin, his son James, on bass, Peter Rowan on guitar and vocals, Don Lineberger on banjo, Bill's fiddler Gene Lowinger and Tex Logan on fiddle. Bill Monroe referred to Gene Lowinger as a Jewish kid from New York, trying to learn to play the fiddle. Again, in that high, soft voice, he said. "I don't know if he'll make a fiddler, or not."

I thought, "Geez, Bill."

We did Mule Skinner Blues, Blue Moon over Kentucky, Wall of Time, Somebody Touched Me, and Bluegrass Breakdown. It was a big thrill getting to play on stage with Bill Monroe at the 1965 Newport Folk Festival.

At one point during the festival, we had a huge jam at the house and it went on for hours. Bill said to me, "Let's go outside." We went out to a bar set up for the entertainers and got a soda pop. That is when he popped the question and I will never forget that high, soft voice, when he said, "I want you to play in my band."

"What...when...?" I stuttered.

"When it's convenient for you," He said.

I told him I had to finish college and that it would take another year and a half.

He said, "Well, that will be fine, just stay in touch. I'd really like you to play in my band."

I thought, "This is great!" As time passed I stayed in contact with him, wanting him to know I was still interested.

On Sunday, July 25 1965, dad and I were first up on the schedule at the Newport festival. They announced us, "A father-son duo from Oklahoma…Lue and Byron Berline." We got Jim Rooney on guitar and Bill Keith on banjo, to back us up and we played several songs, including Crazy Creek, New Broom, Old Logan, and Dusty Miller. I was twenty and dad was seventy.

I did not think anything could equal the summer of 1964, but the summer of 1965 brought even more opportunities and some very good memories.

University of Oklahoma, track, shot put, 1965.

That fall, I entered my senior year at OU. All football players stayed in Washington House and when I changed from football to track, I moved to Jefferson House, the athletic dorm for other athletes.

Harold Keith, a long distance runner and graduate of OU, served as the University of Oklahoma Sports Publicity Director from 1930-1969. He won the 1958 Newbery Medal and the 1964 Lewis Carroll Shelf Award for his historical novel "Rifles for Watie," which is based on the interviews he did for his Master's thesis. He also wrote "47 Straight" about the glory days of Bud Wilkinson at OU. After winning the fiddle Championship in Weiser and returning to OU in the fall, Harold Keith came to my dorm room to do a little interview and take a photograph of me playing fiddle. J.D. Martin, the track coach was there, playing guitar. Coach Martin, Frank Deramus the sprinter, 2-miler, Johnny English, and I occasionally jammed while living at Jefferson House. Harold asked the difference between a violin and a fiddle and with a straight face I said, "A violin has four strings and a fiddle has too."

The article, with a photo, came out the following spring of 1966, right before the Big 8 Track Meet and it was a good article. Harold Keith was a nice person and he enjoyed the athlete-fiddler thing, getting a lot of mileage out of it. The local paper in the town where the track meet was to be held came out with this headline, "OU Brings National Champion to Big Eight Track Meet." Readers assumed it was a track champion. A little part stated it was a fiddle champion.

Harold Keith's son, Johnny, was a banjo player and one night he came out to where I was playing in Oklahoma City. He was not ready to go home yet and wanted to get some more beer or something so I decided to ride along with him.

He said. "I want you to meet somebody."

He said it was Spanky, but I did not know to whom he was referring. Finally, I said, "You mean Spanky McFarland, of the Little Rascals?"

He said, "He's got a club here called, "The Club House."

I could not believe it! We pulled into the parking lot and went inside. There he was...and I got to meet Spanky. He did not look like the kid in the movies, but it was Spanky and I got to meet him. He was a nice person and I remembered all those "Little Rascals" movies.

It was two or three in the morning, but the night was not yet over. Johnny lived way out east of Norman and we drove to his house. I told him I did not think I had ever met his wife. When we arrived, Johnny said, "Now, I want you to go up to the window and play "Black Mountain Rag," so I did and I could see the curtains open a little. His wife, originally from Kentucky, was real pretty and so nice. She got up and fixed us breakfast while most women would have thrown us out. We were officially, little rascals.

I began dating a little, but between studies, track and music, I did not have much time for girls until one night in December of 1965. I came home from studying and went to "Moore Burger," across the street from Jefferson House, the track athletic dorm. I had on a cowboy hat and stood at the counter ordering and Bill Lamb, a great OU wrestler, stood next to me. I looked up and saw a 1963 Pontiac pull up with a girl driving and another girl sitting on the passenger side. I found out later they had been studying and decided to come to "Moore Burger" for some hot chocolate or something.

I told Bill, "Watch this." I went over to the driver's side, tapped on the window and she rolled it down. "Is this your car?" I asked her.

"Yes." She said.

"You know." I began. "I've been wanting to buy one of these...would you give me a ride in it?"

She started rolling up the window. "Wait!" I said quickly. "You go to school here, right?"

"Yes." She replied.

"Where are you from?" I asked her.

"Guthrie." She said.

Finding an opening, I said, "Well, I go through there on my way home."

"Where's that?" She wanted to know.

I told her, "Well, actually, Caldwell, Kansas, on a farm there.

"Oh." She responded. "Do you live in Jefferson House?"

I said, "Yes."

"You're on the track team? Throw the javelin?" she questioned.

"Yes." I said. This was getting strange.

"You play the fiddle?" She asked.

"Yes." I said.

"Your name is Byron Berline, isn't it?" She matter-of-factly asked.

This took me by surprise and I did not quite know how to respond. I looked at her and stammered out, "Well...well, how did you know that?"

"I read about you in the school paper, thought you sounded interesting and I wanted to meet you." She said.

I thought, "That's too much!"

She read the article about me in the OU paper two years before, the one with the photo of me holding a football in one hand, a fiddle in the other and wearing the cowboy hat I now had on my head. For two years, she had wanted to meet me.

Then her friend in the car began talking to me and I asked her the driver's name, but she refused to tell me! The driver did give me a ride, down the block and back and her friend finally gave me the driver's name...Bette Ringrose. I found out she was in graduate school working on her master's degree in music, piano performance. I looked up her name in the university directory and got her phone number then I called her.

"You teach piano and I need a piano lesson." I told her. Shortly after that, I asked her out on a legitimate date. I was a senior and she was in her second year of graduate school. I majored in physical education and loved music. She majored in music and loved athletics. On one of our first dates, Bette went with the band, and me to Caldwell, Kansas and she met mom and dad. Our band played a New Year's Eve party and dance in Caldwell and that is how we welcomed in 1966.

In the spring of 1966, my senior year at OU, I participated in track setting a new OU and state record with a javelin throw of two hundred twenty one feet. I wondered how long the new record would stand.

At the end of that spring semester Bette graduated from OU with a Masters in Piano Performance. I was not quite finished and needed one more semester to do student teaching and take a couple of other courses. The draft board however, said, "You've gone to school for four years and that's enough." I told them I just had one more semester before receiving my degree and asked to do that one semester. I told them I did not mind going after that, knowing after that semester, they would draft me. They totally refused the request stating I was classified one-A. That was it.

Dad was so upset and said, "So what are we going do?"

Medford was the county seat in Grant County, which is where the Berline farm and my draft board were located. Dad began asking people, locals what we might do and they said, "Do you know any senators or other officials that might help you?" Immediately I thought, "Fred Harris," and I said, "I played for him, but he probably won't remember me." I sat down that night and wrote him a letter explaining my situation. I told him I was not trying to get out of being in the service, but simply felt it was important to graduate, and then reminded him I played for his fundraiser in 1963. Harris hand carried my letter to Mr. Hershey who was head of the Selective Service in Washington, D.C. Hershey then called the local draft board in Medford, Oklahoma and told them to change my draft status, which took all of two days and I had my deferment. The following is the letter from Harris confirming my new deferment status.

United States Senate
Committee On
Government Operations
July 28, 1966

Mr. Byron Berline
R.R. #2
Caldwell, Kansas

Dear Byron:

I am enclosing a copy of the report I received from the Selective Service System, and I am pleased to see that you are currently classified with a student deferment to enable you to continue your education.

I wish you the very best, and hope you will keep in touch from time to time.

With kindest regards,
Sincerely yours,
Fred R. HARRIS
U. S. Senate

Sure enough, the following letter made it official.

SELECTIVE SERVICE SYSTEM
1724 F. Street NW.
WASHINGTON, D.C. 20435

Honorable Fred R. Harris
United States Senate

Subject: Byron Douglas Berline
SS No. 34-27-44-29

Dear Senator Harris:

Reference is made to previous correspondence regarding the above-named registrant.

The State Director of Selective Service for Oklahoma informs me that Mr. Berline was classified into Class II-S (Student Deferment) until January 15, 1967, by his local board.

I trust this information will be of assistance to you.

Sincerely yours,
Louis B. Hershey
Director

I thought, "Wow!" It was just a stupid thing to do to a student.

Mom, dad, Bette, and I attended some fiddle contests that summer and in the fall, Bette went to Evansville, Indiana to teach at the University of Evansville while I enrolled at OU for one last semester. I picked up a couple of courses and taught at West Union High School, right there in Norman, which took care of the student teaching requirement.

In January 1967, I graduated from OU with a degree in Physical Education and a memorable part of my life's journey, completed.

Chapter 6
1967: Playing with Bill Monroe

Since our meeting at the Newport Folk Festival in 1965, I occasionally wrote letters or made phone calls to Bill Monroe. I tried to stay in touch and wanted him to know I was still interested in playing with him. Upon graduation from OU in January of 1967, I called Bill and said, "I am coming to see you, when it's convenient for you."

"It looks like it will be the second week in February before I will be in town." He said.

I called Bette in Evansville and asked if she wanted to go with me to Nashville. I drove to Evansville, picked her up, and drove on to Nashville, attending the Grand Ole Opry as Bill's guests. Peter Rowen played guitar for Bill and said that whenever I got to town, look him up and he would take me to the Opry and show me around. Peter Rowen was a little strange. We went back stage at the Ryman Auditorium and listened to them play. Lester Flatt and Earl Scruggs were there as well as the Osborne brothers. A couple of kids, Larry McNeely and Charlie Collins from Indiana, had driven all the way to Nashville to audition.

They said, "We want to play with Roy Acuff."

"Really?" I replied.

Roy did not know anything about this, but he had them play and later on, they got a gig with him. Charlie Collins stayed with

Acuff for several years. Larry McNeely was right out of high school and a very, very good banjo player. He played for Acuff for a while, went on to L.A., and eventually just sort of dropped out. I think he and his wife live in Nashville. She is Doc Harris's daughter. Doc was a real good friend of Roy Acuff, Howdy Forrester and all those people.

I introduced Bette to Bill Monroe and the others back stage. That night we jammed a little with Richard Greene and Peter Rowen at Lamar Grier's house. They were getting ready to leave Bill's band and said they had given him notice.

I drove Bette to Evansville and then went back to the farm in Caldwell. Two weeks later Bill called and said, "I need you here March first."

I drove to Nashville and stayed at the Andrew Jackson hotel. In 1967, I finally had to join the musician's union. Bill Monroe drove me down to the union office where I signed up and paid the $90, hoping I had enough in my checking account to cover it. My very first show with Bill Monroe was the Grand Ole Opry and the pay was a whopping $5 for Friday and $7 for Saturday. That was for one, thirty-minute show each of the two nights. I did not care what it paid or even if it paid, I was so glad to get to do it.

When I got to the Ryman Auditorium that night, Richard Greene was there. He had two or three days before leaving the band and Bill told him to stick around and play until he had to go. Peter Rowen was gone...we did not have a guitar player. Richard asked if I played guitar and I told him I could.

"Why don't you play guitar for us?" He asked. About that time, Bill walked in and I told him that since we did not have a guitar player, did he want me to play?

Up in that high, soft voice he said, "Neu...uuu, "Barn," (he never did figure out how to pronounce my name) "I hired you to play fiddle. We'll get a guitar player. Here, tune my mandolin, will you? I've got to get my shoes shined." There was, of course, no time to rehearse.

I listened to a tuning fork and tried to get his mandolin in tune the best I could. It was not easy because he had the action set up so the strings sat about a half inch above the fingerboard. I am not kidding. I tried to play it a little and thought, "Good gosh this thing is hard to play."

He came back and I handed the mandolin to him, saying, "That action is a little high isn't it Bill?"

"Yeah," he began in that unmistakable voice. "It takes a real man to play that mandolin, Barn."

I said, "I guess it DOES!"

He got a kick out of letting others play his mandolin and then they could not.

He said, "Well, pick out a tune you want to play."

"You want me to play one tonight?" I asked him.

"Yes." He responded. "So pick one out."

I did not know he was going to ask me to play a solo on this first show and the first thing that came to mind was, "Monroe's Hornpipe."

"You want to play that one?" He asked.

"Why not," I asked him. "It's your tune."

"Well, alright, if you want to." He said. "I thought maybe you might play one of those fiddle tunes you play so well."

Therefore, I selected "Monroe's Hornpipe" the one I had practiced.

I was real nervous, never having rehearsed with them, first time on the Grand Ole Opry, no guitar player, just James Monroe, Bill's son, on bass, Lamar Grier on banjo, and me! On the way up to the stage Bill stopped and said to a musician, "Come on up with us." That is exactly what Bill said. This person played the banjo and was a good guitar player in Wilma Lee and Stoney Cooper's group who were also booked on the show that night.

"Jiminy Christmas!" I thought, but the Opry worked this way. Everyone knew everyone else, what he or she played, and played for each other when the need arose. It was a big deal to me, but not to Bill. I was in a panic, but everything was fine; it just added to the anxiety and I was as nervous as a cat.

We got on stage and the first thing we played I could not hear anything! They did not have monitors and the acoustics were terrible. I thought I could hear the microphones going out over the house, but I really could not hear anything; it was like playing against a wall. Everyone said it sounded great over the radio, but on stage, it was total shock. That was the first of many shows I played with Bill Monroe and his Bluegrass Boys and as with that very first night on the Grand Ole Opry, he featured me…on every show, which was very nice of him. He did not have to do that.

Bill wanted Richard Greene and me to work up some things so we did "My Little Georgia Rose" then Bill wanted to do "Mule Skinner Blues" one last time with Richard, before he left the band. I stepped back to let Bill and Richard play while I just chucked rhythm in the background. Richard just stood on stage and glared…he was so disgusted. I looked at him and thought, "What is your problem?" It was, "another fiddler is on stage,"

1967 No Hats Show. L to r; Byron Berline, Lamar Grier, Bill Monroe, Benny Williams, James Monroe.

thing. He was young and not yet initiated in how, professionally, to handle himself.

We thrashed around for a guitar player for a long time just picking up players here and there. We immediately went on the road playing in Ohio and other places where Bill had already booked shows, but we always worked the schedule so we could play the Opry whenever possible. We traveled all over and I had a great time!

In April of 1967, Bill booked us at a big auditorium in Nashville. I had been with Bill about a month when this came up. The inside of the venue was huge, seating at least a thousand people and they had a stage at both ends. The floor was flat, with no bleacher seats, just folding chairs so the stages were raised about six feet off the floor so everyone seated would have a good view of the entertainment. The stages were also flat, wooden surfaces with a railing around the outside. A black curtain hung around the back of the stage. I remember this was scheduled to be a rather formal, evening affair and we all had to rent tuxedos, even Bill. He took the whole band to the rental shop where they fitted Bill, Lamar Grier, Bill's son James, Benny Williams, and me. Benny was sitting in with us because we still did not yet have a permanent guitar player. Back stage before the show, the Nashville Banner took pictures and I wanted to make certain I got one because it was the first time I ever saw Bill Monroe in a tuxedo. It was also the first time we all played without our customary western hats. We took the stage at one end while the Nashville Symphony Quartet took the one at the other end of the building. We took turns playing to the audience; we played about five minutes then they played. It went back and forth like that for about an hour. The guests were all big time…the mayor, maybe the governor. After playing, we all sat down on folding chairs placed at the back edge of the stage. As we would play again, a little later, we did not put our instruments away; we sat quietly while holding our instruments. All in a row, I sat next to Bill and down the row, Lamar, James and Benny.

The speaker came to the microphone at center stage and began addressing the audience. It was absolute silence, only his voice filled the big room. For some reason, Bill decided to scoot his chair back just a little and when he did, his back hit the railing which caused him to bend forward, and chair, Bill and his mandolin fell backwards through the railing, dropping six feet to the floor. A very loud "Crash" interrupted the quiet dignified evening and when I looked, all I could see going over were the soles of Bill's shoes. When he fell backwards, he grabbed at anything to help save him from the fall and it just happened to be my fiddle. He almost pulled it right out of my hand, knocking the bridge right out of it. I said, "Are you alright?"

Bill said, "Get down and help me find a part of my mandolin...I think I broke it."

"Bill, forget about the mandolin...are you okay?" I said.

It was amazing that he had no concussion, broken bones, nothing. Benny came over and he was laughing so hard that tears were running down his face. He said it looked like the whole row of musicians was going to go over like dominos.

I climbed down off of the stage and crawled around, helping Bill find the missing mandolin piece. We found some binding that broke off right at the point of his F5 and the back cracked all the way down.

I remember that Doc Harris was in the audience and came to the stage to check on Bill.

Bill sort of turned his head back and forth, rubbing his neck and said, "You know, my neck felt a little stiff, but it feels better."

Geez, Bill.

Bill Monroe only had one mandolin. We had dates booked and he had no instrument. I lent him one of mine, an E2, which he played a couple of gigs, but he really did not care for it. In the mean time, Gene Martin who was working at the Grammer Guitar factory at this time, offered to repair Bill's mandolin. While we were on the road, someone lent him an F5. When we got back off the road, the next day, Bill went to pick up his mandolin. He told Gene, "I had a dream about the mandolin" then he proceeded to tell his dream. When he finished, Gene said, with a strange look, "I had the very same dream."

It gets stranger, still. I never got one of the photos taken that night, so several years ago; I contacted the Nashville Banner and asked if they had the photo, so that I might copy it. They looked through all their files and there was nothing there. I was so disappointed.

About four or five years ago, I called Brian Sutton or he was in the shop. We wanted him to perform at OIBF. While we were talking, Brian began telling about a friend of his who worked at the Nashville Banner. The newspaper began cleaning out their archive files and knowing this employee liked bluegrass music, gave the employee all the photographs. This friend then called Brian and he made copies of them. He said, "Byron, I've got one of you and Bill in tuxedos."

I immediately knew to which photograph he was referring. He made copies for me and that photo is now on display in my Doublestop Fiddle Shop and in this book.

While I was doing shows with Bill Monroe, mom and dad drove across the country to Paradise, California so dad could enter a fiddle contest. He won second in the contest and "Most Liked Fiddler."

Bill and I always started jamming the minute we got on the bus. He got out his mandolin and I got my fiddle. We played fiddle tunes and started working up stuff. I kept thinking he would tell me how to play after hearing he was a real stickler about the way he wanted things. Only one time, did he ever say anything to me about how to play something and that was about his song, "Uncle Pen" which I learned from somebody who played it some weird way.

"I don't like the way you play "Uncle Pen" Bill said. " All you've got to do is think Grey Eagle."

Doodle de doo. Yep, that was it. I said, "That's easy enough." That is the only time Bill ever asked me to play something different from the way I played it. Since Uncle Pen was Bill Monroe's uncle and Bill wrote the tune, he had the right to have it played the way he wanted.

I do not believe anyone could have been well rehearsed on all the songs Bill performed. There were too many and they went way back. Sometimes in his shows, in the second half, he might take requests and these old, old songs came up. He did not play some of them, but some he did and sometimes he just started singing. The fiddle kicked off everything, unless it was a song I did not know and then I just thought, "Well, I wonder what this one sounds like?" I listened until I caught it then played something that fit into it. I eventually learned the ins and outs and things got easier for me.

Bill Monroe did not like to fire anybody. He would verbally beat you up or try to run you off, but would not fire anyone. He wanted another banjo player, instead of Lamar and he began doing some of that to Lamar. I said, "Bill, why don't you just tell him it's not working out?"

"Oh, no," he said, "Then word would get around that I fire people and that wouldn't do."

All the while, we continued to look for a guitar player. Joe Stewart and Benny Williams played every instrument and they recorded every instrument with Bill except the mandolin. I asked Bill, "Why don't you get those two guys? They play everything, including bass. Get them to play triple mandolin with you and then they can say they recorded every instrument on your recordings"

"I was thinking about that." He quickly said, but he never did do it and I remember Joe Stewart telling me that he wanted to do it so bad. Joe Stewart and Benny Williams should be in the Bluegrass Hall of Fame.

Bill purchased a 1947 GMC bus from Johnny and Jack. Johnny is Johnny Wright, Kitty Wells' husband. He and Jack Anglund traveled, who only knows how many miles and how many years in that bus. When Bill bought the bus, it was twenty years old and worn out. By the time Bill bought it, it was too far-gone to function as a band's travel bus and it never worked when we needed to go out on the road. It would not run...there was always a problem with it and the inside reeked of diesel fuel. That bus was a piece of junk and I remember the very first time I got on it. We did not have a bus driver so Bill's son, James, or Lamar had to drive. About midnight I got tired and asked Bill, which bunk he wanted me to use.

He said, "Just take that one there on the right."

I said, "Okay, well, then, I'll say goodnight."

I went back and looked at the top bunk noticing there was no ladder so I stepped on the other bed, hoisted myself up and over. When I flopped, I heard a big crunching noise of something distinctly breaking. I reached under the mattress, pulled out a paper sack and when I opened it, I saw two or three broken, old seventy-eight records.

I told Bill what happened and he said, "Oh, those were old

Bluebird records of me and Charlie. I found them at an antique store and forgot where I put them."

I felt SO bad. Bill and Charlie Monroe records are collector items and I am sure, meant a lot to Bill. He just said, "Oh well." He was not upset...that was it. No telling how long they had been there. I certainly felt it was a bad way to begin our first trip on the road.

A couple of months into the tour, on May 19, we made a trip to Los Angeles, California to play at the Ash Grove, which was a big club. I looked forward to it because the Dillards, the Kentucky Colonels and other players I knew also lived out there. We got ready to leave Nashville and the transmission went out on the bus. Doug Green, later to become Ranger Doug of the cowboy group Riders in the Sky, was setting in with Bill before he had to go back to college. Bill decided he and Doug had to be out there, so they flew to L.A. and left the rest of us to catch up with them on the bus.

Bill played mandolin, Doug played rhythm guitar and they both sang, so if necessary, they could perform duets. Once there, the Dillards, the Kentucky Colonels and all the other bluegrass groups would be willing to donate their services to fill in. This left James Monroe, Lamar Grier and me, to wait until they repaired the bus and it became road worthy. Oh, and Virginia Stauffer, Bill's girlfriend; he also left her behind. She was to go on the bus with us. Virginia was a songwriter and Bill had covered her, "I Live in the Past" and "Body and Soul"

After a long wait, the bus was ready to go, but they never did get the bathroom toilet to function properly. Bill told us not to use it...we all knew about it and told Virginia. When the bus stopped to get gas, we just got off to eat and used a service station or restaurant's restroom. Inconvenient, but that is what we did.

We got outside of Dallas, Texas and the transmission went out again. Broken down and on top of that...the toilet overflowed, ran everywhere, flooded the isles with raw sewage and it stunk. We had noticed Virginia never got off the bus when we stopped to eat or get gas, but at the time, we did not think too much about it.

We confronted her. "We thought you were NOT to use the restroom."

She did not say anything. James and I cleaned up that filthy, stinking mess and we were so mad at her.

Then, we discovered the bus had no third gear. Most of the Stone Mountain Boys lived in Dallas and while being stranded there for four or five days, we camped out at their houses and different places. Mitchell Land worked in a machine shop and built a bushing to go around that third gear. When he came through with the part, we finally got the bus running.

We got to about Needles, California as it began to get dark so we put on the lights, but nothing happened. We managed to pull into a place and when a serviceman opened the electrical panel, sparks flew everywhere. There was a flash of fire and the stench of burned electrical wiring. They used a fire extinguisher and the resulting white powder went all over the bus, coating everything, but it did put the fire out. I thought, "What else can happen?" They got the thing wired up, taped, and the lights working. We nursed that bus all the way into L.A. and by the time we got to The Ash Grove, Bill had already used the Dillards, Roland and Clarence White and some others to fill in for us.

Roland White had been hanging around with Bill a lot and the Kentucky Colonels were not doing much at that time, in fact, they were about ready to fold. Doug Dillard was there and I had not seen him in a long time so I stayed at his house the first night or so. We only had two or three days to play as we had other bookings to fulfill.

They recorded the show, including the introductions Bill gave his players and as always, he introduced me as, "Barn Berline on fiddle." We played Panhandle Country, Live and Let Live, John Hardy, Put My Rubber Doll Away, Prisoner's Song, Footprints in the Snow, Rawhide, Mule Skinner Blues, Lonesome Road Blues, Dear Old Dixie, When My Blue Moon Turns to Gold Again, Sad and Lonesome Day, Carroll County Blues and Swing Low Sweet Chariot.

I remember sitting with James Monroe at The Ash Grove when Bill said, "I want to see you two on the bus...right now."

I thought, "What now?"

James said, "What's the deal?"

I told him I did not know and I said, "Is he gonna fire us or what?"

We went to the bus and when Bill got on board he said, "You boys need any spending money?"

"Sure," I said.

"We can always use a little spending money." James added.

Then Bill gave us, I think it was twenty bucks. That was nice of him.

Then he said, "What do you think of that little white boy?"

"White boy?" I asked. "Bill, what are you talking about? What white boy?"

"You know," Bill said, "the one that plays the guitar."

Then it dawned on me. The white, had a capital "W."

"You mean Roland...Roland White?" I asked him.

"He says he wants to play with us. Reckon he'd be alright?" Bill asked

"Well, Yes!" I told him. "He sings well too and knows what to do." Bill wanted our opinion, but the way he got us on the bus had us wondering what might happen. Bill was so funny...he would play games with you. Bill hired Roland White, we picked him up, and away we went with our new guitar player.

Bill Monroe and the Bluegrass Boys in 1967 at the First Bean Blossom Festival. 1 to r; Byron Berline, Bill Monroe, Doug Green, James Monroe.

In June of 1967, Bill Monroe had his first Bean Blossom festival in Indiana and of course, we played. We were looking for a banjo player at this time and Butch Robbins, just out of high school, played the festival with us. He was a good banjo player and really wanted to play with Bill Monroe. He came to Nashville to audition and hoped he could play more with Bill's Bluegrass Boys. I was not in town as I had gone to Evansville, Indiana to see Bette during that week, so Roland White told me this story.

Butch liked Don Reno's banjo playing, but Bill did not care too much for that style. They were rehearsing backstage at the Opry and when they began to play Bill asked Butch, "Why are you playing like that?"

"Roland told me to play it that way." Butch said in defense.

"Well, I didn't tell you to play like that." Bill said and then he told Butch to go home and practice...and come back later. He just sent him home.

Shortly after that, we picked up Vic Jordan, a real nice person and a good banjo player. He had been playing with Jimmy Martin until we hired him to go with us. These players stayed with Bill until I left the band: Bill and James Monroe, Roland White, Vic Jordan, and me.

Bill wanted to record while I was still in the band and he knew I would soon be leaving for the army. Bill and I wrote "Gold Rush" and recorded it as well as "Sally Goodin'." This was a 45 rpm and they released the record August 3, 1967. The record got a lot of airplay and I was amazed at the number of players discovering the record and learning to play "Gold Rush" off of it.

After being out on the road, we returned to Nashville to find my draft notice under the door. Roland and I sat down and looked at it, then started having a little party of our own.

I had to report to Army basic training on September 12. One of the last gigs I did with Bill was a show in Hugo, Oklahoma, put on by Bill Grant. My brother Henry came over to see me and I remember it rained like crazy. All the Stone Mountain Boys came up from Dallas and we had a big jam. I still have a tape of that.

Right before going into the army, dad, mom, Bette, and I went to one more fiddle contest in Wellington, Texas. Louis Franklin, a real good player, was my main competition and I think I won that one.

I went to Oklahoma City as ordered, to join the army, but did not know where I would go after that.

Chapter 7
1967-1968: Army Life

I went to Fort Polk, Louisiana in the fall of 1967 and having been in ROTC in college I knew how to march and do that stuff. I had my worst experience at the reception station, which is where they cut off your hair, issue uniforms, and give vaccinations. It was, "Do this, do that" and a lot of testing. We did not know what was going on and they kept us up all hours of the night. We did this for about a week before starting basic training.

The base at Fort Polk has a North and South Fort with training areas in the North Fort. We were in basic for eight weeks and the first thing I heard was, "Don't volunteer for nothin'." In the first place, before new recruits arrive they go over the paper work for each soldier to see if anything stands out, so they already knew a lot about me before I got there. That first day the recruits lined-up and the company commander, a lieutenant about my age, asked for any college graduates. I looked down the row, saw two or three hands go up and figured he already knew about me, so I put up my hand.

He came over to me and charged, "What school did you go to?"

"The University of Oklahoma," I told him.

"Did you play football there?" He grumbled.

"Yes I did." I replied.

"Well, I went to Florida State." He announced. "Remember that Gator Bowl in '65?"

"We might have something in common here." I thought. Usually officers are cold with no personal connection to anybody.

He said, "Well, welcome."

Shortly after that, while still in formation, Sergeant John Pointer training NCO from Chicago, came out to us, walked over, and asked if I could type. I told him I could.

He said, "Okay, I want you to be my assistant. You won't have to march, do any other details and I'll watch out for you, but you may have to work a little later."

He even temporarily, gave me my own quarters. As one of my duties, I drove the first aid jeep and delivered drinking water to all the training sites.

One of the questionnaires I filled out in the reception area asked if I played a musical instrument, to which I entered "fiddle." Then it asked if I played a band instrument and I immediately wrote down sousaphone. At the time, I tried everything to keep from shooting a rifle. About the third week, someone from the base band had obviously read the papers I filled out because he pulled me out of training to try out for the band. I had not played the big horn since high school. They let me warm up a little bit and then this guy put some sheet music down and said, "Okay, now play a little of this." I was terrible, I am sure.

"You play upright bass too?" He asked.

I assured him I did, but I did not read a lick of music and you had to be very good to get in the band. What a disappointment. Shortly after this, sergeant Pointer asked me if I knew anything about music and I told him I knew a little bit. He went on to explain they put him in charge of Family Day at the base and they wanted musicians, drill teams, anything they could think of to show off the company.

I said, "I'll take it over. Let me do the music deal."

I held a company meeting and asked how many musicians we had. Almost every hand went up. They began telling me how great they were. One said he had a Decca recording contract coming up and another said he was a great guitar player. I marched them all down to the entertainment center to check out instruments. The "great" guitar player stood there as I told the clerk he wanted to check out a guitar and I wanted a fiddle, if they had one. The guitar player suddenly remembered he neglected to say he was left-handed so he could not play just any guitar.

"Not a problem." The clerk said. "We've got a guitar strung up to play left handed."

The guitar player took the guitar and just stood there looking down…then walked away. He did not even know how to hold a guitar. Just telling stories…I do not understand that. To be honest, there was not a musician in the whole company, out of two or three hundred men. I tried to pick out the best; we had a horn player, one played a little keyboard and one tried to play the drum. We had no guitar player so I figured I would play that. They gave us time to practice but rehearsals were dismal. Discouraged and having no idea what to do, I asked the company commander if I could recruit some other musicians.

He said, "Sure, you do what you want."

"Thank you very much." I told him.

I thanked him and asked if they had to be soldiers. When he said they did not, I got on the phone and called Tootie Williams, Mitchell Land, Bosco Land, Lonnie Croft and Alan Munde. The Stone Mountain Boys loaded up, came to Family Day, and brought me a fiddle because I needed something better than the one I checked out at the entertainment center. We warmed up in the orderly room and the company commander, now a captain, said, "Wow! I didn't know you could do that!"

I said, "That's what I do. It's what I like to do."

They held the event outdoors and set up a small stage and PA system. They scheduled us to go on at 9:30 a.m. and just before it started someone said, "There's the colonel." A jeep pulled up and, Colonel Reed a full bird colonel got out. He began looking around and saw us holding our instruments, waiting to go on.

"Are we having country music here today?" He asked.

The company commander said, "Yes."

Colonel Reed wanted to know who was in charge of that and the company commander said, "Private Berline, sir."

"Get him over here." Reed ordered.

I hurried over to him, saluted and said, "Yes sir."

"Do you play country music?" He asked.

"Yes sir, we do." I told him.

"Do you know Wabash Cannonball?" He wanted to know.

"We do," I said. That was a Roy Acuff song.

"I might want to sing it with you." He said.

I told him that would be great and then I went back to Alan, Tootie, and Mitchell. "Do you think we can do Wabash Cannonball?" I asked. "The colonel wants to sing it with us." It was no big deal to them. Before we went on, I asked the colonel if he wanted us to call him up on stage or just what. He said, "No, I'll let you know." He was just BS'ing us.

We played all our fast songs like "Orange Blossom Special" and "Rawhide." We only had about fifteen minutes to play, but

Byron 1967 Army photo.

we just tore everything up. You could not have asked for a better audience. The people went nuts and so did the colonel. He came running over to me when we came off the stage.

"Oh, my god…you guys…you've got to play at the Officer's Club!" He was so excited. "You've got to play the entertainment centers. Get right on it!"

There was a lot of excitement in camp and that day we played all of the entertainment centers. Essentially, the colonel told the general about us and the general wanted us to play at the Officer's Ball, which was coming up in about two weeks.

In the mean time, I tried to get in touch with the director of Entertainment Services. Everyone in Special Services wanted me with them, but they did not know if it was possible as the army was in the process of phasing out Special Services.

The Stone Mountain Boys could not come back to play at the ball, but Special Services had a lot of different groups playing so they put me in there. I found this E8 who played guitar…a lot of western swing with bar chords so we worked up two or three songs. I was nervous…I told a joke on my company commander who sat next to the general. I was lucky…they laughed. Camal Kathy, head of the Entertainment division also played drums. He kept the brushes going the whole time we played and I am glad he did…it kept the energy going.

During basic training, no one is to receive special attention, but I could tell it meant a little something, knowing the general, and Camal Kathy. No sergeant gave me any crap! This was weird and I naively decided to test it. One day on the flare testing course, we had an old sergeant I did not know, doing the training. He said, "Now, when we yell, "flare" I want you all to hit the ground.

"Flare!" he shouted. Man, everybody just dropped. I kind of got down, but not in any hurry.

"Alright," he said, "we're going to do this one more time and the last man down is gonna give me fifty push-ups."

FLARE!

Everybody immediately dropped, but I kind of crawled down. The sergeant came charging over, ready to order me and saw my nametag. "Oh, you're the general's boy; I can't do anything to you." He said, and then walked away. You should have seen the looks I got. I decided never to do that again…just finish out my time. I could not believe it.

When you are in the army, you never know where you are going. Out of the two or three hundred men in our company, they assigned ninety percent to the infantry, which meant they would go straight to Vietnam. I got up the morning our eight weeks were up and it was still dark, but before I could get outside to check the assignment board the first sergeant came by saying, "I hope you like Fort Polk, Berline, because you're staying here." I called mom and dad to let them know I was not going to Vietnam and then I called Bette…we were all relieved. A lot of my buddies did not make it back from Nam. They shipped out, got killed…it just made me sick. I remember one sergeant, in particular, in his late forties who had been in the military a long time. I remember he looked a little like Darryl Royal football coach at Texas. This was a neat, neat man. He wanted to retire and only had one year to go. The military of course, wanted him to stay in so they said, "Well, if that's the case, then we're going to send you to Vietnam." They always threatened soldiers with that and he had already done two tours over there. They shipped him out to Nam and he was killed. Again, it just made me sick.

Out of basic training and knowing I would stay at Fort Polk, some other soldiers and I celebrated by riding around in a nearby town called Leesville. We listened to the Grand Ole Opry on the car radio and Roy Acuff was on the air. I told my friends I knew Acuff, but they did not believe me. I said, "Pull over." I got out of the car and went into a filling station, got a couple of dollars in quarters, found a pay phone and called information asking for the backstage number of the Grand Ole Opry. Sure enough, there was such a number so I deposited my quarters and dialed. When the back stage security guard answered, I told him who I was and asked him get Roy Acuff for me. In less than a minute Roy was on the phone. I told him where I was, the story about us listening to the opry and the guys not believing I knew him.

"Well," he said, "I'll fix that. You just listen to the 10:00 pm show and I'll let them know." I made sure we listened to the radio at ten o'clock. Roy came on and began talking about me, what a great fiddler I was and that I was in the Army. He went on and on then dedicated "The Great Speckled Bird" to me. Boy, my shirt buttons could have popped off. The guys could not believe it, which really made me feel great...I will never forget it.

I got in Special Services...the last man in and being there truly was "special." For about the first five months we did not even wear uniforms and then one day, one of our men failed to salute an officer who immediately reprimanded him. While he was at it, the officer questioned why the soldier was not in uniform. The kid said, "Oh, we don't have to wear one." Well, we did after that.

Out of basic training and in Special Services, I had more free time so I went to Leesville thinking I might find a country band to play with on weekends. Jimmy Jeans ran the band at the first place I went and he said I could set in. He thought I played well and said they could use a fiddle player.

"You're not in the service, are you?" He asked.

"Yes, I am" I told him.

"Oh forget it." He said, "Can't depend on them."

Then I tried another place in town called the Pines Club. It was a real big, dark, musty smelling joint. The band consisted of three people, bass, drums, and guitar. They were old...probably in their fifties. I am laughing. They let me sit in with them and liked what I did. Joe, the oldest and leader of the group loved Hank Williams and Hank songs were the only ones he played. I had a good time playing with them...it was kind of a hoot. I told them I wanted to get hired, maybe weekends or something. After the very small audience left for the night Joe said, "We're going to go have a meeting about this. Now Byron, you just stay right here."

They huddled over in a corner, talked about ten minutes then Joe came over and said, "Now here's the deal. We want you to play with us and we're gonna give you five dollars a night. Now wait a minute, that's not all. We're gonna give you a dollar each, out of our pay and that will give you eight dollars, but wait, that's not all...free drinks at the bar...now wait, that's not all. You can get down off the bandstand and dance, any time you want to... now what do you think?"

I will never forget them. I thought that was great, eight dollars a night, free drinks and that's not all...I can get down from the bandstand and dance any time I want. I told them I would think about it. I did not take them up on their offer, but I always tell my band, "Now that's not all."

Jimmy C. Newman was playing at Jimmy Jeans' club so I went there one night, getting there late as they were just finishing up the set. I noticed they had a real good little guitar player with them and I figured he was with Jimmy C. Newman's band. When Newman left, the band did another set. I stood in the audience and Jimmy Jeans said, "Hey, you got your fiddle? You want to go up and play a little?" I got my fiddle out of the car and joined them on stage. The short, little guitar player said, "I guess you play fiddle tunes?" I said I did and he said he knew a few fiddle tunes. We started playing and boy he was a great player. His name is Bobby Whitten and he played in the club's house band. He said he was in the army...I could not believe it. This place turned me down because I was in the service. I told him I thought Jimmy did not hire anyone in the service.

"Well, I'm dating his daughter." He said.

I asked him what he did in the army and he said, "I'm a cook."

"You won't be much longer!" I told him.

"Why not?" He asked.

"Because I'm getting you out of there!" He had only a few months to go and said he would give anything to get out of being a cook, so I went back to Special Services and they immediately cut orders, bringing him in. Bob Whitten and I worked up shows, played all over the post, and competed in a Special Services contest held in San Antonio, Texas, against fourth Army Special Services, which included Louisiana, Arkansas, and Texas. Bob won second and I won first in the instrumental category. Fort Hood won the post contest, which was okay because they could select anyone from the contest to go with them on tour, which was the big prize. They picked Bob and me and we started going to Fort Hood for three or four weeks touring all around fourth Army. The last time I saw Bob Whitten he was playing for Mel Tillis. He is a real good player and we had a lot of fun.

One day I got a call from Lieutenant Garet Von Netzer who was a Big 8 hurdler champion from Missouri. He wanted to put together a track team and he knew I went to OU and threw the javelin and discus. A track team sounded good to me so we began recruiting and getting the word out and the result was an amazing team. We went to the fourth Army track meet and won…I won the javelin and placed in the shot.

When they completely shut down Special Services, either the soldiers played in the marching band or they shipped to Germany. Bill Bailey was the athletic director and he loved music. He said he had a place for me, but it would not have an opportunity for advancement. I was a spec four and could not have cared less because all I wanted was to get my time over and stay state side. Bailey kept his word, dropping one of his men and putting me in that slot so that I could stay with the track team for my remaining year in the army.

With this new position, I knew I would not go to Vietnam, so I called Bette and said, "I guess we can get married now." I took two weeks off and Bette and I were married in Guthrie, Oklahoma, August 23, 1968. When we returned to Fort Polk, Louisiana Bette took a civil service test, scored very high, and immediately got a job at one of the entertainment centers. We rented a little house in Hornbeck a small town about thirty miles from the base. We lived on my pay and saved all the money Bette made.

I had an opportunity to meet some outside players and I met a group called the Southern Bluegrass Boys with Travis Stewart, Gene Alford, and Dennis Lucas. Gene and Travis also lived in Hornbeck. Dennis a banjo player lived in Alexandria, Louisiana. I hooked up with them and we started playing as a band.

Red Corbin invited us to do a TV show in Sulphur, Louisiana, but when we got there, they cancelled the show so we went to Red's house to pick. He set up stereo microphones and we started pretending we were doing a radio show and I played five or six songs on the guitar. Red's son Mitch was about ten years old and not very interested in bluegrass music. He went to another room to watch TV while all of this was going on. Years later, Red played the tape we made that night and Mitch's ears perked up. He decided he wanted to play guitar based on hearing me play guitar on that tape and Mitch became an incredible guitar player. A chance happening that changed a person's life and passed the music on.

Working for Bailey I usually worked with all civilians hired by Army Entertainment. Jim Brisco soldered guitar cords, repaired instruments, and did anything else required. We had one man that made up posters and I distributed them around the base. The entertainment center is where they checked out instruments as you would a library book. My job was to check these instruments in and out. Remember the soldier who needed a "left handed guitar?" This is where I worked. The civilian staff did things a little differently than did the army and the following is a good example. Each morning when I got to work someone said we had better go get breakfast. We left about eight o'clock and came back at nine. I listened to records and messed around just killing time until about eleven thirty. Then someone said that we better go to lunch, so we went somewhere to eat getting back around one o'clock. At two o'clock, I had track practice and that was it...then I went home.

I talked Camal Kathy into having a Bluegrass Festival, which was neat because bluegrass festivals were new to Louisiana and this one at Fort Polk was only the second one in the state. We booked Bill Monroe, the Cumberlands, the Southern Bluegrass Boys, our band played, the Stone Mountain boys came in from Dallas, and I remember they had to get up real early to get there. In addition to Fort Polk, we booked Bill for a whole week in Louisiana...we booked him and the band somewhere every night as there were a lot of little towns near the base. When Bill was there, Kenny Baker stayed at our house and one day I took him with me to work. We were there about forty-five minutes and my boss said, "Why don't you just go on. I'll call you if something comes up." This was military life for the last year or so I was in the service.

When I first met Hank Williams, Jr., he was just starting out and I was getting short, meaning I did not have much longer to serve in the army. I heard Hank was playing at an NCO Club (Non-commissioned Officers) so I could go to that. I had guard duty that night driving an officer around. I told him that Hank Jr. was playing that night and that I sure would like to see him. The officer told me to drive him around a little bit and then he let me go. He did not have to do that. It was a nice thing to do and I will never forget walking into the NCO club, a small place that held maybe two or three hundred people. Hank was playing a banjo and there was an old D28 Herringbone sitting there. I walked up to him, introduced myself and we kind of hit it off. I picked up the guitar and played while he played the banjo. Don Helm, pedal steel guitar player of Hank Senior's Drifting Cowboy Band was there and I got to meet him. Jerry Rivers, Hank Senior's fiddle player was not there and I would like to have met him.

Camal Kathy a GS 10 was a very high-level civil service employee and Director of Entertainment. He booked me into senior centers, theaters...wherever he could. I used Entertainment's PA system, Camal and I split a percentage and while this was great...probably illegal, but great!

I met the Cumberland's Harold and Betty Thom, at one of the local shows we did. Their banjo player Jim Smoak played with Bill Monroe in the 1950's. I jammed with them after the show and had a lot of fun doing folk songs and bluegrass. The Cumberlands lived in Alexadria, Louisiana about fifty miles from Fort Polk and they played at the local Red Horse Inn, a Ramada Inn Club with a bar. They invited me down to sit in with them and we had a great time! They often invited me down for the weekend, gave me a room, and paid me thirty or forty dollars. That was great for me. They let me come down about any time I could get away from the base. They eventually moved to Kentucky and I have very fond memories of the Cumberlands.

All these music things coupled with the track team, really made the time go quickly, also making for some good stories. A fiddler named Jack Kay made his claim to fame playing with Webb Pierce. The Cumberlands thought it would be good to get Jack and me together on stage. It was a night they had some special entertainment and there were several groups including some of the Stone Mountain Boys with Mitchell Land and Tootie Williams. The first set we all got on stage and first thing, Jack Kay lit up a cigarette and stuck it behind his right ear, which I thought was strange and then he lit another one and put it behind his left ear. We started playing Orange Blossom Special and he is... smokin'! What a weird deal. After our set, he sat down at a table and ordered a fifth of vodka, a can of tomato juice, and a bottle of Tabasco sauce...and that is the way he drank. Jack took a big glug of vodka, picked up the can of tomato juice, took a swig and then a swig of Tabasco. Tootie found out the girl with Jack was a prostitute he had hired. He was the weirdest dude I ever saw. That was the first and only time I ever saw him. I thought, "What an interesting night that was."

We occasionally had special shows and got the Stone Mountain Boys to come in and I played with the Cumberlands. We had all kinds of extra players because they lived close by which made it easy to get them there. This was a wonderful opportunity for me to get out and go play with these people.

Journal Entry 1969
Culture Shock - Recording with the Rolling Stones – Dillard and Clark Expedition

Bette began keeping a journal of my shows, recording sessions, and things like that and it has been helpful when doing our taxes, but I never realized how important her journal entries would become until I began this book. Some dates indicate when I received payment for a gig, but most represent the actual date of the event. The journal does not cover all the jams and times I played shows just for fun, or all the many rehearsals I did. This diary of sorts, does give a good idea of the places I have played, with whom, where and when and includes a multitude of road stories.

Journal Entry

May 23 Stone Mountain Boys played at the Red Horse Inn in Alexandria, Louisiana.

May 24 did a Baton Rouge, Louisiana recording session with the Stone Mountain Boys. We did, I Wonder Where You Are Tonight, Bluegrass Breakdown, Love another Man, Rocky Top, and Gold Rush. Mitchell Land is on mandolin, Ed Shelton, banjo, Lonnie Croft, guitar, Tootie Williams, bass and Byron Berline on Fiddle. Then, I was on I'll Live My Lonely Life Alone, Lost Between the Falling Snow, Louisiana, I Can Still Hear You Calling and John Henry with Alan Shelton on banjo, Luke Thompson on mandolin, Travis Stewart on Guitar and Tootie Williams on bass.

May 25 Walker, LA, had a jam session at Old South Jamboree. Fred Robbins recorded this jam session on his Akai reel-to-reel tape recorder. I remember he was backstage and set up the recorder in the bathroom. I also want to give Fred credit for the many photos he took through the years.

I planned to join up and continue playing with Bill Monroe when I got out of the service and Bette had applied for teaching positions in Nashville, but the day before I got out of the Army Doug Dillard called me.

"What are you doin'? He asked.

"Believe it or not," I told him, "I'm getting out of the army… tomorrow."

"That's good." He said, "Because I want you to come out to California and record with Gene Clark and me. We're working on our second album." They had become the Dillard and Clark Expedition and the album was, "Through the Morning, Through the Night." Doug's timing was unbelievable! At that time, Kenny Baker played fiddle for Bill Monroe so I decided to take Doug up on his offer. Later, Bill asked why I did not come back to play with him and I explained that I knew he still had a fiddler…Kenny Baker.

Bill said, "I would have hired you too." He was ready to have me back, but I knew two fiddlers would not work.

The time came to leave the Army and I got an early "out" because dad needed me to help with the harvest, so immediately, mom, dad, Bette and I left for Weiser, Idaho and the fiddle contest. This was the summer of 1969 and that year they invited me to judge the contest.

On June 20, when the fiddle contest ended, mom, dad and Bette took me to Salt Lake City, Utah to catch a flight to Los Angeles where Harry Dean Stanton and Doug Dillard picked me up at the airport. Stanton is an actor and has been in many movies, such as The Green Mile, Fire down Below, Pretty in Pink, Twister, Paris Texas, Christine, Private Benjamin, The Godfather Part II, Cool Hand Luke and many others. Harry Dean was a good friend of Doug Dillard and Gene Clark and enjoyed picking and singing with them. Harry Dean had a garage apartment in the Beachwood area, which is where the HOLLYWOOD sign is located. The street was Beachwood Canyon Boulevard and Doug's apartment was in the same area, real close to Harry Dean. Doug no longer lived in Topanga Canyon…thank goodness. We naturally started jamming right away and Doug pulled out a 1935 D28 Herringbone guitar that he just bought, "from some hippie," he said. We did not have a guitar player so I started playing this guitar, thought it was real nice and I told Doug how I was impressed with it.

First, we went into the studio and recorded on the Dillards' Electra session, Copperfields, produced by Steve Boylan. We were just lying around on the floor listening to the cuts, Doug was drinking beer, and we were talking. "I really do like your guitar." I told him.

"You like it? I'm gonna give it to you." He said.

"No, no…" I said. "I just think it sounds and plays real good."

"Oh, yeah, I want you to have it." He said.

"No, I can't take it." I told him and I said nothing more about it. Then we spent the next two or three days in the studio, recording the Dillard and Clark Expedition "Through the Morning, Through the Night," album and while we were there, Murray McCloud called the studio. He was doing his very first movie score for an ABC Movie of the Week, called "Run Simon Run," and needed a fiddler, but he did not know how to find one so he just started calling recording studios. To find musicians, you call the musicians union and I am glad he did not, because when he called the studio where we were recording, the person on the phone said, "We've got a fiddler in here right now!" McCloud immediately drove to the studio where we met and discussed the project. He said the movie, "Run Simon Run," starred Burt Reynolds as a Native American and in the story, he is running away from something or somebody.

McCloud said, "I want to do this tomorrow. Can you do it?"

"Why Yes!" I told him.

I went into the studio with McCloud the next day and immediately began learning how to score movies. The resulting friendship with Murray McCloud eventually led to my doing about ten made for TV movies with him.

I got another gig while in Los Angeles, another movie score; I could not believe all the work I was getting, all in only four days.

A few days later, when time to leave, I packed up and was ready to have Doug take me to the airport. Moreover, he was sober. As I headed out of the apartment, he said, "Hey, you gotta' get the guitar." He insisted I take it and although I tried to talk him out of it, he would not have it. I picked up the case and took it with me on the plane. I still have that guitar, forty years later and it really does play and sound good.

During the drive to the airport Doug said, "We've decided we want you to move out here to L.A. and join the Dillard and Clark Expedition." I had no idea what kind of work I might find in Nashville, although I could have played with Bill Monroe, then too, Roy Acuff asked me to play with him.

I flew to Tucson, Arizona where Bette, mom and dad were visiting my brother Leonard. I told Bette about the work I found in L.A., movie scores and recording sessions. We talked it over and decided our best opportunities might be in California. After our visit with Leonard, we drove back to the farm in Oklahoma.

Dillard and Clark immediately lined up a tour; it was their first. They drove across country because Gene Clark refused to fly. When they got to Oklahoma, I met them on I-35 about the Bramen area. They picked me up and we drove through Bonner Springs, Kansas where Gene's parents lived. We stopped and ate with them before going on to Chicago. This was July 4, 1969 and two days later, I turned twenty five.

The Dillard and Clark Expedition consisted of Doug Dillard on banjo, Gene Clark on guitar and harmonica, Donna Washburn on guitar, John Corneal on drums, David Jackson on bass and I played fiddle. Donna Washburn was nice, the daughter of a Los Angeles Seven UP executive and Doug's girlfriend…she liked to sing and play guitar. Donna hung around Doug, leaving no room for Bernie Leadon, which was a shame because he was a real good guitar and banjo player so Bernie left the Dillard and Clark Expedition and joined the Flying Burrito Brothers. I did the same, but not until later.

We stayed at a hotel while in Chicago and one day I went to Gene Clark's room for some reason. He offered me a joint, which I declined.

"Oh, come on." Gene said.

He would not take "no" for an answer.

He said, "This isn't gonna hurt ya."

"No, I'm not gonna do it." I told him. He would not let it go.

"Aw, come on, smoke one." He said.

I said, "What part of "no" don't you understand?" He just kept it up until I finally had enough and said, "If you don't stop buggin' me about this I'm gonna kick your ass! That ended it… he backed off and never pressured me again. I wish he could have done the same…he might still be here today.

The first club we played in Chicago was the "Beavers," a small place, nothing fancy, just a place to play. I had never played "live" with the band, only recorded in a studio with them. We set up and did a sound check. The club owner said we could have whatever we wanted from the bar "on the house" and since we did not play for another two hours we all had a couple of drinks before the show started. I remember…Donna Washburn came to me and said, "You better do something," because Doug and Gene were getting too much to drink.

"Really?" I said, surprised. I did not think there was a problem because I did not see them falling down drunk or anything.

The club started filling up real fast…people wanted to hear some good bluegrass and I was anxious to get on stage. I had played before with the Dillards and Doug was just great, but when we got on stage and kicked off the first number, it was as if a light turned off. Doug and Gene acted as if they did not know where they were and I wondered, "What is going on?" It was terrible! Gene played harmonica with his back to the audience, really playing…nothing and Doug had this big stupor grin… people just looked at them. We could not play anything. I could not believe it and could hardly wait to get off of that stage. When I did, I immediately put my fiddle away and went straight across the street to a little bar, ordered a beer and just sat there. David Jackson and John Corneal followed me over there.

"Is this the way it's gonna be?" I said, disillusioned.

"It has before…sometimes, but not always," Jackson confided.

"This is not going to cut it…I am going to get the first bus out of here and go home." I announced. "I can't stand it…it's not right."

"We don't like it either." They agreed.

I knew better than to talk to Doug or Gene that night so I waited until the next day.

"If this continues, I can't play." I told them, but they just hem hawed around. After that, they did a little better; at least we finished the tour. We made it back to Oklahoma and they dropped me off. The Dillard and Clark Expedition still had to get to a gig in Long Beach, California so Bette and I got in her 1963 Tempest, Pontiac, got on Highway 40 and headed for California, trading off the driving. Bette was behind the wheel, I took out my mandolin, and we played and sang as we rode down the highway. We got just outside of Tucumcari, New Mexico and Bette said, "The car just stopped." I told her to pull over to the side of the road. Something was definitely wrong…the car had gas and everything else seemed to be okay, but the car would not start. We were out in the middle of nowhere, about ten, fifteen miles from town and it was a typically hot July day in New Mexico. I spied a little farmhouse about a mile away and decided to walk to it, hoping they would let me use their phone to call a tow. Amid highway construction, I had to walk down the side of essentially, a one-lane deal. It was not long before a pink Mustang went by. It was Donna Washburn's car and Doug Dillard was driving…smoking a cigar. I began waving and yelling and they kept going with no idea this waving person was me. This was before cell phones so there was no way to get a hold of them. Later, they said, "We saw somebody on the side of the road but we didn't pay any attention."

Mr. Crane, a farmer, lived by himself. He opened the door and I explained what happened.

"Oh, I bet your timing chain broke." He said. "That happens to people around here all the time."

We got in his pickup and drove down to Bette, waiting in the hot car. We hooked the car to the pickup and Mr. Crane towed it back to his house. He was very nice.

He asked what I did and I told him I played the fiddle.

He said, "Well, I'm a musician too. I play the saw."

Sure enough, he brought out his saw and played, "Woo, Waa, woo." He was neat.

A garage towed the car to Tucumcari and we stayed there a couple of days before they got it fixed.

We drove into Long Beach and got there just in time for me to play. The gig went well and we still had some recording to do.

July 31, 1969 The Dillard and Clark Expedition did a recording session.

Harry Dean Stanton made a movie in Yugoslavia so Bette and I lived in his apartment while he was away, July through October. He told us to stay there, watch his apartment and it would not cost us anything.

While in the army I really did not keep up too much with the L.A. music scene, as the only time I had been there was recording the Dillards' album in 1964 and then on tour with Bill Monroe in 1967. I knew about the Byrds, Flying Burrito Brothers and that Doug Dillard teamed up with Gene Clark, but no details or anything so it was a culture shock to take in the L.A. music scene. The "anything goes" lifestyle was an even bigger shock for Bette.

In L.A. only a week or two, on August 9, John Corneal said, "Hey, did you hear about all those murders last night?"

"What are you talking about? I asked him.

"Sharon Tate and all those others," He said. "It's all over the news this morning."

We knew nothing about it...it was of course, the Charles Manson murders. Corneal said he was scared to death...I think he knew some of the people involved. Manson had several connections with music people in Los Angeles, as many players knew Manson or his followers or knew people who did.

Two days later, on August 11, reports came out about the La Bianca murders. They told us there was no connection between the two murder scenes, but later we found out that was untrue. Terry Melcher, a music producer, formerly owned Sharon Tate and Roman Polansky's house. Later on, we found out there was a connection between Dennis Wilson of the Beach Boys and Manson. The murders took place in an area where many musicians lived, including the Berlines. Music people in L.A. were very edgy and closely watched the news.

After the Dillard and Clark Expedition tour, we did not have too much lined up. We occasionally practiced, but not much else was going on with the group. Since I was there, Doug wanted to play more bluegrass...Gene became disillusioned by the group's direction.

August 13, the Dillard and Clark Expedition did a recording session for CBS, the title song for the Steve McQueen movie, "Reivers." Alan and Marilyn Bergman wrote the song, specifically for that movie. We walked into the studio and came out with three thousand bucks, which was a lot of money at the time. We were very pleased with the recording...it was good and we felt good about it.

August 18 and 19 the Dillard and Clark Expedition did another session. Also on August 19, I did my first recording session with the Byrds for CBS Columbia on their "Ballad of Easy Rider" album with Roger McGuinn, Clarence White, Gene Parsons, and

John York. Terry Melcher produced the first Byrds albums and at this time became the Byrds' manager as well as producing the "Ballad of Easy Rider" album.

On the website, Byrd Watcher, A Field Guide to the Byrds of Los Angeles, in a review of the "Ballad of Easy Rider" album, they say, "Tulsa County Blues" aka "Tulsa County," written by Pam Polland, is one of the LP's highlights. White's gentle bluegrass-style picking and the mournful fiddle from Byron Berline complement this tale of an unsatisfying relationship."

Those were nice words. Clarence and I always enjoyed playing together.

August 27, did my first recording session with Joe Cocker on his album "Joe Cocker!" for A&M Records.

Lalo Schiffrin, conductor for the "Reivers," scored such movies as, Bullitt, Dirty Harry, Mission Impossible, Enter the Dragon, Jaws, and Cool Hand Luke. A man by the name of Mark Rydell was the movie's director and he decided he did not like Schiffrin's musical score. He canned it all including the title song, which the Dillard and Clark Expedition had recorded on August 13. Wish I had a copy...it must be around somewhere. Rydell hired composer John Williams, to re-score the movie and Williams hired Doug and me to come in and play on the new score. It probably cost a couple of hundred thousand dollars to re-score it. They had to hire the big orchestra, additional musicians like Doug and me and of course, the new composer, John Williams. Williams became known for his work with Star Wars, Angela's Ashes, Close Encounters of the Third Kind, Amistad, Empire of the Sun, Far and Away, E.T. the Extra-Terrestrial, Fiddler on the Roof, and Schindler's List, as well as being the replacement for Arthur Fiedler when Fiedler left the Boston Pops Symphony Orchestra.

September 29, 30 and October 1, Doug and I went into the studio to re-do the music score with John Williams for "Reivers." I had done the made for TV, Movie of The Week, "Run Simon Run," but not a big production movie like the "Reivers." When we got to the studio, they put the odd instrument players over in one corner. They classify odd instruments as things like the jug, jaw harp, banjo, fiddle, etc. The orchestra was in another area and the timpani's, with the pianos, off to the sides. A big screen showed the movie and we played exactly to it...there was an exact place where every note had to go. It was click tracked and all timed out. I really did not have a whole lot to play and did that in the morning. Doug only had to count sixteen bars and "blang!" on the banjo.

Williams said, "Okay, we're going to rehearse this now. Doug, you remember you have got this little splash here. You got it?"

"Okay." Doug said.

The orchestra began and Doug went into one of his dead stares.

I said, "Doug, it is right there. There's the music."

He kept the stare.

"Now Doug," I said. "It is right there in the music...that little thing...just right at sixteen bars."

Williams started the orchestra again and Doug just had a big "I'm lost" grin on his face.

Then Carl Fortina, the accordion player and contractor said, "I'll help you...I'll help you!"

I said, "Doug...you can do this!" I do not think he ever got it.

I said, "Okay, I'm going to count it out and when I point to you, you do it!"

He came in either late or a little early, but he never got it. Finally, due to time constraints, Williams had to go on with the session. Everybody laughed and carried on and of course, Doug made a big joke of it. They booked us for three days, but after this incident, called saying "We don't need those boys any more. We'll pay them anyway, but they don't need to come in."

"Oh, that's great." I thought.

Here is the deal; Doug Dillard has guardian angels. As we walked out of the studio, Doug said, "I don't know, Byron. I'm flat broke...I don't have any money." In that same breath he swept down and picked twenty five bucks, a twenty and a five, off the sidewalk." He looked at me and just rolled his eyes.

I said, "Only you, Doug, only you." He was insane.

Two new television shows began in 1969, Glen Campbell's Good Time Hour and Hee Haw, both featuring country music with some bluegrass thrown in.

When it came time for Harry Dean Stanton to return, Bette

and I began looking for a house to rent. Clarence White said, "If you are looking to rent a house, go out in the San Fernando Valley…that is where all the bluegrass musicians live." That is where Clarence lived, so we decided that sounded okay. We rented a house, at 15113 Lamaida Street in Sherman Oaks, for one hundred eighty five dollars a month. It had three bedrooms and was quite a nice place. We joined the Sherman Oaks First Presbyterian Church and that became our church home for the next twenty-five years. We both became active in the church, made many new friends and Bette worked with the choir.

Bette and I drove back to Oklahoma and rented a U-Haul to make our move to California. One night while we were home, we went into Caldwell, Kansas to visit one of my old school friends. We got back to the farm about ten thirty that night and Mom said a man had called from California and would call back at midnight. Sure enough, the phone rang.

They said, "This is blah, blah, blah, of the Rolling Stones.

I did not understand the man's name.

I said, "Oh, yes, the magazine."

"NO!" He said. "The Stones."

"I bet you are stoned." I thought, still confused.

"The who?" I asked.

"NO!" He was emphatic. (He thought I meant the "WHO.") "The Rolling Stones!"

"Oh, the group," I said. I finally got it. It was Keith Richards and Phil Kaufman. Keith said they wanted me to record with the band.

I said, "Well, I'll be out there in five or six days. Will that be alright?"

"No, no, we need you tomorrow." Keith said.

"Well, okay." I told him. "But you're gonna have to fly me then."

"No problem." He said.

The next morning, October 25, I drove to Oklahoma City, flew first class to L.A. and Phil Kaufman met me at the airport. Phil was the road manager for the Rolling Stones and the one who arranged for the plane ticket and everything. Later on, I learned he was a good friend of Gram Parsons and helped with the Flying Burrito Brothers. Gram Parsons was a good buddy of Keith

Richards and he wanted the Rolling Stones to do more country music. "Let It Bleed," was one of those country records. They wanted a fiddler on it and Gram recommended me.

Phil Kaufman rented Stephen Stills' house on Doheny, off of Sunset Blvd., for the Rolling Stones while they were in the U.S. recording and touring. When we arrived, there were three limousines out front. Everybody including the maids lived in this house. It was a huge, mansion type place. It was early afternoon and there were people playing tennis and people in the pool. The producer, Glyn Johns, said we needed to get right down to Electra studios, which was located on La Cienega Boulevard.

Mick Jagger, Keith Richards, Charlie Watts, Bill Wyman…all the band members were there. I listened to the track and tried to tune my fiddle to it…the best I could. The song was "Country Honk" and the acoustic guitars seemed to be out of tune. After I went through the song a couple of times, Keith and Mick told me to come into the control room. I thought they were going to send me home. Instead, they said, "We have an idea. We want you to go out on the sidewalk to play. We think it will give a different ambience to it." They were experimenting. Art.

Outside they were rebuilding some of the studios and a big bulldozer was moving dirt. It was so loud there was no way we could record anything, so Mick Jagger went out and the bulldozer operator just shut it right off. He did not question Mick at all, just shut it down, got off and construction came to a halt.

The cut I was on, "Country Honk," they decided, needed a real car horn honking. Phil Kaufman paid some woman to drive up and down the street, honking the horn while I was recording.

Instead of headphones, they put a speaker out there and the microphone. By this time, all kinds of people began showing up… The Doors, Bonnie Bramlett, Leon Russell, and others. They all stood around to watch us record that one track. About the sixth or seventh time I went through the song, it began getting dark and a little cooler. The last time I played, the fiddle bow slipped about an inch and went "ziiip."

I said, "Well, we'll need to do that one over."

"No, no." They said. "That's the one. That's the one we want to use."

I asked if they heard the bow slip and they said, "No, no, it's fine."

They kept that one. Geez.

Mick and Keith had to do some vocal over dubs so we went back into the studio. Bonnie Bramlett was there to do some vocals, but because she had been singing too much her voice was shot...she had trouble just talking. When the recording began, they started passing a pint of whiskey back and forth; it was like a live show. I could not believe the gyrations they went through. I guess they had an audience with all those people in there. I do not even remember what song they were doing. I started getting bored with it all and since Doug and Rodney Dillard lived not too far away, I thought I might go visit them. I asked if I might use a car and they said, "Yeah, here's the keys to the limo, take it."

I could not believe it! Here I was driving this big ole Lincoln limousine, right up Beachwood Canyon. I pulled up and Rodney and Doug came out.

"Hi, boys," I said. Then we got in that thing, Doug grabbed some cigars and Rodney's goin', "I want to drive...I want to drive!"

So, I said, "Okay."

We drove down to the Troubadour Club and parked the limo out front. We had a ball with that vehicle and they could not believe I was recording with the Rolling Stones. At the time, it sure did not mean much to me. At that time, I was not a big fan of the Rolling Stones. One of my roommates in college, Chris Forrestburg, loved them and he played their records all the time. In fact, the Stone's were the only records he played. I used to yell, "Turn that crap off!" when I was trying to study. Chris was a freshman and dropped out after one semester. He never went to class so he knew he was not going very far. He would probably freak if he knew I recorded with them.

That was the first and last time I recorded with the Rolling Stones. There was a photographer there that day, snapping pictures. His name is Jim Marshall and he was a very famous photographer. I never did get a picture. Dang! Wish I had a photo from that day. That recording session with the Rolling Stones did a great deal in helping me to get session work. The record, "Let It Bleed," got a lot of airplay; people read the liner notes and checked out who was playing what on the record. I am grateful to Gram Parsons for his recommendation.

At the end of the day, I returned the limo to the Rolling Stones and Phil Kaufman took me to the airport. As Phil Kaufman remembers, it was, "A pretty good day for a country boy." and he is right. I flew back to Oklahoma, got Bette and the U-Haul and moved to California…for the next twenty-six years.

They released the Byrds "Ballad of Easy Rider" album in the fall of 1969 and the "Joe Cocker!" album released that November.

November 25 the Dillard and Clark Expedition got a call asking us to play on Hee Haw in Nashville…it was one of their first TV shows. This opportunity came up real quick and in order to get there in time we had to fly. Gene Clark refused to fly…he said, "Well, I'm quitting the band, anyway.

There was no Clark, so we just called it the "Dillard Expedition." We needed a stronger rhythm guitar player so we hired Don Beck to go with us. We worked up two numbers and when we got there, they said we had to write out the lyrics. We did "Rollin' in My Sweet Baby's Arms" and an instrumental tune Doug wrote called "Hickory Holler." They checked out the lyrics and refused to let us sing them. They said the song was too risqué so we just did the instrumental, "Hickory Holler" and that was it. They are still playing that particular "Hee Haw" show on the RFD television network and you can see it on U-tube. We really sounded good. That episode, #1.14, lists us as the Dillards and sometimes as the Exposition, instead of the Expedition.

The following year Buck Owens recorded "Rollin' in My Sweet Baby's Arms," had a hit with it and the rules regarding that song evidently changed on Hee Haw as a later show had Tammy Wynette and George Jones singing it as a duet.

They released the Rolling Stones' "Let It Bleed" album November 28, 1969.

The Troubadour, owned by Doug Weston, was a very well known venue in West Hollywood and still is. It is located at 9081 Santa Monica Blvd, just down the street from the Beverly Hilton Hotel. Bob Dylan played there, the Byrds, Buffalo Springfield, Joni Mitchell, Richard Pryor, Gordon Lightfoot, Poco, Neil Young, Cheech and Chong, Neil Diamond, Kris Kristofferson, Linda Ronstadt and so many more. One night the Troubadour had a "Hoot Night" and Doug wanted the band to play. The Troubadour is open from 8:00 p.m. to 2:00 a.m. We arrived, but not scheduled to go on until 10:30 pm…it was a repeat performance of the drinking incident in Chicago.

I confronted Doug. "If you're going to perform, you can't get so screwed up you can't play." He just shrugged it off. This was the mentality of all the bands back then. The Flying Burrito Brothers, the Byrds, the Stones…they were all big time partiers; drug users…just could not have enough fun. It was a bizarre time. I was not into drugs and this situation did not thrill me at all…I wanted something better than that.

December 23 did a recording session with Gram Parsons, Chris Hillman, Bernie Leadon, Michael Clark, and Sneaky Pete Kleinow on the Flying Burrito Brothers' album, "Burrito Deluxe," for A & M Records, which was the FBB second album. Their debut album, "Gilded Palace of Sin," released in February of 1969, had no fiddle on it. They cut eleven songs on "Deluxe" and one of them, "Wild Horses," written by Mick Jagger and Keith Richards of the Rolling Stones, ran over six minutes. The following year the Rolling Stones recorded it.

December 24 Christmas Eve, they aired the Hee Haw television show the Dillard Expedition did in November.

The year 1969, was quite something for Byron and Bette Berline. We came for the music and the beach and we enjoyed them both.

Journal Entry 1970

Huckleberry Hornpipe — Charting Music for Charles Manson - Nitty Gritty Dirt Band

A venue at 2020 Addison St. in Berkeley, California opened in 1968 in the Freight and Salvage furniture store…the new owners just added "Coffeehouse" to the original sign. The location moved a time or two, but they are still open. Ramblin' Jack Elliott played there, Odetta, Alison Krauss, Ralph Stanley, David Grisman, David Bromberg, Nickel Creek and many more.

January 7, 8 the Dillard Expedition performed at the Freight and Salvage in Berkley and that is the first time Roger Bush played with the Expedition. That same night I wrote the first song that amounted to anything. Before that, Bill Monroe and I wrote and recorded "Gold Rush" in 1967 and they released that forty-five rpm as a single. This night, picking up the fiddle and instead of warming up playing scales or something else, I began playing a tune. I kept playing it and finally said, "Doug, listen to this. What is this tune?" Then I played it for him.

Doug said, "I don't know. I've never heard it before."

It was "Huckleberry Hornpipe" and it was just lying there. I have never written another one that way. What is unusual is that I did not forget it; then I recorded it.

January 22, 1970 did my first recording session with the Nitty Gritty Dirt Band on their "Uncle Charlie and His Dog, Teddy" album for Capitol Records. John McEuen hired me to do this.

On January 24, I played the Ash Grove. I played with…I do not remember, but got twenty bucks. The Ash Grove, opening in 1958, was another well-established music venue in West Hollywood, located at 8162 Melrose Avenue. It seated about two hundred fifty people and was a favorite hangout, especially for traditional and bluegrass music. I played the Ash Grove in 1967 with Bill Monroe. All the big names performed there, Clarence White, Ralph Rinzler, Taj Mahal, Pete Seeger, Bob Dylan, Doc Watson, Mac Wiseman, Tom Paxton, and David Crosby. They booked country, bluegrass, comedians, old and new acts like

Lenny Bruce, the Byrds, Canned Heat, Flatt and Scruggs, Ry Cooder, Flying Burrito Brothers, Jane Fonda, John Hartford, Kentucky Colonels, Rose Maddox, Joe and Roselee Maphis, Bill Monroe, Nitty Gritty Dirt Band, Gram Parsons and the Weavers.

On January 28, did two recording sessions, one with the Flying Burrito Brothers for their "Burrito Deluxe" album and one session with Linda Ronstadt.

On January 30, 31, the Dillard Expedition played McCabes. This venue is a guitar shop at 3101 Pico Blvd. in Santa Monica, California. It is the guitar shop during the day, but on weekend nights, it becomes a concert venue. Some of the players have included Chet Atkins, Jerry Reed, Mike Auldridge, Hoyt Axton, Norman and Nancy Blake, the Bluegrass Cardinals, Bluegrass Etc., Bryan Bowers, Oscar Brand, Brewer and Shipley, T-Bone Burnett, Jethro Burns, Roseanne Cash, Bill Caswell and the list goes on.

February 6, 7, The Dillard Expedition played a venue in Redondo Beach, California called "House of the Rising Sun." We played there quite often. Tom Keuhl managed House of the Ris-

In 1970 the Dillard Expedition played the Fremont Hotel with Kay Starr. L to r; Doug Dillard, Byron Berline, Kay Starr, Roger Bush, Billy Ray Latham.

ing sun, calling himself "Cowboy Maynard." and he played with a group called "Aunt Dinah's Quilting Party. Mel Durham, part owner of the club, played bass in a band called "Wild Oats" and he played in "Aunt Dinah's Quilting Party." For some unknown reason, whenever Mel saw me coming, he always greeted me as "brother-in-law." Mel loved old time music…we became good friends and played some together.

February 10 –15, the Dillard Expedition played for a week at the Ash Grove and Bette began collecting press clippings. Here is part of one Michael Sherman wrote for the Los Angeles Times on Thursday, February 12, 1970.

> "With musical cross-pollination fast becoming the norm these days (folk-rock, country-pop, et al), it is refreshing to listen to a group which has decided upon its basic idiom and explored it with taste and originality.
>
> Dillard and the Expedition (appearing at the Ash Grove through Sunday) is a bluegrass quintet, which brings talent and polish (not slickness) to its primarily traditional material.
>
> Its impressive combination of instrumental ability and tight three-part country harmony produces an ensemble sound which is both (paraphrasing a commercial) "country-sweet" and "country-fresh."
>
> The set I heard was not only well-paced and varied, but, because the group was so obviously enjoying what it was doing, a warm and friendly atmosphere resulted which is so important to "down home" music whose mood is essentially relaxed and informal."

While playing the Dillard Expedition booking at the Ash Grove, on February 12 did another recording session with the Flying Burrito Brothers for the "Burrito Deluxe" album.

In addition to my music, Bette was busy with hers. Eddie Tickner hired Bette to transcribe tapes for copyright purposes and because Eddie had the publishing of the Byrds, Flying Burrito Brothers and others, Bette had a lot of work. They paid her about ten or fifteen dollars to chart a song. At that time in musical history, you had to write down the notes and everything very neatly, on onionskin paper. You then sent the onionskin copy to the copyright office in Washington, D.C. and that was the copyright process.

In the winter of 1970, the Charles Manson murders were high profile in the news and Manson and his followers, Susan Atkins, Patricia Krenwinkel, and Leslie Van Houten, were in jail facing a court trial.

It seemed like Phil Kaufman was the road manager for everybody and instead of "manager," they called him "Mangler." He was particularly close to Gram Parsons. As a roadie for so many people, Kaufman was around a lot so Bette and I knew him, and he was familiar with the kind of work Bette did. One day Phil came by the house and gave a tape to Bette saying, "I want you to transcribe all the songs on there, then I want to get them copyrighted." There were probably fifteen or twenty songs on the tape.

A few days later, I was in the music room and heard Bette screaming. Wondering what the…? I went to where she was and she said, "Listen to this garbage!"

Upon listening I said, "What is THAT?"

It was the most bizarre sounding "music" you ever heard. Bette wrote it down, the best she could and Kaufman came by to pick up the first completed sheets.

"Okay. What is this…Who is this?" I asked him.

"That's the family jams." He said.

"What family?" I asked.

"That's Charlie Manson and his band."

"You've got to be kidding!" I blurted. "How did you get a hold of that?"

"I was in jail once with Charlie. That's how we met." He explained. "He was interested in music and I was too, so we got to talking. He let me take these tapes and I know what I'm gonna do. When he gets convicted and gets the electric chair, I'm going to put this stuff out and I'm gonna make a fortune."

I said, "Well, huh. You probably will."

This went on for some time; Phil continued bringing tapes to Bette and picking up the completed ones. We found out later that Manson wanted Kaufman to get his music out to raise money for Manson's defense in the upcoming murder trial.

I was not home the first time some of Charlie's followers stopped by the house to pick up the sheets. The second time, I was there when Lynette "Squeaky" Fromm, Catherine "Gypsy" Share and some guy came by the house.

I told Bette, "We really need to talk to these people." Their names were in the news as much as that of Charles Manson so I invited them into our home.

I said, "Well, what do you think about this? What about Charlie?"

They lightly said, "Well, we think he's great."

"Do you have any animosity toward the police?" I asked.

"No we don't." They collectively agreed.

Gypsy said, "You play the fiddle, don't you? Could I see your fid...?"

"Yes!" I quickly said handing her the fiddle, hardly letting her finish the sentence.

I found out many years later, Gypsy played the violin and that is why she was interested in my fiddle. Catherine (Gypsy) Share played violin with other Manson followers, on the album "Family Jams." It was weird...bizarre, having them there. It was a heinous crime, but Charlie Manson's followers were just as nice and polite as they could be.

Terry Melcher, Doris Day's son, was a big time music producer. He produced the Byrds and helped other big names. Charles Manson got some of his "music" to Terry in an effort to get it produced. Manson asked Melcher what he thought and Terry said. "It sucks. It'll never fly." I agree. It sucks. You just cannot afford to offend anyone.

March 1 did a recording session for Harry Nilsson on his ABC Movie of the Week, "The Point." This is an animated movie, directed by Fred Wolf and Nilsson wrote the songs to accompany the story. The narrator/father is the voice of Dustin Hoffman.

March 6, 1970 Phil Kaufman got Charlie Manson's music produced and he released the album called "LIE." They took a cover, similar to LIFE magazine, removed the "F" and that is what the cover looks like. I do not think Phil sold very many.

March 6 – 8 the Dillard Expedition played the Ash Grove again.

March 24, 25 did a couple of recording sessions with Chad and Jeremy. Chad Stuart and Jeremy Clyde, from England, became more successful on the U.S. charts than in Great Britain. Some of their hits include Yesterday's Gone, A Summer Song, Willow Weep for Me and several more. They are still performing and touring.

March 27, 28, the Dillard Expedition played House of the Rising Sun.

In April of 1970, A&M released The Flying Burrito Brothers', "Burrito Deluxe," album...Gram Parsons was no longer with the band.

On April 7 played Hugh Hefner's "Playboy after Dark," backing Linda Ronstadt with Bernie Leadon. Lindsey Wagner was in the audience but we did not know who she was...she had not yet become the Bionic woman.

April 17, 18 played House of the Rising Sun with Tom Keuhl, "Cowboy Maynard."

On April 23 had a recording session with a folk music group called "WE FIVE," but it did not start out that way. I want to thank Jerry Burgan for jogging my memory about this session. Jerry is an original member and played on every WE FIVE album. We FIVE had a huge hit song in the 1960's, "(well I woke up this mornin') You Were On My Mind." By 1970, the group had some different band members working on a new album called "Catch the Wind." They called Doug Dillard to come in and play banjo on one cut, "Never Going Back" and as it would be a quick session, I went along with him to the studio. We got there as they were just finishing up "Milk Cow Blues" and we listened to the playback while the producer began telling Doug what he had in mind for the banjo on "Never Going Back." Then Doug said, "Okay, but Byron ought to play fiddle on "Milk Cow Blues." The producer agreed and told me to get my fiddle and set up in the studio. I played along with the track, approached an obvious break, played a solo then I continued through to the end of the song. Feeling comfortable with it I said, "I like the song and I'm ready to record."

The producer said, "No, we were rolling and that's it." They had already recorded the fiddle track. One take and they were happy with it. Sometimes session work came in the most unusual ways.

May 5 did a recording session for Harry Nilsson's "The Point."

May 8, 9 and May 22 & 23, the Dillard Expedition played House of the Rising Sun.

May 13 did a recording session with Barry McGuire, also

from Oklahoma. He is a songwriter and performer and his biggest hit, "Eve of Destruction," came in 1965. In the 1960's Barry was part of the New Christy Minstrels...his "Green, Green" was a huge hit for them and won Barry his first gold record. McGuire and Hoyt Axton wrote "Green Back Dollar" while doing laundry at a laundromat on Santa Monica Boulevard. At the time of this session, he had just returned to L.A. from New York and the Broadway production of "Hair." This session was for his "McGuire and the Doctor" album for Ode Records. The doctor is Eric Hord, lead guitar player for the Mamas and Papas. Several friends were also on this, with Chris Hillman, Michael Clarke, Sneaky Pete Kleinow, and Bernie Leadon. Barry is still performing and touring; he made a lot of changes in his life... for the better.

May 27 did another recording session for the Byrds.

June 5, 6 The Dillard Expedition played McCabes for two nights.

The Manson Murder trial began June 15, 1970.

June 18 Bette and I went to Weiser, Idaho for the National Old Time fiddle Contest. Mom and dad met us there and my brother Leonard came in from Tucson, Arizona. We had the usual jam sessions, dad, Leonard, all the other contestants and their backing musicians. We really had a good time.

The Weiser Contest had a meeting that year and debated the issue of whether or not to allow professional musicians to continue competing in the contest. That of course, meant I could not participate. I let them know that the amateur or professional status of a fiddler did not matter...the contest is for the best old time fiddler. They tried to talk it down, but apparently, most of the people there agreed with how I felt and as a result, I got to enter the contest. Sixty-eight fiddlers entered and during the four days of competing rounds, the number dwindled until the night of the finals only eight contestants remained. I was among them with backing musicians, Bette on piano (her first time to publicly play that kind of music) and Leonard on guitar. With trophies and prize money to win, I played my best on "Grey Eagle," "Cherokee Waltz" and "Cotton Patch Rag." Apparently, it went okay because I won...a check for six hundred dollars, the big trophy and regained the title, 1970 National Old Time

Fiddle Champion. Friend and fellow fiddler, J.C. Broughton from Sapulpa, Oklahoma, came out of it with fourth place and that guy, Bill Yohey, came in last. We were surprised at the number of newspapers reporting about the contest. Dad, at seventy-seven and I being shy a few weeks, of my twenty-seventh birthday, we sure had a lot of reporters asking us questions. They wanted to know about my fiddle. I told them it belonged to dad and that his friend and fiddle teacher had given it to him. We did have a good time, but it was the last fiddle contest I ever entered.

August 15 judged a fiddle contest in Fort Worth, Texas.

Byron & Bette Berline rehearsing in 1970 at Weiser, Idaho's National Old Time Fiddling Contest. Bette made our matching costumes.

August 18 – 23 they booked the Dillard Expedition for a week at the Ice House, managed by Bob Stane. The Ice House opened September 23, 1960 as a folk music venue, but in the early 1970's it began introducing comedians, such as the Smothers Brothers, Gallagher, and Lily Tomlin. The Ice House at twenty four Mentor Avenue in Pasadena is still open. This was our first time to play the Ice House and Kay Starr was in the audience. Bob Dawes managed Chet Atkins, Floyd Cramer, and Boots Randolph in Las Vegas. When they called Bob from the Kay Starr show and wanted to know if he knew a band that could play for her show, he called Zeke Manners. Manners wrote "Pennsylvania Polka" and he knew Billy Ray Latham and Roger Bush of the Kentucky Colonels. Zeke recommended The Dillard Expedition to Bob Dawes and Bob recommended us to Kay Starr. She had a show opening in September at the Fremont in down town Las Vegas. Dawes and Manners brought Kay out to the Ice House, to see us perform. She loved what we were doing and we immediately began rehearsing because her new show was to open in just a few days. Kay Starr was born in Dougherty, Oklahoma so we immediately had something in common. In addition, she loved country music and the bluegrass music we played.

Her two most memorable hits, both turning gold, were "Wheel of Fortune" and "Rock and Roll Waltz." She heard Roy Acuff's instrumental, "Bonaparte's Retreat," really liked it and decided to record the song. She called Roy in Nashville and apparently had quite a time explaining she needed lyrics; she was a singer, not a musician. They finally understood each other and Acuff wrote some lyrics for her. Kay recorded "Bonaparte's Retreat" and after Capitol released it in April of 1950, it came close to selling a million records. Although her recording popularity declined in the 1960's, her fans came to see her shows in Las Vegas at Harrah's, the Riviera, the Sands, and the Fremont, as well as in Reno, Nevada.

We did a lot of rehearsing and Kay Starr was wonderful. What an entertainer! I remember her telling us that when you are on a big stage you make your motions bigger than you would on a small stage. She taught us to play to the size of the audience. I had never even thought about it and she shared a lot of little things like that. This was quite an opportunity for the band.

September 3, 1970 the Dillard Expedition opened the Fiesta Room at the Fremont in Las Vegas, Nevada with Kay Starr. The deal was, we came out and played for about fifteen minutes, and then she came out and did some songs with us. She ended the show with her signature song, "Wheel of Fortune." That was all we had to do…we got our own spot and then got to do some songs with Kay. Our press clippings indicate the success of the show. The "Variety" had the following to say about our opening night.

> "The Expedition's instrumental session is a rouser with demonstration of trick five-string banjo fretting in "Foggy Mountain Breakdown," a corker of a fiddling workout by one of the southwest's champs on that instrument in the exhilarating "Orange Blossom Special."

The Dillard Expedition got to play Las Vegas. It was a good experience and we had a great time!

September 16 Columbia released the Byrds album.

On October 3, 1970, Janis Joplin died.

October 23, 24, after leaving Las Vegas, we went back to California and the Dillard Expedition played House of the Rising Sun.

November 6, the Dillard Expedition did a recording session for Jimmy Bowen, with Doug Dillard, Billy Ray Latham, Roger Bush, and me, for the movie "Vanishing Point," directed by Richard C. Sarafian. It stars Barry Newman, Cleavon Little, and Dean Jagger. Newman, as Kowalski, works for a car delivery service and he takes a 1970 Dodge Challenger from Colorado to San Francisco with everybody chasing after him. It seemed appropriate to do the song Doug and I wrote, "Runaway Country." I remember playing guitar on the sound track.

November 6, 7, while recording for "Vanishing Point" we also played House of the Rising Sun.

November 13, 14 the Dillard Expedition played McCabes.

November 20, Vault Records released the We Five album, "Catch the wind."

On December 1, the made for TV movie, "Run Simon Run," was first shown on television. That was the first ABC Movie of the Week I made with Murray McCloud, during the summer of 1969 when in Los Angeles doing recording sessions with the Dillard and Clark Expedition.

December 3-31, 1970 and January 1 – 6, 1971 the Dillard Expedition again, got to play Vegas with Kay Starr; this time playing the Landmark. Several years later, they tore down this hotel. When they become outdated, buildings are imploded and new ones built. We played there during the Christmas and New Year's holiday season and Danny Davis and the Nashville Brass shared the bill. We really had a lot of fun and the press was good to us. The following came out in a Las Vegas newspaper:

> "With Christmas fast approaching, the Landmark's Kay Starr Show is the perfect mood setter. Along with Danny Davis and the Nashville Brass, both Kay Starr and Doug Dillard and the Expedition treat nightly audiences to old favorites and modern Christmas tunes."

Farther down in the article it said,

> "The Expedition, a tight bluegrass group which includes the National Fiddle Champion Byron Berline, is a real highlight of the show. They play, they sing and they work well with Kay."

Bette went back to Las Vegas with me on this trip to the Landmark and we had a great time. With all the bookings, session work, and playing Las Vegas, we had quite a busy year.

Journal Entry 1971
The Dillard Expedition - Flying Burrito Brothers

January 1, 1971, Ode Records released Barry McGuire's "Barry McGuire and The Doctor" album.

January 1 - 6 the Dillard Expedition continued playing Vegas with Kay Starr at the Landmark, with Danny Davis and the Nashville Brass. We played there during the holiday season and Bette came with me on this trip. It was a nice get-a-way and we had a wonderful time.

January 14 - 24 after the holiday gig in Vegas, Kay asked the Dillard Expedition to go with her to Hawaii and do some shows at the Royal Hawaiian Hotel. They used a full orchestra and it was wonderful...January, warm...they opened the doors and the breezes came in. Kay came out and sang, Hard Hearted Hannah, Raindrops Keep Falling on My Head, Clouds, I Can't Stop Loving You and of course, Wheel of Fortune. We played our set then Kay came back on stage to do some numbers with the Expedition. Kay Starr and the Dillard Expedition opened January 14 with reviews coming out on the sixteenth.

> "Kay Starr has a large number of fans in the Islands and a good many of them were on hand to cheer her along at the opening of a nine-day engagement at the Royal Hawaiian Hotel Thursday night.
>
> Miss Starr is the headliner of the Monarch Room show which includes a four-man country-western group called the Expedition, Martin Denny at the piano with a good 12-piece orchestra and comic Taf Arnold billed as "the Witty Welshman."

Farther on it read,

> "Then The Expedition - a guitarist, bassist, banjo man and a musician announced as a "three-time national fiddle champion" - was permitted to break loose. The Expedition is a first class C&W group. As the spirited sounds ripped round the room, the elegant guests in the formerly sedate Monarch room stomped their feet and clapped their hands like the gang does at the New Frontier Bar.

It was a historic first for the Monarch Room. Roy Clark, the co-host of "Hee Haw" who is here working military clubs, would have been proud.

Then Miss Starr came barreling back to join the boys with "Frankie and Johnny" and "Wabash Cannonball." Whoopee!"

I agree...it really was a good show.

Doug had a new girlfriend with him, Suzi Jane Hokom, Lee Hazlewood's girlfriend, until she met Doug. Lee, from Oklahoma, is a performer and songwriter. He wrote "These Boots Are Made for Walkin'," a big hit for Nancy Sinatra and "Some Velvet Morning" for Vanilla Fudge. He also co-wrote "Rebel Rouser" with Duane Eddy.

Bette went with me and we were all in Hawaii having a great time seeing the sights, enjoying the food, the beautiful weather, and the beaches.

We played for nine days and noticed that Doug came to the show later and later each night. One night we were back stage getting ready to go on...no Doug. In a panic, we began making alternative plans in case Doug did not show up. It was the last night and he was a no show, while on stage, Kay Starr announced us as four people, not three. She always brought us on and then went to her dressing room to change into another dress while we performed. That night when we came out, she stuck around... standing in the wings. What a class act she is. She wanted to make sure things went okay. She is a real pro. We went through the band's part and then she came out and did the numbers with us. We had to do a little shuffling because Doug sang some parts with her. We made it through the show and it went just fine... we covered everything.

Doug came in when it was over. He staggered around, slobbered while telling us his watch stopped. Suzi and Doug liked to drink and Suzi drank champagne throughout the holidays. That night, wearing cut-offs and a T-shirt she sat in the lobby holding a bottle of champagne. After drinking mai-tai's and champagne all day, Doug and Suzi were toasted. Billy Ray Latham and Roger Bush were totally disgusted. Bush said, "Well, I'm quitting." I said I did not blame him, but the Expedition still had to play a gig at Ledbetter's the very next day, January 25, so we immediately flew back to California. Ledbetter's was a little campus-corner

kind of place in West Hollywood. Fred Walecki has the Westwood Music store at 1627 Westwood Boulevard in Los Angeles
and he set up this little concert. Doug missed the plane. Therefore,
he could not be there. We called Herb Pedersen asking, "Can you
play banjo with us tonight?" We had a ball! The vocals were great
and we zipped right through the show. Herb was leaving the
Dillards, Billy Ray Latham would take Herb's place with them,
and Herb eventually began playing guitar with us.

Also in January of 1971, the Kentucky Colonels did a private
reunion session at Clarence White's house in Topanga Canyon.
Clarence and Roland played, Roger Bush, Billy Ray Latham,
LeRoy Mack McNees, and me. LeRoy, on Dobro, had been with
the White brothers when called the Country Boys.

January 29, 30, the Dillard Expedition played House of the
Rising Sun.

The animated movie "The Point," aired February second on
the ABC television network.

February 9 – 14 the Dillard Expedition played the Ice House
again, but it was not easy. Some pre-press came out to promote
our shows and the headline read, "ICE HOUSE SHOW BY DIL-
LARD SET."

> "Doug Dillard and The Expedition are making their once-
> a-year foray into the Ice House in Pasadena through Sunday,
> says owner Bob Stane.
> The instrumental wizards are said to have been thrilling the
> folks in Las Vegas, of all places, with their singing and world
> famous banjo and fiddle fantastics.
> Dillard is literally a legend with the five-string banjo and
> Byron Berline is the three time national fiddle champion."

At 6:00 a.m., on February 9, the day of our first night at the
Ice House, the Berlines woke to a violent earthquake. It shook
the San Fernando Valley and anything breakable was on the
floor and broken...dishes, lamps, pictures, shelves emptied of
books, records, curios and keepsakes, cupboards and cabinets
opened, their contents dumped out...you cannot imagine the
mess. We had tornadoes in Oklahoma, but not earthquakes and
this was our first. You can occasionally out run a tornado or at
least have some warning. The quake destroyed a new hospital;

there were deaths and many injuries. The integrity of structures still standing were questioned; bridges collapsed, roads became impassable...danger seemed to be everywhere. They began evacuating the Valley, but did not include us. They feared there might be cracks in the dam holding a lake above the valley and as the aftershocks began, fears of flooding increased.

Somehow, the Dillard Expedition made it to the Ice House in Pasadena that night, but back stage we were still feeling the aftershocks. Although it made us uncomfortable, we did the show...every night that week.

Betty Bergholz wrote a nice piece about us.

> "As bluegrass music gains popularity, so does the Expedition...Doug Dillard and the Expedition opened with "Durham's Reel" and then proceeded faultlessly throughout the entire set. They closed with "Orange Blossom Special," an old standard of the bluegrass musicians. The group consists of Doug Dillard on Banjo, Byron Berline on fiddle and guitar, Bill Ray on guitar and banjo and Roger Bush on bass and banjo... They have most recently been performing with Kay Starr in Hawaii and Las Vegas."

Bergholz interviewed Doug. "Doug says he doesn't go up there on stage to make a social comment-he does it to entertain."

Then Doug proceeded with a true Dougism. "If I were doing any protest, it would protest social protest."

When Bergholz asked him for a great social truth, he had another one handy, "The real truth is an extension of the truth."

She ended the article with the following: "Doug Dillard and the Expedition deserve as much recognition as possible as one of the finest contemporary bluegrass bands."

What a week.

February 26, 27 and March 5, 6, the Dillard Expedition played two weekends at Sparks Nugget Inn in Reno, Nevada and Bette and I had a good time. The casino had a circus theme, complete with a live elephant, so Bette took a "ride" on Bertha.

March 8 – 13 and 15 – 20 the Dillard Expedition went to Aspen, Colorado playing two weeks at the Aspen Inn. Bette went on this trip and they put us in apartments, right on the slopes where we tried to ski. This was a fun gig.

March 13 they released the movie, "Vanishing Point." When the movie came out mom was living in Winfield, Kansas. This was after an accident mom and dad had. Mom, my sister Eleanor, her sons Barry and Bart, all went to the movies to hear me play on the soundtrack. Barry was about eleven years old at the time. In one scene the character, Kowalski, played by Barry Newman, is running from the police and stops somewhere out in the desert... you can see the heat waves rising off of the highway. Charlotte Rampling's character is on a motorcycle and she does not have on any clothes. As that scene opened up, Barry said, "Mom, look at that!" Everybody could hear him, "A Honda 250!"

Bette on Bertha in Las Vegas in 1971.

Thinking about that, I still laugh.

March 26, 27 and April 23, 24 the Dillard Expedition played House of the Rising Sun.

April 13 I did another recording session with the Byrds.

April 29 the Dillard Expedition went to San Francisco and played a show with Kay Starr.

May 28, 29 went to Houston, Texas and judged a fiddle contest.

June 4, 5 the Dillard Expedition played House of the Rising Sun.

June 10, 11 had the opportunity to work with Henry Mancini who scored the Pink Panther, Baby Elephant Walk, Days of Wine and Roses, Breakfast at Tiffany's and many others. Mancini called and personally asked me to play on the soundtrack of the Paul Newman movie, "Sometimes a Great Notion." Newman directed and starred in the film with Henry Fonda and Lee Remick. The story is about a bunch of loggers trying to keep their logging businesses going.

June 17 the Dillard Expedition went to Fresno, California and played for the Beef Association.

The Dillard Expedition had one more thing to do, a showcase for a record company. The Smothers Brothers were to be part of it and some other TV shows. Held at the Bitter End West, this was to be a very important night. The manager putting the event together told us to be there at 9 o'clock to do a sound check...no Doug. We did the sound check anyway to get all the mics set and everything and then Doug stumbled in. We suggested it might be a good idea to postpone the showcase for another time, but oh, no...Doug wanted to go on with it. He sat down with some of the band and started drinking, so we knew what was going to happen...all over again. It was a disaster and when it ended, we went home. Roger Bush called and said he did not know about me, but for him, "It was over."

I said, "Me too. I'm done."

I told Doug, "I'm sorry buddy, but I just can't work that way."

He is still out there getting after it. I do not know how, but he made it through. I still think the world of Doug – he really has a warm heart.

I reminded Roger we still had the Kay Starr show and suggested we might be able to do something with it and we did just that. We got Pat Cloud to play banjo on the Kay Starr shows with us. Roger Bush and I wanted to continue playing together although Herb Pedersen could not travel much because his wife would not let him. That was the wife he had at the time. Roger and I wanted to keep it going because we still had dates to play with Kay Starr.

I said, "We'll just call ourselves something else." We looked everywhere for a name to call the newly forming group and Bette found it in a crossword puzzle, "Country Gazette."

Then Chris Hillman called, wanting me to do some things with the Flying Burrito Brothers. I asked him if he knew anybody that could play guitar, sing tenor and play banjo for our new Country Gazette band.

Chris said, "Yes I do, Kenny Wertz."

Chris had played with Kenny in a band called "Scottsville Squirrel Barkers." Chris was just a teenager when he joined that band.

We asked Chris where Kenny Wertz might be and he said, "In Tahoe, washing dishes."

We chased down Kenny and asked if he wanted to come down and play with us. He could certainly sing tenor. He did and we began rehearsing.

July 21-25 Country Gazette played the Bitter End West. This was a big show with Earl Scruggs on it and his sons, Gary, Randy, and Steve. Country Gazette did the first set. Douglas Jones of the Hollywood reporter gave a good review in the Night Club Reviews section of the paper.

> "(Country Gazette)…they are proficient musicians and excellent entertainers…a phenomenal version of "Foggy Mountain Breakdown" consisting of Pedersen, Wertz, and Bush on banjos, standing close together, each one having his hand on a different fret board.
>
> Each musician in the group is extremely versatile and unpretentious, capable of going from one instrument to another with little or no trouble and their virtuosity in each is totally devoid of tricks of flashy pyrotechnics. They will be around for quite a while and a recording company would be smart to sign them up."

July 27-31 did a show and live recording session with Linda Ronstadt at the Troubadour. The Troubadour had the stage, audience seating and at the back of the club, they had little rooms, although I never saw them used for anything. I was on stage setting up equipment for the show and heard banjo music coming from somewhere. I listened and just followed the sound to one of those little rooms. I opened the door and there was just this one man sitting there playing his banjo.

I introduced myself and he said his name was Steve Martin. He said, "I am opening for you tonight."

"Playing banjo?" I asked.

"No, I do comedy, but I use the banjo in my act." He pointed out.

It was opening night and Martin was feeling a little insecure about how he might go over.

John McEuen of the Nitty Gritty Dirt Band and Steve Martin were friends from their high school days and they both played the banjo. John's brother, Bill McEuen managed artists and John talked him into representing Steve Martin.

The night of this opening, John McEuen, banjo in hand, stood in the sound booth. Bette and I were there and we watched Steve do his opening act.

Just to show how differently we remember things, depending on our perspective, here is how John McEuen and I remember the same night at the Troubadour.

The lights dimmed, Steve Martin took the stage with his banjo in hand. He began playing "Foggy Mountain Breakdown" and so did John McEuen. John says they were playing "Sally Goodin'." While John's banjo played over the sound system, Steve played along and smiled at the audience, giving a good performance. Then Steve stopped playing while John continued. Steve sipped a glass of wine. John says Steve took his hands off the banjo and said, "You know, this is really pretty easy." Then he resumed playing with John's music.

Bette and I thought Steve was funny; some of the audience got it while some did not, but they laughed and seemed to enjoy his routine.

Thanks John, for remembering this night with me.

Steve MarChris Bunch reviewed our opening night.

"Silver threads With Golden Needles"…the band was at ease and Ronstadt seemed to have lost most of her opening night nervousness. The song was accented with Berline's fiddle work – fills that were absolutely necessary, but never became solos. The listener wanted more, rather than feeling a surfeit. Both Sneaky Pete (Kleinow), Ronstadt and Berline peaked on "I Fall to Pieces"…"

The reviews were not as kind to Steve Martin and he was concerned.

I said, "The audience laughed, didn't they?"

"Well, yes." He admitted.

I said, "Forget about the critics."

Steve Martin is a neat person.

August 1-7 Country Gazette played the San Mateo Fair.

August 17-22 we played the Ash Grove in a show called "Strings on Fire" and Country Gazette was the featured act. Stann Findelle of the Los Angeles Free Press had some glowing things to say about Country Gazette in the August Seventeenth issue.

This is a long one, but good reviews are sometimes hard to come by…I have read the good ones more than once.

"At the top of the show were the men of the "Country Gazette," featuring the incomparable Byron Berline on fiddle. Lots of people are aware of national championships in basketball or chess, but Berline is the three-time holder of the national championship of fiddle playing and watching him in action makes it simple to see why. Berline,….is one of those rare, captivating individuals who plays his instrument as if it were a natural extension of his arm, where every musical nuance is instantly, flawlessly interpreted. There really aren't enough superlatives to describe his dexterity and dynamics on his instrument. But, it was also fascinating the way Berline meshed with the fine skills of the others in the group, to produce an organic sound of such tightness that it seemed to be created from one mind instead of four.

Throughout a mellow, yet highly stimulating set, the multitalents of Berline, string-basist Roger Bush…and banjo man Herb …were as apparent as the cream floating to the top of pure country milk.

Introduced as the "Crosby, Stills and Nash" of Country Music, which is a title of somewhat adulterated value (this group could pick their teeth with more sheer musical finesse than Crosby, Stills, Nash or Young could ever hope to get out of their guitars, they embarked into a premium set where it was uniquely difficult to distinguish "best" numbers, since all of them were of such consummate fineness.

Especially memorable were some virtuoso bluegrass pieces like "Foggy Mountain Breakdown" with three lightning banjos parts and Berline on guitar. (The Nitty Gritty Dirt Band, who were having a set as flat as a guitar pick across town at the Troubadour, could take a lesson from the energetic control of the Gazette's interpretation of this number...After a genuine encore call, the "Gazette" returned to do "One tear," embellished with delicate violin accents by M. Berline.

For those who like their music organic, untouched by over-seasoning, processing and packaging, the "Country Gazette" would certainly have to be their meat."

Those really were the absolute best audiences and we had guests, David Grisman, Linda Ronstadt, Billy Ray Latham, Bernie Leadon, and Bob Gibson.

They were beginning to notice Country Gazette.

One day in the fall of 1971, Chris Hillman called and said he wanted me to go on tour with the Flying Burrito Brothers. He said he also needed Kenny Wertz because Bernie Leadon left the band. Roger Bush stayed home. He was not invited. They put Al Perkins and Rick Roberts on the tour and I played fiddle.

The Flying Burrito Brothers played country rock and in the middle of the show, Chris Hillman put down his bass and played mandolin on a bluegrass set. That left no one on bass.

In the middle of the tour, I told Chris, "We really need a bass player...Why don't we call Roger Bush and have him go with us?"

He said, "Okay," so I called Roger and he got to go with us after all.

August 18 the Flying Burrito Brothers, preparing to go out on tour, did a radio show for KMET-LA. That was the last time Bernie Leadon was with us. Jim Dickson produced the show and we recoded it at the "Record Plant" in L.A. Bob Gibson sang as a guest on a few songs. The FBB were Chris Hillman, Rick Roberts, Al Perkins, Kenny Wertz, Michael Clarke, Roger Bush, Bernie Leadon, and Byron Berline. They aired the radio show the following day on August 19.

August 23-September 19 The Flying Burrito Brothers had

a tour booked to play clubs and universities taking us up and down the east coast.

August 23, 24 the FBB played Tulagi's Club in Boulder, Colorado. We played this convention where groups and individual entertainers perform and then get bookings for universities and colleges all over the country. We were back stage waiting to go on and heard a couple of comedians on stage so we stepped out to catch what they were doing. The act consisted of two guys called Cheech and Chong and at first, we just did not get it. Al Perkins never did.

The next night, the 25, we played Fort Collins, Colorado. From Colorado, we headed to the Philadelphia Folk Festival and this was the first year they held the festival at the Old Pool Farm in Schwenksville, Montgomery County, Pennsylvania. I still have the driving notes on how to get there. This festival began in 1962, growing considerably by 1971.

August 27-29 the FBB played the Philadelphia Folk Festival. Bill Monroe was also booked and had Kenny Baker in his band. Kenny and I really enjoyed hanging out and Bill had me play with them on the show. I remember that it rained so hard and all the resulting mud.

From there we went to New York City and the FBB played September 2-5 at the "Bitter End" club on Bleeker Street in Greenwich Village. We had an unusual opening act...Cheech and Chong.

Before we opened in Buffalo, New York, the following appeared in the newspaper:

> "The Flying Burrito Brothers will be appearing at the world famed Clark Music Hall and Athletic Arena this Sunday night. According to recent reports, Byron Berline, renowned fiddler and all around wizard, will be playing with them, if you care at all about music, regardless of type or classification, then you should make every effort to hear them."

September 6, 7 we played in Springvale, Maine.
September 8, 9 we played in South Fallsburg, New York.
September 10, 11 we played in Bristol, Rhode Island.
September 12 we stayed in Carlisle, Pennsylvania.
Roger Bush and I wrote "Hot Burrito Breakdown," while on the road...we went up to the hotel room and wrote the tune in

five minutes. The FBB played "Hot Burrito Breakdown" while on tour but did not include it on the album, "Last of the Red Hot Burritos." We played several universities and Jim Dickson did live recordings at three of those concerts. The tapes, then edited, would be released as the album, "The Last of the Red Hot Burritos." They took the best of each concert and made the album from that. We were surprised at the good audience response to the bluegrass set...you can hear it on the album. Bluegrass music was just starting to catch on at college campuses.

September 13-18 we played the Cellar Door in Washington, D.C.

The Flying Burrito Brothers got good reviews for the most part on this tour, including this one by Don Hearn in the Washington Daily News on September 17, 1971.

"Running rather true to form, the Cellar door in Georgetown has come up with another winner.

No sleeper, gang. Currently in residence – the Flying Burrito Brothers.

For the uninitiated (there are always are some, you know), this is NOT a high-wire circus act.

This is some kind of something else. Country-rock. These guys (all six) knock themselves out. It's appreciated, too. All the fans are with them every (Every) night. They scream, whistle, and demand more – more.

I sat thru a pair of shows the other night and left in sort of a state of shock.

Such exuberance is not often encountered.

To grasp their complete, captivating control of country-rock is an experience.

The Flying Burrito Brothers are an extremely well knit group. They know what it's all about and go out to prove it.

Flipping an audience into a semi-trance (vocally and musically) are sure talents as Al Perkins (steel), Chris Hillman (bass and mandolin), Rick Roberts (rhythm guitar), Kenny Wertz (guitar and banjo), Mike Clarke (percussion) and the unbelievable fiddle of Nashville's famous Byron Berline.

Mr. Berline, as far as I'm concerned, just happens to steal the entire show. He's a confident performer, an occasional singer and an artist who treats his violin with all the warming care of an artist who calls himself a ventriloquist.

His fiddle feats are downright amazing and knock the roof right off. Again – they scream and holler for more, more.

It's all beautiful. Certainly, a rewarding evening for anyone hung up on these gentlemen. All in all, a polished performance injected with enough informality to make it seem real."

The Flying Burrito Brothers have a lot of fans on the east coast and their music is catching on at college campuses."

A girl came down and sat in with us while we were playing at the Cellar Door and we were impressed with her singing. She gave us her phone number and her name, Emmylou Harris.

September 19 we played in Sweetbriar, Virginia.

A few days later, we were playing at a university, maybe Charlotte, North Carolina and Gram Parsons walked in. We were surprised to see him and he looked real good...looked healthy. Chris Hillman, Gram and I, just the three of us, sat around talking. Gram said, "I've got an idea to sing some duets. Have you guys got any ideas about a girl singer?"

We said, "Yes. Get Emmylou Harris, she'd be good for you." He had never heard of her either, so we gave Gram her phone number, he called her then flew her out to L.A. That was wild... one chance meeting and just dropping the idea of a girl singer. Gram and Emmylou began recording together and I was involved in all of those recordings. Gram came to the house to rehearse. He played all kinds of music and loved country music, but I never could figure out what he was trying to do. Gram had problems... serious problems and he overdosed. It is so sad...he is still, so very popular today.

September 29, FBB went back on tour and played Bucknell University at Lewisburg, Pennsylvania.

October 4 the FBB played the David Frost TV show in New York City. We did "Six Days on the Road" and you can view this video on U-tube.

October 8 the FBB played Union College in Schenectady, New York.

October 9 the FBB played Spaulding Auditorium at Dartmouth College in Hanover, New Hampshire. The Dartmouth concert is one they recorded for the "Last of the Red Hot Burritos" album. Again, the press wrote positively about the show. Peter Gambaccini wrote the following review:

"A highly enthusiastic Spaulding Auditorium clapped its

hands and slapped its knees to the picking and grinning of the Flying Burrito Brothers Saturday night.

The Burrito Brothers have always included bluegrass music in their concerts but until now have never featured it in the albums. On their current tour, two cornpone characters, Roger Bush (standup bass) and Byron Berline (fiddle) have joined new member Kenny Wertz (banjo) and leader Chris Hillman (mandolin) to produce some excellent "breakdowns," as Bush labeled the selections.

The emphasis on bluegrass by the Burritos was partly a response to its popularity with the audience and largely due to the group's plans to release a live album from their current tour.

...and it was impossible not to smile warmly as you watched Berline, a hulking Okie, towering over much shaggier musicians and having the best time of anybody in the auditorium.

An audience comprised partly of people who had never even heard of the Flying Burrito Brothers, had its appetite satiated with several encores. Back at home, they searched through their record collections hoping they still had their old Flatt and Scruggs albums."

October 11-15 the FBB did a Warner Brothers recording session for Stephen Stills. While we were on tour with the FBB, Stephen Stills contacted us and wanted us to do some session work with him. We took four or five days off from touring and Stephen flew all the Burrito Brothers down to Miami, Florida's Criteria Records studio to begin recording the "Manassas" album. When Stephen decided to record like this, he simply rented out a studio for a month. There were two brothers, Howie and Ron Howard, recording engineers and Stephen hired them to engineer the sessions. We cut "Fallen Eagle" and a bunch of other songs.

October 16 the FBB played Phillips Academy in Andover, Massachusetts.

October 18-22 we flew back to Florida to record with Stephen Stills. This time he asked Chris Hillman, Al Perkins and me to join his band. I was not going to...he was too strange. Talk about a drug infested dude. Stills had his roadies go all the way to Nashville, Tennessee to Gruhn's and bring back a truckload of guitars and other instruments. He went through and culled them, buying a 1924 Lloyd Loar F5 Gibson mandolin, which he gave to

Chris Hillman. He gave away lots of gifts to people he wanted to be his friends, but he did not give anything to me because he was still pressuring me to join his band. I told him Country Gazette was beginning to get going and that we had a record deal.

"He said, "Oh, forget that. I'll get you a record deal with Warner Brothers."

We finished recording and when it was over, the Flying Burrito Brothers went back to California.

The FBB's last east tour concert was as the University of Maryland in Baltimore. When we did the rock set, the rest of the band usually went back to the bus. Sometimes they would call me on stage to do some stuff, but not every song. I might have been on the bus, but whatever the reason, I do not remember the following: Chris Hillman says Gram played a number with us on stage that night. I do not know where I was, but not on stage when Gram was there. Check out Chris Hillman's book, "Hot Burritos, The True Story of the Flying Burrito Brothers."

Stephen Stills called and asked Roger and me to do another recording session. "Manassas" was to be a two record album and Stills was trying to finish the second record. He had Chris Hillman, Al Perkins, with Dallas Taylor playing drums and Joe Lala as percussionist. They flew Roger Bush and I to Florida to record with them...when we went into the studio I never saw such a bunch of zombies. Stephen wanted me to play on this one track, to some obscure song he had written. While listening to the track I started fiddling, figuring out how I wanted to play it.

"Oh, no, no, no," He said. "That's not it," then he sat down and kind of mumbled about how he wanted me to play it. He left the room and was gone about thirty or forty minutes. Chris Hillman was there and said, "I heard it and I thought the way you played it was alright. It sounded good to me."

When Stephen returned I said, "I have it worked out."

"Good," he replied.

I played it just like the first time.

"Perfect." Stephen said. "That's just what I wanted."

This music was so bad...Roger and I knew it was bad...the timing, terrible, but we did the best we could and Stephen sent if off to Ahmet Ertegun, President of Atlantic Records. Warner purchased Atlantic Records, retaining Ertegun as President of their Atlantic Records division. He listened to the Manassas recording once and sent it right back saying, "Do it again." They had already spent a hundred grand on it.

Stephen had huge piles of drugs, ice chests full of alcohol and he made everything available...anything, anyone might want, the whole time we were there. Stephen stayed up four or five days at a time, he never got any rest. I did not want to hang around that nor did Al Perkins or the rest of the people, so we did not do any more of those sessions. The next time he tried to finish it up, Stephen came to L.A. I guess he got it finished, but I do not really know because I did not play on it.

What is amazing is that there are so many people wanting an opportunity to record for a major label. There are a lot of talented people out there that never get that chance, but some who do get the opportunity just blow it up. During the sixties, through the eighties, musicians thought they could get creative if they got screwed-up enough and what a joke that was. It was all so very sad...you can overdo a lot of things.

When the Flying Burrito Brother's tour ended and we finished recording for Stephen Stills, we all flew back to California where Chris Hillman and Al Perkins gave notice...they were both leaving the Flying Burrito Brothers to join Stephen Still's band. The "Last of the Red Hot Burritos" album, not yet released and two members of the band were leaving.

The FBB also had a commitment to complete a pre-booked European tour. One day Eddie Tickner called and asked, "Hey, Bud, you want to go?"

I said, "Sure." I had never been to Europe. "But how...with no more Burrito Brothers?"

He said, "Just put a band together. It's already booked."

Tickner played a FBB tape, recorded from a previous Holland tour. They had Bernie Leadon with them and they played bluegrass. The crowd went wild. They loved bluegrass so we knew we would be playing that plus some Burrito Brothers tunes.

I wondered what would happen when we got there and half the Burrito Brothers were people they had never seen or heard, but I began pulling in musicians. Rick Roberts was out of a job and said he would go. That was one band member, however not an original member of the Burrito Brothers. We had Kenny

Wertz, Rogers Bush, Rick Roberts, Don Beck playing a little steel and mandolin, me on fiddle, but we still needed a drummer.

I also did session work at this time with John Martin, also from Oklahoma. He went by the name of "Moon" Martin and did pretty well. I asked if he knew anybody that could play drums. He recommended Eric Dalton and I told someone to call him. They apparently told him where the band was going on tour because Dalton came into the studio an hour later, wearing a stocking cap, and carrying a six-pack of Heineken.

"He's hired!" I said. "I like him" and that is how we got our drummer. Eric now lives in Oklahoma and is a Rolfer masseuse. The band was almost complete, but although Kenny Wertz played banjo, we needed him to play guitar.

I told Jim Dickson that I knew someone who played banjo and electric guitar and said he might go with us. I called Alan Munde, my OU college-days friend and he joined the troupe. Then I made a tape of Alan and played it for Roger Bush and Kenny Wertz at one of our rehearsals. I told them, "Well, what do you think? This guy can play pretty good."

"Sounds good to me," Roger said. "That'll be alright."

The new Flying Burrito Brothers, finally put together.

November 1, while mixing the music from the three university concerts the Flying Burrito Brothers did while on tour back east, A&M Records called me in to add some fiddle to some of the tracks.

November 19, 20 Country Gazette played McCabes.

November 23, 24 did my first recording session with Arlo Guthrie for Rising Sun Records for his "Hobo's Lullaby" album. Doug Dillard was on this, Clarence White, Hoyt Axton, Ry Cooder, Chris Ethridge, and Linda Ronstadt.

December 9 did a recording session with Jack "Moon" Martin. He grew up close to the Oklahoma-Texas border, played rock and roll, and wrote songs, then he came to L.A. and did session work for Linda Ronstadt, Gram Parsons, and Del Shannon. Jack is the one who recommended Eric Dalton for the FBB European tour.

December 15 we did a FBB recording session.

December 31 on New Year's Eve, the new Flying Burrito Brothers left California for a European tour. The line-up included Rick Roberts, Eric Dalton, Alan Munde, Don Beck, Roger Bush, Kenny Wertz, and Byron Berline. Robert Firks, a young roadie went on this tour with us.

Journal Entry 1972
United Artists Signs Country Gazette – Flying Burrito Brothers Tour Europe – Traitor in our Midst

January 1-30 1972 The Flying Burrito Brothers on tour in Europe.

The rest of the band did not even meet Alan Munde until we met at the airport in New York City on our way to Holland. We played together just a little bit at the airport, then boarded our flight to Holland and began the European tour of the new Flying Burrito Brothers.

Our greatest fear was that of being "booed" off of the stage… we felt the audience would not accept the band with new players in it. Chris Hillman was not there and he had been a big part of the original Flying Burrito Brothers.

Our first show was at Breda, Holland on January 1. We played the show and everyone did fine, including Alan Munde. The audiences really loved the bluegrass stuff…they just loved bluegrass. The show was a success, the audience loved it, and there was not one word regarding the new configuration of the band. One person did ask about Chris Hillman, so I explained he was with Stephen Stills…that was the end of it. This fan just noticed Chris was missing.

On a previous tour of the Netherlands, the Flying Burrito Brothers had stayed at the Hotel Wiechmann in Amsterdam, Holland. A former Oklahoman, Ted Boddy, went to Amersterdam while in the military, met Nicky, whose parents owned the Hotel Wiechmann. Ted and Nicky got married and began running the hotel. On our very first trip to Holland, the new Flying Burrito Brothers also stayed at the Hotel Wiechmann, which is very old and furnished with Boddy family memorabilia. The band members were young and did not mind climbing the narrow staircase up to our rooms. The hotel is located on a corner intersection, on the Prinsengracht Canal…a beautiful old world setting. The Boddy's, so kind and hospitable, allowed us to jam in the lobby and they became big Flying Burrito Brothers and Country Gazette fans.

We toured Holland, Sweden, Norway, Denmark and they all loved bluegrass. It was quite an experience, but when the FBB played Amsterdam, we had a dilemma. We knew there would be people recording the concert, resulting in bootleg records. Ariola Records wanted to record and release the show as a live FBB album and although we really did not want a live recording made, we said okay, knowing they would bootleg it anyway.

When we returned from our first "Flying Burrito Brothers" tour of Europe, Country Gazette began to emerge, separately, from the FBB. Eddie Tickner and Jim Dickson were involved with the band and we went to the office of the President of United Artists recording company and explained why we wanted to record. We told him about the things Country Gazette had been doing and told him we felt a recording would fit right in.

He said, "Okay." Dan Bourgoise signed "Country Gazette" and "Asleep at The Wheel" to United Artists on the same day in 1972.

February 1, 1972 I do not remember with which group, but I remember playing St. Cloud, Minnesota.

February 18, 20, 1972 The Flying Burrito Brothers played a benefit concert at the Fox Theater in Long Beach. Also on the bill were the New Riders of the Purple Sage.

March 13-15 I had the opportunity to work on the sound track for the MGM movie, "Junior Bonner," directed by Sam Peckinpah, starring Steve McQueen, Robert Preston, Ida Lupino, Ben Johnson, and Joe Don Baker. The story is about a rodeo cowboy trying to make a comeback. It is really a good movie.

March 22 Country Gazette played Disneyland and doing several shows a day, the band quickly became tight. While we were doing the Disney thing, we also went into the studio to cut our first album, "Traitor in Our Midst."

March 23, 29 Country Gazette did a recording session. Country Gazette included Roger Bush, Alan Munde, Kenny Wertz, and me. Herb Pedersen came in and did some singing on that album. We did, "Hot Burrito Breakdown," the tune Roger Bush and I wrote for the "Flying Burrito Brothers." Kenny Wertz played banjo when we were on tour with the FBB, but the tune really did not sound like we wanted. When Alan Munde got a hold of it, he really brought it to life.

The engineer said, "Take One" and when we messed up he said, "Take two" and so on. When he said, "Take twenty-seven," we got a little discouraged and by late afternoon, things just would not fall into place. We finally decided to just forget it, come back the next day and the following morning we did it in one take. Engineers do not do that anymore...thank goodness. It wears on you. Today you just go through it until you get a good take.

Jim Dickson brought in different people to come in and play on the record. Al Perkins played a little steel here and there, Leland Sklar came in and played bass along with Roger Bush's slap bass, and it just sounded great.

Country Gazette played a show at McCabes with Linda Ronstadt. Linda did all the lead vocals and we told a lot of stories. They quickly arranged this gig and we did not have time to rehearse.

March 25-April 1Country Gazette played Disneyland.

Atlantic Records released Stephen Stills' "Manassas" album.

April 10, 13, 20, 25 Country Gazette continued recording sessions and although "Traitor in Our Midst" turned out to be a very good recording, we spent more money on the album cover than we did recording it. The cover had a comic book look to it and Norman Seeff, previously a brain surgeon, did the photography. As in comic books, the back cover had this Charles Atlas type character and we had a leopard skin thing for that pose that I wanted Alan Munde to wear, but he refused. Then the rest of the band said, "You do it." so, I did. We hired a model to come in and it was not easy lifting her up on my shoulder because she was not little and of course, Bette was there, watching this whole thing. "Watch out now..."

When they released the album, a lot of people saw the cover, read the liner notes, heard the music and that is what made it a hit record.

In 1972, CBS/FOX released the movie "Welcome Home Soldier Boys," also known as, "Five Days Home." Country Gazette did a few songs in it, including "Farther Along."

A&M Records released the Flying Burrito Brothers' "Last of the Red Hot Burritos."

April 30-May 1, 2, 3 did recording sessions with Gene Clark on his "Roadmaster" album.

May 19 I did a recording session with Rick Roberts. Rick left the Flying Burrito Brothers and this was his debut solo album, "Windmills" on which he wrote all but one song. Chris Hillman was on it, Don Henley, Bernie Leadon, and Randy Meisner. Some other players included David Crosby, Jackson Browne, Al Perkins, Dallas Taylor, Leland Sklar, Joe Lala, and Mark Benno.

May 31 did a recording session with singer and songwriter, Wendy Waldman, for her solo album "Love Has Got Me" for Warner Brothers and produced by Charles Plotkin. Maria Muldar and Linda Ronstadt were on this recording.

June 1, 1972 United Artists released Country Gazette's debut album "Traitor in Our Midst." From that, they released the single "Keep on Pushin'." This is a Gene Clark song and on the B-side, they released "Hot Burrito Breakdown," the tune Roger Bush and I wrote. "Keep on Pushin" received a lot of radio airplay and as a result, we had a hit!

June 1972, Ariola released the Flying Burrito Brothers' album, "Live in Amsterdam."

Beginning about June 18 Country Gazette played the rest of the summer at Disneyland. Our gig to play for twelve weeks was to open Bear Country. Walt Disney's "Disneyland" theme park in Anaheim, California, opened in July of 1955 and they were always adding new rides and attractions. They placed Bear Country in Frontier Land, which resembled the Pacific Northwest; with tress, a river and of course, there were bears. The first attraction in Bear Country was the Country Bear Jamboree, which became the forerunner of similar productions such as Chuck E. Cheese and Show Biz Pizza Place's animatronic music shows. Country Gazette played outside the Country Bear Theater doing several shows a day. Inside, frames covered with fur, came to life as bears playing musical instruments with a country flavor. I do not know if we were imitating them or they sounded like we did.

The Disneyland gig for Country Gazette occurred during the 1972 summer Olympics, August 26 to September 11. They held the games in Munich, in what was then, West Germany. I remember running to catch a glimpse of the games on TV, between our sets at the amusement park.

June 19, 20 began working on a Disney picture.

June 23 played with Linda Ronstadt again at Knott's Berry Farm.

July 16, 1972 played with Stephen Stills at the Hollywood Bowl. This outdoor venue opened in 1922 and it holds over seventeen thousand people.

July 20 did a recording session with Tom Keuhl, "Cowboy Maynard," on his "Uncle John O'Neal" album, for Rural Rhythm Records. The recording studio in East Los Angeles was an 8-track studio and located in a not so great neighborhood. The upstairs control room looked down over the studio of musicians and background singers; this was a big band. We had to do the entire album at one time with no over-dubs. When we arrived, the engineer sat with his feet propped up, a cigar in his mouth and a case of beer on the floor beside him. The studio did not have headsets (monitors.) The engineer said, "You don't need em'…just follow the drummer." We could not hear in that huge studio. It took a long time to record one track and the whole session quickly became a nightmare…the most unorganized session I had ever done. At long last, we finished and when ready to leave, discovered the President of Rural Rhythm Records, Jim O'Neal's Cadillac, was gone.

July - August Country Gazette continued playing at Disneyland. Bette was pregnant, it was hot, I was tied up at Disneyland every day, and we found a house to purchase. Our new place had one window air-conditioner for the whole house and Bette did so much of the work. We only moved about a half mile away, keeping the same house number, but on a different street, at 15113 Weddington St. in Van Nuys.

August 2 MGM released the Steve McQueen movie, "Junior Bonner."

August 18 practiced with Gram Parsons at my house for his solo debut album "GP" on A&M Records.

August 18, 19 did a recording session for the ABC movie, "Bounty Hunter." "The Bounty Man" starring Clint Walker as a bounty hunter originally aired October 31, 1972. The cast included Richard Basehart, John Ericson, and Margot Kidder. When work begins on a movie, it has a working title, which often changes during production.

In September of 1972, A&M Records released Rick Robert's "Windmills" album.

September 1 Stephen Stills flew Roger Bush and me to Orlando, Florida for a recording session.

September 7 did a recording session for Brush Arbor on Capitol Records for their debut "Brush Arbor" album. This Christian-country band played a lot in southern California.

September 7, 8, 11, 12, 13, and 25 had a lot of recording sessions with Gram Parsons on his solo debut album, "GP," for Reprise Records. He had a lot of good players including Emmylou Harris singing duets with him, musicians included Barry Tashian, Ric Grech, John Conrad, Ronnie Tutt, John Guerin, Sam Goldstein, Glen D. Hardin, James Burton, Al Perkins, Buddy Emmons and Alan Munde and me. We did some rehearsing at my house.

September 8 Twentieth Century Fox/CBS released "Welcome Home, Soldier Boys," also known as "Five Days Home." Richard Compton directed the movie starring Joe Don Baker, Paul Koslo, Alan Vint, Jennifer Billingsley, and Billy Green Bush. The plot revolved around some Green Berets returning from Viet Nam. They went across the country and violently took over a town. Ken Wannberg was the music supervisor and Country Gazette worked on the sound track.

September 14 I did a recording session for the ABC movie "Rolling Man." Peter Hyams directed this Movie of the Week, starring Dennis Weaver, Don Stroud, and Donna Mills. Jimmy Dean was in it, Sheree North, Slim Pickens, and Agnes Moorhead. The story is about a man in prison whose children disappear; upon release, he searches for them.

September 15, 16 Country Gazette played McCabes.

September 17- October 14 Country Gazette rented a Chevy station wagon and went on our first road trip playing Denver, Colorado, the Winfield, Kansas, Walnut Valley Festival, Cleveland, Ohio and Minneapolis, Minnesota.

September 29, 30 - October1 Country Gazette played Winfield, Kansas Walnut Valley Bluegrass Festival. They had an amazing line-up that first year that included Lester Flatt and The Nashville Grass with Lester Flatt, Paul Warren, Haskell McCormick, Roland White, Johnny Johnson, Jack Martin, and thirteen–year-old Marty Stuart. I remember he stayed at my sister, Eleanor's house there in Winfield, during the festival. Others on the bill that year included Jim, Jesse, and the Virginia Boys with Jim and Jesse McReynolds, Vic Jordan, Jim Brock, and Carel

Johnson. Doc and Merle Watson performed, the Lewis Family with Miggie Lewis, Roy "Pop" Lewis, Talmadge Lewis, Wailkes, "Little Boy," Jamie Lewis Phillips and Polly Lewis Williamson. Country Gazette played with Alan Munde, Kenny Wertz, Roger Bush, and me. They booked New Grass Revival with Sam Bush, Ebo Walker, Courtney Johnson, and Curtis Burch. Also on the bill were Dan Crary, Norman Blake, and the Stone Mountain Boys with Mitchell Land, Eddie Shelton, James Durham, and Tootie Williams. Jimmy Driftwood performed, Art Eskridge, and the Bluegrass Country Boys with Jack and Mike Theobald, Joe Payton, Jay Yount and Dan Kochs and Minnie Moore (many more.)

Jack Theobald brought bluegrass music to Kansas. I first met Jack in 1958 and that was the first time I heard live bluegrass music. At the 1972 Winfield Festival, Jack's son, Mike, played with him. The Bluegrass Country Boys had Jack on guitar and lead vocal, Mike on banjo, Joe Payton on mandolin and vocals, Jay Yount on fiddle and Dan Kochs on bass and vocals.

Stuart Mossman lived in Winfield, Kansas, made Mossman guitars and was three times, named Luthier of the Year. He decided a national contest/festival would bring together the country's best pickers and that would be a good way to showcase his line of guitars. I remember Stuart calling and inviting me to play at this little thing before they had the first Walnut Valley Festival and that was the first time I met him. At this first Walnut Valley Festival, Stuart hired Dan Crary, Norman Blake and me, as judges. When it was all over, Stuart went out to his guitar factory at Strother Field, picked out three guitars and gave one to each of us for judging the guitar-picking contest. I will never forget it...they were Great Plains models and I thought, "How neat that is!" At a festival a few years later, Stuart offered us Golden Era model guitars and the only one who took his at the time was Alan Wald. I just told Stuart I would get it later. Dan and I never got our guitars. Alan took his right then and that is what Dan and I should have done.

Dad had a good friend and bones player, Cecil Hiatt and they played together a lot. Cecil learned to play the bones from a fellow that worked in a medicine show. When my nephew, Barry Patton was about seven or eight years old he saw Cecil play the bones. By 1972, watching Cecil play with dad, the bones really caught Barry's attention. At the end of the festival, while getting ready to leave, Cecil was talking to Barry and accidently shut Barry's fingers in a car door. Cecil felt so bad...he gave Barry a set of oak bones and one quick lesson. This was a very serious accident and Barry almost lost a finger. According to his mother, Eleanor, when Barry got home he went straight to the basement and using his good hand, he rattled those bones for a long, long time. It helped keep him occupied while the other hand healed, which took almost a year. Then Barry began playing the bones with the injured hand, no doubt, serving as good therapy. Eventually, he put bones in both hands.

Cecil Hiatt taught Barry how to play the bones and Barry did the practicing...night and day. He wore out our records and left the radio on all night; when a song came on that sounded like he could play the bones to it, he got up and started playing. He still does this.

Larry Frost, my co-author's husband also attended that first Walnut Valley Festival in 1972. I will let him tell this story.

Larry Frost: Sam Onjes was in partnership with Stuart Mossman and they were both friends of mine. I had Stuart make a Flint Hills model guitar for me (No. 55) when I returned to the states after getting out of the air force. Sam Onjes and I had played in a high school folk group in Hutchinson, Kansas. On Friday night of the festival, Sam and I went to Bob Redford's house, where they fed all the performers and we ate with Byron and the rest of Country Gazette.

On Saturday night, Sam had a big picking party planned for the artists playing at the festival and when giving the players directions to his home, he made it clear that drugs "would not be tolerated" and everyone showed up except Norman and Nancy Blake. This was a huge jam and during a lull, someone began softly singing "Amazing Grace." One by one, everyone joined in with beautiful harmony. That was quite a memorable chorus.

This is also the first time I met Sam Bush. I had seen and heard Doc Watson at the 1965 Newport Folk Festival and I had heard Ian Tyson on a record, single string pick a guitar, but I had never seen anything like the way Doc Watson, Dan Crary, and Norman Blake played that first year at Winfield.

Byron: Do you remember how cold it got? Wind blowing

40 miles an hour and my parents were there in the audience all bundled up.

Larry: Someone went around selling big plastic trash bags as Rambo Raincoats. That is about the coldest I have ever been.

Byron: Country Gazette, with their brand new debut album, Traitor in our Midst, parked near the stage and bleacher seats. After our set on stage, we opened up the back of the station wagon and sold albums. Years later, Joe Carr and I were talking about that festival and he said, "I know who bought the very first "Traitor in our Midst" album."

I looked at him and said, "Who?"

"I did!" He said.

Larry Frost: I too, was in that line and I know my music pursuits took a new direction, as a direct result of seeing and hearing Country Gazette play live and listening to that album. This was over thirty years ago and although Stuart Mossman has passed on, his festival continues to bring together many fine musicians.

Capitol Records released the "Brush Arbor" album in October of 1972.

October 4 ABC released the Movie of the Week, "Rolling Man."

October 31 – November 2 Country Gazette played a gig in San Francisco.

Also on October 31, the ABC Movie of the Week, "The Bounty Man," aired for the first time on television.

November 17-December 2 Country Gazette played Cotati, California, Houston and Dallas, Texas and Boulder, Colorado.

Also in November, the magazine "Bluegrass Unlimited," Vol. 7 No.5, featured Country Gazette. The article is lengthy and in depth with regard to the band and each member's contributions. At the end of the article, I stated, with regard to the success of Country Gazette, "It's almost complete. I'm just waiting for my first child to be born and teaching him to fiddle."

I had no way of knowing it would take another generation for that dream to become a reality.

December 5, 6 did another recording session with Brush Arbor for their "Brush Arbor 2" album.

December 8, 9 Country Gazette played McCabes. I played the show, but with concerns about leaving Bette that Saturday night, as the baby was due any time. The next morning, Sunday, December 10, 1972, Bette went to church and late that night Becca Diane Berline was born.

December 18 did a recording session for Michael Nesmith on his "Pretty Much Your Standard Ranch Stash" for RCA.

December 29 did a recording session with Stephen Stills from 9:00 p.m. to 3:00 a.m....an all-nighter and never paid for it.

Journal Entry 1973
The Year the Music Died - Clarence White - Gram Parsons

January 10-12 did a recording session for Michael Nesmith.

January 14 did a recording session with Doug Dillard for his solo "Duelin' Banjo" album for 20th Century Records, produced by Doug's brother, Rodney. It is "banjo" instead of the Deliverance "Banjos" because there is just Doug playing. I played fiddle on this with Andy Belling on keyboards, Billy Ray Latham on guitar, Buddy Emmons on steel guitar, Colin Cameron on bass, Dick Rosmini on guitar, Doug played banjo and guitar, Jeff Gilkenson on bass, Paul York on drums and Rick Cunha on guitar. We were all setup in the studio, ready to record when Doug said, "Wait, I've got a cramp in my head." Someone should be collecting these gems.

January 16 Country Gazette had another recording session for our "Don't Give up Your Day Job" album.

January 18 did another Doug Dillard session.

January 19 Country Gazette played UCA at San Diego.

January 24, 30, 31 did Country Gazette recording sessions. We recorded my tune, "Huckleberry Hornpipe" and Clarence White took an amazing break. I have a picture of us briefly going over that at our house. We did not have much time to rehearse but, when we went into the studio to record, the first take sounded good.

Clarence said, "What do you think?"

I told him I thought it was fine, but asked, "Did you want to do it again?"

We did and he nailed it! I used to tell Clarence, "I made you a star, letting you record my song."

Following "Huckleberry Hornpipe," we did a tune we had not played in a long time and I had to play guitar on it. The tune, written by Country Gazette for a Mazda commercial, we titled "Deputy Dalton" and decided to record it on the album.

I felt so weird sitting there playing lead guitar, so I told Clarence, "Why don't you play this?"

"I don't know this song." He said. "I'll just play rhythm for you."

I felt kind of silly…Clarence White played rhythm guitar, for me…that is a special memory.

February 1-March 10 did European tour, co-billed as the "Hot Burrito Review and Country Gazette," this time including Sneaky Pete Kleinow on steel guitar, replacing Don Beck. The line-up included Kenny Wertz, Rick Roberts, Alan Munde, Eric Dalton, Sneaky Pete Kleinow, Roger Bush, and Byron Berline.

In Holland, we again stayed at the Boddy's Hotel Wiechmann and they became very good friends, watched after us and went to all our shows. Mrs. Boddy, Nicky, lined up some of the tours we did and made sure we got most of the money. The press was always there doing interviews. It was a blast.

Country Gazette had a hit single with "Keep on Pushin'" from our Traitor in our Midst album and as a result, fans followed us around, the press was everywhere, we did radio and television interviews and every concert was a success. We played the Concertgebouw, a big, very old concert hall, the most prominent venue in Holland; all the great classics played there. It seats about two thousand and we packed it. This is where they recorded the live show and later released it as the "Live in Amsterdam" album. After the show, Roger Bush and I walked out with a paper sack full of Guilders…probably ten or fifteen thousand dollars. We felt rather strange carrying a paper sack full of money, which was a small fortune to us.

Barend Toet picked up Alan and me to do a radio interview in Hilversum, a small town nearby, where the Dutch national broadcasting system had a studio. We got there expecting an interview and Barend asked us to bring our instruments saying he wanted us to play, so we took a banjo, guitar, fiddle and mandolin. We did a sound check with the instruments and microphones then Barend left us in the studio.

I asked the person in charge, "What do you want us to do?"

He said, "Just go ahead."

Alan and I looked at each other. No one asked us a single question. We did not know what to do, so, finally we started interviewing each other…it just got so funny and this was not something they edited later…it was going live over the air. We went back and forth. "Now tell me, Alan..." and then he did the same with me. So, Byron..." We got tickled, started laughing and as a result, the program director got a lot of calls wanting to know what was going on. The calls, of course, were in Dutch and apparently, he got some complaints. I have a tape of this show and it is hilarious; I will never forget it.

Ted and Nicky Boddy enjoyed having bands stay at their hotel and wanted to become even more involved in the music business. Ted built "Boddy's Music Inn" for Country Gazette and all the bands staying at their hotel and we opened it for them on February 25, 1973. The Eagles were also staying at the Hotel Wiechmann as well as a Canadian band called "Stampeders" who had a huge hit with the song "Sweet City Woman." The Boddy's daughter, Nicolette, remembers all the bands staying at the hotel and playing at the Music Inn.

> "February 25, 1973, There to open the club, which had live music every nite, were three bands; the bluegrass group Country Gazette, who first came over as a part of the Flying Burrito Brothers, but later garnered their own large following of loyal fans in Northern Europe and included Byron Berline, Kenny Wertz, Alan Munde and Roger Bush.
> Also playing was the Canadian band the Stampeders, who were touring Europe and staying in the Hotel Wiechmann, as were most of the touring musicians when they hit Amsterdam in those years."

Rounding out the night's line-up were the Eagles, who were on their first European tour. The Eagles at that time included Glen Frey, Don Henley, Randy Meisner, and Bernie Leadon, who has the auspicious honor of having been a member of the Flying Burrito Brothers, which was the very first band to stay with the Boddy's at Hotel Wiechmann.

Ted and Nicky Boddy were very nice people and most American groups stayed there while performing in Holland. Their son Jan now runs the Hotel Wiechmann.

Holland prints the names of towns, streets, and public buildings in Dutch. Remembering that the Dutch colonized New York City, we recognized names like Breukelen (Brooklyn.) Amsterdam is an amazing city and we had quite a time walking along the canals and seeing the artwork. The Dutch love dogs and every household has one…they also have an affinity for bicycles. I had never seen so many bicycles in my life and on the album cover of "Live in Amsterdam," they refer to the Boddy's daughters, Nicolette and Patricia Boddy, bringing their bicycles into the hotel. Nicolette remembers, "We kept our bicycles in one of the utility areas, where we kept the extra office supplies and soft drinks and beer. In order to access this room, we had to bring our bicycles in the front door of the hotel and straight through the lobby. Every morning we took them out, and upon our return from school in the afternoon, we brought them inside and into the utility room. Our bicycles were as pampered as we were."

We also went to Norway, Sweden, Denmark, England, and through the years, we returned to visit. This second, co-billed tour, "Hot Burrito Review and Country Gazette," was as successful as the Flying Burrito Brothers tour in 1972. We went back to Holland several times, each time filling every major hall with people who sang along with every song. It was like the big time with the press covering everything we did and being on all the major radio and television shows. It was quite a time for us and we truly felt like Rock Stars. The people of Holland are the nicest people and to this day I will meet someone and they will say, "Hey, I remember seeing you in 1972 or 1973. I was one of those that followed you guys around."

Capitol Records released the "Brush Arbor 2" album in February of 1973.

March 28 did a recording session for Brush Arbor.

March 30, 31 Country Gazette, played the Palomino.

I have a CD of a show Country Gazette played with Linda Ronstadt at McCabes in March of 1973. I do not have a journal entry for it, but we really had a good time that night and it is fun to listen to the show after all these years. I remember that we did not have a lot of time to rehearse for this show. Linda giggled a lot and talked to the audience between songs. We did some gospel numbers, which are so much fun to harmonize and this was such a treat because we seldom got to do such a laidback kind of show. We had a rather unique encore, we sang an old song Doug Dillard taught me, and we sang it in pig Latin. I wonder if Linda remembers this.

April 6, 7 Country Gazette played McCabes.

Flying Burrito Brothers in Holland in 1973. front row l to r: Sneaky
Pete Kleinow, Roger Bush. back row l to r: Kenny Wertz, Byron
Berline, Rick Roberts, Alan Munde, Eric Dalton.

Roland White quit Lester Flatt's band and came to California from Nashville. Clarence left the Byrds and he, Roland and Eric White, decided to reform the White brothers into the New Kentucky Colonels. They played up and down the west coast and went on tour on the East Coast. We did some things together, everybody was doing session work, and we rehearsed at my house.

Clarence and Roland White, Herb Pedersen and Roger Bush came to my house and we rehearsed for a gig at the Ash Grove, stuff for Country Gazette's "Don't Give up Your Day Job" album and Clarence's solo album. The Kentucky Colonels were preparing for a European tour and Wim Bloemendaal, who hosted radio/television shows in Holland, asked me to tape an interview with the Kentucky Colonels and of them playing, for use in promoting their tour. We also did some recording at this session and I sent it all on to Wim. We taped John Henry, Willow Garden, Hard Hearted, If You're Ever Gonna Love Me, Wicked Path of Sin, If I be Lifted Up and some other tunes.

April 7 did the "Guitar Workshop" for Bob Baxter, with Clarence White. Bob Baxter produced bluegrass banjo contests, including giant, all-day shows at Japanese Village, Devonshire Downs and at the Santa Anita Racetrack in Sierra Madre. In addition, Baxter also had this television show on CBS called "Guitar Workshop." The show had a live audience and Bob interviewed guests as well as having them perform on the show. Bob had some interesting shows with Linda Ronstadt, Ry Cooder, Mason Williams, and many others. Clarence White was his guest guitarist for this show. After the interview with Clarence and his playing some solo work, Roland White, Alan Munde, and I came out and played with him. They taped the show and I believe it is available commercially.

April 9 did a recording session for Dorsey Burnett, a performer and songwriter.

April 13 did a recording session for Bill Danhoff and Taffy Nivert Danhoff, for RCA. They formed the Starland Vocal Band and wrote, "I Guess He'd Rather be in Colorado" for John Denver.

In addition to recording sessions, Country Gazette rehearsed and played everywhere we could. Bette stayed home to take care of Becca while I was out traipsing around.

April 14 Country Gazette played Cal State at Fullerton and played in Santa Monica.

April 16-19 gig at Disneyland.

I played with Linda Ronstadt for a week at the Troubadour in April of 1973. I remember the date because the following Saturday I was leaving to judge the California State Fiddler's Contest. I remember Richard Bowden played with us. Don Henley, Glen Frey, and Sneaky Pete Kleinow were part of this Troubadour thing; the Eagles had not yet started...they were just rehearsing and did not have any money, nothin'. They had holes in their jeans and they were not making a fashion statement. I remember Bernie Leadon was involved with them.

April 20, 21 judged the California Fiddler's Contest in Fresno.

April 22, Easter weekend, Roger Bush, Alan Munde, Herb Pedersen and I, with Clarence, Roland, and Eric White, performed at the Ash Grove. We had a lot of guest musicians jamming on stage with us.

April 24 did a recording session for former Byrd, Roger McGuinn for CBS.

April 25, 27 did Country Gazette's last recording session to finish up "Don't give Up Your Day Job." Actually, I thought our second album was better than our first. Jim Dickson produced both records and it was neat, being on a major label, but who knows how many albums they sold...we never did figure it out because they keep things pretty complicated...on purpose.

May 2, 10 am to 1 pm did a recording session for Brush Arbor. That afternoon I did a recording session with Clarence White. Country Gazette wanted to play more bluegrass and more acoustic and so did Clarence. He had played with the Byrds and wanted to get his chops back up by playing more acoustic and bluegrass. Clarence had a three record contract with Warner Brothers and this was his first solo album. Jim Dickson produced this and musicians included Roger Bush, Herb Pedersen, Roland White, Leland Sklar, Ry Cooder, Ed Green, and Byron Berline.

The Dillards, scheduled to go on tour to Europe, cancelled a couple of weeks before they were to leave. Eddie Tickner called the Whites and asked if they wanted go on the tour, replacing the Dillards. The New Kentucky Colonels decided to go and got Herb Pedersen to go with them. They had Clarence on lead guitar, Roland on Mandolin, Eric on bass and Herb playing banjo.

Herb had played on and off with Johnny Rivers and Rivers

happened to be touring Europe at the same time as the Kentucky Colonels. Johnny invited Herb to go with him, Pedersen left the Whites, stranded in Holland without a banjo player, and they were supposed to record a live album in Sweden. Eddie Tickner called wanting to know if Country Gazette was booked for those dates and I told him we were not. He asked if Alan Munde could go to Sweden to finish the Kentucky Colonels tour and live recording in Sweden. Alan Munde went and it is Alan playing on their "Live in Sweden" album, The New Kentucky Colonels – Live in Sweden 1973, released in 1976 by Rounder Records.

Monday, May 7, my dad, Lue George Berline, died at the age of seventy-nine in Caldwell, Kansas. Losing a parent is never easy and our family was very close.

In April of 1973, rehearsing in our home in Sherman Oaks, California. l to r; Clarence White, Byron Berline, and Roland White.

May 13 Country Gazette played Cal State at Long Beach.

June 1, 1973 United Artists released Country Gazette's "Don't Give up Your Day Job."

June 1-3 Country Gazette played McCabes.

June 8-10 Country Gazette went back on the road to play the Culpeper-Warrenton, Virginia Bluegrass Festival. We had a jam with Vassar Clements with me on fiddle, Alan Munde on banjo and guitar, Bill Keith on banjo, Sam Bush, David Grisman, Bill Kenner on mandolin, Roger Bush on bass and Grant Boatwright on Guitar. Fred Robbins recorded this jam and took the photographs.

June 29 did a recording session with Clarence White for his solo album. We had recorded about five or six songs. One time at Clarence's house, he put on a tape someone had sent him and he said, "I've got somebody I want you to listen to." One of the first songs on the tape was "Gold Rush" the tune I wrote with Bill Monroe, which was released as a single in 1967. After six years, that little 45-rpm record of Gold Rush really made the rounds with bluegrass players and it is still a popular bluegrass tune.

I said, "Well listen to that!"

Clarence said, "He's pretty good, isn't he?"

I said, "Well yes."

He said, "Well, you can have the tape." That was my introduction to the guitar playing of Dan Crary.

It began to look like everyone was going to start recording for Warner Brothers. Clarence White and Gram Parsons both had projects going with Warner and it just seemed like that was the direction of things to come. With the involvement of Eddie Tickner and Jim Dickson, we were all very busy.

June 30-July 10 did the Warner Brothers, Country Rock Tour to Annapolis, Maryland and Philadelphia, Pennsylvania. Country Gazette opened the show, with former Byrds following, then former Flying Burrito Brothers. The New Kentucky Colonels were there with Clarence, Roland and Eric White, then Gram Parsons and Emmylou Harris did their duets. As a finale, every performer came back on stage to play. The tour had Country Gazette, the Kentucky Colonels, Emmylou Harris and all these former Byrds and Flying Burrito Brothers:

Clarence White former Byrd

Gram Parsons Former Byrd and FBB
Gene Parsons former Byrd and FBB
Sneaky Pete Kleinow former FBB and sometimes Byrd
Chris Ethridge former FBB
Country Gazette had Kenny Wertz, Alan Munde, Roger Bush, and Byron Berline, all former FBB

It was a great line up! These shows lasted three hours and we had so much fun. We all knew each other and had played together so although there was no time for rehearsals it was a great show. Warner Brothers wanted to see if the audience reception would work with this kind of show and if the players thought it would work. They were right on both counts. The audience loved these "test" concerts and the musicians had a ball! Warner Brothers immediately began staging an extensive Country Rock Tour to begin in the fall.

While we were on this pre-tour Kenny Wertz told us he wanted to leave the band so we immediately began looking for a guitar player and tenor singer to replace him. Tony Rice had contacted us wanting to play with Country Gazette. Roger knew Tony and I knew of him. At the time, Tony was in Kentucky playing with J.D. Crow. We flew Tony to Annapolis and when we began rehearsing, realized he could not sing tenor. That kind of disillusioned him and us…it just did not work out. He could sing, just not tenor. Tony Rice went back to Kentucky and we continued looking for a guitar player and tenor singer.

I remember the last show we played. We all stayed in hotels and motels when on the road and after a show, especially the last one, players wandered up and down the halls. As you might expect, there was a lot of partying going on. Chris Ethridge and I went from room to room and as we walked down the hall we passed by Gram Parson's room. The door was wide open and we saw Gram sitting on the edge of the bed, kind of hunched over a little, with a fifth of Jack Daniels in his hand. He looked like he was dead.

It seemed as if everyone was recording solo albums, Skip Battin, Clarence White, Doug Dillard, and Gram Parsons. We did recording sessions for Skip Battin's second solo album "Topanga Skyline," Gram Parson's "Grievous Angel," Clarence White's album and Doug Dillard's "Duelin' Banjo." We rehearsed and did some recording at my house.

Everyone had been touring all over the United States and Europe and by June of 1973, the momentum of Los Angeles country-rock-bluegrass emerged as a force we could all feel...the players, labels and all involved in the music industry. It was such an exciting time and all of us felt it building. Audiences loved the music...records, concerts, and festivals. I cannot express the excitement we felt.

July 11 we returned to California on Wednesday after the successful test Country Rock Tour and Clarence said, "Let's get together Saturday night. We aren't booked anywhere so why don't we go out to Nashville West and jam?"

Nashville West was a Club out east of L.A.

Clarence said, "We'll get Roland and whoever else wants to go."

I remember us talking about Chris Ethridge going, Roland, and Sneaky Pete.

I said, "Okay, just give me a call."

Saturday, July 14 came, but Clarence did not call.

Sunday, July 15, Roger Bush and his wife, Yvonne, had access to a house on Manhattan Beach and that morning, Bette and I were getting ready to go meet Roger and Yvonne, at the beach house to have a cook out. About nine or ten o'clock, the phone rang. Chris Etheridge, an original FBB, was a bass player and had been on the Country Rock Tour with us. Chris, from Mississippi, talked with a real southern drawl. When I answered, Chris was on the phone and slurring his words. To be honest, I thought he was drunk, I could hardly understand him.

He managed to get out, "Clarence got killed."

I thought, "Now what is this?" I really did think he was drunk or something. As he kept talking, I began to understand what had happened and although I no longer wondered why Clarence had not called, I could not believe it.

Clarence had a very nice house in Palmdale and a friend of his called and told him some windows had been broken out. As Palmdale is just north of L.A., Clarence and Roland decided they better not go to the jam at Nashville West and instead, go up to Palmdale and see about possible damage to his house.

They checked out the house damage and then went over to their mother's house, also in Palmdale and ate dinner with her. Gib Guilbeau was playing at a club in Palmdale so they decided just to go to the club and jam over there. About two AM (Sunday), they were getting ready to leave the club, putting amps and stuff in the van as cars were zipping up and down the road.

Clarence told Roland, "We better get out of here. We're libel to get killed."

Roland said that was the last thing Clarence said to him. A woman came through there about sixty miles an hour, ran off the road, hit Clarence, knocking him about a hundred feet down the road, which killed him. Roland was also injured and taken the hospital. Clarence was 29 years old and so was I. Losing Clarence was terrible and many people felt his loss; he was a good friend and a good musician, whom I would miss a lot.

Steve Weitzman wrote an article about our final show at the Tower in Philadelphia. He gave the Country Rock concert a good review and included his interview with Clarence and Roland White after the show. It was Clarence White's final performance and I think he summed it up rather well.

> "Entering a tiny backstage dressing room in which there was an uproar emanating from at least fifteen people, I was informed that, amid all the distractions and after a long show, Clarence would love to do an interview. I found him on one end of a couch sipping a Heineken. Resting next to him were his brother Roland and Sneak Pete.
> "Clarence explained about Roland being his older brother and his following after him, musically, bringing home blue-grass records. He indicated it could have been different.
> "If he (Roland) had brought home Elvis Presley records instead..."
> Feeling uncomfortable with all the credit, Roland added, "We all started together, really."
> "And we're all going home together," proposed Clarence, taking a deep breath and slowly pulling himself up from the couch."

Clarence had just finished his final concert and we all went home together. It was not easy for any us to go on with things.

July 17 did a recording session with Skip Battin doing bluegrass stuff. Skip left the Byrds and this was for his second solo album "Topanga Skyline" on Atlantic Records, produced by Al Hersh. Roger Bush, Alan Munde, Herb Pedersen, Roland White, Chris Ethridge, and I were on this. Clarence White had rehearsed with us, but never made it to the studio. Al Perkins came in to fill-in for Clarence on this recording.

July 18 did a recording session with Kay Starr on her "Kay Starr Country" album for Capitol with Cliffie Stone producing. Kay did the "Frankie and Johnny" duet with Tex Williams, instead of Doug Dillard, Oklahoma Hills, Your Cheatin' Heart, Tie A Yellow ribbon, Something's Missing, Saturday Night, Rangers Waltz, Blue Grass, Odds and Ends and Pain Down Deep. Kay also had an orchestra conducted by Billy Liebert.

On Thursday, July 19, Bette and I attended Clarence White's funeral and sat with Skip Conover, Roger Bush and their wives. The whole church filled with musicians. Kris Kristofferson and Rita Coolidge were there and all of the Byrds. The service started and in walked Gram Parsons and Phil Kaufman. They sat right in front of us, about two pews up. I remember Gram wore jeans and a jean jacket. This was a Catholic Church funeral, a high mass, with the priest never once mentioning Clarence's name and there was no music. It was so impersonal and we had to sit through about an hour of this nothin'. Everyone there expected and wanted more than that...we wanted something that really honored Clarence.

Gram told Kaufman, "When I die, we aren't going to go through this crap. Just take me out to the desert and burn me. Okay?"

"Alright," Phil told him.

This was not a quiet, private discussion.

After the mass we went out to the gravesite and Clarence's wife Susie, was there and the children. There still was no music. Gram was standing there, Bernie Leadon, then me. They started singing "Farther Along," a song Clarence sang with the Byrds. Everybody tried to sing with them, but when I tried to sing nothing would come out. I got so choked up...I could not sing a lick. They sounded great and I was so pleased they did that. It was something Clarence would have appreciated...I know we did.

It was not easy, but everyone somehow carried on. We immediately asked Roland White to join Country Gazette. Roland said "Yes" and that is who played guitar with us the rest of 1973.

July 21, 23 we did another Skip Battin recording session.

July 26-August 19 Country Gazette with Roland White, played the Hugo, Oklahoma Bluegrass Festival, a show in York, Pennsylvania, Austin, Texas...we played all over the country. The following is an Austin, TX review of our show at a club called Castle Creek:

"Only rarely will you find four musicians in the same group as talented as those in Country Gazette.

What would you do if you had a million dollars?

Byron: "I'd keep on playing bluegrass until the million dollars ran out!"

Country Gazette played New York City and on August 16, the Village Voice had the following review:

> "He plays what sounds to be a combination of bluegrass and traditional, old Texas-style long bow fiddling. He is really a transcendent virtuoso. With the consistent whine of double-stopped harmonies and the wild flutter of crazed arpeggios occurring simultaneously, it seemed as if two fiddlers were on stage with ghosts and angels, doing the old invisible square-dance meeting in the air. As in the words of Bill Monroe's "Uncle Penn," he "played the fiddle, you could hear it ring, hear it talk, hear it sing." Berline played old Sally Goodin, Lost Indian, Rawhide, and closed with Orange Blossom Special. If it all had occurred fifty years ago I would have wound up drunk on corn likker, yelling, "Hell, that boy can fiddle!" and slapping myself on the knee till my goddamed false teeth fell out."

August 15 did a recording session with Gram Parsons and Emmylou Harris for Gram's "Grievous Angel" album on A&M Records. This would be my last recording session with Gram Parsons.

We were always looking for good players and good jam sessions. Don Parmley, of the Bluegrass Cardinals lived in California and we got together occasionally to jam. Someone asked if we had heard of the Hickman Brothers and I had not. When Don said they could not sing I did not pay too much attention to what he said, but I remember thinking, "They probably can't play a lick." Michael Nesmith and Red Rhodes were playing at Mc-

Cabes and Alan Munde and I went down to hear them. I knew Red Rhodes from the Palomino and Michael Nesmith from the "Monkees" and I had done session work with both of them. The Hickman Brothers and Scott Hambly were also on the bill. The Hickman Brothers turned out to be good pickers, so we went backstage and introduced ourselves. After that, we started jamming with them a lot. That was the first time I met John Hickman and we are still playing music together, after almost forty years.

In California, at that time, the music community was small and it was easy to get to know all the pickers, especially if you were a session player. These were all the "A" players and it was quite a feat, just getting into that click.

August 24, 25 Country Gazette played the First Annual Colorado Rocky Mountain Bluegrass Festival. Bill Monroe was on this thing, Lester Flatt, The Bluegrass Alliance and many other acts.

All of the bands involved in the Country Rock Tour decided to proceed and continue with plans for the extended tour although we knew it would not be easy without Clarence White.

September 13-November 10 Country Gazette began an east coast tour before going on another tour to Europe.

September 15 Rick Roberts opened for Country Gazette in Cleveland, Ohio at the Smiling Dog Saloon. During the Gazette's last set, Rick came up and told me that Gram Parsons had over dosed. I thought, "What's next." Gram Parsons was twenty-six years old. It was so sad…such a waste.

We did not attend Gram's funeral…they did not have one. Phil Kaufman kept his word to Gram. Phil rented a hearse, went to the Los Angeles airport, and stole Gram's body…casket and all. He drove to Joshua Tree, which is out in the desert, built a fire, and cremated Gram's body, just as Gram wanted. To know more about this episode, you might want to read Phil Kaufman's book, *Road Mangler Deluxe* or see the movie, Grand Theft Parsons. Phil is quite a character.

Up to this point, everyone had wanted to continue with Warner Brothers' big Country Rock tour, but not now, not after losing both Clarence White and Gram Parsons. Such a tragedy and affected the lives of so many people. Then, there was Emmylou Harris. What was she going to do? Gram Parsons is missed and I know Emmylou misses him a lot.

After shows on the East coast, Country Gazette went back to California to prepare for our second tour to Europe in 1973, which they billed only as Country Gazette, no Flying Burrito Brothers. Becca was nine months old and Bette and I took her with us to Europe. Country Gazette toured September 30 through October 30 doing several shows in England, Holland, Belgium, Sweden, Denmark, and Brussels. United Artists had their own booking agency called "The Iron Horse Agency" and this is who handled the Country Gazette tour. The following is the itinerary they provided us prior to our departure.

ITENERARY - England and the Netherlands

September 30, Sunday, Grand Ole Oprey of England at Newmarket.

October 1, Monday, Country Style, we did two radio shows

October 2, Tuesday, Old Grey Whistle Test, BBC2 TV program

October 3, Wednesday, Sounds of the Seventies, a radio program

October 4, Thursday, In Concert, a radio program

October 5, Friday, Bristol Polytechnic Concert

October 6, Saturday, London School of Economics Concert

October 7, Sunday, Bluegrass Club of London Concert

October 8, Monday, this was hand written, "open." We must have had a day off.

October 9, Tuesday, Lanchester Polytechnic Concert in Coventry

October 10, Wednesday, the Nashville Rooms Concert in London

October 11, Thursday, University of East Anglia Concert

October 12, Friday, Sussex University Concert at Brighton

October 13, Saturday, Manchester Polytechnic Concert

October 15 – October 21, Monday - Sunday, is held for SWEEDEN

October 22, Monday-Tuesday, October 30, held for Belgium and Holland:

October 23, Tuesday, Leuben, Belgium

October 24, Wednesday, Gent, Belgium

Either Monday October 29 or Tuesday, October 30, Brussels. The "NME GIG GUIDE" is an entertainment publication in England. Country Gazette had a full-page advertisement in their September 29, 1973 edition. It promoted our "Traitor in Our Midst" album and printed a schedule of all our appearances in England.

Sunday, September 30, we played the "Grand Ole Opry" at the Kingsway Cinema in Newmarket.

Friday, October 5, we played the "Polytechnic" in Bristol.

Saturday, October 6, we played the "School of Economics in London.

Sunday, the October 7, we played the "Bluegrass Club" at Walthamstow Assembly Hall in Walthamstow.

Tuesday, October 9, we played the "Polytechnic" at Lanchester.

Wednesday, October 10, we played the "Nashville Rooms" in London.

The Iron Horse itinerary states that we were to play the University of East Anglia on Thursday, October 11. NME Gig Guide stated we would be playing the North London Polytechnic. I do not remember which one, but we did play at least one of them.

Friday, October 12, we played Sussex University at Brighton.

Saturday, October 13, we played the "Polytechnic" at Manchester.

Sunday, October 14, they added the "Rainbow Theatre" in London.

October 15 Bernie Leadon bought old instruments and one time he and I were jamming at the Hotel Wiechmann in Amsterdam, Holland. He had just purchased an old mandolin and I was playing it. We were really getting after it when I strummed, looked down and realized I had caused a long scratch on the instrument...it was not even mine. I felt so bad because I am usually, so careful with musical instruments...mine or someone else's. I just felt so bad. Leadon just shrugged and said, "It'll buff out. Don't worry about it." Man, I sure felt bad about that.

That same evening, the Eagles called and asked me go into the studio and record with them. The Eagles were on tour and doing some recording in London. They too, stayed at the Hotel Weichman while in Holland. They needed a fiddler and I went in and did the session. I remember discussing things to play because they really did not have anything specifically in mind, just trying out the idea of having a fiddle in the band. I do not know if they ever used those tracks. It is too bad it did not work out... that would really have been something. This session is unusual because they did not record with musicians other than the Eagles.

After gigs, late at night, we would all come back to the Wiechmann Hotel and Ted Boddy would open up the bar so we could play poker. We played with gilders, what the musicians called "little Dutch money" that looked like nothing more than tokens. You could play poker for hours with this "pocket change" and never run up a big pot, it was just something fun to do.

Rick Roberts liked to play some funny poker games such as High and Low Chicago. Most of these, called carnival games, typically involve a wild card, which adds an element of risk to a variation of stud poker. Ted Boddy came to me and explained that one night Rick had gotten caught-up in one of these poker games and ended up losing about 400 dollars. Ted said everyone playing that night felt so bad about it that they wanted to get a new game going and let Rick win his money back. They let him win his money, but it was not a lesson well learned.

We all continued touring and went on to London where another poker game opportunity arose, this time, with the Eagles. The tour up to that point had been very good to Country Gazette and we each had about fifteen hundred dollars in our pockets. This was a great deal of money because all of us, including the Eagles were on a shoestring, so to speak. We were not making the millions of dollars that some of the more established groups brought in. This time, the Eagles took Rick to the cleaners, fifteen hundred dollars...every penny he had and of course, would not give it back.

I said, "You dumb ass! Didn't you learn anything in Holland?"

The Eagles soon became one of those established groups, taking in millions of dollars and I believe they still do.

Country Gazette did concerts in England, Holland, Belgium, Brussels, and Sweden completing the tour. Upon returning to the states, we still had some bookings to do, wrapping up the tour on November 10.

November 2, Country Gazette opened for the Steve Miller Band at the Tower in Philadelphia. The following is from an interview we did on October 30, prior to the concert.

THE DRUMMER, BLUEGRASS BREAKS THROUGH

"Country Gazette, who will be opening for Steve Miller at the Tower theatre this coming Friday, are well on their way to becoming the most important contemporary bluegrass band around."

Reporter: "What does Bill Monroe think about Country Gazette's music?"

Roger Bush: Well, Bill Monroe doesn't get real excited about anything. Byron and Roland used to work for him. I worked for him once and have known him for a long time. We just did a festival with him in Denver and around me, it was just, "Boy you fellers sure did a fine job." That was the extent of it. If he does compliment anyone, he means it. A little from him is a lot. He likes most of our stuff though.

Reporter: Well, we've got some pretty good material now.

Roger: "Good" he said, eyeing the tape recorder as if it were some kind of chaperone. "Turn that thing off and we can do some drinkin'."

November 11, 1973 the Ash Grove burned.

November 30 did a recording session with Dorsey Burnett, a songwriter and performer.

December 3, 4, 5 did another ABC movie made for TV for Murray McCloud. Its U.S. working title "Children of God," upon release, was re-titled "Can Ellen be Saved?" It starred Michael Parks, Leslie Nielsen, Katherine Cannon, and Louise Fletcher and directed by Harvey Hart. The story line revolved around a fictitious family involved with the real life cult known as "Children of God." Alan Munde and I were actor-Musicians on this and we worked all day, every day of shooting.

December 7, 8 Country Gazette played Long Beach College.

December 8 did an Arlo Guthrie session.

December 8 Country Gazette played the Anaheim Convention Center, opening for Crosby, Stills, and Nash. The Convention Center "sold out" and we played to a crowd of nine thousand.

I spent December 10, 1973 at home, celebrating Becca's first birthday.

December 12 Country Gazette played the Palomino.

December 13 did a recording session for Bill Wyman. Bill was the bass player for the Rolling Stones and this session was for his debut solo album, "Monkey Grip." Other players on this included Lowell George, John McEuen, George Terry, Joey Murcia, Danny Kootch, Jackie Clark, William Smith, Duane Smith, Leon Russell, Hubie Heard, Mac Rebannack, Peter Graves, Dallas Taylor, Joe Lala, Betty Wright, George McCrae, Gwen McCrae and Abigale Haness.

After the summer and fall of 1973, the momentum was gone. We all did what we had to do, but it was not easy. Although 1973 began as a year of excitement and anticipation, many of us were glad to see it go and looked forward to a new year.

Journal Entry 1974
130 Days on the Road with Country Gazette

January 4, 5 Country Gazette played McCabes.

January 8-13 Country Gazette played Denver, Colorado at a club called Ebbets Field named after the Brooklyn Dodgers ballpark. Ebbets Field, located at 1025 15th Street, was a small club that held a little over two hundred people. They recorded most of these shows and played them on DKPI and KFML in Denver. Some of those having played there include Asleep at the Wheel, Brewer and Shipley, Gene Clark, Commander Cody, Ry Cooder, Dr. Hook & the Medicine Show, Dan Fogelberg, Peter Frampton, Emmylou Harris, Ozark Mountain Daredevils, Willie Nelson and Pure Prairie League.

January 18-February 2 Country Gazette went on a road trip. Week of January 27 WHN aired an album radio show that Country Gazette pre-recorded. We were guests on the Lee Arnold show "Country Cookin'." We played Down the Road, Teach Your Children, and an instrumental, My Oklahoma, Honky Cat, and Lonesome Blues Tonight with Lee interviewing us between songs.

February 5, the ABC Movie of the Week, "Can Ellen Be Saved?" aired for the first time.

February 9 Country Gazette played in Muncie, Indiana.

February 20-March 3 Country Gazette did a Texas tour.

March 8 Country Gazette played California State at Long Beach, Bristol Bay.

March 12-17 Country Gazette played the Boarding House in San Francisco.

March 20-22 did a recording session with Red, White, and Bluegrass.

March 22 did another session with Red, White, and Bluegrass playing twin fiddles with Vassar Clements.

I played as a guest musician on the "Docker Hill Boys" demo recordings. Musicians on these sessions included Gene Parsons, Joel Scott Hill, Chris Ethridge, John Barbara, Michael T. Lawson, Eric White, and Byron Berline.

March 23-27 Country Gazette toured Texas and Kansas.

April 1-May 4 Country Gazette toured the east coast and was on the road for a month.

April 27 Billboard named Country Gazette the top U.S. group at the 1974 Billboard/Record & Radio Mirror Country Music awards show during the Country Music Festival in Wembley, England. Unfortunately, we were on tour in the U.S. and could not attend.

May 10 Country Gazette played McCabes.

May 11 Country Gazette played a benefit show with Linda Ronstadt, Honk, and Lonesome Dan Hicks at USC's Cromwell Athletic field. Tickets were only five dollars and the show was billed "An Afternoon on the Grass."

We were all still reeling from the loss of Clarence White and Gram Parsons. I remember talking with Eddie Tickner and he was so concerned about Emmylou Harris. "You're hooked in with Warner Brothers." I told him. "Why don't you get Emmylou her own record deal with them?" I could not believe he did not think of it himself.

Emmy had a band already put together, so she went back to Washington D.C. and got them going. When Emmy played McCabes in L.A., she used this band whose bass player she was dating at the time.

Eddie went to Warner Brothers and they thought signing Emmylou Harris was a good idea, but said they wanted to put together a "Hot" band to back her up. They got James Burton on guitar, Glyn D. Hardin on piano, players that worked with Elvis Presley, so these were session players. Emory Gordy played bass, Rodney Crowell auditioned and they hired him and they wanted me to become part of that, but Country Gazette was going strong.

Eddie told Emmylou what was up with Warner Brothers and that she was going to have to get rid of her band, which certainly was not easy for her. She had to tell her boyfriend he was not going to play for her any more. I thought those musicians were good.

In addition to her Hot Band, Warner had different people come in to do recording sessions with her. Herb Pedersen sang with her, I did some things and Hank DeVito played on some stuff. She had a piano player and I remember Ben Keith came in. Gram had put these players together when he flew her out to record with him.

Warner chose Brian Ahern to produce Emmylou. Ahern produced "Snow Bird" with Ann Murray and everybody thought he was a genius because he recorded just Ann and her guitar, then added strings and everything to her track. That record was a big hit so he was quite a popular producer at the time. He came to California from Canada and brought a semi-truck, which was his studio. He had a control room in it and you could record toward the back end of the truck. He hauled that truck up Cold Water Canyon Boulevard to Ania Lane. You could barely drive a car up there, let alone a semi. They rented a house way up at the top of this windy road paying over a thousand dollars a month in rent and that was a lot of money in 1974. That semi is where he did all of his recording and every time Emmy released a new album they had a release party at that house. All the Warner Brothers people came and other invited guests. They provided food and of course, everyone came to listen to the new album. I went to about every one of those parties. In addition to fiddle, I did a lot of mandolin playing on her records such as "If I could only Win Your Love."

May 18-21 Country Gazette played Washington D.C.; we were on the road for a week.

May 29 did another Red, White, and Bluegrass recording session.

June 3, 4 did a Michael Nesmith session.

June 7-9 Country Gazette played in Toronto, Canada, or it could have been Bluegrass Canada at Carlisle, Ontario. Dan Crary was there and indicated he was moving from Louisville, Kentucky to Fullerton, California about fifty miles from where I lived. Dan said he would be teaching there and I told him we needed to get together.

June 13 did a demo recording session with Red Rhodes.

June 16 I played the Troubadour with the Nitty Gritty Dirt Band and again, Steve Martin opened for us.

June 21-23 Country Gazette played the Couschatta, Louisiana Festival. On June 27 in the Bossier Press, Word Nutt reviewed the festival.

"...you talk about four guys who could put out some music and put on a show they could. Naturally, I had to meet the leader and ask him a few questions, because these opportunities don't come along very often. His name is Byron Berline. He's a tall, big guy, handsome and has the charisma and wit it takes to make it big in the music and entertainment business."

This is of course, one of my favorite reviews.

July 5-7 I played Joe Hutchison's bluegrass festival at Powder Horn Park in Langley, Oklahoma. I met Mark O'Connor when his mother brought him to this festival and "The Byron Berline Fiddle Contest." I was thirty years old and Mark was twelve. I had never heard of him before then. I remember being out back playing guitar when this kid, wearing a cowboy hat, came up and said in his kid's voice, "Would you play guitar with me?"

"Sure." I said. "What can you play?"

The night before someone told me, "Wait until you hear this kid from Seattle, Washington, he's really good." I have heard that a lot, but I am always ready to hear a new player. Mark started playing "Grey Eagle" and I went, "Gee." I thought, "Man, he can really play." He took lessons from Benny Thomasson and then he stayed with J.C. Broughton until he learned everything he could from J.C. Mark picked up everything so quickly…it was amazing.

Another kid at that festival was seventeen-year-old Vince Gill, playing with a band of teenagers called "Bluegrass Revue," but I never got to hear them play.

My brother Leonard came in from Arizona, driving a 1971 Dodge Charger with a beautiful red paint job and he spent a good deal of time carting people back and forth from Disney, Oklahoma to the festival at Langley. He brought my sisters, Eleanor and Janice, Mom and other people. A reserve officer as "acting officer" for the festival, watched this bright red car with Arizona plates, make many trips in and out of the festival grounds and he became suspicious. We were celebrating my birthday by sitting in a car at the campground, having a beer. A cousin, Bruce Sloan who was underage, also had a beer. We noticed this "acting officer" across the way, harassing my sister Eleanor and her husband Irvin, so we all decided to go over and check it out. The "acting officer" decided he wanted to search our vehicle.

"Whhaaaat?" We said. Leonard immediately got upset because he had a fifth of Wild Turkey locked in the trunk. The "acting officer" wanted to take the car nearer a light pole so he could better see, but he could not get the car started. He told Leonard to drive it over there by the light. Leonard got in, started the engine, and just took off. He drove a ways and then threw the Wild Turkey off the side of the road although it was legal to have liquor in the trunk and besides, Leonard did away with the evidence. They arrested Leonard, took him to Pryor, Oklahoma, and put him in jail. It took all of us pooling our money, to come up with the five hundred dollars bail to get him out of jail. Some festivals are more memorable and expensive than others.

July 13, 14 Country Gazette played the Milwaukee, Wisconsin Festival.

July 23 Country Gazette played the Sundance Saloon on Mulholland Valley Drive Circle in Calabassas.

July 27, 28 Country Gazette played Harrison, Arkansas.

Linda Rondstadt and I rehearsing at our home in Sherman Oaks, California. Note Bette's photo on the mantle and my lamb chops.

July 30 did a recording session with Murray McCloud for the made-for-TV-movie "The Rookies." We recorded from 10:00 a.m. to 7:00 p.m.

August 2 Country Gazette played the Bluebird Café in Santa Barbara.

August 3 Country Gazette headlined with John Hartford at the Japanese Village in Buena Park. Thinking about where we were at the time; I remember Roger Bush and I drinking a lot of sake before our show.

Bob Baxter produced this event and had a big banjo contest in conjunction with the festival. They advertised the "Banjo Band Contest will be held all day with the finals after dark." They offered $1,000 for first prize, five hundred dollars for second place and two hundred fifty dollars for third place.

Country Gazette on tour in Holland in 1974. l to r; Roland White, Byron Berline, Alan Munde, Roger Bush.

In addition to Country Gazette and John Hartford, they had another group called "Corn Bred." Their lineup included John Hickman on banjo, his brother George on bass, Darrell Boom on guitar, Jody Sifra on fiddle and Tom Sauber on mandolin. John Hickman had never been in a banjo contest and decided to enter. Their Corn Bred band entered the band contest. Corn Bred won and received a thousand dollars. John Hickman won the banjo contest and received a $1,000 custom-made banjo from McCabe's guitar shop in Santa Monica. I guess that was enough because that was the only banjo contest John Hickman ever entered.

John Hickman: I won. I didn't need to enter another one.

August 7 did a session for "The Rookies" movie.

August 8-11 Country Gazette played in San Francisco then went on to a festival in Hugo, OK where it rained like crazy.

August 20-24 Country Gazette played in Illinois and the second Annual Colorado Rocky Mountain Bluegrass Festival in Denver. Bill Monroe was on the show, Ralph Stanley, Lester Flatt, James Monroe, Bluegrass Alliance, McClain Family, Dudley and Deanie Murphy and Minnie Moore.

August 30 Country Gazette did a Midwest tour.

September 24-October 13 Country Gazette toured Texas, New Mexico, Colorado, Canada, Arkansas, and Austin, TX.

October 18 did recording session with Mike Post who did music for TV commercials. Herb Pedersen did some things for Mike and Herb called me in to do some session work with them, but it was not an easy session, working all afternoon on just one song. He had me do some twin fiddle stuff, which meant recording everything twice, thus taking twice as long and for doing that, a musician receives double pay. I did feel positive about the session and looked forward to bigger and better things, doing commercials, etc. with Mike Post.

When we finally finished, Herb said, "Let's settle up."

I said, "Well, why don't you just go through the union?"

He said, "We usually, when we do these things...we just sort of do them and then see how it goes...which ones do well."

I thought, "Oh, this is great. I'll probably get about half scale." I got 30 bucks...not even half scale.

October 31 did a recording session for the ABC Universal made for TV movie "Night Stalker." This movie received the highest ratings of any TV movie at that time. In 1973, they released a follow-up movie called "The Night Strangler" and in the1974-75 television series, another titled "Kolchak: The Night stalker."

November 1, 2 Country Gazette played the Palomino.

November 7 Country Gazette played Santa Barbara.

November 8, 9 Country Gazette played McCabes and recorded our Live at McCabe's album. Jim Dickson produced this and released it on Transatlantic, released in NL (Netherlands) on Ariola, Japan on Trio Records and in the U.S. on Antilles Records. Musicians included Alan Munde, Roger Bush, and Roland White with Skip Conover on Dobro and me on fiddle. We recorded Black Mountain Rag, Roses for a Sunday Morning, Blue Day, To Prove my Love to You, Lonesome Road, Will You be Lonesome Too, Only Way Home, Sally Goodin', My Baby's Gone, Sunday Sunrise, Laughing Guitar, Never Ending Love, Holland Holiday and Down in the Bluegrass.

November 14 Country Gazette played San Francisco.

November 15, 16 Country Gazette played in Long Beach.

November 18 I did the Bear Country TV show with Gene Bear.

December 4-12 Country Gazette toured Texas.

December 9, 10, 11, 13 Mason Williams, my Oklahoma friend, became head writer for the Smothers Brothers TV show and he asked John Hickman and me to be guests on the show. We rehearsed for a few days and then were to tape the show December 15-17.

December 10, 1974 Becca turned two.

Just prior to taping the Smothers Brothers TV show, one night John Hickman was at our house and we picked until very late. I told John he better not drive, but he said, "Oh, I'll be alright." He was not drunk, just sleepy. He fell asleep at the wheel and a seven-car pileup resulted. It threw John out of the car and he slid on his butt down the 405 freeway. It tore up his jeans… took both pockets right off and did not even hurt him, but it broke his banjo. They took him to the hospital, just to check him over; a highway patrol officer brought his billfold, which had $200 in it…just what John had before the accident. Although not seriously injured, they were not sure John would be able to play the Smother's Brother's Show.

December 15-17 John Hickman borrowed a banjo from Alan Munde and we did the show.

Most of us spent 1974 trying to get on with our careers, although it was not easy. Losing Clarence and Gram was unsettling, but we scheduled the tours, set concert dates, booked recording sessions, just going through the motions.

I spent 130 days on the road in 1974 and I had a lot to come home to.

Journal Entry 1975
Arnold Schwarzenegger – Sundance – L.A. Fiddle Band

January 2, 3 did a recording session with Emmylou Harris.

January 18 did a recording session with Jerry Riopelle who wrote songs for and produced "WE FIVE" and "Brewer and Shipley."

January 21-February 17 Country Gazette went on what would be our last European Tour. We recorded a Swedish TV show at Mosebacke Establissement in Stockholm, Sweden.

Roland White lived in Nashville and Alan Munde lived in Texas. Country Gazette came in off the road one day and Roger Bush's wife was there to pick him up. She said, "Oh, by the way, we've moved to Parker, Arizona, just thought I'd let you know." That is the way she was. There was no one left in L.A. and the only time we got together was when we were on the road. I became disillusioned. No one seemed to be having any fun and if you do not enjoy it, then it is not worth doing. It just was not the same and I missed a lot of recording sessions because I was gone too much. The time had just come to end the band. While on tour, I gave Country Gazette notice that I would be leaving the band. Alan Munde was upset and there was some tension in the band on that tour because they did not know what would become of the group. Our manager, Eddie Tickner wanted to fold the band, but they wanted to keep it going, so Eddie helped them stay together.

All the country music labels such as United Artists, MCA, and RCA...all the major labels had offices in Los Angeles. In 1974 and 1975, much of that changed when they began moving to Nashville and as a result, a lot of the acts started moving to Nashville, too. There were still a lot of commercials and movie scores to do, but major country sessions were no more. Emmylou Harris stayed out there for a while and I recorded on all of her records. Most of the session players stayed in L.A. I remember that J.D. Maness went to Nashville only lasting one year, but he did not like it, so he came back to the coast. J.D. was a good friend and he played steel with Buck Owens, later on, with the "Desert Rose Band" and he also played in "Sundance."

In February, Country Gazette recorded songs with new Dutch singer "Sari Schuwer" (aka Sari Martin). The songs included "The Bramble and the Rose" and Gram Parsons' "Still Feeling Blue."

February 25-March 6 did a recording session with Red, White, and Bluegrass and played a stage show with them.

March 25 rehearsed with Emmylou Harris.

April 4, 5 Country Gazette played the Sundance Saloon in Thousand Oaks.

April 20 Country Gazette played a festival at Long Beach.

April 24-May 17 I was asked to work on the movie "Stay Hungry," starring Sally Field, Jeff Bridges and a body builder and actor named Arnold Schwarzenegger. Someone from the studio called so see what I would charge to teach Arnold how to fake playing the fiddle. I told them I would not charge anything. We set a time, had him come over to the house and I found him to be very nice. I took him to the music room (converted garage) and began showing him how to hold the bow and fiddle. I immediately knew he was very coachable. I asked if he knew what songs he would play to in the movie and he said, "Orange Blossom Special."

I said, "No, that's not a good idea. If it was a dance scene and you could move around a lot maybe, but it would be better to do something less active...so it will look like you are really playing."

As we worked on his fiddling and got to know each other, I found he had a sense of humor. I pulled out Country Gazette's Traitor in our Midst album and turned it over so he could see the back. I wanted him to see me in that Atlas leopard suit with that gal on my shoulders.

I said, "If you want to see a real body builder, look at this."

We got along from the very beginning.

In that unmistakable accent, Arnold said, "Byron, I've got to get you into this movie somehow."

A day or two later someone again called from the production company and asked me to come in and meet with Bob Rafelson the director and Harold Schneider the producer. Before going to the meeting, I made a cassette tape of some of my fiddle playing and put it in my pocket anticipating they might want to hear a sample. When I arrived and ushered into the meeting, they began laughing.

I said, "What are you laughing at?"

They replied, "Arnold said you would be perfect for the part."

"What part is that?" I asked.

"An eighty-five-year-old man." They said.

I did not look the part, yet.

I took the cassette from my pocket and played it for them and they responded with, "That's exactly what we are looking for."

They were considering a group to pre-record the music, but after our meeting, they decided to hire me. They also thought I

On the set of the STAY HUNGRY movie in 1975. Byron Berline on stage playing fiddle, directly beneath him on the dance floor, very young Jeff Bridges and Sally Field.

would get along well with those they hired locally in Atlanta and I would teach Arnold how to play on the fiddle. It was a good break...always...being involved in a major movie.

There was to be a scene that involved some bluegrass musicians and the film's director Bob Rafelson, asked me to help him arrange for that scene. I found all the musicians locally, including a young boy who was a very good fiddler. I played on the soundtrack and was in the scene with Arnold where he is supposed to be playing the fiddle. We got together and I showed him how to put his fingers on the strings and how to bow. The scene turned out great and Arnold did a good job of faking on the fiddle.

"Stay Hungry" is available on home video and includes a narrative by the director Bob Rafelson and Sally Field.

STAY HUNGRY-MGM

"We had the premiere fiddle players in the world, Byron Berline number one. And he is in this. Byron gathered up all these players from all over the south. The track here is live. There's Byron, a wonderful man and the greatest fiddler in the world. I have to tell you, If there is a scene in a picture of mine I'd want to take to the grave, it's that one. I'm serious, because the scenes both touch me and make me feel good.

We shot it in one take, using one angle, all in one afternoon."

Bob Rafelson

Party scene
Bob Rafelson: "It also took a lot of work on Arnold's part, to play the fiddle."
Sally Field: "I always wondered how he did that."

They filmed the movie in Birmingham, Alabama and some actors, crew, and I, road a bus from the airport to our hotel. During the bus ride, I met R.G. Armstrong who lived in L.A., was born in Birmingham and he was an actor in the movie. Armstrong and Frank Crumpton were friends and knew each other before making "Stay Hungry." Frank Crumpton was a real pool hustler. He also hustled ping-pong and other games. He asked me what I did and I told him music. He said, "Maybe I can help you." and he did. I had to put together musicians, find a studio in which to record and other things. Crumpton took me all over Birmingham and we found everything I needed. Frank sold a pill to an undercover cop; they sentenced Frank to one year's probation and as a result, did not allow him to leave Birmingham. He could not get a pool game because everybody in Birmingham knew he was a hustler. He really was good and did all kinds of trick shots.

Sally Field wanted a ping-pong table so the studio set one up near the swimming pool at our hotel. One day Sally, Arnold Schwarzenegger, Frank Crumpton, and I were there and a man wandered over. He wanted to know if he could get in the ping-pong game and Frank said, "I think we can work something out." Frank beat him five straight games at five dollars a game. Frank said, "I think you need to pay me."

Nothing happened. Schwarzenegger came up to this person and in his unique accent, said, "I think you better pay the man."

The man immediately began fumbling around for his billfold. He said, "Ping-pong's not really my game...I like pool." They went to a nearby pool hall, but I missed the game...I had to go to work. When I arrived I found out Frank did not hustle the man, but he did beat him and got about $20.

When we finished the movie, I went back to California. Five years later, I was in a studio in L.A. with some musicians. I had not even thought of Frank during those years. I do not remember why, but his name came up in conversation. The studio phone rang...it was Frank Crumpton. We all just looked at each other. That was so strange and it was the last time I talked to him.

We had a great time making the movie and as a result, Arnold and I became friends.

June 10 continued to work on "Stay Hungry."

June 20, 21 Country Gazette played McCabes.

June 20 did a recording session for Terry Asher.

June 21 did a demo recording session with T. Bone Burnett.

June 21, 22 continued working on "Stay Hungry."

June 26 did a demo recording session with Al Perkins.

June 27, 28 Country Gazette played the Bluebird Café in Santa Barbara.

After leaving Country Gazette, I just wanted to play with someone. I had been jamming some with John Hickman and when Dan Crary moved to Fullerton, he played with us. I met

Allen Wald and Jack Skinner at different places and heard them on the radio. We had some great jams. Jack Skinner had written a lot of songs that lent themselves to bluegrass. We got together at our house, either in the living room or out in the music room (garage.)

Jack had a little 4-track Teac recorder so we went to his house and recorded about seven or eight songs. We decided they sounded good. We called ourselves "Byron Berline and Sundance," and we began performing around the Los Angeles area.

July 4-6 I played Joe Hutchison's bluegrass festival in Langley, Oklahoma.

July 8 did a recording session for "Stay Hungry."

July 12 did a recording session for Terry Asher.

July 19 did another recording session for "Stay Hungry." I also played with Red Dog Weber at the L.A. Marina. I met Red, in Aspen, Colorado. He was a big burley man who played a boom bass, which is a very unique instrument and people loved it.

That summer, Country Gazette also played Bluegrass Canada at Carlisle, Ontario located about an hour's drive west of Toronto. The lineup for this festival also included Norman Blake, R.F.D. Boys, Josh Graves, Kentucky Grass, Country Store, Bryan Bowers, Seldom Scene, the Country Gentlemen, and Bill Monroe, along with several excellent local, Ontario bands.

July 21 did a recording session for Terry Melcher for RCA Records.

July 23, 24 did a recording session with John Denver.

July 25-August 9 Sundance played Birmingham, Alabama, Oak Street Bar, Horse Pens Forty area, the festival was at the park. Mark O'Connor was there and Sam McGee. I remember... Terry Ryan's brother played in "Three on a String."

We went back to our small motor home after Sundance did a show and lined up our instruments along the outside of the RV. We all decided to take off in different directions so we put all the instruments inside the RV. John Hickman and I decided to wander through the campground. We stopped at one camp and started playing with them using borrowed instruments. Eventually John decided to go back to the motor home to get his banjo and my mandolin, then I went back to get my fiddle, but it was gone. I thought it must be a joke or something. We walked the campgrounds late into the night looking for anything suspicious. I had a Jagger double fiddle case with two fiddles in it. One was dad's favorite fiddle, Italian, including a W.E. Hill bow with gold mounted tortoise frog. The other fiddle in the case was a Harwood and I used it for off tunings such as "Black Mountain Rag." It also had a bow with it. I lost the case, both violins and the two bows. The next morning, Dan Crary's guitars were gone. He had a 1952 D 28 and a (Stuart) Mossman guitar. Someone had broken into the motor home and crawled through the window, leaving mud on the dinette table. I never saw those fiddles again and I do not think Dan ever got his guitars.

August 2 did a "Stay Hungry" session.

August 22 & 23 Sundance played the Bluebird Café in Santa Barbara.

August 27-30 Sundance played the Oxford Hotel in Denver, Colorado.

August 31 I played with Emmylou Harris at Malibu. Bobby Kimmel, who was in the Stone Pony's with Linda Ronstadt, managed McCabes and Bobby set up this concert. Brian Ahern was there and Rodney Crowell, John Wear played drums and Emory Gordy was in Emmy's band. Bette and Skip Conover went with me. We could not believe it! They expected about 500 people to attend and ten thousand screaming fans showed up. When we did "Orange Blossom Special," I thought they would never let us leave the stage. They never had the event again.

September 4 I did a recording session with The Band, for their "Canadian Driftwood" album for Capitol Records. The band session included Band members Levon Helm, Rick Danko, Robbie Robertson, Richard Manuel, and Garth Hudson. I was the only guest musician on this.

September 15-Oct 2 Sundance played Birmingham, Alabama, Indiana, Virginia, Baltimore, Maryland, and Washington, D.C.

October 4 Sundance played UC at Riverside.

October 10 I played at Long Beach with Emmylou Harris.

October 11 Sundance played the Pumpkin Festival at Chatsworth, out in the San Fernando Valley. Lloyd Segal, fresh out of law school, asked if we had a recording deal. We told him we did not.

He said, "Well, let me see if I can get you one."

We said, "Well, okay." and he did!

We gave him a tape; he sent it to Bob Davis a vice president at MCA and Bob just loved it. He signed us and gave us twenty five thousand dollars in front money. We got five thousand dollars a piece and we started recording. We thought, "This is cool."

October 14 did a recording session for Terry Melcher for RCA Records.

October 18 Sundance returned to the Pumpkin Festival at Chatsworth.

October 18, 19 Sundance played the Orange County Festival.

October 21 did a recording session with Leroy McNees who played Dobro with Clarence and Roland White in the Kentucky Colonels.

Sundance in 1975. l to r; John Hickman, Jack Skinner, Dan Crary, Alan Wald, Byron Berline.

One time we had a pickin' party at John Hickman's house. I remember planning to go to Bakersfield to a big fiddle contest the next day. Dennis Fetchet was a good fiddler that played all around and Bruce Johnson who did some contests. They were both good fiddlers. I told them they were welcome to go with me to Bakersfield if they wanted to and if so, they could meet at my house the next morning. They spent all night jamming at Hickman's house, but showed up at my house the following morning and rode with me to Bakersfield. When we arrived, we took out our instruments and immediately began working out fiddle parts. We were not in the contest, just there to hang out with other fiddlers, jam and have fun, but they put us on stage playing these three fiddle part things and the audience liked it. That was too much fun, so when we returned to L.A. we began getting some other players together and as a result, formed the "L.A. Fiddle Band."

October 25, 26 Sundance played Norco and it was one of those nights...we tore the house down! What a great audience.

November 1 Capitol Records released The Band's album, "Canadian Driftwood."

November 4 did a recording session for the "Starsky and Hutch" TV show.

November 5, 6 Sundance played the Lighthouse, down on the beach.

November 15, 16 did a recording session with Emmylou Harris.

November 19, 20 did a recording session for Guthrie Thomas for the movie "Bound for Glory" starring David Caradine as Woody Guthrie. Warner Brothers rented a big apartment for Thomas and bought all kinds of sound equipment for him. He had me hire all the musicians...we needed someone on piano, banjo, guitar, etc. I got John Hartford, Doug Dillard, John Hobbs, and some others. We arrived in the morning to a very nice studio and found Thomas in the control room. He froze...did not have a clue what to do. I took over and we managed to get through the session. After they completed the movie, David went to Germany and found a bass player whose playing he added to the sound track. The music was terrible and RCA called, asking if we could salvage the sound track. We over-dubbed and tried to make it sound good.

November 23 I played the Palomino.

November 24 did the Guthrie Thomas session again, but they never used the music we recorded.

November 24 did a recording session with Emmylou Harris.

December 2, 3, 16, 17 Sundance played the Palomino.

December 10 Becca turned three years old.

December 21, 22 Sundance played Fullerton, California.

December 28 Sundance played Laguna Beach.

I finished playing booked dates with Country Gazette, got Sundance going, and formed the L.A. Fiddle Band. Recording sessions and movie scores also kept me busy. Oh, and I had a lot of fun.

Journal Entry 1976
Bluegrass Symphony — Kris Kristofferson — Vince Gill

January 4 did Chris Hillman session, "Take Me in Your Lifeboat," for Asylum Records. I sang on this and played some too.

January 6 did Ken Mansfield session. He produced our Sundance album.

January 9 did a session with Doug Dillard and Vaughn Meader for their "Dillard and Meader" album. Vaughn did impersonations of John Kennedy's voice and had a hit with "The First Family." We started the session at midnight and went until 5:30 a.m. What we did...I do not know.

January 9, 10 played Bob Baxter's TV show, "Guitar Workshop."

When we moved to California I occasionally saw Mason Williams, but we did not play together. Mason is from Oklahoma City, also came to the west coast to pursue his musical career. He has done very well. He is good at writing comedy and the Smothers brothers, Tommy and Dick, recorded some of his comedy songs. Mason also played guitar on those recording sessions and the Smothers brothers' managers began managing him. Mason began writing comedy for the "Roger Miller" TV shows. He also became head writer for the "Smothers Brothers Comedy Hour" TV shows for which he received an Emmy Award. He came up with the "Pat Paulsen for President" thing. When he wrote and recorded "Classical Gas," it became a number one hit song.

Mason got the idea of merging symphony orchestras with bluegrass and his concert consists of a bluegrass band and full orchestra. He scored all of the arrangements and in 1974, premiered his "Concert for Bluegrass Band and Orchestra" at Red Rocks Amphitheater in Denver, Colorado. It did well in Denver and Mason proceeded to repeat the concert in cities all over the country. After seeing Sundance perform, Mason invited us to come to Oklahoma City to play with the Symphony Orchestra. He had his own band, made up of Rick Cuhna and some other players. Sundance was special; we were to do some of our own music and then set in with the orchestra. Mason just thought that would be neat. It was and I have been playing with Mason Williams ever since. That is when we started doing several of these bluegrass symphony gigs. We also played bluegrass shows and we still do. Mason is such a neat person and so funny! He gets an idea for something and just runs with it…works on it for days. He is just hilarious.

January 14-17 played the Mason Williams' Bluegrass Symphony Concert with the Oklahoma Symphony at the Civic Center Music Hall in Oklahoma City.

Sundance, with Dan Cray, John Hickman, Jack Skinner, Allen Wald, and Byron Berline, did a whole set as Sundance and then we sat in and played with the symphony orchestra. Barry Patton played bones with us. This was a big deal for Sundance; this was our first exposure to the Bluegrass Symphony. I remember that Mike Clark picked us up in Oklahoma City after the show and took us to Shawnee, Oklahoma to a bluegrass show.

This was also the first time I had the chance to hang out and spend some time with Rick Cuhna. Rick has a recording studio in Van Nuys, California. He is a neat person and we are about the same age; I am eleven days his senior. He wrote "YO YO Man" the theme song for the Smothers Brothers, sort of. Rick is a good songwriter and singer.

We used to have picking parties during this time in our music room (garage) and people came out of the woodwork…it was amazing. I invited ten or so very good players, they brought their wives or girlfriends and we had thirty people there. We had food, beer, soft drinks and I guess these parties became popular as word got out about them. Those people were the only guests I invited, but one time, over a hundred people showed up, parked all over the place and I did not know most of them. One pulled in the driveway…someone blocked him in and he could not get out. He did not ask them to move their car. He instead, drove through the yard, over our sprinkler system and took out some of our neighbor's rose bushes while driving through their yard. We did not have too many pickin' parties after that.

January 22-24 Sundance played another Mason Williams' Bluegrass Symphony Concert, this time with the Sacramento Symphony and the Eugene, Oregon Symphony. They held it at the Community Center Theater in Sacramento, California.

January 27, 28 Sundance played the Palomino.

Also on the 28 played with Mason Williams at the Marathon in Eugene, Oregon.

January 29 did session for J. Edward who wrote "Red Rocking Chair" and other songs.

January 29, 30 Sundance played the Golden Bear at Huntington Beach.

February 4 did a recording session for Johnnie Rivers. Fred Walecki managed Westwood Music and he got a session job for me with Johnnie. They needed a mandolin on one track and when I got there, I listened to the track and although it just did not seem to fit mandolin or fiddle, I tried to do something to make it work.

The producer said, "Oh, I really like that."

Rivers said, "No, let's try something else."

This went back and forth for two hours, going from frustration to ridiculous. Finally, I said, "I'll do it one more time and then I'm walkin'." Nope, they did not like it. I walked…the only time I ever walked out of a session. They offered to pay me, but I said, "No, no." They wasted my time and I evidently wasted theirs.

February 7 did the ABC Special, John Denver TV show.

February 7 did a recording session for the movie "Stay Hungry" for United Artists, 9 am to 7 pm.

February 13 did the movie score for "Dixie Dynamite" staring Warren Oates and Christopher George and directed by Lee Frost.

February 19 did a recording session with Rod Stewart. Unable to get the studio they wanted, they rented a mobile unit, drove it to Rod's house, set everything up in his game room, which had animal heads on the walls. I do not know if he is hunter or what. That was really a fun recording session.

February 20, 21 Sundance played McCabes.

February 22 Sundance played the Palomino.

February 23 did a recording session for the movie "Stay Hungary."

February 26, 27 Sundance played the Sweetwater Café at Redondo Beach. Others who have played there include Emmylou Harris, Levon Helm, Juice Newton, Sweethearts of the Rodeo and Pure Prairie League when Vince Gill was with them.

February 28 Sundance played UC at Riverside. I also played Mason Williams' Marathon Concert at the Valley River Center in Eugene, Oregon.

March 3 did a recording session with Gene Clark.

March 5, 6 Sundance played the Palomino.

March 8-21 Sundance played in Alabama and Kentucky.

March 27, 28 Sam Bush and I did a recording session with Mark O'Connor. Mark's mother wanted a recording of Mark with Sam and me. I remember when Sam was 13 and winning the Junior National Fiddle Contests at Weiser, Idaho. I met Mark O'Connor when he was twelve and here Sam and I were watching Mark come into his own.

I remember Sam saying, "That Mark, he's really going to be something."

I said, "He sure is." It is a wonderful thing to pass the music on.

One time Mark, his mother and his sister came out to California and stayed at our house. Mark played the piano and Bette reminds me that Mark brought his skateboard and rode up and down the street showing us all the tricks he could do on it.

March 30 Sundance played the Palomino.

April 9, 10 Sundance played McCabes.

April 12 did a Manhattan Transfer recording session.

April 12 -14 Sundance played the Lighthouse.

April 19, 20 Sundance did a recording session for our album "Byron Berline and Sundance" on MCA Records. We recorded in a very nice studio and Ken Mansfield, who produced Waylon Jennings, produced the album. Jack Skinner played bass and sang lead vocals, Dan Crary played acoustic guitar, John Hickman played banjo and Allen Wald played electric and acoustic guitars, pedal steel, and vocals. We got Skip Conover to come in to do Dobro and vocals and Dallas Taylor played drums. Jack skinner wrote six of the songs, Bill Withers wrote one, one by Rodney Crowell, one by Rick Cunha and included "Storm over Oklahoma" that Dan Crary and I wrote.

April 21-25 Sundance toured Colorado and Arizona.

April 27 Sundance did a recording session.

April 28-May 2 Sundance played the San Francisco Boarding House.

May 3-6 Sundance played San Francisco area cities.

May 7, 8 Sundance played McCabes.

May 8, 9 played Mason Williams' Bluegrass Symphony Concert with the Eugene Symphony at MacArthur Court in Eugene, Oregon. The next day we played the concert at the Oakridge Elementary School.

May 16 did a recording session for Guthrie Thomas' solo album.

May 18, 19 Sundance played the Troubadour.

I used to get calls at all hours of the day and night to do recording sessions. I guess they got wound up on adrenalin, drugs, or whatever and called me in the middle of the night. One night about midnight, Doug Dillard called. He was at A&M studios doing a recording session with Gail Davies and they needed a fiddle. I got up, dressed, drove to the studio and we finished up at 4:00 am. I am quite glad I did as that session led to another one with Gail.

One time I did a recording session with the Byrds. Terry Melcher produced the Byrds and during a recording session, they needed a fiddle and Melcher called me, "You get down here." When I got there, Roger McGuinn was trying to play a guitar break. I sat down by Clarence White and after several McGuinn attempts at the break, I said to Clarence, "Why don't you go in and play it?" I knew he would just do it once, that would be that and we could get on with the recording session.

Clarence said, "No, give him a chance," so we sat there all night. I never took my fiddle out of the case and they paid me double. That was Clarence.

Another time, while in the studio recording our Sundance album, in the same building, but in a different studio, George Martin was producing a session. He came in to the studio where I was recording and said, "Would you come in and record on this thing I'm doing?"

I did and they paid me. Allen Wald was there and said, "Do you know who George Martin is?"

"No." I said.

"George Martin produces the Beatles." He informed me.

May 21, 22 played UC Riverside at The Barn, a folk music/bluegrass place near the campus.

May 25 did a recording session with Kris Kristofferson at A&M studios for his album, "Surreal Thing" for CBS Monument Recording Co. They wanted our vocals, Jack Skinner, Allen Wald, and mine, on Kris's next album. We thought that was kind of neat, to just sing. I remember that Leland Sklar played bass. David Anderle, the producer, is a great person and neat to work with. He heard Sundance somewhere, liked the way our voices blended and thought we had a good sound. When we arrived, everyone was really partying and the three of us were stone sober. Gary Busey, the actor who played Buddy Holly in the movie was there, singing and being a part of all of this.

Jack Skinner said, "I need something for my voice."

The producer sent out for a fifth of Jack Daniels and when it was gone, Kris sent out for another bottle of Jack plus one of tequila. We began recording and cut about six or seven songs. I looked up and Kristofferson, smoking a joint, took a swig of Daniels and chased it with a shot of tequila. I had never seen that done before.

Kris was not only conscious, he was aware of how things were going, picking up immediately if things did not sound just right. This was actually a fun session...we just sang and never played a lick.

June 7-10 Sundance did a recording session.

June 14-July 6 Sundance went on tour to Nebraska, Illinois, Kentucky, Alabama, and Tennessee.

July 11 did a recording session with Mary Kay Place. They called her TV show "Fernwood Tonight." "Baby Boy" was a hit she sang on her show and I played on those sessions for Columbia Records.

July 12-14 did a Rose Maddox recording session and I enjoyed that so much. They do not make them like Rose Maddox any more, or Patsy Montana...real troopers.

July 17 played Mason Williams' Bluegrass Symphony Concert with the Denver Symphony at the Denver Center in Denver, Colorado.

July 18 I played the Palomino alone.

July 24, 25 played the Corral in Topanga Canyon. It was on Horseshoe Bend at 2034 Topanga Canyon Boulevard.

August 4, 5 Sundance had a big showcase at the Roxy for MCA Records. Dallas Taylor played drums with us on the album and this showcase. The show did not flow well...the sound was not too good. Things just did not go as well as we wanted.

August 6 did recording session with Sonny Curtis, a member of Buddy Holly's Crickets. Sonny wrote some hit songs, such as, I Fought the Law, More Than I Can Say (co-written with J.I. Allison), Walk Right Back, The Straight Life, and I'm No Stranger to the Rain.

August 13, 14 Sundance played Santa Barbara.

August 16-September 19 Sundance went on a big tour ending in Winfield, Kansas. When it came time for Sundance to tour Dan Crary was teaching so he could not get away a lot to go with us, therefore we had to augment somebody else for him. I remember we got Skip Conover who played Dobro or rhythm guitar while Allen Wald played guitar and that worked well. When the album came out, we had a thirty-day, thirty-city tour lined up on the east coast, which turned into another fiasco. I did not know much about Jack Skinner's background up until this first Sundance tour. We got to New York City and Jack said, "You know, I've never been with a band more than a year." I thought, "Well, so?" He was our lead singer and front man and I think he was afraid of success, although I do not know that for a fact. We played this one place and he was out of tune. He was playing his Hoffner Beatle bass and you could not tune the thing. I went down to Mannie's Music store and bought him a Fender bass and a strobe tuner. I told him that if we were going to use that bass on stage we needed to make sure it was in tune.

We went to a big festival in Kutztown, Pennsylvania. Jack had to get about half sloshed before he would get on stage and that night he got a little over served. There were 20,000 people there…it was a huge festival and they put a massive screen way up high so everyone could see the shows. The Nitty Gritty Dirt Band was coming on right after us so, during our encore Skip Conover came up to the mic and said, "The Dirt Band is coming right up so stick around." This made Jack mad to think Skip promoted the Nitty Gritty Dirt Band. We went off stage, came back on, did an encore and then we left stage again. We went back to these little trailers they had for us and began putting instruments away when we heard, "Bam! Bam! Bam!" We found Jack hitting the wall with his right hand. He said, "You'll have to get another bass player…I just broke my hand." Then he got into it with Skip and they started yelling at each other. I had instruments on a chair between them and I thought I had better get those instruments out of there before something happened to them. Skip was huge and could have killed Jack with one blow. I was mad at him, but I felt sorry for him in a way because his head was on crooked. I do not know that this has anything to do with it, but he was into scientology.

We were playing the Cellar Door and Country Gazette was playing nearby, so I got Roger Bush to come in and fill in for Jack. We had to change our whole repertoire because we could not do half the songs on the album. Jack finally wandered in with his hand in a cast. He decided to play that night so Roger did not have to sit in. It was the last night he played with us…Sundance had to finish the tour without him.

Later, we got together to record a solo album for him on a Sheffield Direct to Disk album with Larry McNeely, Jack and Geoff Levin. Direct to Disk is an interesting way of recording. You have to go straight through without making any mistakes because there is no tape. As you perform, the music records on a disk. That means if there is a problem with the third tune that you record, you have to start all over again. The whole side is done in one continues take without editing.

Sundance still had one more gig to do on this tour, the 1976 Walnut Valley Festival in Winfield, Kansas. We got there and Dan Crary showed up and joined us. Chris Fisher worked for Stuart Mossman at the Mossman guitar factory and he sat in with us playing bass. We got through the Winfield Festival and headed home to California to face revamping the band. Sundance still had to find a lead singer and Allen Wald said he knew a couple of people. We knew we wanted a drummer and we ended up hiring a couple of players from the Redondo Beach area; Joe Villegas played bass and Marc Cohen became the drummer; they were quite good. We just needed a lead singer and we tried out a lot of musicians for that spot.

At a festival the summer before, we met this kid who sang with Bluegrass Alliance. This was Lonnie Pierce's band and it seemed that everybody had been in that band at one time or another, including Dan Crary, Sam Bush, Tony Rice, and a bunch of others. I really did not spend any time with Vince when we met, I just watched him on stage. I liked his Dobro and banjo playing.

He also played mandolin and guitar. I was impressed with his singing and he played good. I remember asking him where he was from and was quite surprised when he said, "Oklahoma City." He was a teenager right out of high school. We remembered him when we were in search of a lead singer for Sundance and I said, "What about that Gill kid? He was good. I wonder if we can get him out here."

When Bette and I came back to Oklahoma for a visit in the later part of 1976, I got out the Oklahoma City phone book and started calling "Gills." There were about seven families listed and finally, I got Stan Gill.

I said, "I'm looking for the home of Vince Gill...is this where he lives?"

"Yes," Stan said. "You've got the right one. I'm his dad, but he's not here. He's in Birmingham, Alabama playing at the "Oak Street Club."

I said, "Well, I know where that is...I've even got their phone number."

I called the club in Alabama, got Vince on the phone, and asked if he would be interested in coming to California. He knew we had a major record deal with MCA. We were the only bluegrass band at that time that had a major record contract.

"He said, "Sure!"

I told him I would send him the Sundance album and that he needed to learn some of the songs off of it when he came out to California. Every day we continued auditioning a number of musicians. When Vince flew in Bette picked him up at the airport. We held auditions in our garage/music room and there were some players already there when Vince arrived.

Later, Bette said that Vince told her, "I've never had to try out for a band in my life."

He was only 18, but he did not think that was cool.

He knew every song on the album and after he sang only two songs, I said, "That's enough. You've got it as far as I'm concerned." Allen and I looked at each other...done deal. Vince Gill moved to California, but having such a young player in the band was a chore. He was very talented but a loose wire in a way. I introduced him to Albert Lee and J.D. Mannes. We went to the Troubadour one night when Dolly Parton and Emmylou

Harris were in the audience and I introduced them. He just stood there; he thought that was great. Sundance was a good experience for him.

When we were putting Sundance together, we considered various players. Fred Walecki, of Westwood Music said, "You know...Albert Lee wants to be in the band."

"Who's that?" I asked.

"He's one of the new ones...a good guitar player." Fred said.

I thought about it and said, "No, I don't think so."

I did not know who he was. We got Vince Gill.

August 21 played Mason Williams' Bluegrass Symphony Concert at the Lane County Fair in Eugene, Oregon.

September 29, 30 did a James Taylor recording session produced by Peter Asher.

October 7, 10, 20-3 Sundance went on tour.

November 1 did an Electra demo session for Electra Records for Mason Williams in Los Angeles.

November 6 played twin fiddles with John Hartford on Mason Williams' album for Electra Records.

November 17 did a recording session with Michael Parks. I met him when I did some sound track work for the movie "Can Ellen Be Saved?" and again when Michael starred in the made for TV movie "Along Came Bronson." This recording session was for an album he was making. One time he flew me to Kansas City to record with some jazz musicians.

November 24, 25 Sundance played the Troubadour.

December 2-5 Sundance played in the San Francisco area.

December 9 did a recording session with Keith Caradine.

December 10 Becca turned four years old.

December 22 did a recording session with Mickey Mouse for Disney...no kidding.

December 28 Sundance played the Palomino.

Journal Entry 1977
Dad's Favorites - Mary Kay Place - Elvis

January 7, 8 Sundance played Sweetwater.

January 15, 16 John Hickman and I played Humboldt College in Humboldt, California and Bette went with us. I remember having a Chevy Monte Carlo at the time and when we got on campus I drove up a little cart path to get close to the place we were going to play. Campus security came by, all upset.

I said, "Can you tell me how to get to highway 5?"

"It sure the hell isn't here!" He said.

"I'm kidding...we're going to play, just right over there." I said, pointing. He finally calmed down and it was all okay.

January 18 played USC in L.A.

January 21 Al Bruno is a session player from Canada and this session was for his solo album. Stuart Mossman of NAMM (National Association of Musical Merchandisers) asked Sundance to come in and play

January 26 Sundance played the Palomino.

January 31 did a recording session with Bruce Langhorn for his album "Outlaw Blues." Bruce did the orchestration for the "Stay Hungry" movie I worked on with Arnold Schwarzenegger.

February 4, 5 Sundance played Sweetwater.

February 8-13 Sundance played the Troubadour. I think Vince was in Sundance by then and we were booked to open for Gene Clark. We did our set and ended it with "Orange Blossom Special." Doug Weston, owner of the Troubadour, was about six feet seven or eight inches... real tall and real gay. That night he was also real drunk. He had a drink in his hand when he stumbled to the front of the stage just as we finished our set. He slurred, "Playorangeblossomspecial."

"We just played it." I told him.

Emphatically, he said, "Well, playitagain."

I said, "You give me your drink and we'll play it."

He handed me his drink, I set it on the stage and then, to appease him, we played just a little of the song. He wanted his drink back. When I picked it up and handed it to him, he tried to kiss me. I shoved him away, then he turned around, staggered over to the stairs and up he went...to Gene Clark's dressing room. He tried the same thing with Gene...Gene slugged him.

February 15 did a recording session for the movie "Smokey and the Bandit," starring Burt Reynolds and Sally Field.

February 18 played with Rose Maddox at McCabes.

February 21 did a recording session with Country Gazette.

Becca, Bette and Byron Berline in 1977.

February 22, 23 played the Troubadour.

Feb 26-Mar 28 Sundance went on a big tour to Louisville, KY, Illinois, Michigan, New York, and Massachusetts.

February 24 did a recording session with Hoyt Axton.

March 3 played Mason Williams' Bluegrass Symphony Concert with the Edmonton Symphony, held at the Jubilee Auditorium in Edmonton, Alberta, Canada.

April 1-3 Played with Mason Williams at Blitz Bluegrass Festival at the Lane County Fairgrounds in Eugene, Oregon.

April 9 Sundance played at Riverside, California.

March 30 did a recording session with Chris Hillman for MCA Records.

April 15, 16 Sundance played Sweetwater.

April 22, 23 played UC Davis and Fresno State.

April 28 did a recording session for Olivia Newton John.

May 1-20 Sundance went on a southern and mid-western tour.

June 1 played Mason Williams' Bluegrass Concert at The Little Bear in Evergreen, Colorado.

June 3, 4 Sundance played Sweetwater.

June 5 Sundance played the Palomino.

Sundance performed and recorded for about three years and we tried to get a major recording contract again, but could not seem to do it. We stayed busy and traveled all over everywhere. We got a new Dodge Maxi van for touring. We built a bed in the back with room underneath for all our stuff. Five could ride in it or two could sleep. It worked out good. As soon as we got the van, Sundance headed to New York.

June 13-26 Sundance played Rochester, New York.

Allen Wald was married to a Swedish girl at that time. She was a flight attendant and as her spouse, he could fly for little or nothing, so Allen said he would fly and the four of us would drive the Maxy van. We drove straight through in fifty-three hours and it really was not bad as two of us could sleep while two were awake to switch off driving every four hours. Nobody got overly tired…it worked out well. We knew when Allen's plane would arrive, but when we got to the airport, we did not know where to park, so we just pulled up next to the curb, stopped and put it into park, just as Allen walked out the door. He had just gotten there, got his bags, and walked out front.

We just said, "This is amazing."

Fifty-three hours with stops and we got there just as he did. Sometimes you have to wait, just picking up someone locally.

June 24 played Mason Williams' Spree '77 Park Concert in Denver, Colorado.

I also released a solo album in 1977 on the Rounder (0100) label. Its title, "Dad's Favorites," was just that. I did Coming from Denver, New Broom, Grey Eagle, B & B Rag, Redbird, Ragtime Annie, Limerock, Miller's Reel, and Arkansas Traveler. Bette played piano on the record, Vince Gill played some rhythm guitar, and there were five banjos…just because Dad liked the banjo so much.

June 26 Sundance played the Fourth Annual Telluride Bluegrass Festival in Telluride, Colorado.

June 28, 29, 30 played with Mason Williams at the Telluride Festival.

July 1, 2 Sundance played the Palomino.

July 1, 2 Played with Mason Williams at the Oxford Hotel in Denver, Colorado.

Roland White and I getting tangled up. I was playing guitar and fiddle and so was he.

July 3 Played with Mason Williams at the Steamboat Village Inn in Steamboat Springs, Colorado.

July 5 Played with Mason Williams at the Hungry Farmer in Boulder, Colorado.

July 6 Played with Mason Williams at The Nu Gnu in Vail, Colorado.

July 8, 9 Sundance played McCabes.

July 15, 16 Sundance played Sweetwater.

July 17 did a recording session with Hoyt Axton.

July 27 did a recording session with David Frizzell.

July 31 Sundance played the Truckee Festival. Bette and her dad went on this trip. John Hartford was there and a lot of local L.A. groups. Truckee, California is a town up in the mountains about six thousand feet in elevation. It was so hot! Our instruments, which were sitting on chairs behind us on stage, were so hot we could hardly pick them up.

August 15 did a recording session with the Nitty Gritty Dirt Band.

August 16, 17 did a recording session with John McEuen in Aspen, Colorado. I remember that Tony Rice was also on the session and Bette and Becca went with me. We drove to Colorado and listened to the car radio on the way. As we pulled up to the studio we got the news before we even got out of the car; Elvis had died. I wanted very much to record with Elvis Presley. James Burton, who is a friend and a member of Elvis' band, and I had discussed the possibility of recording with Elvis. I had James on the phone only the week before. We were doing some session work together and I told him to get Elvis to cut some country/bluegrass stuff so I could play on it. Burton said he had and Elvis seemed kind of interested in the idea. It was a missed opportunity.

August 19, 20 Sundance played Sweetwater.

August 24 did a recording session for John Denver's ABC TV Special.

August 25-27 Sundance played Cotati in San Francisco.

August 31-September 25 Sundance went on tour to

Kansas, Illinois, Wisconsin, Pennsylvania, Colorado, and Kentucky.

September 19-23 did a Sheffield Direct Disk recording session, two sessions per day.

October 14, 15 Sundance played Sweetwater.

October 22, 23 Sundance played Magic Mountain in Valencia, California.

October 26 did a recording session with Slim Pickins… quite an unmistakable voice and during this session, he talked more than he sang.

October 29 played UC Riverside.

November 4 did an episode for Mary Kay Place's TV show "Forever Fernwood." The first time was a session only.

Sundance in 1977. l to r; Joe Villegas, Vince Gill, Marc Cohen, Byron Berline, Alan Wald.

October 31 did another recording session with Slim Pickins.

November 4 did episode for TV show "Forever Fernwood" for Mary Kay Place. This was a spin off from "Mary Hartman, Mary Hartman." Mary Kay Place is from Tulsa, Oklahoma and she played a country music singer named Loretta Haggers. I was in a scene filmed in a very small trailer, with Emory Gordy on mandolin, Rodney Crowell on guitar and me on fiddle. Mary Kay was right in the middle, all of us crammed into that trailer and we were supposed to be her band. They cued us to begin so we started playing and Mary Kay began to sing. Somehow, her hair caught in Emory's mandolin keys, but we kept playing while Mary Kay tried to reach up and hold her hair to keep from ruining the scene. We finally had to stop and get her hair untangled before we resumed filming. She was upset about it, but Mary Kay was usually very nice about everything.

November 11, 12 Sundance played the Palomino.

November 17 did a recording session with Randy Meisner, the Eagles founding bass player, for his solo album.

November 25, 26 played the Zen Crook Festival.

December 2 did Leon Medica session for "Louisiana Man." Leon wrote this song.

December 2, 3 Sundance played Sweetwater.

December 10 Becca turned five.

December 12 did a movie session for Universal Decca.

December 13 did a recording session of Christmas songs for a 20th Century Fox movie.

December 13 Sundance played the Saloon in Thousand Oaks.

December 20 did a recording session for a Hoedown album with John Hobbs. J.D. Manes and some other players were on it recording a bunch of fiddle tunes. Eventually a man in Denmark sent a copy to me and said, "I think this is you." I had forgotten all about it.

Journal Entry 1978
Filming "The Rose" with Bett Midler

January 7 played the Blue Ridge Pickin' Parlor.

January 14 Sundance played in San Luis Obispo.

January 21 played Big Bear Festival with Jack Skinner, Larry McNeely, and Geoff who put this thing together. Bette went with me.

January 26 did a Dan Crary session.

January 29 played Shrine Auditorium with Vasser Clements, Brush Arbor, and John Hartford.

After filming "Stay Hungry" with Arnold Schwarzenegger, he became a Sundance fan and began going to our shows. He brought his mother, from Austria, and introduced her to me. At the Shrine Auditorium show there was a photo opportunity and as a prop for the picture, the female photographer borrowed Vince Gill's Ovation guitar, put the strap around Arnold's neck, but as it was not tightly fastened, it came off, and the guitar crashed to the floor. Vince was not very happy and Arnold stood there wondering, "What just happened?" It could have been worse.

After the show, the party continued at our house. The band was there, Vasser Clements and Dennis Fetchet. When we converted the garage into a picking room, we occasionally held "all nighters" and this is one of those times. We played all through the night and one by one, the players departed. About daylight, only two of us remained, Dennis Fetchet and I. Becca was five years old and about 7:00 a.m. she came into the picking room and told me, "Momma said you might ought'a come in and go to bed."

Bette has put up with a lot and for a lot of years.

February 1 Played Mason Williams' Bluegrass/Symphony Concert with the Hamilton Symphony at Hamilton Place in Hamilton Ontario, Canada.

February 3, 4 Sundance played Sweetwater.

February 12-18 I played Mason Williams' Bluegrass Symphony Toronto, Canada.

February 22 Sundance played the Palomino.

February 23 Sundance played at UCLA.

February 26-March 5 played Club Med Playa Blanca. We got expenses but no pay...a working vacation. Dennis Fetchet on fiddle, Dave Dias on Dobro, Craig Smith on banjo, Vince Gill on guitar and I played fiddle. A banjo player named C.W. Mundy worked there and he got us the gig. Bette went with me and we rode horses for hours...I got a blister on my hind end. We played music around the pool, ate very well and the rooms were nice.

March 10, 11 Dan Crary and I played Golden West at UC Riverside.

March 14 played USC Fullerton, California.

March 18 played McCabes with Dan Crary.

March 18, 19 judged the Fiddle Contest at Knotts Berry Farm.

March 20-26 Murray McCloud, "Sting Ray" movie session... one of the worst movies I have ever seen, and I did the whole score for that thing.

April 1 I played Knotts Berry Farm.

April 2 Sundance played Cal State Northridge on Devonshire St. I remember Arnold Schwarzenegger was there.

April 22 played at Country Fest with Al Bruno president of ACM in California.

April 25 did a Leroy McNees session. Vince Gill played guitar on this.

April 28-30 Sundance played the Oregon Festival.

May 15-17 shot "The Rose" movie scene in three nights. Mark Rydell, who directed the "Reivers," also directed "The Rose," with Bett Midler. He felt bad that they knocked us out of the Reivers thing, so he asked Doug and Rodney Dillard, Harry Dean Stanton and me, to be in "The Rose." Harry played the straight laced, country music dude and Doug, Rodney, and I were his band members. I tried to size up what real life character Harry Dean played and to me; he seemed patterned after Ernest Tubb. Bett Midler was great and when off the set, we would start singing. The movie set was north of L.A. in the desert, but it was bitterly cold. When the sun goes down it does not take long to get very cold. We shot this in a small travel trailer, which only had one side so that cameras had room to shoot the scene, so the wind just ripped through it. To make things worse, they spritzed us with water to make it look like we just came off the stage sweating. Oh, it was cold! We did that for three nights, just shooting that one scene. Doug and I were to be in another scene, but we really did not have any lines. We were just to "be" there in the scene and it was another bitter cold night.

Rydell said, "We've got to do something to get this chill out of here." Then he told some of his crew, "Go get that brandy."

Rodney has this little shaking of the hands, which the cold amplifies. Someone handed him the bottle of brandy and Rydell says, "Pour me a little, will you?"

Rodney's hands began to shake and Rydell said, "Are you that cold or have you already had…Here, let me pour it." The conversation could easily have gone, "Drink a lot?" "No, I spill that much."

Doug had been on the wagon for several weeks, but it did not take much for him to be feelin' no pain and once he got that first one in him, he just could not stop. At the same time, the director and Harry Dean Stanton were having a debate about how the scene should go. It was a heated debate, but that was normal, as they did that all the time. Right in the middle of it, Doug jumped up and ran over to Harry Dean. He got right in his face and said "Iyagreewithyou, Harry Dean." Rydell looked at Doug and I thought he was going to run him off.

May 17 did a Doug Dillard session.

May 18 Snuff Garrett movie for Warner Brothers probably Clint Eastwood's "Any Which Way but loose"

May 25, 1978 Brian Ahern asked me to do a session on Rodney Crowell's new album. We did "Leavin' Louisiana in The Broad Day Light."

Bennie Thomason the great Texas fiddler, occasionally came to California to visit. At the time of this session, he was spending a week at our house and went to the studio with me that night. Bennie was in the control room having a beer. It spilled on the console and ran down the faders and everywhere. Brian cleaned it up the best he could and it did not short-out anything. I felt kind of bad about it, but things happen.

May 28 played in Santa Barbara. Stuart Duncan was there and Jim Messina.

June 1 did session for Bill Knopf a banjo player.

June 3, 4 Sundance played Santa Barbara and San Luis Obispo.

June 10, 11 Sundance played Six Flags' Magic Mountain in Valencia, California.

June 17 played Seaside Cal State University Northridge.

June 30 Sundance played the Melodrama in Oceana, California.

July 4 played Woodland Hills' fireworks.

July 6-16 BCH (Dan Crary, John Hickman, and I) toured Japan.

July 18-31 judged the Missoula, Montana Fiddle Contest. Bette and Becca went with me and I played some other towns in Montana.

August 14 did Doobie Brothers session.

August 18, 19 Sundance played the Sundance Saloon…neat pairing.

September 1 played a Seattle Show.

September 18, 20 I rehearsed two shows 9:00 p.m. to 2:00 a.m. for Michael Murphy (not Michael Martin Murphy) for CBS.

September 21-26 Sundance toured Oregon and Washington

September 30, October 1 Sundance played the Chino Festival in Chino, California in San Bernardino County.

October 2-8 Sundance played Mason Williams' Bluegrass Symphony with the Sacramento Symphony at Rancho Murieta in Sacramento, California. They held this outdoors and I remember being upset because OU played Texas that weekend and I missed watching the game.

October 14, 15 Sundance played Magic Mountain, Six Flags in Valencia, California

October 15 did a session for Jesse Ed Davis a session guitar player from Oklahoma who died young. He played with the Rolling Stones, Bob Dylan and many others.

October 17, 18 played Austin City Limits with John McEuen, Mel Durham, and Vasser Clements. I called Dave Ferguson (with Country Gazette at the time) and he came to Austin, they put him on the show and we did some triple fiddle stuff. Elizabeth Cotton who wrote "Freight Train," was on the show. This song is a classic and she was only twelve years old when she wrote it.

October 29 I played with Wild Oats.

November 1 did an Andy Williams demo session.

November 11 I sat in with someone at the Palomino.

November 17 Sundance played the Irvine Festival with Emmylou Harris.

November 28 did a Doug Dillard session.

December 1 did a Dan Crary session.

December 2 played UC Riverside.

December 4 did a Dan Crary session.

December 9 BCH (Berline, Crary, and Hickman) played Houston, Texas. Stuart Mossman's sister Martha, loved BCH, and she got this gig for us. Martha worked for Frito Lay and we played for their big corporate party at the Woodlands Club House. After the gig, Hickman and I played pool with some dude and we almost got into a fight. It was very late when we got back to our room and we had only been asleep a couple of hours when Dan woke us up. We were late and almost missed our flight.

December 10 BCH played Santa Cruz and Becca turned six.

December 12, 13 Doug and I started playing some together again and we played this gig at the Palomino.

December 15, 16 L.A. Fiddle Band played McCabes.

Journal Entry 1979
The Palomino - Other Road Stories

January 5 did an Emmylou Harris session.

January 8 did a session for the movie "Every Which Way but Loose" starring Clint Eastwood and produced by Snuff Garrett. Clint is a neat person. He came in the studio and sang a song on the soundtrack.

Hank Penny, a banjo player, singer, promoter who performed with Spade Cooley, co-founded the Palomino in 1949 with Armand Gautier. Tommy Thomas purchased the Palomino from Hank Penny.

The Palomino Club was famous and lent itself to occasional use in movies. One time they were filming some scenes at the club and Clint Eastwood was the star. I knew Clint and when I walked behind the club, I saw his trailer. I noticed he was there and he said, "Hey, come on in and have a beer with me" so, I did.

I played with Tommy Thomas many times and knew him well. For some reason, maybe jealousy, he got it in his head that I was bothering Clint, but Clint said, "No, no." He settled it right there.

Tommy made a big production of every star and celebrity that came to the Palomino. He stopped whatever he was doing and gave exaggerated welcomes to them, which was a little embarrassing for everyone involved. I do not know why, but many of the club owners were like that. Club owners were typically grey and pasty because they stayed in the dark all the time at the clubs and most of them seemed to be paranoid. Tommy had various house bands through the years and Red Rhodes ran the house band for a time. Tommy paid each band member separately, which is unusual as clubs more commonly pay the band and then they divide the pay among themselves. Tommy had each musician go to his office and pick up his or her pay. He said such things as, "Now, you watch out for so and so." He was always stirring up animosity and trouble.

Monday was a slow night so to drum up business Tommy hired a band and gave out complementary tickets. These comp tickets would ensure the place would have a good crowd and the patrons in turn, would spend money at the bar. We played on one of these nights and the place was not packed but had a full crowd. Tommy jumped all over me saying, "Not enough comp tickets came in, I can't make any money like this."

I told him, "What are you talking about? The club is full and everybody is having a good time and drinking?" I just did not get it. He acted as if he was not making a penny and it was all costing him...everybody knew he was making money.

When Doug Dillard and I played the Palomino, we iced down beer in our dressing room because we could not afford to pay bar prices. Some of our friends started coming backstage and we offered them beer. Tommy saw this and then called me saying, "I'll comp your drinks at the bar." He did this to keep us from bringing in our beer and giving it to friends. The next night he did comp our drinks and we ran up a four hundred dollar tab. He should have known better with Doug Dillard in the band.

Tommy called and said, "We can't do that anymore."

From then on, we brought in our own beer and I guess Tommy just looked the other way.

Glen D. Hardin was a regular at the Palomino and often brought guests with him. He always ran a tab and paid it every week or whatever arrangement he had. One time Tommy called Glen frantically saying, "You've got to get this tab paid! I can't run a business like this!"

Glen knew he had paid the tab or most of it, but he drove down to the club. The tab was $6.50. That was Tommy...he got upset over the simplest things.

January 11-19 BCH went on tour in Tennessee, Alabama, Washington D.C., Kansas, and Hawaii.

There was a Bluebird club in Santa Barbara and they opened another one in Hawaii. We were booked there in January, a wonderful time to be on the islands. Jim Dickson lived in Hawaii at that time and he knew a couple that had a big fishing boat. The boat owner's wife was heir to the Levi Straus family. We were booked for three nights and the last night Jim and his friends came to the show and offered to continue the party on his friend's boat. Employees of the Bluebird came, the band, all of us. They audiotaped the show and played the tape while we were on board the boat. We had the best time that night…it was really a lot of fun. I worked with Jim Dickson for many years and that night in Hawaii was the last time I saw him.

February 3, 5 Doug Dillard, Emmylou Harris, and I played the Palomino.

February 10 played the Fullerton Chili Cook Off.

February 13 I went to El Paso, Texas to a memorial concert for Charles and May Harding's son. Cecil Hyatt came and played the bones, my brother Leonard played guitar, Wayne Shrubshall played banjo and Hans Kaiser played Dobro. This became an annual event.

February 23, 24 BCH played Portland, Oregon and Seattle, Washington.

March 1 I played the Banjo Café in Santa Monica. This is a small room for 50-60 people where bluegrass musicians went to play.

March 4 "Cowboy Maynard" Tom Kuehl and I played Huck Finn's in Long Beach.

March 8 I played the Banjo Café in Santa Monica.

March11 Tom Kuehl and I played Huck Finn's in Long Beach.

March 15 I played the Banjo Café in Santa Monica.

March 18 Tom Kuehl and I played Huck Finn's in Long Beach.

March 20 Sundance played the Melodrama Theater in Oceana, California. They had music on off nights and this was the last show with Vince Gill in the band.

March 24 played Santa Monica College with one of the bands I was with at that time.

March 25 Tom Kuehl and I played Huck Finn's in Long Beach.

March 30 played the Long Beach Festival.

March 31 played the Sundance Saloon at Thousand Oaks.

April 1 BCH did a live radio show on KPFK. That night I played Huck Finn's with Tom Kuehl.

April 7 did a show with Mark O'Connor and Dan Crary at McCabes.

April 7, 8 played Knotts Berry Farm.

April 8 Tom Kuehl and I played Huck Finn's in Long Beach.

April 10 did a movie session with Murray McCloud.

April 12, 13 did "Dad's Favorites" session.

April 15 Tom Kuehl and I played Huck Finn's in Long Beach.

April 19-24 Northern California tour with Doug Dillard, Ray Park, Bill Bryson, Billy Constable, and Skip Conover.

April 26 did a "Dad's Favorites" session.

April 27, 28 BCH played the Banjo Café or I played with the L.A. fiddle Band. I cannot remember which group.

April 29 played Cal State at Long Beach and I was well paid.

May 5, 6 played the San Diego Folk Festival.

May 8 played the Oceana Melodrama Theater.

May 12-15 played Mason Williams' Bluegrass Symphony Concert with the New Orleans Symphony at the L.W. Higgins High School in Marrero, Louisiana on the fourteenth. The next day we played the concert at Grace King High School in Metairie, Louisiana.

May 16 played UCLA.

May 18, 19, 20 played the Blitz Bluegrass Festival with Mason Williams at the Lane Country Fairgrounds in Eugene, Oregon.

May 20-28 Mr. Tanaka booked BCH and we did a Japanese tour.

May 30 did Bernie Leadon session.

May 31-June 26 did a road tour with Doug Dillard. We played Bluegrass Canada at Carlisle, Ontario. Also featured that weekend were Lester Flatt and the Nashville Grass, New Grass Revival with Courtney Johnson, Curtis Birch, Sam Bush, and John Cowan. Country Gazette also played, with Roland White, Alan Munde, Joe Carr, and Mike Anderson. Also included on the bill were The Pinnacle Boys, Don Stover, Hotmud Family, R.F.D. Boys, and Boys from Indiana.

We did a show on June 17 at the "Great Northern Opry" in Bloomington, Minnesota, held at the Carlton Celebrity Room. Norman Blake was on the show, Peter Land, the Doug Dillard Band and me. It was one show only and we made a live recording that night.

We played Telluride, Colorado where we cut a live album called "Jack Rabbit." The players included Doug Dillard, Skip Conover, Ray Park, Billy Constable, Bill Bryson and me. It was Doug's kind of deal. Doug Dillard is an experience; you never know what is going to happen next.

July 11 did a Molly Hatchet session. Played a fiddle sound effect that took no time at all and they paid double scale.

July 16 Tom Kuehl and I played Huck Finn's in Long Beach.

July 20 played Knotts Berry Farm.

July 27 played in San Francisco with Doug Dillard and his band. While there, I played with another group at a winery.

August 3, 4 played Atlanta, Georgia with Doug Dillard and his band. We arrived to find our opening act was the Danny Gatton Band with Buddy Emmons. We could not believe it! Buddy Emmons is a steel guitar legend as was Danny Gatton, on guitar. How this came about we never knew. We could not believe these great artists were opening for us, but bluegrass purists in the audience had no interest in electric instruments, so they went to the lobby until we came on. We watched their opening set and were mesmerized. They had such high energy and when their set was over, we were exhausted, just watching them. We should have been opening for them. After the show, they stuck around and we jammed with them for about forty minutes. What a pleasure.

August 6, 11 toured Missouri and Illinois with Doug Dillard and his band.

This is a reminder of a 1968 story while I was in the army. Red Corbin is Mitch Corbin's dad. While I was in the army, Red invited the Southern Bluegrass Boys band to tape a show to be played on the radio. His son Mitch is the little boy not interested in bluegrass until years later, when he heard me play guitar on that tape we made in his living room back in the 1960's. Mitch went to Chicago and took lessons from Jethro Burns. In 1982, he took first place in mandolin and guitar at the Winfield, Kansas National Flat-picking Championship and was the first person to take both titles in one year. Mitch Corbin became an incredible musician. At this festival in Illinois Mitch Corbin asked me to do a recording session with his girlfriend and they set up the recording equipment in their house. I remember that Suzy Bogguss was so appreciative. She is so talented and this was one of her very first albums.

August 12 played the Palomino.

August 18-26 toured Wisconsin, Tennessee and Colorado with Doug Dillard and his band.

August 29 did session with Robbie Weaver, Dennis Weaver's son. I also did a session with Larry McNeely and Mike Cassidy.

September 1 did Mike Utley session. He played a lot with Kris Kristofferson.

September 5 played the Crescendo with Tom Kuehl.

September 7 did Mike Cassidy session.

September 23 played the Crescendo with Tom Kuehl.

September 28-October 6 BCH played Kansas and El Paso, Texas.

October 7 played the Peninsula Music Fair.

October 10 did session for the TV show WKRP in Cincinnati.

October 12-14 BCH played Bullhead City, Arizona.

October 20 played Santa Barbara and Lancaster, California.

October 22 played the Palomino.

November 19, 20 played Huck Finn's with Tom Kuehl.

November 4 played the Crescendo.

November 25 played the wrap party for the "Long Riders" movie. Stuart Mossman was in the film with the Caradine and Keach brothers. Stuart played a train engineer and he had one line, "Who are you...Jesse James?"

November 26 played Huck Finn's with Tom Kuehl.

December 3 played Huck Finn's with Tom Kuehl

December 6-9 played Mason Williams Bluegrass Symphony Concert with the Kansas City Philharmonic at the Music Hall in Kansas City, Missouri.

December 10 played Huck Finn's on Becca's seventh Birthday.

December 17, 17 did a Stuart Margolin session. Stuart played Angel Martin in the James Garner TV show "Rockford Files." He was a good friend of Murray McCloud and Murray, also was an actor. Garner persuaded Warner Brothers to give Stuart this record deal.

I gave Stuart the book about my hero Pistol Pete and asked, "Can we get a movie made of this?

Stuart said, "It would make a good thirteen week series." We never got it made. Stuart Margolin went on to direct episodes of M.A.S.H., the Mary Tyler Moore Show, Northern Exposure and other TV shows. I think he and his wife live in Canada.

December 17 Tom Kuehl and I played Huck Finn's in Long Beach.

Toward the end of Sundance in late 1979, approaching 1980,

we were still playing, but not doing too much. One day Vince Gill came to me and said, "I've got a chance to go with Pure Prairie League and I just don't know what to do."

"Well, I do." I told him. "You go do it! If they are getting ready to record, there's no question about it."

He went to the Pure Prairie League audition with a buddy he had met on the beach. Once at the audition, Vince sang for them and they hired him. Pure Prairie League had a hit record with Vince singing several songs that he had written. One of the songs, "Let Me Love You Tonight" he did not write and it became a Top Ten hit, which changed Vince's life and career. Most of the songs on that album were for teenyboppers and as a result, Vince thought he should continue writing those types of songs. It took him about ten years to wake up.

The "L.A. Fiddle Band" did a live album on Sugar Hill Records in about 1979. We had Roger Reed, a very good guitar player and singer. Roger's voice reminded me a lot of Tony Rice's. Skip Conover played Dobro and John Hickman of course, on banjo. We used various bass players. George Hickman John's brother, played with us some. Joe Villegas played with us sometimes as well as Vince Gill. We just rotated a bunch of people in and out. Roger Reed's brother Dennis played bass on the recording.

We did the L.A. Fiddle Band for fun, but we got booked here and there. We played at Winfield, Kansas during their winter series of concerts and went to Langley, Oklahoma to their festival a few times.

Between the L.A. Fiddle Band and BCH, I stayed busy and I kept Sundance going.

Journal Entry 1980
Outrageous — You Bet Your Life

In 1980, I recorded a solo album, "Outrageous" on the Flying Fish label (227). I did Barndance, Fall Creek, Passin' By, Don't Put It Away, Coming Home, Jack Rabbit, Stampede, Byron's Barn, Outrageous, Skippin' Around, Oklahoma Stomp, and Funky Deer. Dan Crary, John Hickman, Skip Conover and Vince Gill played on it, J.D. Maness played pedal steel, John Hobbs on piano and Lee Skylar on bass. Before the album came out, I had a copy of it in my car. Kenny Baker and I were riding around one afternoon and I put the "Outrageous" cassette in the player. I wanted to see how Kenny would like it and he did.

"Byron," he said, "You've got to have Bill (Monroe) hear this." I am thinking, "No, I don't think so." "Naw," I mumbled.

Kenny was insistent. "Oh, I think he'll really like it."

I knew Bill would not like it because of the nontraditional sound. "I don't think he would." I cautioned Kenny.

"Oh, yeah, he'll love it." Kenny kept at me.

We pulled up to the motel where Bill was staying. His room was on the second floor and he was standing on the balcony. Kenny yells up at him, "Bill, you gotta hear this."

I knew what would happen. Sure enough, one cut and Bill said, "That pedal steel just ruins the whole thing." Bill and I had been personal and professional friends for many years and we jabbed each other a lot. He said, "Your dad wouldn't like you playin' that kind of music."

Being from Oklahoma I grew up on Bob Wills' western swing music and there was always a lot of pedal steel in it. I said, "Bill, dad was listening to western swing before he ever listened to your music."

Later on Ricky Skaggs recorded Bill's "Uncle Pen" and it became a big hit for him. It too, had pedal steel in it. Bill came to California about that time and I questioned him about Ricky's recording. I asked Bill, "How did you like Ricky Skaggs' recording of "Uncle Pen?"

"Mighty fine." He said. "I just think it's real good."

"There was a pedal steel break in there." I told him. "Did you hear that? Well, I don't think your uncle Pen would have liked it played that way."

January 26 Played Mason Williams' Bluegrass Symphony Concert with the Louisville Symphony at Louisville Gardens in Louisville, Kentucky. The Cumberlands Harold and Betty Thom were playing in town. I played with the Cumberlands while I was in the army. Ed Boutwell, who I met while working on the "Stay Hungry movie," owned a studio and he was there. Barry Patton played bones with us and after this, Mason wanted Barry to be in every show. We started jamming after the show and Ricky Skaggs showed up without an instrument, so he borrowed my mandolin. They eventually kicked us out and we continued the party at the hotel. While playing I realized my mandolin was missing. Someone remembered seeing Ricky putting it behind the big bleachers back at the venue. Ed and I went back to the building, went inside and there was my mandolin right behind the bleachers. Barry was about nineteen or twenty and his bones playing went over very well. It was quite an exciting time for him to witness.

One time in 1979 Sundance played at McCabes and a Japanese promoter, Robert Tanaka from Tokyo, was there and saw us perform. He then called and wanted to know if Dan Crary, John Hickman and I, just the three of us, could go on tour to Japan as "Sundance." He indicated he could not afford to bring the whole band. We thought that sounded interesting. We did that trip to Japan and that is how we formed our group, "Berline, Crary, and Hickman." We realized we could do that, just the three of us, and sound good. We did that for ten or eleven years. During the decade we performed as "Berline, Crary, and Hickman," "Sundance" was going and I also kept working on movie scores and did session work.

Michael Martin Murphy's song, "Wild Fire" came out in 1975 and it was very popular. The movie "Urban Cowboy," came out in 1980 and I got to record on the soundtrack album. The movie starred John Travolta and Debra Winger. As a result, I got the idea to put together a group that could play bluegrass and country. I formed another band and kept the "Sundance" name. I got Steve Spurgin to join the group. He lived way up north in Ridgecrest and played drums with a group called "Wild Oats." We played Huck Finns in Long Beach every Sunday night and Steve drove all the way from Ridgecrest to Long Beach...one hundred fifty miles one way. We played the show, went somewhere to eat and he tried to sober up then drive back to Ridgecrest. He got home a little after daylight and he did this for fifty bucks. We did this for a year or more and had so much fun! One of the reasons we did this was because on Sunday, few musicians were booked so we always had many great players sit in with us. Steve Spurgin played drums for us and we got Rick Cuhna to join us. I met a kid named Pete Wasner a keyboard player and good singer. We got Don Whaley a bass player and very good singer, Skip Conover on Dobro and lap steel and me. That was the new Sundance band. This band cut one album, released it on an Italian label in Italy and of course, no one ever heard of it again. This Sundance band was excellent and we really tried to get a record deal, but could not. MCA almost signed us, but signed the "Whites" instead. They called us two or three times and said it was between Sundance and the Whites and they said they did not know what to do. Ultimately, they picked the "Whites." The new Sundance continued playing on and off for quite a while.

February 11 Played Mason Williams' Bluegrass Symphony Concert with the New Orleans Symphony at the Thibodeaux Civic Center in Thibodeaux, Louisiana.

The L.A. Fiddle Band released an album in 1980 on the Sugar Hill label (3716). We did Roanoke, Dixie Hoedown, I'll Just Stay Around, All the Good Times, Jack Rabbit, Sitting on Top of the World, Red Haired Boy, Don't Put It Away, On and On, Brown County Breakdown and Uncle Pen.

After Bruce Johnson left the L.A. Fiddle Band and moved to northern California, he and Steve Spurgin got together and they started a band. Bruce went to fiddle contests and we occasionally played together.

February 23 played Mason Williams' Bluegrass Symphony Concert with the Arkansas Symphony at the Convention Center Music Hall in Little Rock, Arkansas.

I performed at the Pacific Christian College Theater in May. This was a benefit show for an organization aiding Mexican Orphanage Refugees, a non-denominational and non-profit group.

They used the funds raised at the benefit to provide clothing and shelter for the children.

We played Flapper McGee's in San Jose. We had John Hickman on banjo, Ray Park on guitar, Ray's son Larry Park on bass and fiddle, Ted Smith on mandolin and me on fiddle. There was a Japanese fiddler in the audience and he audiotaped the show. He introduced himself and said he came to see me at both of my previous tours to Japan. The audiences were quite large in Japan and while in California on a trip, he discovered I would be playing in San Jose and arranged to be there, at the much smaller venue. I asked him to join us on stage and we played fiddles together on a few songs. It made his day and mine too. Sometimes we forget how far-reaching our talents may become.

They nominated Emmylou Harris's "Blue Kentucky Girl" for a Grammy and she and her Hot Band, including Ricky Skaggs, were playing the same weekend at the nearby Catalyst.

June 15 played with Mason Williams at the Northwest Charity Horse Show held at the Lane County Fairgrounds in Eugene, Oregon.

June 21 Played the Kerrville Country Fair with Mason Williams in Kerrville, Texas.

In the summer/autumn issue of Old Time Music, they had a review of my "Outrageous," Flying Fish FF227, album.

"As music for the car cassette, as an example of how some of the greats in the field behave when free to cut loose, this sort of LP is seldom bettered. Play it 1000 times and I almost guarantee on the 1000th playing a new break will emerge to take over from last week's favorite."

Here is a part of an Oakland Tribune review: "Not trying to be anything pop, schlock, Nashville smooth or anything other than a non-stop hot playing session with the finest studio musicians around, this album is down-right hot summer fun that should have even grandmothers dancing. There's a bit of bluegrass some Western swing and a lot of country dance tunes (all written by Berline.)"

This is something from a review by Rich Kienzle from the Country Music periodical.

"One can tell a lot about a musician from the way he plays behind others, but to realize a player's true depth, a solo album like this, where they can stretch out, is the key. Berline tackles bluegrass, rock, jazz and various combinations with a group built around ex-Emmylou Harris guitarist Albert Lee, former Elvis lead man James Burton (the man who played lead with Ricky Nelson on all those dance scenes on the old Ozzie and Harriet TV shows,) pianist John Hobbs, L.A. pedal steel master Jay Dee Manness, rock bassist Lee Sklar and banjoist John Hickman. They not only do a great job of backup, but their solos seem to inspire Berline to greater heights on each of his original tunes, most of which were cut live in the studio."

December 10 Becca celebrated her 8th birthday.

You probably remember a popular television show that ran from 1950 to 1961, called "You Bet Your Life" starring Groucho Marks. After the show's ending, they reintroduced it with Buddy Hackett as the host and this show ran for two seasons. I do not remember which year I was on the show. They always had one male contestant and one female. Buddy interviewed us on the show and then we played a true or false quiz of five questions in a particular category. I answered the first correct answer to a question and won twenty-five dollars. The amount doubled with each correct answer and I got all the way to the end…all five questions. After the fifth question, I could choose to try and answer the sixth question and triple my winnings or keep the money I had won.

I went for it! The sixth question came from the science category: beetles.

I might have won if it had been the Beatles.

Journal Entry 1981
Cecil and a Fugue – Tex Williams – Scotland and Ireland

January 5 did Dennis Weaver, Hoyt Axton session for "Don't Fence Me In" produced by James Burton. This was a fun session.

I got Dennis Fetchet a gig with Hoyt Axton and this is how it happened. Hoyt and I played together some and became good friends. One time he called and asked if I knew a fiddler he could use in his band. I suggested Dennis Fechet and Hoyt said he would try him out.

A decade later I asked Hoyt, "How's Fechet?"

Hoyt said, "I'm still tryin' him out."

Another time, at the Palomino, Hoyt's bus was in back and he was inside the club doing a sound check. He told Tommy Thomas owner of the Palomino, "I want a whole wash tub of beer iced down back stage."

Tommy said, "I can't do that."

Hoyt said, "Okay boys, load up we're getting out of here."

Tommy quickly said, "It will be right here."

Hoyt played the date.

January 7-20 BCH toured Pennsylvania, Washington D.C., Alabama, Tennessee, and Oklahoma.

January 22 did Peter Alsop session. This was a children's deal.

January 23 did Lee Holdridge session for the "Freedom" movie. Lee was the conductor or director for John Denver and several others.

January 27 did Doc Watson session.

January 28-31 new Sundance played the Saddle Bronc Club. The band included Rick Cuhna, Skip Conover, Steve Spurgin, Pete Wasner, Don Whaley and me.

February 4 the L.A. Fiddle Band played the Banjo Café.

February 5-8 the L.A. Fiddle Band played the Lone Star Saloon. Gate Mouth Brown was an African American fiddle player. He and his band played first, followed by L.A. Fiddle Band. Everyone left, but we stuck around to hear Gate's second set. He played guitar that set and blew us away. He was very,

very good. If he had played the guitar on that first set, everyone in the club would have stayed for his second set.

February 11 played the Banjo Café.

February 14 Rick Cuhna and I played a club we had never heard of before, the "Rawhide" in Burbank. It was Valentine's Day and it did not take long for us to figure out it was a gay bar. It had a high stage where our feet were eye level to the audience. Rick had on some rather fancy western boots and they caught one man's eye. He got on stage and started rubbing Rick's boots... caressing them. I think Rick wanted to kick him. I did play at the "Rawhide" again, that time with Rose Maddox and Jann Brown. Jann's most requested number was Tammy Wynette's, "It's So Hard to Be a Woman." Boy, am I laughing now just thinking about it.

February 17 did Arlo Guthrie session for Warner Brothers. The Warner studio had a big basketball goal and we played until we got tired and then started recording again.

February 18 BCH played Sweetwater, a little club in Redondo Beach where we played all the time. John Hickman is here, helping me tell this story.

Byron: We arrived at the club and began getting out our instruments. Dan Crary opened his case and...no guitar. He left it at home. Dr. Dan Crary the absent-minded professor. Vince Gill was there to listen to us play and because he did not live far from the club, he went home and got his guitar for Dan to use.

John: We had become accustomed to Dan always forgetting things...leaving a trail of stuff everywhere we went. He dropped his passport, plane tickets...important stuff. We were in Europe one time and Dan left his briefcase containing all our contracts, in a phone booth. When he noticed it was missing and figured where he left it he went back to get it, but it was gone.

Byron: He never did find it, did he John?

"Nope. Never did." John says shaking his head.

Byron: John Moore is the same way. Scatter brained...I forgot about that.

February 20 did Janis Ian CBS session, did another session that afternoon, and played the Ice House that night.

February 27 played 20th Century Wrap Party.

March 4-8 played Mason Williams' Bluegrass Symphony concert with the Eugene Symphony at the Lane County Fairgrounds in Eugene, Oregon.

March 3, 10, 11 played Saddle Bronc with new Sundance.

March 13 played Rawhide with new Sundance.

March 14 played El Coriso Golf Course Club.

March 15 played Cowboy Club in Anaheim. Anything "Cowboy" became very popular, including boots, hats, etc. Country music finally began to grow in popularity and with that, the pay for country bands got better.

March 16 did Art Masters session. Did the song "Second Fiddle" and liked it so much I recorded it on my "Fiddle and a Song" album. Jann Brown sang it on the album. Art was a neat person.

March 18 did Lee Hazlewood session.

March 19-23 toured the West coast with new Sundance.

March 26-April 3 played Mason Williams' Bluegrass Symphony with the Tulsa Philharmonic at the Performing Arts Center in Tulsa Oklahoma on the seventh. That was a lot of fun. Then we went on to do another one in Spokane, Washington, with the Spokane Symphony at the Spokane Opera House.

When we did Mason Williams' Bluegrass Symphony in Tulsa, Oklahoma the chairs on the front row were for the "Bones" section, Cecil Hyatt and Barry Patton. We played "Fisher's Hornpipe" for our encore and when it came the orchestra's turn, they played a fugue and we were to stop playing and let them play. We stopped, they played, they stopped, and we played…that is how we did the set. Cecil however, did not understand the process and when the band stopped playing and the orchestra began their fugue, Cecil just kept on playing….right through the orchestra's part. After the show Cecil said, "Byron, did you notice they got completely off? The fellow with the stick pointed at me and I just held the beat…pretty soon they got back on it."

I never told him the orchestra was playing a fugue. I just enjoyed the memory. It reminds me of a song, "Stop, stop. What's that sound?"

April 4 Peter Rowan and I played McCabes.

April 5 played the Lone Star with new Sundance.

March 6-11 played the Crazy Horse with new Sundance.

April 7 played the Glendale community College with the

L.A. Fiddle Band. Larry Cudney, a math professor, got us the booking and we played during the noon hour when students were active on campus. We did this every year in the spring. In 2010, he and his wife attended OIBF (Oklahoma international Bluegrass Festival) in Guthrie, Oklahoma.

Cudney worked for Howard Hughes, but never met him. Hughes always hired Mormons because he thought they were clean.

Larry had lots of horses and while my siblings were in L.A., we went riding in the foothills and we got lost in the fog. Henry got on his horse and first thing, it started bucking. He said, "Guess I'll break him before I ride him."

Eleanor and Janice were there and Eleanor was scared to death. She just knew she was going over one of those drop offs and Janice messed up her back. When we finally got back to where we were staying, Janice got in the hot tub.

April 16 I played the El Paso, Texas Festival.

April 17 played the Banjo Café.

April 20 played the Cowboy in Anaheim, California. It was a benefit for Tex Williams who had a huge hit, "Smoke, Smoke, Smoke, That Cigarette." Over fifteen hundred people attended the benefit and there were three or four bars. They scheduled Tex and his band, with his nephews, to play on the show. About 10:30 p.m., Tex came in, feelin' no pain and he kept a big grin on his face.

He said, "We stopped at a bunch of bars on the way over. You gonna play with me tonight?"

He wanted me to play "Sally Goodin'." I was playing an electric fiddle that night so a microphone was not necessary. I started playing and he hoisted the microphone and stand, way up high so it would pick up my fiddle. It got close and I could just see it hitting my fiddle.

When it was over I said, "Let's get out of here."

We did "Smoke, Smoke, Smoke That Cigarette" and when he started to walk off of the high stage I grabbed him, telling him to go off to the left, but he turned and walked to the back of the stage. The drum riser was about thirty inches high and in front of that were all the amplifiers, which were still on. He fell across the amps and you can imagine the noise it made. I looked over and Tex was facedown, horizontal, on the amps...with one leg sticking straight out behind him. I did not know he had a wooden leg. There were people waving from the wings to get him out of there, so I got him up and off the stage.

April 23 did a French bluegrass session with Francois Vola.

April 24 Sundance played the Bel-Air Bay Club. Bruce Johnson had played keyboards for the Beach Boys and he sat in with us that night.

April 25 did Kit Thomas session and I played Sweetwater that night.

April 26 Sundance played the Cal State, Long Beach Festival. These were big budget deals. Emmylou Harris was there, Buck White, Ricky Skaggs, Jethro Burns, and Jerry Douglas.

Sundance played Huck Finn's, that night. This is the club where Steve Spurgin played with us every Sunday night. Everyone who played the Long Beach Festival showed up and we had a great time.

April 30 Greg Humphrey is a bass player and I played the Barn with his band. Later on, he played in Jo El'Sonje's band. Jo El' is a Cajun accordion player.

May 1 BCH played Cal State at Fullerton. After the show, a review came out in The Daily Titan and staff writer, Becky Goalby said the following:

"It's hard to believe three middle-aged men playing guitar, banjo and fiddle could generate as much enthusiasm as Don [Dan] Crary, Byron Berline and John Hickman did in the Pub Wednesday."

We were in our thirties.

Goalby went on to say:

"Crary didn't prowl or growl. Berline didn't leap about or smash his fiddle, Hickman didn't leer at the girls. They just played great bluegrass music. And the audience loved it."

She got that right.

May 3 we played Huck Finns every Sunday if we were in town and if there were no scheduling conflicts.

May 4 Hal Southern had me play Newport Beach.

May 8 did Beverly Hillbillies session with Earl Scruggs.

May 8, 9 played the Cal State Old Time fiddlers Association.

May 10 played Huck Finns.

May 13 & 14 BCH played Stockton, California.

May 17 played Huck Finns.

May 20 did "Hangin' On" movie session for Warner Brothers.

May 21 did session for Cher's Show in Las Vegas. We did background music and I remember that one of the songs was "Devil Went down To Georgia." We continued to receive checks from the session for quite a while.

May 21 played a club in Lancaster, California. Another time we played there the wind was so strong it blew Steve Spurgin's cymbals around and I could hardly keep my bow on the strings.

May 22, 23 played Fresno, California.

May 24 played Santa Barbara and Huck Finns that night.

May 28 played a club in Lancaster, California.

May 29 played the Banjo Café.

May 30 played the Pico Rivera Festival with one of the bands. Being involved in several bands, sometimes I get confused about who played where and when. I remember…Rex Allen asked me to play fiddle with him.

May 31 played Huck Finns.

June 6, 7 Sundance played the Chino Festival in Chino, California. The last day we had a three-gig day. Sundance played the Chino Festival, opened the "Stardust" in Hollywood, and played Huck Finn's until 1 am. I rode with Rick Cuhna and I do not know how we made it…antifreeze I guess.

June 12-21 BCH played somewhere.

June 25-28 BCH toured Canada and Colorado.

July 1 did Rob Walch session. Rob did music for Warner Brother's Bugs Bunny cartoons.

July 4 played Molly Halloran's wedding. Her Mother, Ella Rose an organist, wrote music for the Sherman Oaks Presbyterian Church. This is where Bette, Becca, and I attended church and Sundance played the wedding reception.

July 5 played the Cowboy Club with Sundance.

July 10-12 BCH played Good Times Canada at Carlisle, Ontario.

July 18 played the Mason Williams & Friends Concert at the Rocky Mountain Opera in Denver, Colorado. We repeated the concert the following day at the Winter Park Resort at Winter Park, Colorado.

July 16-19 BCH played a Denver, Colorado festival.

July 19 played with Mason Williams for the Madrid Supply Company in Madrid, New Mexico.

July 21-Aug BCH toured Europe and Bette went with me. When BCH went to Scotland and Ireland, Bette and I drove all over everywhere to see the sights. It came time to leave and we had a gig booked immediately in Detroit, Michigan at a bluegrass festival. Bette and I flew out of Ireland's Dublin airport while Dan Crary and John Hickman were scheduled to fly out of Shannon Airport.

August 15, 16 BCH played the Detroit, Michigan Bluegrass Festival. Dan and John's flights were cancelled, or something. When they finally got to the airport in Detroit, they rented a car and got lost on the way to the venue, arriving just in time to play the final set. Bette and I got to Detroit, but without Dan and John, BCH was just B. Bill Box and his band were there and the first set they backed me up, but they had to be paid. The promoter worked something out and took some of BCH's pay to help cover paying Bill. The set went okay, but was not smooth or anything…it felt a little edgy. In the afternoon, Don Reno and his band were there and I told them my story.

Don said, "You play with me and we'll play with you." It was a done deal. We had such a good time. Don is such a great performer and such a nice person.

Don's son Dale and I took a little time off while in Detroit and went through the Henry Ford Museum. I discovered Henry Ford was a fiddle player and started the Ford Fiddle Contest. Ford sponsored fiddle contests at his Ford car dealerships and after all these regional contests; he had the national contest in Detroit, pitting the regional winners against each other. The winner in Detroit got a new Ford Lincoln, a thousand dollars in cash and gigs booked all over the east. That little side trip Dale and I took was quite interesting. Each time I won the National Fiddle Contest (three times) and I got about six hundred dollars and a trophy.

August 18 did a Yamaha session for a commercial.

August 18-22 Sundance played the Crazy Horse.

August 23, 24 Sundance played the Mustang Club in San Diego.

August 25 did a five-hour session with Bill Caswell.

August 26 did Corine and Steve Gillette session.

August 27 played the Lone Star Club.

August 28 did a Harry Shannon session.

August 30 did a Mazda commercial session.

September 8-11 played the Crazy Horse with Sundance.

September 12-20 BCH on tour in Kentucky, Alabama and the Winfield, Kansas Walnut Valley Festival.

September 13 played the Nike Marathon with Mason Williams at Hayward Field in Eugene, Oregon.

September 21 did Rod Stewart session from 8:00 to 11:00 p.m.

September 27 played The Horn with BCH.

October 3, 4 played the Chino Festival. They paid Ralph Stanley, but it took the whole budget so the rest of the bands got nothing. We got zip.

October 8 played Glendale College with the L.A. Fiddle Band and that night we played Lancaster.

October 9 played the Rawhide Club.

October 10 played the Colton Festival.

October 11 played the Phoenix, Arizona Festival.

October 15 played Lancaster.

October 16 played the Swallows Inn, San Juan Capistrano with Sundance. What a surprise! I figured it would be fancy, but not at all. It did end up being quite a fun place to play and we went there many times. Swallows Inn is still there and having music and fun. They are at 31786 Camino Capistrano.

October 21-November 9 toured Europe with some Dutch players.

November 13 played Lucadia, California.

November 14 played in Redlands.

November 21 played a Rick Cuhna Benefit.

November 22 played with Al Bruno.

November 23 did El Newkirk session.

November 24 played the Cowboy Club.

November 25 played the Kickers club.

November 27-29 played the Charles Harding thing again in El Paso, Texas.

December 6 played The Barn in Riverside, California.

December 7 played with Al Bruno.

December 10 Becca turned nine.

December 14 did M. Murphy 10:00 a.m. to 3:00 p.m. session for Capitol Records and played the Barn that night.

December 16, 30 played Kickers.

Journal Entry 1982
Youllneverplaythevalleyagain – Moonshine

January 4-7 did a session in Nashville with Earl Scruggs and Tom T. Hall. I recorded with them and sang tenor, Earl sang baritone and I had the most fun!

Earl Scruggs' youngest son, Steve, was a banjo player and Johnny Warren, Paul Warren's son, was a fiddler, like his dad. Steve and Johnny were at this recording session and they were excited when they came into the studio because they were playing together and were about as good as their dads. They really were good and I encouraged them, but it never happened. Steve's untimely death prevented their success. Johnny went on with his career and made an album with Charlie Cushman, who played banjo. On their 2009 album, Johnny and Charlie played a tribute to Johnny's dad, "Fiddlin' Paul Warren." One of their guests was Earl Scruggs. I imagine Earl was sitting in for his late son, Steve. This is a bittersweet memory. If you would like to see and hear Johnny Warren and Charlie Cushman perform, I believe there are some videos on U-tube. The CD is a nice tribute and Paul Warren was a very good fiddler.

January 8-16 BCH on tour.

January 19-23 Sundance played the Crazy Horse.

January 27 played Kickers.

January 29 played Sweetwater.

January 30 played the Banjo Café and did a Kit Thomas session.

February 4 played the Banjo Café.

February 12 played somewhere with Chris Hillman.

February 20 played the UC Irvine Festival and Swallows Inn the same night.

February 21, 22 Cowboy Maynard and I played somewhere.

I was always looking for new places to play and one day, while driving around in Calabasas, California, I saw a place called "Castle Peak Inn" and decided to stop in to see if we might be able to play there. Castle Peak is a mountain in California's Sierra Nevada and is in the Tahoe National forest.

I met the manager, told him who I was, who I played with and asked if we might get a booking and he said we could play the following Monday. When I got home, I called and asked if they had a PA system and he said, "no, but I can get one."

Skip Conover and I made flyers and put them up all over the Valley and then we started calling people. Monday came and we were scheduled to play at 9 p.m., so we arrived about 7 p.m. to check on the PA system and do a sound check. The manager was not there, but his mother was…drunk and tending bar.

"Oh boy." I thought. "What about a sound system?" I asked

"Idunno." She managed to get out.

By eight o'clock, a lot of people were coming in, but the manager still was not there and there was no PA system. I called Howard Yearwood and asked him to bring his PA system. He and the PA system showed up at 8:55. We had five minutes to start playing. Getting Howard to bring in his PA system saved the manager fifty dollars, who finally came in drunk and happy. We played the show and all through it, people came up on stage and played with us. On the last set, the manager walked up to the stage, downed a shot, and then threw the shot glass to the floor. He got on stage, threw down a microphone and stand and I told him to get off the stage.

He said, "Itsmyplace, Idonhavto."

Rick Cuhna said, "Get off, you asshole" and then helped him off the stage. We finished the set, put our instruments and the PA system away and I went to the manager's office to get paid. I told him we needed to settle-up and then he started to write a check.

"Cash Only," I said. "No checks."

"You'll never play the valley again," he shouted.

I was so mad! I intended to shake his desk a little, but instead, I pulled the whole thing on top of him, the telephone, everything. By this time, Rick Cuhna and Bill Caswell had joined me. The owner of the building came in demanding to know what was going on. When we told him, he ordered a waitress to get our money and then the manager and the owner got into a fight. I got our money and as we were leaving, the owner locked the door from the outside, which kept the manager locked inside.

He pounded on the door, yelling, "You'llneverplaythevall eyagain!"

We never played there again!

February 26, 27 Sundance flew to Mexico City and played a Mexican version of the U.S. Hee Haw type show on television. The show featured country music and had various guests. The first night we were off, so after checking into our rooms we began hunting for mariachi bands by asking the desk clerk who in turn sent us to a park where nothing seemed to be happening. We got a taxi, a big ole Plymouth Fury, all six of us got in, and the taxi driver took us to the city square…Mecca of Mariachi bands. He did not charge us much to do this. There were many bands there, for hire. They would leave for a couple of hours, go somewhere to play and then return. Someone hired them to play a party and off they went again. We really had a great time.

Made the cover of Frets Magazine, March 1982 issue (p 26-31) including a nice article.

March 4-6 played Mason Williams' Bluegrass Symphony with the Eugene Symphony at the Lane County Fairgrounds in Eugene, Oregon.

March 7 BCH played Riverside, California.

March 17 played the Longhorn Saloon in the San Fernando Valley.

March 20 played the Banjo Café.

March 21-27 Sundance did a session for an Italian label, recording at a studio in Topanga Canyon. I did a session with Lee Hazlewood and Sandy Clark on 27 and played at Cabelas. It was another three-gig day.

March 30 played with Chris Hillman and played with Sundance.

April 1 Brian Ahearn called and asked me to do a session with Karen Brooks for Warner Brothers.

April 2 played McCabes.

April 3 played Knotts Berry Farm and judged their fiddle contest.

April 4 played the Rib Rack.

April 15 played Glendale College with L.A. Fiddle Band.

April 17 played the Longhorn Saloon.

April 18 played the Lone Star.

April 23 played the Banjo Café.

April 24 played the Silver Saddle.

April 25 played at Calamitys.

April 27 Dennis Caplinger and I played Carlsbad Pizza with Sara and Sean Watkins and Chris Thile, all of Nickel Creek. They were just kids and they came down and sat in with us.

April 29 played Lancaster, California.

April 30 played the Palomino.

May 2, 3 played at Calamitys.

May 7 played Knotts Berry Farm.

May 8 held the Mariners Church social. When Bette and I moved to Sherman Oaks, California we joined the First Presbyterian Church, which sponsored a group called the "Mariners," organized mainly for fellowship. We came up with different things to entertain the group and because our house had a very large backyard, we hosted a Mariners get together. Two or three hundred people attended and they brought chairs or sat on blankets spread on the ground. Cecil Hyatt came to visit us quite often and he was there when we had this party, Sundance played, we had a lot of food and a keg of beer.

Sundance was booked to play the Banjo Café that night and the next morning we had to be up early to leave on a northern California tour. We were gone a week and when I finally got home Bette informed me that the family next door had found some music equipment in their back yard shed.

When I opened the door to our picking room to investigate, all my equipment was gone...the PA system, microphones... everything. There was my mandolin, sitting right there...they did not take it. Months later, I walked home from the gym after working out and an African American man approached me and said he might have some of my things. I got my PA board back, but I never did find out what the real deal was on all of that.

May 19 played in San Diego with Dick Tyner who produced Norco festivals and recorded with Bluegrass bands.

May 20 played the Belly Up Bar with Sundance. This place is south of L.A., almost to San Diego.

May 21-June 8, BCH played the World's Fair in Knoxville, Tennessee. Dan Crary, John Hickman, and I stayed in an old Victorian house where the three of us shared the same room with each having a single bed. We played every day at the Fair and our nights were free. This house also had some African American blues musicians staying there who got up at dawn and began playing and carrying on. We were probably just getting to bed.

One night we played an area festival where they offered us iced tea, which we knew meant moonshine and they poured us a big glass. John Hickman took it back to our room and set it on the floor beside his bed. He knocked it over and it stripped the varnish right off the floor.

Cas Walker invited us to be on his local TV show in Knoxville. Walker had a friend in the hospital and he went into this big

1982, Hee Haw's Million Dollar Band, front row l to r; Byron Berline, Roy Acuff, John Hartford, Norman Blake, back row l to r; Earl Scruggs, Marty Stuart, Roy Clark, and a staff bass player.

production of pleading with the viewers to donate blood. "He's gonna die if he doesn't get the blood." He pleaded. Think about the poor man in the hospital watching this on live television. Then he introduced BCH "We got three guys here to play." When we began to play, Cas's little dog got loose and ran right over to our feet. Cas walked into the set, right between the camera and us, got the dog, and carried him out.

June 9-13 toured with Sundance and then went back to Nashville. Sundance had a one-day gig to play a festival in Knoxville, Tennessee. Pure Prairie League was there and Jerry Jeff Walker. My brother Leonard, went with us and we arrived in the morning. Bill Caswell lived in Nashville and he drove from Nashville to Knoxville, about two hundred miles, to be there. This was Saturday night and people started arriving, filling up the place. They had beer and food for us back stage and then it began to rain. A local band played first and it was almost dark by that time. We did a couple of songs and a deluge began. It just poured and shut everything down. We quickly got about half of our pay. Nobody got to play, Jerry Jeff Walker or Pure Prairie League and the audience demanded their money back. No one else got paid. We got out just in time and drove back to Nashville.

Sunday we appeared at Opryland's Grand Masters Fiddle Contest. That night we played the Station Inn in Nashville.

June 16, 17 went to Nashville and played on Hee Haw with their Million Dollar Band, which included Roy Acuff, John Hartford, Norman Blake, Roy Clark, Earl Scruggs, Marty Stuart and me. We all wore overalls, except Norman. This was a lot of fun!

June 18, 19 played Mason Williams' Bluegrass Symphony with Eugene Symphony at the Hui Concert in Saginaw, Oregon.

June 22, 24 played Mason Williams' Bluegrass Symphony with the Kansas City Philharmonic at Starlight Theater in Kansas City, Mo. Starlight Theater is a huge outdoor pavilion.

July 2 played Palmdale with Roger Reed.

July 3, 4 played Chino Downs Festival in Chino, California. Played the night of the fourth at Ukaipa, California.

July 15 did Kathy Bee session.

July 17 played Lancaster, California.

July 23 played Ashland, Oregon.

July 24 played the Bel-Air Bay Club in Malibu.

July 26 did Snuff Garrett session with Shelly West and David Frizzell, "You're The Reason God Made Oklahoma." Doug Atwell and I played twin fiddles. J. D. Maness was on that session and Tommy Alsop played guitar. Larry Collins and Sandy Pinkard wrote the song for Clint Eastwood's movie, "Any Which Way You Can."

Felice and Boudleaux Bryant wrote "Rocky Top." After "You're the Reason God Made Oklahoma" came out people began listening to it and they took notice of the songwriters, because "You're the Reason God Made Oklahoma" and "Rocky Top" are the same melody. The tempo and some things are different, but the song is the same.

August 2 played Swallows Inn.

August 7 played Cal State at Long Beach.

August 12 played the Market Place.

August 20-22 played Denver, Colorado's Tenth Annual Colorado Rocky Mountain Bluegrass Festival, held at the Adams Country Fair Grounds. This was a BCH (Berline Crary Hickman) and Country Gazette reunion. The Country Gazette Reunion had Roger Bush, Alan Munde, Roland White, and me. Also in the lineup were the Dillards, Hot Rize, the McLain Family, Big Country and many others.

August 27 played the Banjo Café.

September 4, 5 BCH played the Strawberry Festival near Yosemite National Park. Bill Monroe was there and asked me to play on his set. He told me to get some fiddlers together...I got Sam Bush, Dennis Fechet and Glen Duncan. Glen played in Bill's band at this time. Sam Bush was thrilled...he finally got to play with Bill Monroe. Sam, Dennis, Glen, and I played and Bill sure was tickled with what he heard.

September 6 played the Topanga Festival.

September 10-12 BCH played the Louisville, Kentucky Fried Chicken. It was all free and really, a neat deal. Bill Monroe was always there. Doug Hutchins (bass player with Bill) organized this and we gave Bill a Birthday present. Bill came on stage, put his hat on my head, and joined us. He sure was excited!

September 18, 19 played Grass Valley, California.

September 24, 25 did east coast tour in Boston, Massachusetts and we played Lincoln Center in New York City. Bill Monroe was there and they booked several other acts like the Lewis Family and Del McCrory. We did a sound check then a photographer wanted to take a group shot of everyone in the show. I purposely stood next to Bill…knowing how he could be. I remembered the time someone tried to take his picture with a little Brownie camera. They asked him to step back and Bill said, "You move back."

This time the photographer climbed up a ladder attempting to get this big group in the shot. Sure enough, she said, "You, with the hat on…" that was Bill. " Would you move over?"

I could feel Bill bristle. He said, "We don't have time for this."

October 5-11 did a Holland Tour with the Dutch players and John Hickman or Skip Conover may have gone with me.

October 14 played Glendale College.

October 14-16 did Sundance Tour.

October 20-November 1 did a Sundance tour through Texas, Oklahoma, and Kansas. While in Oklahoma, Ken Munds asked the whole band to do a recording session. Ken played with the Brush Arbor band in California. He had moved back to Oklahoma and wanted us to cut an entire album with him in one day…the whole band. We went to the Christian World Studio and arrived in the morning. The engineer was also a drummer named Steve Short, who played all over everywhere and at one time, was Reba McIntyre's drummer. We got him in trouble because we had beer cans scattered around this Christian studio. I will tell the rest of that story when we come to it, in 1995.

November 2 played the Banjo Café with BCH.

November 5 played San Juan Capistrano.

November 6 played Banjo Café with BCH.

November 7 BCH did a live radio show on KPFK in Los Angeles. Dan Crary drove his BMW and while we were in the studio, someone broke into his car and stole his radio. This had unfortunately, happened to him before.

November 9 played the Banjo Café with BCH.

November 12 BCH played the Old Time Café, a neat place.

November 13, 14 played Knotts Berry Farm.

November 16-20 played the Crazy Horse with Sundance.

November 21 played the San Bernardino Community College.

November 23-26 played the Longhorn Saloon.

November 27 played Cabelas.

November 30 played the Banjo Café with BCH.

December 2, 4, 5,9,12,16,17,18 did the play "Other Woman's Child," which has a lot of bluegrass music in it.

December 3 played the Banjo Café with BCH.

December 7 played the Belly Up Club in Solano Beach.

December 10 played the Banjo Café with BCH on Becca's tenth birthday.

December 11 played the Crazy Horse Bluegrass Festival.

December 19 played the Great American Music Hall in San Francisco with BCH. This was a benefit for Sam Bush, now a cancer survivor.

December 21-28 played the Banjo Café.

December 31 played New Year's Eve with Sundance at the Swallows Inn and that is how Bette, my brother Leonard and I rang in the New Year.

Journal Entry 1983
Australia – Africa – China – Canada

January 5, 6 did a session for Delia Bell produced by Emmylou Harris.

January 7 played Old time Café with BCH.

January 5, 8, 9 did the play "Other Woman's Child."

January 11 played the Banjo Café.

January 13 did another Delia Bell session.

January 15, 20, 21 did the play "Other Woman's Child."

January 18 played the Banjo Café.

January 24 did a sound track session for the play "Other Woman's Child."

January 25-February 14 toured Australia with John Hickman and Vince Gill and Bette went with me. They invited John, Vince and I to be presenters at their nationally televised Country Music Awards show, which was a very important deal. I did my line, then, John looked at the next line and said, "Vince, you haven't had much to say, why don't you read this next nominee."

It was some long, complicated name and John could not figure out how to pronounce it. Vince handled it all right.

February 18 played Swallows Inn.

February 19 played Banjo Café.

February 22 BCH played Carlsbad Pizza Place.

February 23-March 20 did European Tour.

March 23 played the Belly Up Club.

March 29 played the Banjo Café.

April 1 BCH played the Old Time Café.

April 5 played the Banjo Café.

April 6-10 played Mason Williams' Bluegrass Symphony with the Arkansas Symphony at Robinson Music Hall in Little Rock, Arkansas. Governor Bill Clinton showed up and played a comb at a pre-show get together.

April 12 did M. Murphy session for Capitol Records.

April 15, 16 BCH played South Plains College at Leveland, Texas for Alan Munde and others teaching there.

April 17 played Mason Williams' Bluegrass Symphony

with the Longmont Symphony at the high school in Longmont, Colorado.

April 19 played Glendale College.

April 20 played with Howard Yearwood, a good guitar picker.

April 22, 24 played San Antonio, Texas.

April 23 played Bakersfield.

May 29 played with Mason Williams at Riverfest at the Riverfront Park in Little Rock, Arkansas.

May 3-June 11 did USIS Tour (United States Information Services) in Northern Africa. Roger Reed, John Hickman, and I went on this tour. Roger was a good guitar player and singer and he had been in the L.A. Fiddle Band. They only speak French in Northern Africa and we had a fellow who spoke French, with us the whole time. Our first stop was Katmandu, Nepal. We went to Tunisia, Israel, Jerusalem, Algeria, and Morocco. We got a Moroccan rug, of course. On our Nepal stop, I met a kid from Caldwell, Kansas, my hometown. His dad delivered gasoline to our farm when I was growing up. His son was in Communications for the government.

While there, they asked what hobbies we might have and of course, I told them "Golf." They took us to play at a two-hole course and cow patties were everywhere. A little native man wearing a golf hat came by.

"Where do you play?" we asked him.

Pointing to the two holes, he said, "Here and over the there." He motioned back and forth.

The agency made sure we had plenty of time to site see and we took many pictures. It was a third world country and we were amazed at how people can live.

We were outside at this Buddhist temple area, when a fifteen-year-old boy came by and began playing this three stringed, board instrument, shaped like a fiddle and cut out of a log. He used his fingernails to play it and the music sounded Cajun. As he was trying to sell this instrument, we noted he spoke English rather well. He made it by hand, did a good job, and only asked $15, but I did not want to carry it with me on the tour, so I turned him down. He kept dropping the price and finally got it down to $2. While sightseeing, I visited several shops seeing similar instruments, not nearly made as well and were much higher in price. I wish I had purchased his.

We played for the locals, although they had no idea what we were doing. We also played for some expatriates that an ambassador invited to various parties. Ambassador Reed had a palatial home in Morocco where he entertained big wigs. There were beautiful Moroccan rugs all over the house, patios, on the grass and around the pool...everywhere. This was quite an elaborate affair and everyone in attendance was a rich oilman or rich something. The big guest was a man from Nebraska.

Famous for playing the "Rifleman" on American television, Chuck Connors also attended the party. His son played country music in L.A.

Ambassador Reed did not have a clue what bluegrass was or what we did. He worried that neither we, nor our music, would go over with his guests. As it turned out, everyone loved our music, which considerably relieved Ambassador Reed.

When we went to Jerusalem, a Franciscan priest took us through the Stations of the Cross, retracing the walk Jesus made on his way to the crucifixion. This was quite a moving experience. The Muslim prayer towers, which are tall spires with conical crowns, were quite something. A loud recording of a singing/buzzing prayer came over loud speakers out of the towers as the call for prayer and everyone stopped what they were doing. This happened five times a day, dawn, noon, mid-afternoon, sunset and night.

We went swimming in the Dead Sea and because there is so much salt concentrated in it, you cannot sink...we just floated.

The Moroccan King had a forty-five-hole golf course and it is one of the most beautiful, immaculate, flower-studded courses, I have ever seen. It cost $10 to play a round and when Roger Reed, John Hickman, and I rented clubs...we were the only ones on the course.

The next day we went to another eighteen-hole course, touted to be much more difficult than the first and this course required caddies, all of which were French speaking. We picked a couple of caddies to go with us. About the fourth or fifth hole, I hit one into the woods and my caddy took out a nine iron and began looking for my ball. Another caddy, holding a stick, went with him and when he threw the stick into some bushes, two cobra snakes reared up. We immediately got back on the golf course.

Roger and I decided to play more golf while in Tunisia. There was a small man who was a concierge at the hotel where we stayed and when we asked for a taxi, he had to run all the way down the drive to the main street in order to get us one. He told the taxi driver we wanted to play golf, but the driver took us right down town. Roger and I just looked at each other. We saw a man carrying a tennis racket, coming out of a building and we motioned him over to the taxi. We held up a golf ball. He told the driver we wanted to play golf.

The driver said. "Goof."

He immediately took us to a goof course where all the fairways and greens were sand. Roger got a forty-year-old caddy, but my caddy was only about fifteen. Our caddies were a lot of fun and we ended up playing with them as a foursome. We had a ball.

We got hot and tired and inquired where we might get some cold drinks. The caddies climbed a fence, went into a shop, and came out with some cold orange drinks. They climbed back over the fence and we continued to play. When we got back, we tipped them $10 and they thought they hit the mother lode. It was a great day on the goof course!

June 14 played somewhere with Chris Hillman and I played the Banjo Café.

June 16 played with Tom Taffy.

June 17 played the Old Time Café in Carlsbad, California.

June 19 played the Anaheim Convention Center.

June 21 played the Banjo Café.

July 1, 2 played the Rapid City, South Dakota Festival with BCH.

July 3 played a party in Spokane, Washington.

July 15-26 toured China. This was an Oklahoma Friendship Force sponsored thing. A lot of people from Oklahoma went on this trip. Bette's brother and his family went and Becca remembers eating a lot of rice. Becca and Bette worked up some piano things and planned to perform, but they did not get the opportunity because there were no pianos in China…outlawed, pianos had been destroyed during the Revolution. Sometimes we forget to count our blessings.

July 30, 31 BCH played the big Indianola, Indiana Festival. Jethro Burns was on the bill. Red Rector a mandolin player and Cecil Hyatt were there. The last set we got them all on stage to play with us.

August 5-8 played with Mason Williams at the Edmonton Folk Festival in Edmonton, Alberta, Canada.

August 9 played the Banjo Café.

August 11 played the Market Place.

August 12 played the Swallows Inn and did Harry Shannon demos.

August 15 did Simon Grace demos and Dave Diaz Dobro demos.

August 16 played the Banjo Café.

August 19-21 I played the Denver, Colorado Adams county fairground, Eleventh Annual Rocky Mountain Bluegrass Festival, Country Gazette Reunion, and Berline Crary Hickman. Country Gazette had Alan Munde, Roland White, Roger Bush, and me. Billy Ray Latham played a few songs with us, as did Dan Crary and John Hickman.

August 25 did movie sessions.

August 30 Banjo Café

September 2 Strawberry Festival

September 2, 3 played with Mason Williams and opened for the Smothers Brothers at the Turn of The Century in Denver, Colorado.

September 4, 5 played the High Sierra Festival.

September 9-19 did BCH tour in Kentucky and Winfield, Kansas Walnut Valley Festival.

September 22-26 played Washington D.C. with BCH and on to Puerto Rico, via Miami, Florida.

September 27-October 4 played the Banjo Café with BCH.

October 7 played the Old Time Café with BCH.

October 8 played the Banjo Café with BCH.

October 13 did a Paramount movie score.

October 16 played a picnic in Topanga Canyon.

October 18, 22, 25 played the Banjo Café.

October 29 played Norco with Sundance.

November 1-3 did a San Francisco recording session with Don Reno and his kids. Tony Rice played the first day and was suppose to record with us on the second day. They called him, but he said his fingers were too sore. We called him "No Show Rice."

November 8 played the Banjo Café.

November 11-13 played Ashville, North Carolina.

November 16 did session for George Highfill, a good songwriter from Bartlesville, Oklahoma who lived in California. I also played Port Hueneme, California.

November 20 did a workshop at the Blue Ridge Pickin Parlor in Conoga Park.

November 22, 29 played the Banjo Café.

December 3 played the Swallows Inn.

December 4 did a Jo El'Sonje session.

December 10 Becca turned eleven.

December 11 played the Bakersfield Melodrama.

Journal Entry 1984
Jo El' Sonje – My Last Beer

January 3, 7 played the Banjo Café.

January 5 played the Smoke Eye.

January 8 played the Sportsman's Lodge in Van Nuys, a great place to play.

January 29-29 BCH toured Ohio, Texas, and San Francisco.

February 3-5 BCH toured Tennessee and Washington, D. C.

February 7 did session with Michael Stanton a guitar player. That night I played Banjo Café.

February 10-12 BCH toured North Carolina and Virginia.

February 14, 20, 21 BCH played the Banjo Café and again on the 24.

March 4 played the Branding Iron.

March 6 played the Banjo Café.

March 13-15 did Don Reno session in San Francisco.

March 17 played the Banjo Café.

March 20-27 L.A. Fiddle Band toured Texas, Kansas, and Colorado. When we drove back to California from Denver, I was driving and John Hickman was in the front passenger seat. The landscape, covered in snow, was so bright I had on sunglasses. I could see a little black speck in the distance, so I took off my sunglasses thinking I might have something in my eyes or maybe on the lenses. As I drove on the speck got bigger. As we got closer, we could see it was a big truck tire and it was coming right at us. It crossed the highway, barely missing us. Whoa!

April 7 did Jo El'Sonje rehearsal.

April 10 played Glendale College.

April 11, 12 did twenty hours total in Jo El'Sonje sessions. He had very good musicians on this including Garth Hudson, Glen D. Hardin, Albert Lee, and Steve Duncan. Sneaky Pete Kleinow called and said, "Byron, you've gotta come down and be on this. This is better than anything we've been on." By this point in time, Sneaky Pete and I had been on every major recording session in L.A., so he was saying a lot. Moreover, he was right.

I played a show with Jo El'Sonje at a huge club at Stanford

University in Palo Alto, California. Back stage, before the show Jo El' came out in an all white outfit from head to toe. He said, "I've got bugs in my stomach." He was nervous and he meant butterflies.

He said, "I don't feel so good."

We got on stage, plugged in and began moving around. It was almost time to play, but Jo El' was not yet on stage. The audience began clapping while waiting for us to begin. Finally, he came out and I noticed he was sweating. He apparently had a last minute attack of diarrhea just before time to go on. I stood behind him, noticing there was a huge brown spot on the seat of those snow-white pants...it was hard not to burst out laughing.

April 20 played the Banjo Café.

April 24 played Vista Pizza.

April 26 played with Jo El'Sonje.

April 27-28 played Bakersfield.

May 4-7 BCH toured Ohio, Texas, and Massachusetts.

May 9 did a session with Frank Richard who played guitar with Emmylou Harris.

May 10 did Steve Goodman session. He was dying then. He was neat, so pleasant to be around and quite a songwriter.

May 11-13 played somewhere in Michigan.

May 15 did a Bear Country session. I contracted the musicians for Disney and this session was to redo some music. Ralph Hall music editor for the movie "Stay Hungry," also worked for Disney studios in Burbank. Every day they had a jam at noon and he invited me to join them. I distinctly remember...he played a sousaphone. I also met George Wilkins who worked in Disney's music department. He heard me play at the jam and said he might have a job for me. It ended up that I contracted all the musicians for the Bear Country Jamboree music, for the U.S. as well as France and Japan. We also did a Christmas thing.

The bears were big, fur covered animatronics. We recorded the music and the engineers synchronized the bears' movements to the music. Every so often, we redid the recording and put new music out for the bears.

Jack Daniels and I played this gig for Disney and it led to other things. Jack played guitar and was in the Highway 101 band.

May 18-20 toured Virginia and Washington D.C.

June 1 played the Banjo Café.

June 10 played Albuquerque, New Mexico.

June 18 played the Palomino.

June 21-24 toured Colorado and New York.

June 28-July 1 toured Oklahoma, Ohio, and Wisconsin.

July 4 played the Starlight Theater in Kansas City with Mason's Bluegrass Symphony.

July 5, 6 played Mason's Bluegrass Symphony with the Oregon Bluegrass Symphony Orchestra.

July 8 played Polliwog Park in Manhattan Beach, California.

July 14-21 toured New York, Pennsylvania, and Canada.

July 29, 30 played the USOOC Olympic Village. Jack Daniels and I got to play for all the athletes. First thing, this athlete in a USA training outfit claimed to be a sprinter on the USA team, but he was just not convincing. An Australian swimmer was there and he sang along with us. It did not take long for the Australian swimmer and I to figure out this fake athlete was not on the U.S. Olympic team. He just walked across the street and right into this thing we were doing. Security certainly was not what it is today.

August 3, 4 BCH played Dallas, Texas and Hugo, Oklahoma.

August 8-12 played with Mason Williams for the 25 Year Retrospective Concerts/ Gallery Showing at the Arvada Performing Arts Center in Arvada, Colorado.

August 13 did session for producer Jerry Fuller.

August 17 played the Twelfth Annual Colorado Rocky Mountain Bluegrass Festival, held in Denver at the Adams Country Fairground. In addition, the lineup included the Seldom Scene, Doyle Lawson and Quicksilver, The Bluegrass Cardinals, Hot Rize, Last Kansas Exit and many more groups.

August 22 played Knotts Berry Farm with the Doo Wah Riders.

August 25 L.A. Fiddle Band played Cal State at Long Beach for the Soroptimist Club. I drove up and it turned out to be the place I played when I first moved to California. It was the trip Bette and I made in her car, had car trouble, and barely made it to the show. That was in 1969 when I was on the first tour with the Dillard and Clark Expedition.

September 1-3 BCH played the Yosemite Park Strawberry Festival.

September 3 BCH played the Kerrville, Texas Folk Festival.

September 5 played the Palomino.

September 7-9 toured Virginia, North Carolina, and Georgia.

September14-16 played Winfield, Kansas Walnut Valley Festival.

September 19 played the Palomino.

September 23 played San Luis Obispo.

September 24 did session for Michael Stanton, one of the "Bud Girls" in the Budweiser commercials. These men dressed up like women to do the commercials and they really were funny.

September 29, 30 played the L.A. Street Scene with Jo El'Sonje. Stages were set up on the streets and different bands came in to play. On September 29, I also played the Baja 1000.

October 2 did "Fame" movie session for MGM.

October 2-4 judged the Redding Fiddle contest.

October 5 BCH played the Old Time Café in Carlsbad.

October 7 played the Sportsman's Lodge.

October 9-21 on 12 played Mason Williams' Bluegrass Symphony Concert with the Tucson Symphony at the Community Center Arts Center in Tucson, Arizona.

October 19, 20 played with the Alabama Symphony at the Jefferson County Civic Center in Birmingham, Alabama.

October 21 played with Jerry Chase/Daniels.

October 21 played the Palomino with Jason Richards. Jason's dad, Rusty Richards sang with a later version of the Sons of the Pioneers.

November...not much booked for this month.

December 2 played the Sportsman's Lodge.

December 10 Becca turned twelve.

December 14 played the Pizza Place with John Moore.

December 26 played with the Limelighters and the same day played the Freedom Bowl (now called Holiday Bowl) in San Diego with John Jorgensen.

December 27-31 BCH toured Georgia and Tennessee.

Dec 31, 1984 BCH played in Alexadria, Virginia on New Year's Eve. We were booked on the show with the Seldom Scene and the Johnson Mountain Boys. After the show, John Hickman and I got a pitcher of beer and he said, "Let's have a chugging contest."

I said, "Okay, but that's the last beer I'm ever gonna drink."

And it was. I never said anything to anybody about it...I just did it. A few years earlier, I had done the same thing with smoking.

Journal Entry 1985
Traveling the Globe

January 6 played the Sportsman's Lodge.

January 7 played with Al Perkins.

January 19-23 played with Jo El'Sonje and his band in San Francisco.

January 30-February 1 played the Longhorn Saloon.

February 7 played Santa Barbara.

February 13 did Brian Ahern truck studio session.

February 22 played the Old Time Café at Carlsbad.

February 23 played the Crazy Horse.

February 27 played the Melodrama.

February 28-March 5 played Mason Williams' Bluegrass Symphony Concert with the Spokane Symphony at the Opera House in Spokane, Washington. On March 4, I played with Mason for the Community Concert at Thompson Falls, Montana.

March 10 played the Sportsman's Lodge and every teenage boy's heartthrob, Annette Funicello, came in to see us. Her husband came in a little later and they stayed to watch us play.

March 21, 22 played the Rosemont School at Yorba Linda. After auditioning, the school board hired me to give workshops to the fourth and fifth graders...entertain them as well as teach them the parts of the fiddle and the different things it can do, such as birdcalls and train sounds.

March 23, 24 Country Gazette played in Denver, Colorado.

March 27 played the Crazy Horse Saloon.

March 29 played Rosemont School.

March 30 played Lakeside.

March 31 played Knotts Berry Farm.

April 10-13 played Mason Williams' Bluegrass Symphony Concert with the Sacramento Symphony at the Community Center Theater in Sacramento, California. We played two concerts, one on the 12 and on the 13.

April 23 L.A. Fiddle Band played Glendale College.

April 27 played Santa Barbara.

April 28 played the Sportsman's Lodge.

April 30 I sat in for Ray Park at the Mule Lip Saloon, at 1067 N. Mount Vernon in Colton, California.

Mule Lip was a grocery store, converted into a huge county music club. The night we were there, it was talent night. An African American got on stage, all decked out with western hat and boots. He sang, "I'm the Black Sheep of the Family." We thought it was funny and it showed he had a sense of humor, because he laughed too.

May 5-7 played the California Trail Ride in San Ynez Valley. This was a huge event with over 700 riders and they divided the riders into various camps. It was an all men trail ride that lasted a week. The riders were all very important people...governors and the like. Someone pointed out that one fellow looked a lot like Prince Charles...and it was.

May 10 BCH played Leucadia.

May 11 played the Crazy Horse Saloon.

May 15-19 played in Colorado.

May 21 Country Gazette played the Pickin' Parlor.

May 22-30 toured Japan with Country Gazette.

June 2-13 I began a tour of Australia. I got with Chris Duffy over there and we played a Melbourne Jazz Club where two brothers, real outback cowboys, were celebrating their birthdays. They had a great time! They were so appreciative...one gave me his hat and the other, his belt, which he made from harness. I still wear them.

June 15, 16 played the Grass Valley Bluegrass Festival.

June 18 played the Crazy Horse Saloon.

June 20-25 BCH played a festival in Alaska.

July 2 played the Crazy Horse Saloon.

July 4-7 L.A. Fiddle Band and BCH toured Texas and the Langley Festival in Oklahoma.

July 8, 9 did some Disney sessions.

July 9, 16 played the Crazy Horse Saloon.

July 18-28 BCH toured Oregon, Washington, and Canada. We played the thirty-fourth Vancouver Folk Music Festival. Also on the bill were Nanci Griffith, Mike Seeger, Trapezoid, and Riders in the Sky.

July 30 played the Crazy Horse Saloon.

August 2 did session for CBS's Knotts Landing TV show.

August 3 L.A. Fiddle Band played Cal State at Long Beach.

August 8 played the Market Place.

August 9, 10 played the Old Time Café.

August 11 played Palos Verdes City Hall.

August 14 played in Santa Barbara with Tom Ball a harmonica player.

August 17, 18 BCH played Denver, Colorado's thirteenth Annual Colorado Rocky Mountain Bluegrass Festival. They had a big lineup of groups, including the Johnson Mountain Boys, Dave Evans, Riverbend, and Hot Rize with Red Knuckles and the Trailblazers and many others.

One time John Hickman and I played golf at Tory Pines, which is a long course right along the ocean. We got up real early and were the first to arrive. As other golfers began showing up we noticed they lined their golf bags along the building. We were there a long time watching others play ahead of us. We did not know they determined the playing order by lining up your clubs at the door. I sure was mad about that.

Aug 27 began the Brad Boatman project. Brad's dad, Bob Boatman, was one of the directors for the Hee Haw television show. Brad was also a producer and we decided to team up and put together a television show. We called it "Way out West." We wanted to shoot different shows, bluegrass festivals, and rodeos. Our first venture took us to a show in Bakersfield headlined by Doc and Merle Watson. Others booked included Tim O'Brien with his Red Knuckles and the Trailblazers, New Grass Revival and BCH. We filmed live performances, did interviews and then edited the show and put music behind it. Bob Boatman did the voiceovers… it was a wonderful show. Bob's wife was head of programming for the Nashville network and Brad presented our new show to her.

She said, "No, that would be nepotism."

She would not even pitch it to the network. We still have that taped show. We really thought it would fly...something the Nashville network audience would like.

August 29-September 1 BCH played the Strawberry Festival.

September 3 played the Crazy Horse Saloon.

September 4 played the Alpine Village.

September 6-8 BCH began a tour and played Kentucky Fried Chicken in Louisville.

September 12 BCH played Nashville, Tennessee.

September 13, 14 BCH played Washington, D.C.

September 19-26 BCH played Concordia and Winfield, Kansas Walnut Valley Festival.

September 28 played the L.A. Street Scene with a band I put together.

September 29 played with Paul Bowman. I also played the Sportsman's Lodge.

BCH band in 1985, John Hickman, Dan Crary, Byron Berline.

October 4-6 played the San Diego Harvest Festival with Ray Park and Mel Durham.

October 15 played with Rick Cuhna.

October 21-November 21 BCH flew to Point Barrow, Alaska beginning a statewide tour. I bought a video camera, took many hours of video, edited it down to a two-hour video, and put music behind it. We played logging camps, which held most of the events in local high schools. Our transportation was usually via seaplanes, which had pontoons allowing us to land on water. Some of these trips were rather scary…one in particular. While stranded at a logging camp, because things moved in Alaska based on the weather, we missed a couple of dates, but finally got another pilot from a nearby town to fly us to Tanenau, Alaska. He arrived in late afternoon and we knew it would soon be dark and planes do not land on water in the dark. We stood on shore with our suitcases, records, instruments…everything we had to take with us.

The pilot took one look and said, "Can't take all that."

He had a single engine, four-seat seaplane and did not want to take all our stuff and us. I made up my mind that if he said another word, I was not going. We crammed everything in the plane including ourselves. We must have looked like sardines, squished in there with all our stuff. We could not move…could barely breathe. He tried to take off, but could not get high enough. He made another swing around, revved the engine, barely getting high enough to clear the treetops. There was absolute silence during the trip…no one said a word. The sun went down and it was dark when we arrived in Tanenau. He circled the town as a cue for everyone to come outside and turn on their car headlights so we could see to land on the water.

The pilot tried to land, but pulled the plane up saying, "Shit!"

There was a big log in front of the plane. We did finally land, floated to the dock and we were so glad to get there. We got out of the plane and unloaded everything, but the only way up the steep bank was on a snow covered narrow plank with a ten or fifteen-foot drop on both sides. We all loaded up with luggage, records, instruments and everything else we had and began the treacherous walk on that plank. It was a good thing it was dark… we never would have made it if we had seen what we were doing. The next day I looked down at that plank and wondered how we ever made that walk.

Someone drove us to the two-story log hotel where the three of us would stay.

We played at the High School and the band teacher from Seattle, Washington, showed us around. We had a jam with the locals and met Joe Folger who played a homemade mandolin. He opened the case, inside was a cheap mandolin and a six-pack of Hams beer. The Eskimo natives seemed to drink a lot.

Every so often Joe would say in a low voice "Want a beer?"

I would say "No, thank you" each time…this went on until midnight. We had to get up early to get to the airport, so John, Dan, and I went upstairs to bed. We slept in parkas with blankets over us and were still cold; there was very little heat. At 5 am, we awoke to loud hollering and a fight downstairs. It seems the band teacher had insulted a student and some of the student's relatives were there. It is a wonder they did not kill him.

Dawn finally broke and we got up. They suggested that we might enjoy going to the airport by way of a dog sled, but they really could not do so as there was not enough snow. They hooked up a Volkswagen body to the dogs, which is what they used to train them in the summer months. We were drinking coffee and the dogs outside were hyper. It was not long before a man grabbed the latched door and yanked it open hardware and all. He tore outside and went after dogs that had broken loose, pulling the Volkswagen body behind them. I had my video camera running the whole time and got it all on tape.

December 10 played with Tony Trishka and Becca became a teenager.

Journal Entry 1986
Stone's Rag — Double Trouble — Cinderella

January 19 played the Sportsman's Lodge.

January 25 played the Old Time Café.

January 26 played the Sportsman's Lodge.

January 30 played with Harry Shannon.

February 13-20 BCH toured the Northwest part of the U.S. and Canada.

March 13 John Hickman and I flew to Oklahoma City and played for the National Indoor Track meet, which was set up and hosted by my track coach J. D. Martin. J. D. plays guitar and is a good friend.

March 19 played the Crazy Horse Saloon.

March 22, 23 played Knotts Berry Farm.

March 23 played the Sportsman's Lodge.

April 10 played with Harry Shannon.

April 12 BCH played McCabes.

April 13 played in San Diego.

April 23-27 played in Washington, D.C.

April 29 played the Glendale Community College

May 1, 2 played in El Paso, Texas.

May 2 played in Ojai, California with Pete Feldman.

May 3 played Laguna Beach.

May 4 played the Sportsman's Lodge.

May 5-7 played the California Trail Ride at Rancho Vistaderas.

May 10, 11 BCH and/or L.A. Fiddle Band played a festival at the Calico Ghost Town.

May 17 played the Mule Lip.

May 18 played with Archie Francis a drummer living in the L.A. area. Archie played a lot with different people. I also played Bandstand the same day.

May 25 did a TV show Paul Bowman produced for a local network. Don Whaly was on it and some other artists, including Jack Daniels and I remember Steve Duncan played drums.

May 26 played the Sportsman's Lodge with Sundance.

May 31 played with Jason Richards.

June 3 did demos with Steve Duncan a drummer in Chris Hillman's band, with John Jorgenson, Bill Bryson, and Herb Pedersen.

June 6 BCH played the Old Time Café.

June 7 did Paul Bowman TV show.

June 8 played the Palomino.

June 11-14 played Mason Williams' Bluegrass Symphony with the Denver Symphony at the Denver Center's Boettcher Hall in Denver, Colorado. We played two concerts, one on the 12 and on the 14.

June 17 did the Paul Bowman TV show.

June 20 BCH played the Telluride Festival.

June 21 played with Mason Williams for the Napa Country Arts Council Benefit at the Clarion Inn in Napa, California.

June 24-26 did session with T. Bone Burnett for MCA.

June 29 did a three-gig night at Long Beach, Manhattan Beach, and the Sportsman's Lodge.

July 4, 5 L.A. Fiddle Band and BCH played Joe Hutchison's festival in Langley, Oklahoma,

July 6, 7 L.A. Fiddle Band and BCH played Nacogdoches, Texas Festival.

July 10-13 BCH played Winnipeg, Canada Festival.

July 15 did T. Bone Burnett session.

July 18-20 BCH played Atlanta and Ohio.

July 24 played the Market Place.

Jul 25-27 played Jackson Hole, Wyoming.

July 31-September 1 toured Europe the month of august.

September 13 played McCabes.

September 14 played the Sportsman's Lodge.

I played a Norco festival during the summer of 1986. I have this little deal here, a broken piece of a bow glued to cardboard and it reads…it is a little faded, "This is the remains of Bruce Johnson's fiddle bow after attempting "Stone's Rag."

It was about one o'clock in the morning and I was walking through the campground in Norco's Prado Park. Terry Carroll, who worked on my fiddles and everything, Bruce Johnson, Dennis Fetchet, and Steve Langford were just sitting around talking. Steve was playing around on the guitar. Terry Carroll saw me carrying my fiddle case and said, "Get that out, and play "Stone's Rag."

I took out my fiddle, we started playing, and it all sounded real good. I guess Bruce had been drinking because he got his fiddle and started playing..."Cotton Patch Rag" instead of "Stone's Rag." I admit they are in the same key and have the same chords.

I said "Oh, Cotton Patch Rag."

"Is that what that is?" He said.

"That's all right. Play it," I told him.

"No, I want to play "Stone's Rag." Start over."

We did and he got off on "Cotton Patch Rag" again...Bruce was definitely upset. He said "God Damn it!" then proceeded to break his bow on the back of a chair, then turned around and stomped off. The next morning I walked to where we were the night before and saw that piece of bow. I thought, "I want this. I'm going to mount it and someday put it in my fiddle shop."

Bruce knows about it. I told him "I've got that broken piece of bow hanging up in my shop, hanging up, just to remind me of what you did."

"Aw, I know it." He growled.

September 18, 21 BCH played Winfield, Kansas Walnut Valley Festival.

September 27 played a radio show and fair in Denver, Colorado.

September 28 played Follows Camp Bluegrass Festival.

October 2-5 played Tucson, Arizona Festival.

October 6 played with Doug Thomas.

John Hickman and I recorded an album of duets on the Sugar Hill label called "Double Trouble," which they released in 1986. We recorded this at Boutwell Studio in Birmingham, Alabama and Weddington Studios in Van Nuys, California. We did Double Trouble, I Don't Love Nobody, Cajun Waltz, Tugboat, Liberty, Blackberry Blossom, Indian See Saw, The Old Rugged Cross, Sugar In The Gourd, Time Changes Everything and of all things, the Funky Chicken.

October 7, 9 played with Patsy Clark, a bass player.

October 12 played the Sportsman's Lodge.

October 23 did Michael Stanton/Jay Turnbow session.

October 24 played with Steve Duncan at the Troubadour.

October 31 did Rosie Flores session for Warner Brothers, produced by Steve Fischel who played steel with Emmylou Harris.

November 3 did Steve Stone session.

November 15 played Santa Barbara.

November 16 played with T. Bone Burnett.

November 29 played with Jason Richards.

December 4 played with Mark O'Connor.

December 10 Becca turned 14.

December 11 BCH played the Old Time Café.

December 13 played for a Kris Kristofferson Party.

December 16, 17 played for Disney for six hours.

December 19 did a Vince Gill session for RCA. He sang, "Cinderella" and I played on this recording. I remember he borrowed my mandolin to do some over-dubs.

Journal Entry 1987
Dealing in Instruments — Europe — Woody Paul

January 12 did M. Glodell session.
January 24 BCH played McCabes.
January 27 played the Palomino.
January 31 played the Longhorn.
February 4 played with Russ Gary.
February 7 played the Pizza Place in Vista with John Moore and Dennis Caplinger. John Moore's sister, Julie, played guitar and sat in with us sometimes. When John, Julie, and Dennis were children, they played together and made an album, which I produced. This is another special memory of "passing on the music."
February 14 played with Evan Anderson, a mandolin player with Wild Oats.
February 20-22 played Dallas, Texas.
February 26 BCH played the Old Time Café.
March 12-15 played Oklahoma City.
March 16 played with Duke Davis a cowboy singer.

John Hickman and I had a friend named John Graf who dealt in stringed instruments and he was always checking swap meets, newspaper ads…anywhere he might find instruments. One day in March of 1987, he called and asked if I wanted to go with him to a friend's house to see some fiddles. His friend had a stroke and needed to sell his instruments. His friend, John Plata, played tenor banjo…he played jazz. After the stroke, he could not use his right arm. He could talk, but could no longer play the banjo. Graf cautioned that if Plata liked you, he would do right by you, but if he did not, he could be cantankerous. When we entered the home of Mr. and Mrs. Plata, the musty, old instrument smell was overwhelming. I remember Plata's wife, in her nightgown, lying on the sofa eating chocolates while smoking a cigarette and watching a black and white television set. Now, couple that with the overpowering smell. Plata showed me through an open bedroom door. The room was stacked from floor to ceiling…I am not exaggerating, with stringed instruments…it was amazing and Graf and I spent some time going through many of those instruments.

After a while, Plata said, "Maybe we should go to the garage and really show him (me) something."

We went to the garage and overhead, in the rafters alone, there were over 200 fiddles, some of which Plata had not looked at for over twenty or thirty years. Plata was a stringed instrument-swap meet addict. Daily, for forty years, he left his home, went to swap meets, garage sales, estate sales, anywhere he might find instruments or parts of instruments and never came home empty-handed. He also had over 10,000 records. John Graf and I began climbing through the stacks and going through fiddles covered with mud dauber nests, dust, and dirt. I remember getting sick from going through this stuff.

Dad dealt in fiddles for many years and when he died, he had thirty…I have some of them today. I never had the desire to deal in fiddles until the day I met John Plata. I picked out thirty fiddles that day, many of them in disarray. I asked him how much he wanted for them and Plata said "Oh, $800." I took them home and began cleaning and putting the pieces together, setting them up the best I knew how.

Plata knew that I wrote articles for "Frets" magazine for several years and he showed me an old magazine from the 1920s… called "Frets," but was not connected to the current day publication of the same name. It was very interesting.

I went back to John Plata's, took some of his instruments home with me and as a favor to him, I set them up and then took them back to him so that he could sell them at swap meets and other places. When he finally decided to move to Colorado, I helped him dispose of bag after bag of necks, tailpieces and other instrument parts. It broke my heart, but it had to be done…he had to get rid of everything.

One time I called someone to repair something on my fiddle and he wanted a thousand dollars to do the job. I called a friend of mine, Terry Carroll who repaired stringed instruments and he said, "Bring it over and I'll fix it."

I of course, wanted an estimate.

He said "Oh, don't worry about it."

Well I did worry about it. With all said and done, he charged me nothing. He also said, "Anything that needs fixing, I'll take care of your instruments."

Without his help, I never would have been able to turn those thirty fiddles into the number of quality instruments I have today. I have been dealing in instruments ever since, learning so much along the way. Bette reminds me that when we left California in 1995, we carried out of the house, thirteen guitars, one hundred and thirty fiddles, three or four banjos, twelve mandolins, and those are what I used to open the Doublestop Fiddle Shop in Guthrie, Oklahoma. During the years since 1987, I have continued dealing in instruments...buying, selling, and trading, but it all began with those first thirty fiddles and yes, it can be addictive.

March 17 played with David McElvey a harmonica player who played on "You're The Reason God Made Oklahoma." I also had him do some stuff on Bear Country. David was an often sought after player.

March 19 BCH played in California at a show that celebrated the state of Kentucky. Ned Beatty, the actor, was there and Florence Henderson sang. Ned loved bluegrass and came to the Banjo Café to see us. Dustin Hoffman dropped in to see us, too.

April 1, 3 did George Highfill session for Warner Brothers. George is from Oklahoma.

April 4, 5 played the L.A. Country Scene. This was a huge festival and they booked the L.A. fiddle band and every group of which I was a member. They booked over fifty acts. The man heading this up worked for the L.A. Times and he helped get lots of folks in there. We did this a couple of years and if a group was good...they were there.

April 9-11 played Humbolt State.

April 12 played in San Francisco.

April 25 played Red-White Alumni OU Football game. My friend and former track coach, J. D. Martin and I played two or three tunes at half time on the fifty-yard line.

April 28-May 19 John Hickman and I played a fiddle festival in the Shetland Islands and toured Europe with Dutch musicians.

May 20 played with Al Perkins.

May 25 played with David McElvey.

May 26, 27 played the Longhorn Saloon. Also on the 27, I played with Ed Freeman.

May 28 Peter Feldman and I played somewhere.

Here is a story about one time when Peter and I played together. I will let him tell you how he remembers it.

Peter: Byron and I have enjoyed working as a duo from time to time, as well as with full bluegrass bands. Here is a musical moment from a parking lot show from a city function way back in the last millennium. We were on a temporary stage set in a shopping center parking lot. Our audiences included walk-ins and drive-bys, with people honking their horns for applause. There's no business like show business.

May 30 played with Jason Richards.

June 2 played with David McElvey.

June 3 played with the Doo Wah Riders.

June 6, 7 played the Follows Camp Festival with the L.A. Fiddle Band.

June 9 I played with Eddie Dunbar a very good bass player, singer and songwriter. He looks just like Mel Gibson and he is a crazy man who I like a lot, although he was a loose wire. I used him in the L.A. Fiddle Band and every time I needed a good bass player. He played on my album "Jumpin' the Strings." Eddie ended up playing a year or two with the Doo Wah Riders and they played a lot. He even got a major recording contract, but Eddie had one problem...he could not keep his mouth shut. When this record deal came up, we told him to, "Just go along with whatever they want...don't fight them. Do whatever the label wants you to do." He blew the whole deal...we knew he would because he just could not keep his mouth shut.

June 10 played the Longhorn Saloon, probably with the Doo Wah Riders

June 12 played McCabes.

June 13 played Porterville, California Festival.

June 14 played the Alpine Village Festival.

June 19 BCH played the Telluride, Colorado Festival.

June 26, 27 BCH played the South Dakota Black Hills Festival.

July 2 played Nacogdoches, Texas.

July 3, 4 played the Langley, Oklahoma Festival.

July 5 played UC at Riverside.

July 25 played "Music from Bear Valley" at the Bear Valley Lodge in Bear Valley, California.

July 8 played with Brush Arbor.

July 18-20 BCH played Vancouver, Canada Folk Festival.

Woody Paul, of Riders in the Sky is a very good musician. He is a weird dude and I like him, a lot. One time we were playing in Vancouver, Canada at a Folk Festival. Someone set up a golf game and the next morning John Hickman, Woody, and I planned to play. The night before the festival ended, they had an after party with all the musicians and friends, invited. It was after midnight when John and I were getting ready to go to our rooms because we were going to play golf early the next morning. As we were leaving the party, Woody Paul walked in.

Woody said, "Byron, I can't get in without my name tag and I don't have it with me. Can I borrow yours?"

"Why sure!" I told him. "I'm going to bed. I'm not going to use it anymore."

He said, "Wake me up in the morning when you're ready to go."

The next morning about 7 am, I knocked on his door and when he finally opened it, I asked if he had a late night.

"He said, "Yeah, I met this girl and we ended up coming up to my room." Then he said, "I never did use my real name."

That girl thought Woody Paul was Byron Berline, because of my nametag. "You dog you!" I told him.

July 24-26 played with Mason Williams and his band at Bear Valley.

July 31-August 1 BCH played the Grass Valley Festival.

August 8 BCH played Seattle, Washington.

August 20 BCH played the Old Time Café.

August 21 played Mammoth, California.

August 22, 23 played the Bluegrass Expo. Also on 22, I played Carona/Hot Springs, California.

September 6, 7 Played with Mason Williams' Symphony Bluegrass Concert at the California State Fair in Sacramento.

September 9 did a session with Judy Robinson. Judy and her sister were very good singers.

September 11, 12 BCH played Johnson City, Tennessee at the Down Home Pickin' Parlor.

September 13 BCH played Louisville Festival.

September 17 BCH played Wichita, Kansas and Winfield, Kansas Walnut Valley Festival.

October 4 played the Peninsula Fair.

October 7 played Bob Wills Jr. show…not. A man called saying he was Bob Wills Jr. and he said this to everyone he met. He was big, probably 300 lb and about six feet four inches tall. He wanted to put on a benefit show in an old hotel in downtown L.A. He had rehearsals at his house and when we arrived, there was a bus parked out front with "Bob Wills and the Texas Playboys" on the side. Something just did not ring true. Inside the house, there were no family photos. I called Johnny Gimble and he said Bob had no son…unless an illegitimate one. Bob Wills had no son.

He hired Joan Kassel to judge a contest thing, had uniforms made for all of us, cooked steaks for us, and hired a disc jockey from a radio station to emcee the show. We did the gig, but it was a flop with only about fifty people in attendance. I was the first in line to get paid and he did pay me, but the others complained they never got any money. We never again did anything with this person.

October 10 played the Fret House, a music store in Covina.

October 17 played McCabes.

October 18 played the Riverside Barn.

October 29 BCH played the Old Time Café.

November 12 did session for the TV series "Dallas."

November 17 the L.A. Fiddle Band played Glendale College.

November 29 played with Jann Brown.

December 10 Becca turned fifteen.

December 12 played a House Concert.

December 14 played with Johnny Pierce.

December 19 played with David McElvey.

December 20, 22 played the Bandstand with Jann Brown.

Journal Entry 1988
Kevin Costner - Texas Trail Ride - Indian Reservation

January 9 did demo with Bernie Leadon.

January 30 played with Jason Richards.

February 2 did Kevin Costner session for his "Simple Truth" album. Kevin called his band Roving Boy and he got a recording contract in Japan, which is where they released the album.

February 7 did a workshop at Blue Ridge Pickin' Parlor.

February 8 played with Larry Dean a country singer.

February 10 played with Russ Gary.

February 12-21 John Hickman and I played along the west coast, just banjo and fiddle.

February 20 played the Crazy Horse.

February 22 played with Al Bruno.

February 24 did Kevin Costner session for his Roving Boy band's "Simple Truth" album. They liked the first session and asked me to come back and play on the rest of it. You can hear the "Simple Truth" cut on U-tube.

February 28 played in San Diego.

March 1 played with Al Bruno.

March 11 played with Jann Brown.

March 12, 17, 18, 20 played with Jason Richards.

March 23 played with Ken Orick. Stuart Duncan was in his band.

March 26 played with the Doo Wah Riders.

March 27 played with Jason Richards.

March 31 played with Eddie Dunbar.

April 5 played with Jerry Marcellino.

April 6 did another Kevin Costner session.

April 10 played with Al Bruno. I also played that day with Jason Richards.

April 11 did a session with Cliffie Stone producing.

The rest of April I played with Jason Richards and Eddie Dunbar.

April 28-30 played the Arvada Center in Arvata, Colorado.

May 3, 4 played with the Smothers Brothers.

May 8-11 played the California Trail Ride.

May 12, 14 played with Jann Brown.

May 16 did Santa Barbara session with Tom Ball and Kenny Sultan, ole time blues players. Also on 16, I played with David West.

May 17 played with David West. I also played with Peter Feldman somewhere.

May 18 played with Joey Rand, a keyboard player.

May 21, 22 L.A. Fiddle Band and every group I was with, played Country Fest. This year they wanted some of the older acts, so we got Bill Monroe, Rose Maddox, Hank Thompson, and Leon McAuliffe. I had to put together a band to back Leon... we had Dennis Fechet, John Hobbs and I played fiddle. Red Stegall's band came over and joined us and we doubled every instrument...we had four fiddles. Leon was in tears he was having such a good time.

April 7 L.A. Fiddle Band played Glendale College.

May 22, 29 played Heroes.

May 30 played with Eddie Dunbar.

June 4, 5 played the Follows Camp Festival.

June 8, 9 played with Jason Richards.

June 11 played with the Doo Wah Riders. I also did a gig with David Durham and his Bull Durham band.

June 12 played Brentwood and the Sportsman's Lodge.

June 13 played with Duke Davis.

June 14-18 played the Crazy Horse Saloon.

June 20 played with Richard Green.

June 22 played with Chris Light.

June 23-26 John Hickman and I played the Coushatta, Louisiana Festival.

June 27, 28 played with Jason Richards and Eddie Dunbar.

July 4 played Long Beach.

July 5 did a session for Capitol Records with Pete Anderson producing. Pete, a very good guitar player, played in Dwight Yoakam's band.

July 10 played Polliwog Park in Manhattan Beach.

July 12 played Knotts Berry Farm.

July 21 played with George Wilkins who did some things for Bear Country.

July 22 played McCabes.

July 23 played in San Diego.

July 24-29 BCH played in Cannon Beach, Oregon. We did a weeklong workshop, 9 a.m. until later in the afternoon, six or seven hours a day. Most tiring, taxing workshop we had ever done. Usually, a workshop is about an hour.

Fletcher Bright from Chattanooga, Tennessee had the longest going bluegrass band "Dismembered Tennesseans," starting the band when he was in High School. He came to Cannon Beach and that is where we met. He paid his money, signed up for my workshop...for one reason. He wanted to learn about my bowing. In about an hour, I showed him...he got it and then I asked him to help me teach at the workshop, which he did! He was a very good player.

July 30 BCH played Sand Point, Idaho.

August 5-8 BCH played the Mole Lake, Wisconsin Indian Reservation. Native Americans ran this festival...they had their own security, everything. Their budget for this event was probably in the neighborhood of $300,000 or $400,000...it was a huge festival. The headliners included Dwight Yoakam, Desert Rose Band, John Hartford, Doug Dillard, Buddy Spicer, BCH and several others. There were about 2,000 people in the audience, all adults, as this was not a family event, and they had vendors in booths, selling liquor. The campground was another story. There were 40,000 drunks in the campground and no one dared go there. Performers considered the campground, off limits. This was summer and when the girls removed their shirts and sat on the boy's shoulders, they used fire hoses to cool off everyone. We played the show and the audience paid attention to us or they did not...we did not sell any cds. This was one wild party.

August 9 did session for Bernie Taupin a songwriter having written for Elton John.

August 12, 13 played the Arvada Center, Colorado with Mason Williams and his band.

August 19, 20 L.A. Fiddle Band played Canton, Texas.

August 27, 28 played Cal State at Long Beach.

September 10-14 played the Texas Trail Ride with John Hickman. This was my first year there. The Texas Trail ride is a smaller version of its California counterpart. It is located not far from Kerrville and they call it Tejas Vaqueros Ride. It was always booked right before we played the Walnut Valley Festival in Winfield, Kansas.

Park Meyer worked for Howard Hughes and was still on his advisory board. Park was president of the Trail Rides in California and Texas and always went to the California Trail Ride. He invited us to play…sponsored John and I and paid our way. He showed us around to all the camps. Each one had a president, etc. Park Meyer is a big man, weighing probably three-hundred pounds. The various camps made great big wooden chairs for him.

At the California Trail Ride, I got to visit with Park and get to know him a little. He bought maybe a $100 of my tapes and gave them out to his friends. I found out he was a UT Longhorn and I asked where he was from, originally.

He said, "I went to High School at Caldwell, Kansas."

My hometown…what a surprise! His senior year, in 1936, he played football for Caldwell High School. It really is a small world.

September 17 played with John Moore.

September 20-24 played the Crazy Horse Saloon.

September 29 did Paul Bowman TV show.

October 12 helped produce/mix for Larry Struble. He lived in Denver, Colorado and he had two daughters that played violin/fiddle. He recorded them and then needed a place to mix the recording so he asked me to do it.

October 21, 22 played Albuquerque, New Mexico and Phoenix, Arizona with Mason Williams and his band.

October 25 played the Palomino.

October 27 played Casey Kasem's American Top 40 weekly radio show He always signed off by saying, "Keep your feet on the ground, and keep reaching for the stars."

October 28-30 played Charlotte, North Carolina with Mason Williams.

November 4 played a benefit show for Rose Maddox.

November 5 & 6 played with Heather Miles.

November 7 played a Palm Springs private party.

November 13 played with Jann Brown.

November 19 played Corbin Burnstein's wedding. Corbin

is an actor who played "Arnold Becker" in the TV series, "L.A. Law."

Tommy Morgan played harmonica and he had a whole case of them. He had done mainly studio work reading charts, but had not done many parties, which are casual, so you never know what you are going to play.

He said, "What do I do? There's no sheet music?"

He was in a panic. I told him, "Just get the key and go with the flow."

November 25 played the Rawhide club with Jann Brown.

December 10 played the Fret House in Covina. Becca turned sweet sixteen.

December 14 played with Jeff Rough, a banjo player.

December 16 & 18 played the Rawhide with Jann Brown.

December 17 played somewhere with John Moore.

December 22 played the Palomino.

Journal Entry 1989
Doo Wah Golf – Walk in the Irish Rain – South Pacific

January 5-8 played the Swallows Inn, Capistrano.

January 11 Doo Wah Riders played Simi Valley.

January 13, 14 played the Rawhide with Jann Brown. I also played with David McElvey that day.

January 17 played with Doo Wah Riders.

January 20-22 played Blythe, California.

January 23 played with Jack Arnold.

January 24 played with Jann Brown.

January 25 played for Disney.

January 27 played the Gene Autry Museum of Western Heritage at 4700 Western Heritage Way in Los Angeles' Griffith Park. We played in the museum among various displays of artwork belonging to Phil Anchuts. It is a wonderful place to play and visit.

February 4 played with John Scholoker, a banjo player.

February 5 played the Lighthouse.

February 7, 8, 9 played the Crazy Horse Saloon.

February 10, 11 played the Rawhide club.

February 21-25 played with the Doo Wah Riders.

February 27 played with Al Bruno.

February 28 played with Jay Silverman.

March 1, 2 played with the Doo Wah Riders.

March 3-5 BCH did a Northwest Tour.

March 7 played with Jann brown.

March 10, 11 played the Rawhide.

March 12 played with David McElvey. I also played Gene Autry's Museum of Western Heritage.

March 14-17 played with Jann Brown.

March 22-26 played the Blue Bayou with Dale Watson a good singer and songwriter. He always picked me up when we went to these gigs. I remember telling him one time that I had a song title, "If You Don't Leave Me Alone, I'll Find Somebody Who Will." The next day he wrote the song and performed it that night.

March 29 played with Jenny Richards at the Roxy. Jenny was Jason's sister and Rusty's daughter.

March 30 Hit By Car. This is not a band. I really did, get hit by a car. I tried to run when I could, to help stay in shape and one day while jogging a car hit me. I hit the windshield post; "Wham!" which resulted in a big basketball bruise on my thigh and it got my elbow. I hit the side mirror and it flipped me right up in the air, but it just was not my time. I do not know how I ended up with such relatively minor injuries. The first thing I did was check my fingers to make sure they were all okay. Bill Jackson a fiddle player and a friend I had not seen in a long time, as fate would have it, happened to be there in traffic at the time this happened and saw the whole thing. He got out of his car and said, "Byron, are you alright?'

I told him to get the name and address of the woman that hit me, which he did, but it was bogus information. When the cops arrived, they got all the correct, necessary information such as the driver not even having insurance. I went to the hospital to have x-rays taken. It was a short night because I had to get up at 5 am to catch a plane to Salt Lake City, Utah for a show that night.

April 31played the TV show in Salt Lake City, but I could barely lift my arm…I could not lift up my fiddle. I had to place it in my left hand, using my right hand and then lift my left arm up to shoulder height with my right hand. My shoulder hurt so bad I could barely play. I remember Steve Spurgin became upset because he had not been with Sundance very long and was afraid I would not be able to play the show.

April 4, 5 Doo Wah Riders played the Crazy Horse Saloon.

April 6 played with Jason Richards.

April 7-9 played with Eddie Dunbar.

April 11 played Glendale College and the Palomino.

April 14 played with Jann Brown.

April 16 played with John Moore.

April 18 did a John Hobbs commercial. I also played with Randy Frank.

April 19 played Knotts Berry Farm.

April 21-22 played Guthrie, Oklahoma's 89'er Day 100th Anniversary of the Land Rush. I remember…Barry Patton was there and his bones guru, Cecil Hyatt. I rode in a parade with

Robert Ringrose, Bette's brother and I played live as we rode in the parade. It was so windy we could hardly keep our hats on. Bette rode a horse in the parade, with other past Queens. Her senior year of High School in Guthrie, Bette was the 1960, 89'er Celebration Queen. I remember we also played on a stage set up along Cotton Creek in Mineral Wells Park.

April 24 did Disney movie session for David Anderle who produced Kris Kristofferson.

April 27-30 BCH plus Steve Spurgin toured the coast playing San Francisco, Davis, San Diego, and McCabes.

May 4-6 played Swallows Inn in Capistrano.

May 7-10 played California Trail Ride with Steve Spurgin, John Hickman, and Roger Reed.

May 11 & 12 Sundance played on a train booked by John Green, who worked for Phil Anchuts, President of the Southern Pacific Railroad. For this particular event, they usually booked the Nitty Gritty Dirt Band, but for some reason that was not possible and as a result, Sundance got to play. He arranged a railroad trip from San Diego to Bakersfield. We rode the train, played along the way and people lined the tracks to see the train. This was the year Steve Spurgin joined Sundance and was with us on this trip.

Also on 12, we played San Luis Obispo.

May 13, 14 played the Calico Ghost Town Festival.

May 16 played with Eddie Dunbar.

May 17, 18 played with Jason Richards.

May 19-21 BCH plus Steve Spurgin played in Ohio.

May 26 did a session for Julie Wingfield a good performer and singer who worked a lot at the Calico Ghost Town. I also did a Jann Brown session for Curb Records.

May 27 played with Ray Winkler originally from Oklahoma City. Ray ended up playing bass with the Doo Wah Riders.

May 28 played at City Limits.

June 1 did session for Katy Gadette a singer.

They released the "Now We Are Four" album in January of 1989. Musicians included Dan Crary, John Hickman, Steve Spurgin, and me. I remember that Dennis Fetchet came in to do some twin-fiddle work on it. We recorded this at Juniper Studio in Burbank, California. We did Big Dog, Train Of Memory, Weary Blues From Waitn', Moonlight Motor Inn, They Don't

Play George Jones On MTV, Speak Softly You're Talking to My Heart, Santa Ana, Leave Me the Way I Am, Kodak 1955, and Hallelujah Harry.

I still worked some with Sundance and the L.A. Fiddle Band, but I mainly did things with BCH. Dan, John, and I always made it a point to play traditional fiddle tunes, putting a different twist to them in our arrangements. Dan is such a good guitarist at playing fiddle tunes. I have always thought that Alan Munde and Dan Crary were the tops at playing note for note fiddle tunes.

BCH traveled more. We went to England and to Ireland's Balcher Folk Festival. We traveled and performed all over Europe. I always enjoyed seeing and meeting the many bluegrass groups from the various countries when we toured. I thought it would be a neat idea to bring them to the United States to perform. I believed it would be a good experience for them and audiences here would certainly enjoy their music. I presented my International Festival idea to Joe Hutchison who ran the festival in Langley, Oklahoma and suggested we also might want to have a headliner…maybe someone like Bill Monroe. Joe liked the idea but at that time, we just talked about it.

June 4-18 did European Tour with BCH plus Steve Spurgin. We went to Ireland and I took Steve to various pubs where we listened to a lot of local musicians. These musicians always wore shirts and ties and one of them owned the local music store. They never introduced us around as we stayed a couple of hours, listening to the music. When we were about to leave they asked me to play a tune. I told them I did not have my fiddle with me, so they offered me one of theirs. I heard them talking about the tune I wrote, "Huckleberry Hornpipe." I explained that I did not know much Irish music and they said, "Oh, we want to hear your music." I played "Huckleberry Hornpipe." They wanted one more and I said, "This one is a traditional tune that fiddlers play a lot at home" then I played "Limerock," a bouncy, happy tune. When I finished, a gorgeous girl of about eighteen came out of nowhere. I had not seen her in the audience or anywhere. She had coal black hair and the bluest eyes I have ever seen. She approached me, tears streaming down her cheeks and said, "That's the most beautiful thing I've ever heard in my life."

I looked at the fiddle I was holding and just…thought, "Did I do that?"

It was from this first trip to Ireland that Steve Spurgin was inspired to write, "Walk in the Irish Rain." I think he captured it all in that song and it has almost become an anthem in Ireland.

June 20 did Will Ray session. Will was a wonderful guitar player and his specialty was bottleneck on the telecaster. He was the best at this. Later on, he was in the "Hellecasters" with Jerry Donahue and John Jorgenson.

June 22-July 26 USIS Tour of the South Pacific with BCH plus Steve Spurgin. Like the previous USIS tour, we had an official escort who took care of us and this time we had a soundman. Our first stop was New Zealand then we played Auckland, Wellington and other places.

July 4 they of course, do not celebrate our Independence Day, however Americans living there do and they had a celebration of their own and we played for them.

We went to the Kingdom of Tonga and played for the King. On Sunday everything shuts down…there are no shops open, no drinking, swimming…no anything. We decided to hang out on nearby Kings Island. Although it is fifteen miles from Tonga, the water is so shallow that in theory, you could walk the distance. The escort, soundman, Dan, John, Steve, and I took a ferry. The King's son the Prince was there with his entourage. Some Americans and maybe some New Zealanders, told us about the Prince. It seems he was next in line for the throne succeeding his father as King. There was, however a problem with this. The Prince, rumored to be gay, rejected an arranged marriage. Speculation indicated his younger brother would probably take the throne.

We visited the American Samoan Islands and played for people, then toured Fiji and on to Guadalcanal. Americans are familiar with Guadalcanal and the heavy fighting there between American and Japanese troops during World War II. They shelled the island many times during 1942 and 1943. An official took care of us and made a tour available. He sent a kid, a historian, to go with us and he told us about everything we saw. This little tour was quite interesting. The official then suggested that if we wanted to take a hike we might enjoy going to the falls. This sounded pretty good to Dan and I and the soundman. We began the trek, about four or five miles one way and took notice of several loud explosions and booms off in the distance. The war had been over for forty years, but munitions experts were still finding and discharging explosives. The foxholes dug during the war years were still visible and we could see them while hiking along the trail. It was very hot and humid and about half way there, Dan who was just too exhausted to go on, said, "You all go on. I've got to stop and rest."

We thought we would never get to the falls, but the rest of us went on eventually coming upon a steep ravine...straight down and I could hear the falls on the other side. We were getting into the jungle where it was hot, humid and we were very tired and thirsty. For some reason we did not take any water with us and at that point, I did not want to go on. The official and our escort said they would go down the ravine and check it out. Ten minutes went by and we heard nothing from them. We yelled, but heard nothing in return. The soundman was tall and big but had little feet, maybe size eight or nine and he was clumsy, always tripping. He said, "I'm going down there."

I told him, "I wouldn't do that." The bank was wet, steep and straight down...very difficult to climb and I knew what would happen if he tried it. He took two steps and slid on his butt all the way down. I do not know how he missed hitting trees and killing himself.

The official and the escort eventually made it back up the ravine.

I said, "That's enough for me. I've got to find Dan." Dan Crary was lying down resting with his handkerchief shading the bald spot on his head and he said he thought he had about three poisonous snakes crawl over him. We found a place that sold us cold drinks and waited about forty minutes until the others showed up. What a trip! It kind of tarnished the glamour.

Transportation was limited to half-worn-out jets that backfired. Steve Spurgin was not totally comfortable...at all. The last trip out of there was very tense. We thought we had plenty of time with a day to fly back to the states, California, Sacramento and then on to a gig we had booked at Grass Valley and as headliners, it was a good paying gig. The planes only had certain times of day they could come in and not at night because they did not have working lights. The day came for us to leave and the planes could not come in, so we could not make our connection. We were getting frantic so I called Bette and told her we were trying to let Grass Valley know we might be late, if we were going to be there at all. There is a big military base there and we contacted Communications and asked if they could help us.

"There's a flight that leaves tomorrow for Guam, but it's full." Someone told us.

I do not, and do not want to know how, but he got all four of us on that plane including our luggage, records, instruments, and everything. Dan, John, and Steve checked their instruments; I carried mine on the plane. We called Grass Valley and let them know we were going to be late, but would definitely be there. The four of us did not sleep for forty-two hours. When we finally made connections and landed in Sacramento, we got off the plane to find the only things coming out on the baggage cart were four instruments; no luggage, clothes, nothing else...just instruments. We rented a car and drove on to Grass Valley and although really rushed for time we knew that we could still do the show. We arrived, tuned up, went on stage and played... right on time. It was nothing less than amazing.

July 22 played Mason Williams' Bluegrass Symphony with the Sacramento Symphony at Hornet Stadium CSUS in Sacramento, California.

August 5 played a gig with Kenny Blackwell a wonderful mandolin player and a very nice person.

August 8 played with Jann Brown.

August 11 played with John Pierce.

August 14-21 played Mason Williams Show in Oregon.

August 24 played with Chad Watson, a bass player.

August 26 played with the Doo Wah Riders.

August 27 played City Limits.

August 29 played the Palomino.

September 1, 2 played the Strawberry Festival with BCH plus Steve Spurgin.

September 3 played Pasco, Washington.

September 4 played with Johnny Pierce.

September 5 received payment for work I did on the movie "Blaze" with Paul Newman. Benny Wallace was music director on this and I worked with him in rehearsals to figure out what music to use in the movie. Benny also played saxophone. I remember James Burton played guitar on the sound track as well as Dr. John. Inside the studio, instead of having a huge screen to watch the film footage as we played, we had small monitors. We played "You Are My Sunshine" real slow. There is a nude scene in the movie with Lolita Davidovich. She chose this particular day to visit the studio to see what was going on. She was just gorgeous on the screen.

Upon her arrival at the studio Burton said, "I almost didn't recognize her."

Without the movie makeup and all, the glamour was gone.

A man, calling himself Dr. John, played keyboards for a lot of these sessions. At another one of the "Blaze" recording sessions I

Now They Are Four in 1989, l to r; Dan Crary, John Hickman, Steve Spurgin, Byron Berline.

did some recording alone and kept hearing a funny noise in the headsets. Then the director heard it and said, "What's that noise?"

I got down on the floor from where I thought the noise originated. Dr. John was comfortably asleep on the floor under the piano. The tape was picking up his snoring and I had to get him up and out of there. He just wanted to take a quick nap.

September 6 BCH plus Steve Spurgin played in Los Angeles and I did a Will Ray session.

September 7 played with Dick Wells.

September 9 BCH plus Steve Spurgin played the Tulsa, OK Chili Cook Off.

September 10-13 BCH plus Steve Spurgin played Kerrville, Texas.

September 15, 16 BCH plus Steve Spurgin played Winfield, Kansas Walnut Valley Festival.

September 24 played with Jann Brown and played Canyon Country, out of L.A.

September 26 did Benny Wallace "Blaze" movie rehearsals.

September 27 played with Jason Richards.

September 28 played with D. C. Snyder, only this one time.

September 30 did a thing for Brian Ahern for WEA in Canada.

October 4 did Benny rehearsal, paid seventy five dollars for rehearsals.

October 5 did "Keaton's Cop" TV show.

October 7 played with the Doo Wah Riders.

October 8 played Santa Barbara, probably something with Peter Feldman.

October 10 did "Blaze" session for Disney.

October 14 I played the San Luis Obispo Festival.

October 15 played with Howard Yearwood.

October 16, 17 did another Disney "Blaze" session.

October 18 played with Al Johnson.

October 19-21 played another big celebration in Oklahoma City.

October 22 played City Limits.

October 23 did Disney "Blaze" session,

October 26 played with Susan Raye.

October 28 played the Fret House in Covina.

October 29 BCH plus Steve Spurgin did KPFK radio show.

October 30 played with Glen Clark.

November 3-5 performed and did workshops at South Plains College in Levelland, TX.

November 13 did Disney "Blaze" session and finished at three p.m. I also had a Rehearsal at the Palomino.

November 14 played with Larry Park (Ray Park's son).

November 21 did another Disney "Blaze" session.

November 30 did a TV documentary session.

December 1 did Mark Herd session.

December 10 Becca celebrated her seventeenth birthday.

December 13 did movie Will Orlis session for "RIP."

December 14 did Mike Lloyd session for Arista.

December 17 played KMPC L.A. Country Show…old time with sound effects and a live band. I sat next to Pat Buttram who said things under his breath that just cracked me up. What a funny man.

December 27-31 played the Silver Bullet with the Doo Wah Riders on New Year's Eve.

I played with the Doo Wah Riders because I enjoyed them, liked going to Florida and because some of them enjoyed playing golf.

Kenny Liebenson prefers Kenny Lee Benson so as not to emphasize his Jewish name. Kenny is a real good friend and a lousy golfer. I tried to help him with his game because he wanted so much, to play with the others and me. He just wanted to play so bad.

Disneyworld in Orlando, Florida had a place called "Pleasure Island" and on that island they had a club called the "Neon Armadillo." Instead of hiring local bands to play there, they hired California bands. The Doo Wah Riders and Dave Durham and his band Bull Durham, were booked and they alternated bookings. The Doo Wah's played a week or two, came home and then Dave Durham and Bull Durham would then fly down and play a week or two. The bands rented a house in Kissimmee because the rent was quite reasonable and certainly a lot cheaper than staying in a motel.

During one of the Doo Wah's gigs there, Kenny Liebenson and I went golfing. It was a miserably hot summer day and therefore it was cheap at ten or fifteen dollars to play a round, which included a cart. It was too hot for tourists, but not for us.

In Florida all the homes with swimming pools have them enclosed with a huge screened in thing, almost like a room. There was a house along the side of the golf course and the pool, right up next to the house had one of those screen enclosures.

For some reason, everything Kenny hit jerked left. That is unusual as most people jerk to the right. Kenny hit a couple of balls that did not really connect. The third one took a 45° turn and went like a bullet, straight to the house with the pool. He hit it hard…it was ten feet off the ground and just screaming. It hit the house with a loud BAM! We were 200 yards away and it sounded that loud. We rode the cart up to the house not knowing if anyone was home and as we walked up to the screened room I noticed a dent in metal flashing on the house. A naked lady, lying down and covering her breasts with her hands, was giggling. Kenny's golf ball was lying next to her head. Her husband clad in a g-string bathing suit came out of the house, picked up Kenny's golf ball, and handed it to him, saying in his British accent, "Here's your ball."

This English couple was renting the house. The ball hit the flashing and dropped straight down, which could never happen again in a hundred years.

Even if you do not know Kenny or me…or play golf, for that matter, these stories are hilarious!

I never paid for a round of golf at these fancy country clubs. I either knew someone there or met someone…they always comped my golf and I have played some very nice courses. Kenny and I were playing one day in Palm Springs and his drives just did not work. I told him to try the three-wood off the tees and on the fairways. He hit the ball every time, but it only went about thirty or forty yards. He just could not make contact. On the last of the 18 holes' par 5, he made six shots with the three-wood. I was across the fairway hitting my approach when I looked up and realized Kenny was only about ninety yards from the green… using that three-wood.

I yelled "Nooooo!" but it was too late.

FINALLY, he made contact with the ball. It went over the

green and into a parking lot full of Mercedes and Cadillacs. Bang, boing, bang. It made the darndest noise.

Kenny said, "Should I go find my ball?"

"Don't you even look over there...just keep goin'!" I told him. Kenny really is the greatest person.

Then there was the time Kenny and I played the Dinah Shore Golf Club whose grounds are meticulously groomed...it is quite a place. We left about 11 a.m. for our tee time at 1 pm. Kenny had on sweat pants, sweatshirt, and tennis shoes. He did not bring appropriate golfing clothes; in fact, he did not even have his golf clubs with him. I wore slacks, a golf shirt, golfing hat, golf shoes and I had my clubs. These kinds of courses are very particular about what one must wear while on their courses and Kenny's attire was absolutely, unacceptable.

I asked if he was going to change clothes. He said, "No."

I asked him if he had golf clothes he could put on. He said, "No."

We got to the golf course, walked up to the entry gate finding the person I needed to see. "I'll do the talking." I told Kenny, thinking that maybe he would not be noticed.

Immediately, Kenny said, "I'll need some clubs."

"We can take care of that for you." The man said. "You're going to change clothes aren't you?"

"Oh, sure." Kenny replied. We had thirty minutes. We took off and found a K-Mart and as we were short on time, I told Kenny to get a shirt and slacks. He did, paid for it then changed clothes in the car as we drove back to the golf course.

We played the round and on the eighteenth hole Kenny said, "These pants are a little tight."

I said, "Just take them back."

He took back the pants and the shirt and got a full refund. When the clerk asked why he was returning them Kenny said, "My girlfriend doesn't like the color."

That is the end of Doo Wah Golf.

Journal Entry 1990
A New Band Called California

January 4 did Richie Podler session for Bon Bon. Richie produced Three Dog Night.

January 4-6 played Palm Springs with the Doo Wah Riders.

January 12, 13 played the Crazy Horse Saloon.

January 14 played City Limits.

January 16, 17 Doo Wah Riders played the Longhorn.

January 23 Doo Wah Riders played the Silver Bullet.

January 24 did Harry Shannon session.

January 27 played with John Moore.

January 28 played with George Clinton.

January 30-Feb 3 played the Silver Bullet with the Doo Wah Riders. While on stage playing, Lindy Rasmussen and I noticed a woman about thirty years old, who had a physical tic of some kind that caused her head to nod from side to side. When the music played, other people nodded their heads up and down with the beat while hers went from side to side. When Kenny Liebenson introduced me, he said, "We are going to feature Byron Berline on fiddle." He asked the audience, "Do you all like bluegrass?" This woman, of course, nodded side to side, which Kenny interpreted as "No," she did not like bluegrass. He went on and on saying things like, "Why don't you like bluegrass?" and she kept nodding her head, "No."

Lindy and I tried to convey to Kenny what the deal was, trying to stop him from going on, but it was not until after the show that we could explain what had happened and he felt so bad about it.

The Doo Wah Riders is one of the hardest working bands in the business. They had to learn all of the top 40 songs plus everything they wrote. The Doo Wahs are still out there playing and Kenny is the one heading them up.

February 1 I did a movie session for CBS "Seven Stories," from 1 - 4 pm.

February 5 played with Marty Blair.

February 7-11 Played Mason Williams' Bluegrass Symphony

with the Colorado Symphony Orchestra at Boettcher Hall in Denver. We did two concerts, one on the eighth and one on the ninth. We also played the concert on the tenth at the Pikes Peak Center in Colorado Springs.

February 13 played with C. Price.

February 14, 16 played with Duke Davis.

February 17 played somewhere.

February 24 played H. Saloon in Palmdale.

March 3 played Borego Springs.

March 4 Doo Wah Riders played the Longhorn.

March 11 played the City Limits.

March 13-16 Doo Wah Riders played the Silver Bullet.

March 17 played with Katy Gadette.

March 18 played with Gary Bright.

March 20 did Bobby Vinton session.

March 23 performed with Bill Webb.

March 27 played the Melodrama at Bakersfield.

March 28-April 1 Doo Wah Riders played the Longhorn.

March 31 John Moore, Dennis Caplinger, and I played the Mojave Narrows for the Southwest Bluegrass Club.

April 4-7 Doo Wah Riders played Cactus Corral in Palm Springs.

April 8 played the City Limits.

April 17-20, 22 played the Western Convention in the Riverside area.

April 18 did session for the movie, "Back to the Future."

April 21 I played with Alan Munde at Laguna Nigel.

April 23 did a Bobby Vinton session.

April 24 did session for the Dillards/Heartland for Vanguard. I also played the Pizza Place with John Moore and Dennis Caplinger.

April 25 played the Academy of Country Music party.

April 26-28 Doo Wah Riders played the Silver Bullet.

April 29 Doo Wah Riders played the Redondo Frontier.

May 1 did a Will Ovis session for an HBO movie.

May 2-5 Doo Wah Riders played the Calico Saloon.

May 3 played Glendale College and did a Will Ray session.

May 4 played with David Ferguson.

May 6-10 played the California Trail Ride.

May 11 California played McCabes. John Moore joined the BCH plus Steve Spurgin band and we renamed the group, "California."

May 12, 13 California played the Calico Ghost Town at Barstow.

May 14 did Lucinda Williams session.

May 15, 17 played somewhere with Dave Durham.

May 16 played with Peter Feldman at Santa Barbara Zoo.

May 18 played with the Doo Wah Riders.

May 20 Doo Wah Riders played the Crazy Horse Saloon.

May 22, 24, 25, 27, 28 Doo Wah Riders played the Bandstand.

May 28 played with Pete Martin.

May 29 played a Helen Bartlett party. Helen produced movies and her boyfriend was director Tony Bill. Helen loved our music, came to some of the places we played and she was convinced we should be in movies. Helen was always trying to get that worked out. She threw a big swanky dinner party and hired us. I put together a combination of players and she rented a big meeting room at the Santa Monica Airport. She had the room beautifully decorated and dinner, catered. She really wanted us to "Wow" her guests, but we did not. She clapped her hands and tried her best to get them into it, but they really did not and she just could not understand why.

May 30 did a Bobby Vinton session.

May 30-June 1 Doo Wah Riders played the Longhorn.

June 2 Doo Wah Riders played the San Diego Rodeo.

June 7, 8 Doo Wah Riders played the Silver Bullet.

June 9, 10 played the Follows Camp Bluegrass Festival.

June 12 BCH played Bakersfield.

June 14-18 played Albuquerque, New Mexico, Tucson, Arizona, and El Paso, Texas.

June 21 played at Corona.

June 23 played Pierce College in the San Fernando Valley.

June 24 played with Harry Shannon.

June 25 played the Gene Autry Museum of Western Heritage at Griffith Park in Los Angeles.

July 7, 8 played the Hollister, California Festival.

July 13, 14 played Fairfield and Salt lake City, Utah.

July 17-21 Doo Wah Riders played the Silver Bullet.

July 18 did session for a Will Ovis movie. I did this eerie sound effect on a five-string violin. I pulled the bow across the strings and it sounded kind of strange. He used that sound effect in several movies he produced and I continued to get paychecks for it.

July 21 played Tenecula. David Jackson played bass with the Dillard and Clark Expedition when I joined the band. On the Tenecula gig, David played bass, John Moore played guitar and I played fiddle. Many times, I got a gig and just put together a band of players who were available at that time.

July 22 played New Port Park.

July 24 played with Jeff Steele who later on formed a band called "Boy Howdy" with Larry and Cary Park. I also played the Pizza Place with John Moore.

July 25-27 Doo Wah Riders played the Crazy Horse Saloon.

July 28 the L.A. Fiddle Band played Cal State at Long Beach.

July 29 the L.A. Fiddle band played Polliwog Park in Manhattan Beach.

July 31-August 4 Doo Wah Riders played the Longhorn.

August 2 did a Bob Nitsik session.

August 3 did a Michael Mish session.

August 5 played San Jose.

August 10 played with Wayne Foster in Sacramento.

August 14 played with Mason Williams at the Summer Pop Series at Hospitality Point in San Diego, California. John Hartford was there.

August 17 played with Red Dog Weber.

August 18 Doo Wah Riders played Hollister.

August 21, 22 Doo Wah Riders played the Silver Bullet.

August 27 did a Will Ray session.

August 28 played somewhere with John Moore.

August 30-September 2 California played in Ohio and Kentucky.

September 4 did a Jim Scott session for Virgin Records.

September 8 played a Tony Bill private party. Tony Bill, movie director and Helen Bartlett's boyfriend, had a restaurant with Dudley Moore. Tony also had parties at his house and we played on a balcony. I put together available players and that was the band.

September 10-12 played the Texas Trail Ride with John Hickman, John Moore, and maybe Steve Spurgin.

September 13-15 played the Winfield, Kansas Walnut Valley Festival.

September 22 played the Dana Point Inn.

September 23 played the City Limits.

September 25 played the Pizza Place.

September 28 played McCabes.

September 29 California played the Yucaipa, California Festival.

September 30 California played the Live Oak Festival in the Santa Barbara area.

October 1 played with Jenny Richards.

October 3 did a Michael Stanton session.

October 3, 4 Doo Wah Riders played the Silver Bullet.

October 6 Doo Wah Riders played a private party.

October 7 Doo Wah Riders played the Bandstand.

October 10 played with Louis Roche.

October 12-14 California played Calgary, Canada. They had three clubs, one bluegrass, one folk music and another one. These were run by organizations and individuals offered to put us up in their homes. The first night we played the bluegrass club, the second night the folk music club and the other one on the third night. We packed the places all three nights.

October 15 did another gig with the Doo Wah Riders and we played golf.

October 16 played with Larry King. I also played the Silver Bullet with the Doo Wah Riders.

October 17 played with Jim Lesley.

October 18, 19 John Moore, Steve Spurgin, John Hickman, and I played Mesquite, Nevada's Grand Opening of the Virgin River Inn. They had a nice golf course and Steve Spurgin, John Hickman and I, played it. It was terribly windy that day and about 11 am we stopped to get a bite to eat. Spurgin set his hot dog on the golf cart and it blew away. That was enough for him, but Hickman and I finished eighteen holes.

October 20 played the Gene Autry Museum of Western Heritage in Griffith Park.

October 22 played with Chad Watson.

October 23 played the Pizza Place.

October 25 played the California Trail Ride and I met Buck

Bean who lived in San Juan Capistrano. He is a neat person and I remember playing a party with him.

October 26 played the Gene Autry Museum of Western Heritage in Griffith Park.

October 27 played Borrego Springs with Steve Spurgin, John Moore, and Dennis Caplinger.

October 28 played a Helen Bartlett party.

October 30 did a Billy Swan session. He had a big hit in the 1970's with "I Can Help."

October 31 played the Gene Autry Museum of Western Heritage in Griffith Park.

November 1 did a Dave Pearlman session. Dave is a steel player and he had a studio in his garage. We did sessions there with Frank Stallone, Sylvester's younger brother. I also played the Bandstand with the Doo Wah Riders

November 2-4 Doo Wah Riders played the Cat Ballou.

November 6-8 Doo Wah Riders played the Bandstand.

November 9 played Buck Bean party.

November 10 did a Will Ray session and received payment for Will Ovis "Gabriel's Fire "movie.

November 13-17 Doo Wah Riders played the Silver Bullet.

November 18 played the Gene Autry Museum of Western Heritage in Griffith Park.

November 19 did a session for the movie "One Cup of Coffee" for F. Capp.

November 20 played a Litton corporate party.

November 25 did a John Cornet session.

November 28-December 2 Doo Wah Riders played the Crazy Horse Saloon.

December 5-8 Played with Mason Williams And Friends at Maxwell House in Idaho Springs and the Thornton Recreation Center in Thornton, both in Colorado. We also played Mason's Bluegrass Symphony with the Cheyenne Symphony at the Civic Center in Cheyenne, Wyoming.

December 10 Becca turned eighteen.

December 11-13 did an Eric Bikales session and played the Academy of Country Music rehearsal and show.

December 16 Doo Wah Riders played the Queen Mary ship.

December 18-23 Doo Wah Riders played the Longhorn.

December 27 Doo Wah Riders played a private party.

December 30 Doo Wah Riders played Bandstand.

December 31 played the Silver Bullet on New Year's Eve with the Doo Wah Riders.

Journal Entry 1991
A Killer Waltz-Basic Instinct-Christmas in Connecticut

January 2-5 Doo Wah Riders played the Silver Bullet.

January 7 played with Tom Ball and Kenny Sultan. From Santa Barbara, they are the best white blues players anywhere and I did several recording sessions with them. We played a place that was an old stagecoach stop. Bikers came in and it turned out to be a fun place to play.

January 8 Doo Wah Riders played the Bandstand.

January 9, 10 Doo Wah Riders played Palm Springs. As with most bands, the Doo Wahs occasionally had players out for one reason or another, so when I needed to play and they needed a player; I filled in and became their floating fifth player.

January 15-20 Doo Wah Riders played the Longhorn Saloon.

January 14-16 did a Jim Calvin session and helped him put the album together.

A publication came out on Tuesdays in the L.A. area, called the Recycler. I often looked in the stringed instrument section, as did other musicians. I was trading/buying/selling instruments at this time and sometimes I found something then followed up on it.

Jim Calvin had some instruments listed and when I called him, he knew who I was. He played banjo, fiddle...anything with strings on it. Jim is a big burly looking man, with a beard... looked like a mountain man, yet he was conservative and super nice. We started trading/buying/selling instruments with each other and sometimes went together to look at instruments. That business became addictive. It got into us like a rusty fishhook and once in, it was hard to get out. Years later, Jim Calvin and his wife attended the very first OIBF (Oklahoma International Bluegrass Festival) in Guthrie, Oklahoma. They performed and Jim emceed at the festival.

January 17 did a Marvin Heard session.

January 22 played the Pizza Place.

January 23-27 Doo Wah Riders played the Crazy Horse Saloon, as we had many times. As result, we got to know the patrons that came in to dance and see us perform. On breaks, they played my CD's and people got to know my music. One night someone in the audience said, "Byron, play "Honeymoon Waltz," which is a tune I wrote. It is a nice dance tune and uniquely, only has two chords. While playing the song, a man just fell down on the dance floor on his partner's feet and almost knocked her down. They called the paramedics and everything just stopped for about forty-five minutes. The man died right there…he was only fifty years old. After they removed the body, things calmed down, we began to play again, and people resumed dancing. No one knew the man, but we learned he was from Wichita, Kansas and was on a business trip. He stayed at a hotel across the street, noticed the Saloon, and decided to check it out. His dance partner, Abby, did not know him. Abby looked like a Barbie Doll, blonde, shaped like Barbie and everything. This man simply asked her to dance and she accepted.

The rest of the evening people said the oddest things and as serious as the situation was, they were funny.

One person said to the man's dancing partner, "They were falling at your feet tonight."

Another man said, "Byron…that was a killer waltz you played."

January 29 did a session for Marc Evans who was a drummer and engineer at City Recorders where Dan Crary, John Hickman, and I recorded.

January 29, 31 Doo Wah Riders played the Alpine Village.

January 30 played with Jeff Knoll.

February 3-March 2 Doo Wah Riders played a month long gig at Disneyworld, Orlando, Florida Neon Armadillo on Pleasure Island.

Harry Shannon worked with a movie production company and I had done several recording sessions for him. He was looking for a country band to be in a movie and somehow, he got the name of the Doo Wah Riders and the phone number at the house where we stayed in Orlando, Florida. Kenny Liebenson, leader of the Doo-Wah Riders, answered the phone. From the living room, I listened to Kenny's side of the conversation. I asked him the name of the person on the phone and he said, "Harry Shannon."

I said, "Well, give me the phone."

"I said, "This is Byron."

Harry said, "Are you down there?"

I told him, "You don't have to look any further. This is the band you want."

We talked a bit and then I hung up.

"There you go, boys," I said. "That's how you do business." They could not believe it!

March 10 William Tapia owned a violin shop in Pasadena and he was a very nice man. I went in, always looking for fiddles. He asked me to do some workshops in his shop and he had cookies, coffee...it was very nice. He helped me acquire a very nice Italian violin and a French bow...at a good price. He eventually retired to Arizona.

March 12,13,15,16 Doo Wah Riders played the Silver Bullet.

March 14 played somewhere with Peter Feldman.

March 13 did a Mike Klink session.

March 18 did a Bill Medly session for his solo album. Bill was one part of the Righteous Brothers; the other member was Bobby Hatfield.

March 21, 22 California played SXSW (South by Southwest) in Austin, Texas.

March 25 Doo Wah Riders played Knotts Berry Farm.

March 26 played the Pizza Place.

March 27-30 Doo Wah Riders played the Crazy Horse Saloon.

March 31 Doo Wah Riders played Knotts Berry Farm.

April 1 did a Michael Stanton session.

April 2, 4 played the Alpine village.

April 6 Doo Wah Riders played Knotts Berry Farm.

April 7 Doo Wah Riders played the Bandstand.

April 8 did a Bobby Vinton session produced by Mike Lloyd for Curb Records.

April 9-11 Harry Shannon flew the Doo Wah Riders to San Francisco where we shot our bar scene in "Basic Instinct" starring Michael Douglas and Sharon Stone. We did get to do an original song, but the camera just panned over us and that is all you see of the Doo Wah Riders. "Basic Instinct" was the last movie I did and I did enough acting in it that I finally got my SAG (Screen Actors Guild) card. I still get a little royalty check from that movie. Michael Douglas is very nice and I have a picture of him upstairs in the Music Hall.

April 13 played Barrego Springs.

April 16-21 Doo Wah Riders played the Longhorn Saloon.

April 24 Doo Wah Riders played the Academy of Country Music rehearsal and show.

April 26-29 California played Fallon, Nevada. The last set the sun went down and it got so cold Dan Crary could not hold on to his pick...he could not feel it. John Hickman's finger picks fell off of his fingers and he did not even know it. It is the coldest I have ever played...the temperature was in the 20's.

May 2-4 Doo Wah Riders played the Crazy Horse Saloon.

May 5-9 played the California Trail Ride.

May 11, 12 played the Calico Ghost Town.

May 13 played the Melodrama in Bakersfield.

May 14-17 went to Nashville with the Doo Wah Riders to try and help them get a record deal. We did showcases at the Bluebird Café, but for Jimmy Bowen, president of Capitol Records, we did a special show at a sound stage including snacks and everything. Everybody at Capitol wanted him to sign the Doo Wah Riders...they really liked our music. I knew Jimmy Bowen from working on the movie "Vanishing Point" in 1970 and the song we wrote for that movie, "Runaway Country," because he did the publishing on that. When we did this showcase for him, I saw him in the back of the room and knew he was not at all interested, leaving before we finished. He did not want to sign the Doo Wah Riders because it was not his idea.

May 18, 19 played the Santa Margarita Rodeo.

May 18 played a Bobby Simpson Party.

May 19 played a party with John Moore.

May 20 did something for Disney.

May 21-26 Doo Wah Riders played the Longhorn Saloon.

May 24, 1991 Gene Clark died...he was forty six years old and so was I.

May 28 played the Pizza Parlor.

May 29-June 1 Doo Wah Riders played the Silver Bullet.

June 2-17 Doo Wah Riders played Disneyworld Orlando, Florida Neon Armadillo on Pleasure Island.

June 18, 19 did a commercial for the Southern Pacific Railroad. Phil Anschutz called on me again, this time to record a commercial for the company. I remember Steve Spurgin wrote the number and we recorded it, then Southern Pacific used the recording for things such the music used when customer phone calls were placed on hold.

June 24-28 California did recording sessions every day, 10 am to midnight.

June 29, 30 California played a Bluegrass Festival in San Diego.

July 4-7 played in Oklahoma.

July 10-14 Doo Wah Riders played the Crazy Horse Saloon.

July 18-21 California played Oakland, California and Vancouver, Canada.

July 23 played the Pizza Place with John Hickman and Dennis Caplinger.

July 24-27 Doo Wah Riders played the Longhorn Saloon.

July 30 did a session, but do not know with whom.

July 31 played the HOP with the Doo Wah Riders.

August 1 Doo Wah Riders played the Alpine Village.

August 2 Doo Wah Riders played the Dance Party.

August 3 Doo Wah Riders played Mission Viejo.

August 4 L.A. Fiddle Band played Polliwog Park.

August 6-10 played Mason Williams and Friends concert at the Denver Zoo in Denver Colorado on the seventh, the Hilton in Grand Junction, Colorado on the ninth, and the Gold Hill Inn in Boulder, Colorado on the tenth.

August 11 California played the Las Vegas Bluegrass Festival.

August 14 did a Will Ray session.

August 15 did a Michael Stanton session.

August 14-15 Doo Wah Riders played Crazy Horse Saloon.

August 16-18 I went to Montana and probably judged a fiddle contest.

August 21, 22 Doo Wah Riders played the Crazy Horse Saloon.

August 23 played the Chili Cook Off in a little town north of L.A., with the Doo Wah Riders and I judged the Chili Cook Off.

August 24 California played the Crestline, California Festival.

August 25, 26 played the Santa Monica Jazz and Folk Festival at the Santa Monica Hall in Santa Monica, California. The next day I played the Mason Williams and Friends concert at the Vaudeville Melodrama Theater in Bakersfield.

August 27 played the Pizza Place.

August 28 did a Will Ray session.

August 30-September 1 California on tour; we played in Ohio and Rhode Island. Rhode Island had a Cajun-Bluegrass festival that was a fun gig!

September 6-11 California played Texas.

September 20, 27 California played the Station Inn in Nashville, Down Home Pickin' Parlor in Johnson City, Tennessee, and IBMA in Louisville, Kentucky.

October 3 went to San Francisco for John Reishman session produced by Charles Sawtelle of Tim O'Brien's Hot Rize Band.

October 7 did something for Disney from 9 a.m. to 12 p.m.

October 12 California played the Pasadena Ambassador Auditorium.

October 13 California played Santa Barbara.

October 14 California played Bakersfield.

October 16 did a Dan Baird session for Warner Brothers.

October 19 played Santa Barbara.

October 21 did a John Reishman session in San Francisco.

October 22 played the Pizza Place.

October 27 California played Creston, California Festival.

October 28-30 Doo Wah Riders played Palm Springs and Las Vegas.

November 2 Doo Wah Riders played the Silver Bullet.

November 5 played the Palomino.

November 6 did a Michael Stanton session.

November 9 Doo Wah Riders played the Crazy Horse Saloon.

November 11 did the "Christmas in Connecticut" movie with Arnold Swartzenegger. Arnold directed this remake of the Barbara Stanwick movie of the same name. Arnold called and said, "Byron, can you still play the fiddle, or what?" Then he told me what he was doing with the movie. There was a dance scene with Dyan Cannon and Kris Kristofferson where dancers would be doing a Virginia reel style of dance. I told him he would need a banjo player and guitar picker so I got John Hickman and John Moore. We did "Rag Time Annie," which was gratifying to me because it was the second tune dad taught me to play on the fiddle. I also recorded "Honeymoon Waltz," but I do not know if they used it.

November 13 did Hot Country Nights TV show, NBC with Dick Clark. I played with the house band, which included J.D. Maness, John Jorgenson, John Hobbs, and Steve Duncan.

November 14-18 California played Calgary, Canada.

November 19-23 played the Silver Bullet with the Doo Wah Riders.

November 26-December 1 Doo Wah Riders played Bandstand.

December 3 did Hot Country Nights, NBC, for Dick Clark.

December 6-8 Doo Wah Riders played the Crazy Horse Saloon.

December 7 did a Michelle Shocked session.

December 9 Played with David Pearlman.

December 10 Becca turned nineteen.

December 10, 11 did Hot Country Nights, NBC, for Dick Clark.

December 12-15 Doo Wah Riders played Palm Springs.

December 17-22 Doo Wah Riders played Riverside.

December 21 Doo Wah Riders played the Elk-B. Park.

December 31 played the Silver Bullet, New Year's Eve with the Doo Wah Riders.

Journal Entry 1992
California's Traveler

January 2, 3 Doo Wah Riders played the Silver Bullet.

January 4, 7 did Dick Clark's Hot Country Nights for NBC.

January 8, 11 Doo Wah Riders played the Cowboy Boogie.

January 9 Doo Wah Riders played an NBC party.

January 12 Doo Wah Riders played a private party.

January 14 did a session for the made for TV movie "Broken Chord," directed by Ken Olin, who starred in "Thirtysomething." The movie is about a man named David Moore, played by Jimmy Smits, who adopts a Native American little boy who has medical and emotional problems. The plot revolves around the David Moore character coming to grips with the boy's problems.

January 15-19 Doo Wah Riders played the Crazy Horse Saloon.

January 15, 16 did some school programs.

January 20 did a John Goux session.

January 21 turned into a three-gig night with a Dennis Agajanian session, a session for Dee Dee Ward for Disney, and I played the Palomino.

Dennis Agajanian did a lot of Billy Graham Crusades. He was a real red neck and could not stand any man that looked gay; Dennis was very conservative. His moniker was the "Fastest guitar alive." He did play everything lightning fast and he was actually a very sweet person.

January 22-26 Doo Wah Riders played the Longhorn Saloon.

January 23 did Dick Clark's Hot Country Nights for NBC.

January 28 did four school programs.

January 29 Doo Wah Riders played Cowboy Boogie.

January 30 Doo Wah Riders played the Alpine Village.

February 3 the "Broken Chord," made for TV movie first aired.

February 3-14 Doo Wah Riders played Disneyworld, Orlando, Florida at the Neon Armadillo on Pleasure Island.

February 2 played with Peter Feldman.

February 15 went to Alaska for maybe a film I worked on.

February 19 did some school programs.

February 21 did a M. Reed session for Columbia.

February 22 did a session for Alan Rich, Charlie Rich's son. Charlie had a big hit with "Behind Closed Doors" and Alan could sound just like him. I remember that Alan and Billy Swan did a lot of things together.

February 23 played Albuquerque, New Mexico.

February 26 did a Bob O'Connor session.

February 28 did a Bob Nitsik session.

The March 1992 issue of *Frets magazine* (FR 23) had my picture on the cover and inside, a feature story about me.

In 1992, California released the only album we ever recorded together, "Traveler," on the Sugar Hill label. We recorded Steve Spurgin's, "Walk in the Irish Rain." We also included Bill Monroe's Uncle Pen and John Penn's Sasquatch (complete with sound effects), Scissors, Paper & Stone, My Sweet Blue-Eyed Darlin', Spurs, Farmer's Son, California Traveler, I'll Dry Every Tear That Falls, Whiplash, and Band of Angels.

It may seem I was never without work, but there were times...Bette reminds me that I might go a month without anything.

They released "Basic Instinct" in March of 1992.

March 6-8 California played Northern California.

March 11, 12 did a children's recording session for Disney with Herb Pedersen and David Grisman.

March 13-15 California played in Santa Rosa.

March 17 another three-gig day with a Jan Buckingham session, Bob Nitsik session, and the Doo Wah Riders played the Alpine Village.

March 18-22 Doo Wah Riders played the Cactus Corral in Palm Springs.

March 23 did a Chris Hillman session. By this time, Chris and I had been playing together for twenty years.

March 25-29 I did some school programs and played the Crazy Horse Saloon with the Doo Wah Riders.

April 2, 3 Doo Wah Riders played the Silver Bullet.

April 4 played the Gene Autry Museum of Western Heritage in Griffith Park.

April 7 Doo Wah Riders played Pamona.

April 9-19 California toured Pennsylvania, Washington, D.C., Virginia, and Tennessee.

April 21 did a Michael Stanton session.

April 22 did a Glen Spreen session.

April 24 Harry Shannon's movie "Universal Soldier," released. Roland Emmerich directed and it stars Jean-Claude Van Damme, Dolph Lundgren, and Ally Walker. This is a kind of sci-fi movie about soldiers killed in Viet Nam.

April 21-25 Doo Wah Riders played the Longhorn Saloon.

April 30 L.A. Fiddle Band played Glendale College.

May 8 played Solvang. This gig was usually booked right after the California Trail Ride.

May 9, 10 played Calico Ghost Town.

May 11 played the Melodrama at Bakersfield.

May 12-27 went on a European tour.

May 30 Doo Wah Riders played the Silver Bullet.

June 10 played or did a session with Liz Hooker.

June 12-13 I performed and judged a contest for Floyd Warren, in Ohio. Floyd was a fiddler and top gun engraver in the world. We met at the Walnut Valley Festival in Winfield, Kansas in the 1980's and became good friends. We have the same birthday, except that he is twenty-seven years older than I am. He engraved mandolin tailpieces, armrests for banjos, plaques, all kinds of metal things. He made a plate with my name on it and I have it on the wall in my fiddle shop. He made a mandolin tailpiece with Sam Bush's picture on it and I have that too. He made a banjo armrest for dad with "Lue Berline" on it. These are beautiful pieces of work. Floyd gave me a fiddle one time and several things over the years. Sometimes I went to Ohio to see him and we talked on the phone...I loved hearing the stories he had to tell. After his death, I bought all of his instruments from the family.

June 16 did a session for Sue Nikas a singer and guitar player.

June 17 did a Sally Stevens session.

June 20 did a Dennis Agajanian session and played the Huck Finn Festival and Contest, at Mojave Narrows. I judged the contest.

June 21 played Polliwog Park.

June 24-28 played the Zoo-Grass Series with Mason Williams

at the Washington Park Zoo in Portland, Oregon. The next day we played the Britt Music Festival at the Peter Britt Amphitheater in Jacksonville, Oregon.

June 29 did a Julie Wingfield session.

July 3, 4 played Grove, Oklahoma 4th of July weekend at Fiddler's Park.

July 10-12 did a session for Ann Murray's "Snowbird." Shortest recording session of my career...went in the studio at 1:00 and out at 1:05.

July 15-26 California toured Virginia, Pennsylvania, and Winterhawk in Utica, New York. They held Winterhawk in the Berkshires on the Roth Boss Farm and Vasser Clements and I did a Fiddle Workshop in conjunction with the festival.

July 31-August 1 California played the Minnesota Bluegrass Festival.

August 3-10 went on tour in Colorado and Wyoming with Mason Williams. We played the Mason Williams and Friends Concert at the Arvada Center in Arvada, Colorado on the fourth

Byron Berline and Jane Frost, July 4, 1992 in Grove, Oklahoma.

and at the Manitou City Hall in Manitou Springs on the fifth. We went on to Cheyenne, Wyoming and played Mason's Bluegrass Symphony Concert with the Cheyenne Symphony at the Cheyenne Civic Center on the seventh. The next day, the eighth, we headed back to Colorado and played the Mason Williams and Friends Concert at the Breckenridge Music Institute Tent in Breckenridge. On the ninth, we played the Mason Williams and Friends Concert at the Gold Hill Inn in Gold Hill, Colorado.

August 12 California did a European Tour.

September 7 California did an east coast tour, playing New Jersey and Rhode Island.

September 11-17 California played the Tulsa, Oklahoma Chili Cook Off. I judged the chili contest and then we went on to Texas.

California band in 1992 back row: John Moore, Steve Spurgin, front row: John Hickman, Dan Crary, Byron Berline.

September 20 did a Mark O'Connor session for "Gold Rush." Dan Crary, John Hickman, and Bill Monroe came in and played on it.

At the session Bill says, "Now what are we doing here?"

I said, "We're doing a song called "Gold Rush," you remember that one?"

Bill always stopped in a session while we were recording and thought of something else he wanted to do, such as "This would be good to do twin fiddles right here."

I said, "Let's do this one first."

Mark O'Connor videoed everything at this session. It was done in Nashville and all done live with no overdubs.

October 3, 4 played the Follows Camp Festival.

October 7 did a Bobby Utal session

October 9 did a Chris Clark session.

October 16 did a session for John McEuen's "Wild West" TV series or special.

October 19 I worked for David Schwartz, the music director for the TV show "Northern Exposure" and he wrote me into the show weekly, to do music. In addition, they used songs I recorded from the "Jumpin' the Strings" CD.

October 24, 25 played the Pumpkin Festival.

October 26 California played the Bakersfield Melodrama.

November 1 did a show at the Old Fiddlers in San Jose and played a House Concert near Santa Cruz. John Lytle put this together and the house concert was at his house. I remember buying six fiddles from John. I tied a rope around the bundle, carried them with me on the plane, and flew back to L.A.

While in Santa Cruz, I did a session with Joe Weed a good musician and producer. He produced a DVD documenting the history of the song, "Westphalia Waltz" titled "The Waltz to Westphalia" and it is fascinating. I carry it at the Doublestop Fiddleshop.

November 3 did a Northern Exposure TV session.

November 5 Doo Wah Riders played the Alpine Village in Torrance.

November 7 played the Bluebird Café in Santa Barbara.

November 9 did a Northern Exposure TV session.

November 10-14 played the Silver Bullet with the Doo Wah Riders and did a Janet and Judy session.

November 18, 23 Doo Wah Riders played the Cowboy Boogie.

November 19 did an Eddie Dunbar session produced by Jerry Fuller, a session for Northern Exposure and I played the Alpine Village in Torrance with the Doo Wah Riders.

November 20-22 played the Stone Mountain Boys Reunion, Auditorium show in Garland, Texas with Alan Munde, Ed Shelton, Mitchell Land, Tootie Williams, and everybody that had been involved with the band.

November 24 did a recording session with Alvin and the Chipmunks, recording their version of "Boot Scootin' Boogie." John Boylan produced this and he produced/managed Linda Ronstadt. He also produced the Urban Cowboy album and I played on that.

On the set of "Christmas in Connecticut" movie in 1992, directed by Arnold Schwarzenegger. Front row, l to r, John Hickman, Byron Berline and John Moore. Arnold Schwarzenegger is directing the scene.

November 27, 28 played the Longhorn Saloon with the Doo Wah Riders.

November 29 I played Running Springs.

November 30 did a J. Silverman session. Also on 30 played with or did a session with Wayne Cook.

December 1 did something with David Hamilton.

December 2-5 played Palm Springs with the Doo Wah Riders and on the fifth, played the Mason Williams' Bluegrass Symphony Concert with the Eugene Symphony at Hult Center's Silva Hall in Eugene, Oregon.

December 7 did a Northern Exposure TV session.

December 8-11 Doo Wah Riders played the Cowboy Boogie.

December 10 Becca turned twenty.

December 12 played the Fret House.

December 16-19 Doo Wah Riders played the Crazy Horse Saloon.

December 20 Doo Wah Riders played a private party.

December 31 Doo Wah Riders played the Silver Bullet on New Year's Eve.

Journal Entry 1993
John Hickman Philosophy

We lived in California for twenty-six years, but never had any relatives living there. It was just Bette, Becca, and me and every time we wanted to see family, we had to come back to Oklahoma or someone would have to come out to California.

When Bette's parents died, they left her their house in Guthrie, Oklahoma and we just left it closed...only occasionally coming back. When we came to Guthrie to visit I would think, "I'd like to have a little old store front where I could get instruments out of the house and I could go to the fiddle shop to do business." That way, I would have a place to put up some of these instruments. I just decided in about 1993 and told Bette, "I'm ready to get out of here if you are."

"I'm ready," she said. "I'm ready."

I said, "We might as well head back to Guthrie. That nice house is sitting there and we can sell-out here." It was my idea... not hers.

As Becca was out of college and had a job, we began making plans.

January 1, 2 Doo Wah Riders played the Silver Bullet.

January 4 did a session for a Pabst Blue Ribbon Beer commercial.

January 5, 7 Doo Wah Riders played the Silver bullet.

January 9 did work on a Jerry Fuller-Eddie Dunbar project.

January 10 played the Bluebird.

January 11-14 Played Mason Williams' Bluegrass Symphony Concert at the Music Hall in Kansas City, Missouri. This is a story about John Hickman and I will let him tell you the way he remembers it.

John Hickman: One time we played a show in Kansas City and the night before, I began working on the bridge of my banjo. When I woke up it was almost time to be on stage...I overslept. I was in a panic! I cut some grooves for the banjo strings, didn't shave or nothin', threw on my clothes and ran all the way to the venue, losing my billfold somewhere along the way. I got to the back stage, tuned the banjo, and went on stage. The banjo kicked the set off so I took off and everything went fine. I was okay once we started playing…we sounded good that night.

Byron: John is full of banjo wisdom and here is some I will share with you.

"You can't get a banjo loud enough."

"There is a banjo part in every song."

"If musicians were paid by the note, the banjo player would win."

"Every band needs a banjo."

"Some flat pickers start out slow and then taper off."

January 16 did a John Hobbs session.

January 17 Doo Wah Riders played Phoenix, Arizona.

January 18 did an on-location scene for Paramount Studio's, "The Thing Called Love," movie released July 16, 1993, directed by Peter Bogdanovich and starring River Phoenix, Samantha Mathis, and Ermot Mulroney. This was River Phoenix's last movie. The scene takes place at the Bluebird Café in Nashville, but they actually did the filming at the Paramount studio in Los Angeles. It took all day, from 11 a.m. to 11 p.m. to film that scene. I played music for the movie and I was in the movie. I remember Jo El'Sonier was there too.

January 19 did a Capitol Records session for "The Thing Called Love" movie.

January 20, 21 Doo Wah Riders played the Crazy Horse Saloon.

January 26-31 Doo Wah Riders played the Long Horn Saloon.

January 28, 29 did two Matthew Sweet sessions.

January 30 did a Dana Walden session and played a private party with Bill Bryson.

February 1 did a session for the Northern Exposure TV show.

February 5 Linda Ronstadt called me to record on a Jimmy Webb album she produced. We did the recording session at George Lucas's studio Skywalker Sound, at his Skywalker Ranch in Marin County, California. Herb Pedersen was on this too and Lee Sklar played bass. This was a gospel thing Jimmey wrote for his dad.

February 8 did a Kit Thomas karaoke tapes session.

February 10 did something with Sam Ward.

February 11-13 played in Michigan for maybe, the Saline Fiddlers.

February 15-28 Doo Wah Riders played Disneyworld in Orlando, Florida. March 3 did a Will Ray session.

March 6 played the Bluebird in Santa Barbara.

March 9 did a Tim Goodman session.

March 11-14 played Mason Williams' Bluegrass Symphony Concert with the Oklahoma City Philharmonic at the Civic Center Music Hall in Oklahoma City. We did two concerts, one on the thirteenth and one on the fourteenth.

March 22 did a Gary White session.

March 23, 24 Doo Wah Riders played the Silver Bullet.

March 28 Doo Wah Riders played the Cowboy Boogie.

March 29 Doo Wah Riders played Palm Springs.

April 1-3 Doo Wah Riders played a private party in Tucson, Arizona.

April 5 Doo Wah Riders played Knotts Berry Farm.

April 8 did a Mel Harker session.

April 16-18 played Knotts Berry Farm with Jason and Jeany Richards.

April 18, 19 did a Beverly Hillbillies Reunion Show. They did this in Topanga Canyon. We were the band, Roy Clark, Earl Scruggs, John Moore, and me. I remember driving into the parking lot and having my car radio turned on and breaking news came on, about a fire in Waco, Texas. The Branch Dividian Seventh Day Adventists compound in Waco had been under siege since February 28 and on April 19, the siege ended when they burned the compound.

April 20, 23, 26 Doo Wah Riders played in Phoenix, Arizona.

April 24 Doo Wah Riders played in San Diego.

April 29-May 1 played Merle Fest on the campus of Wilkes Community College in Wilkesboro, North Carolina. Doc Watson hosted the festival, named for his son Merle.

May 4-6 Doo Wah Riders played the Silver Bullet.

May 6 did a session for twins, Janet and Judy.

May 8, 9 California played the Calico Ghost Town Festival.

May 10 California played the Melodrama at Bakersfield.

May 11 I played Glendale College. The same day, the Doo

Wah Riders played the Academy of Country Music Awards Show and party.

May 12-14 Doo Wah Riders played the Silver Bullet.

May 15 Doo Wah Riders played Knotts Berry Farm party.

May 18 played a live radio show with Ronnie Mack at the Palomino. Ronnie was a hillbilly/rocker and this was a fun show.

May 20 played with Billy Block a drummer, at the Troubadour. It was a zydaco type thing.

May 21, 22 played with Jann Brown.

May 23 Doo Wah Riders played the Cowboy Boogie.

May 27 California played the Ambassador Auditorium in Pasadena with The Masters. I had to buy a white tuxedo to play with The Masters. The band had Eddie Adcock, Kenny Baker, Josh Graves, and me. I took Jesse McReynolds' place and played mandolin. California came on first and we did our set, then I changed into the white tux and went out with the Masters. I never wore the tux again and The Masters never performed again.

May 28 did an Eric Bikela and Becka Mosher session.

May 30-June 11 played with the Doo Wah Riders Disneyworld in Orlando, Florida.

June 13 did something with Brian Braff. I do not remember what I did, but it was a nice payday.

June 25-July 18 California toured Europe, West Virginia, New York, and Arizona.

July 20 Doo Wah Riders played Knotts Berry Farm.

July 21 Doo Wah Riders played a private party.

July 21-24 Doo Wah Riders played the Orange Country Fair.

July 25 played Warner's Center.

July 26 did a session with an eleven-year-old named Stern.

July 28, 29 Doo Wah Riders played a Universal Studios Show.

July 31 played the Mason Williams and Friends concert at the Sammy Davis Festival Plaza in Las Vegas, Nevada.

August 1 Doo Wah Riders played the Starlight.

August 2 did a Richard Bowen session and played the Mason Williams and Friends Concert at the Vaudeville Express Melodrama Theater in Bakersfield, Colorado.

August 4 did another session with eleven-year-old Stern.

August 5-8 California toured Cumberland, Maryland, and Colorado.

August 11 did a John McEuen session.

August 14 California played the Sun Valley Festival.

August 17 did a Clancy Dunn session.

August 21 California played the Crestline Festival.

August 22 played Polliwog Park.

August 29 California played Park City, Utah Festival.

August 30 did a session for the "Picket Fences" TV show which ran from 1992 through 1996. It was about a fictional family from Wisconsin, but they shot it in California.

September 2-6 California played the Strawberry Festival, a Cajun bluegrass festival in New Jersey and another festival in Yucipa, California.

September 7 did a Northern Exposure TV session.

September 9-12 California played the Tulsa Chili Cook Off and then my hometown Caldwell, Kansas, for the Centennial Celebration of the 1989 Land Run. We played in a ball field and I remember Barry Patton's dad drove his John Deer tractor down to the ball field where we had the show. This was a big deal and a lot of fun.

September 13-16 California played Winfield, Kansas Walnut Valley Festival.

September 20-26 California attended the IBMA (International Bluegrass Music Association) annual awards and picked up the "Instrumental Group of The Year, 1993" award.

September 28, 29 Doo Wah Riders played the Alpine Village in Sorrento.

September 30 Doo Wah Riders played Canyon County.

October 2 I played northern California folk/bluegrass festival at Half Moon Bay.

October 3 played the Santa Cruz workshop and house concert for John Lytle.

October 5 did a Dana Walden session and a Duane Stork session.

October 7 played for a Japanese reception.

October 8 did a D. Michaels session and played McCabes.

October 9 California played Santa Barbara.

October 10 California played Bakersfield.

October 12 did a Robert Jason session.

October 14 did a Will Ray session and an Eddie Montana session.

October 15 did a Lee Hodges session and an Arthur Lee session.

October 19-November 1 Doo Wah Riders played Disney-world in Orlando, Florida.

November 5-7 California played Minnesota.

November 12, 13 played Dallas, Texas.

November 17-21 Doo Wah Riders played Temecula, CA.

November 22 did a session for Dana Walden record producer. I did a lot of sessions with Dana in his studio and he is a very neat person.

November 23, 24 Doo Wah Riders played the Alpine Village in Sorrento.

November 25 played a Japanese reception and did a Barry Fosman session. Barry produced the music for "Fame."

November 27 did a Cherie Hayes session.

December 1-3 Doo Wah Riders played in Palm Springs.

December 4 played the Gene Autry Museum of Western Heritage in Griffith Park.

December 6-7 played the American Music Shop TV show with Mark O'Connor, Jerry Douglas, and Bill Monroe. We played "Gold Rush" and that clip is on U-tube.

December 8-12 Doo Wah Riders played the Crazy Horse Saloon.

December 10 Becca celebrated her twenty-first birthday.

December 14 Doo Wah Riders played the Alpine Village in Sorrento.

December 16 Doo Wah Riders played the Country Music Association.

December 17 did a "Hearts of the West" session for Water-man/Baker.

December 17 did something with Greg Dorman.

December 18, 19 Doo Wah Riders played Riverside.

December 28 did a David Hamilton session.

December 31 Bette and Becca went with me to Disneyworld in Orlando, Florida where I played the Neon Armadillo on Pleasure Island with the Doo Wah Riders. What a great place to ring in the New Year.

Journal Entry 1994
Nickel Creek-Burt Reynolds-Earl Scruggs and Bill Monroe Recording Together

January 11, 18, 19 Doo Wah Riders played the Alpine Village.

January 12-16 Doo Wah Riders played the Crazy Horse Saloon.

January 24 did something with John McEuen.

January 25-27 Doo Wah Riders played Bronco Billy.

January 28 did a Will Ray session.

January 31-February 14 Doo Wah Riders played Disneyworld, Orlando, Florida at Pleasure Island's Neon Armadillo. While in Florida, I also did a recording session for Full Sail Film School, for their sound department, from 11 a.m. to 11 p.m.

February 16 did a Russell Carter session.

February 18 did the "Evening Shade" TV show with Burt Reynolds from 11 am to 11 pm.

The first movie I did in L.A., with Murray McCloud, was a Burt Reynolds movie "Run Simon Run" an ABC Movie of the Week. I ended up doing several Burt Reynolds movies and was involved in all the "Smokey and the Bandit" movies. I did the music...I was not in any of the movies and as a result, I never met Burt.

Just before we moved back to Oklahoma, Burt had a television show called "Evening Shade." On one of the last shows, they invited me to the set to be in the show and play my fiddle. In this episode, Tammy Wynette has these sisters and they all were going to Nashville. Tammy sang and I was part of the band. When I arrived on the set, we went through some stuff and then took a little break. Check this out. Burt came up to me and said, "You played football at OU, didn't you?"

"Yeah..." I said, surprised. He wanted to talk football, then had me play the fiddle, all by myself, for the whole cast. I thought, "What is this?" I later asked the director, "How in the world did he know I played football for OU?"

He just said, "He knew who you were."

I got to know another member of the "Evening Shade" cast, but I did not meet him on the set. This is a strange story, too. Burton Gilliam as "Virgil Mosley," was a regular character on Evening Shade and you might also remember him as "Bubba," from the "Duke's of Hazard" and from being in other movies such as "Back to The Future" and of course, "Blazing Saddles." He is also synonymous with the commercial, "This stuff is made in New York City." Burton is originally from Waco, Texas, but after becoming an actor, he moved to California. I met him at a celebrity golf tournament at the El Cariso Golf Club in Los Angeles. This was about 1987 or 1988 and was a "Toys for Tots" fundraiser tournament. I will never forget...Burton showed up wearing cowboy boots with spikes. I had never before seen that.

Someone introduced us, "This is Byron Berline."

"Berline?" Burton questioned. "Are you any relation to Becca Berline?"

"Yes!" I told him. "She's my daughter."

"Oh, man," he said. "I follow her in softball in the newspapers, all the time!"

Becca was a sophomore in high school at that time. She was a very good softball player and made All City and All State that year. I admit, her name was in the newspaper, a lot! We are very proud of her accomplishments. What a hoot! Burton and I became friends and after that, I saw him quite a bit.

Another celebrity tournament participant is Mickey Jones. We enjoyed playing golf, but I knew him best as a musician when he played drums for Kenny Rogers and the Second Edition.

February 20 did a San Diego Bluegrass thing.

February 22 did a Will Ray session.

February 28-March 28 did a European tour with some Dutch boys.

March 5 did a Lanny Cordola session.

March 6 Doo Wah Riders played the Alpine Village.

March 8 did a Northern Exposure TV show session.

March 9 John Moore hired us to play for his parent's anniversary party.

March 11 did a Warner Brothers session for the movie "Maverick," starring James Garner, Mel Gibson, and Jodie Foster. In the movie, inspired by James Garner's TV role in the series

"Maverick," Mel Gibson plays James Garner's Maverick role and Garner plays a marshal. Richard Donner directed the film and Randy Newman handled the music. Herb Pedersen was on it, Vince Gill, Reba McIntyre, and many others.

March 12 did a David Messenger session.

March 15-17 California played Calgary, Canada.

March 20 Doo Wah Riders played the Alpine Village.

March 21-23 Doo Wah Riders played Bronco Billy.

March 24 played Santa Barbara with Peter Feldman.

March 27 Doo Wah Riders played Santa Barbara.

March 28-30 California played Park City, Kansas.

April 19 Beverly Hillbillies Reunion TV special aired.

May 3 Doo Wah Riders played the Country Music Association party.

May 4, 5 Doo Wah Riders played Country Fest.

May 6 California played McCabes.

May 7, 8 California played the Calico Ghost Town.

May 9 California played Bakersfield.

May 10, 11 played the California Trail Ride.

May 12-15 Doo Wah riders played the Orange Country Fair.

May 16 did a Chris Thiele session for his first album when he was about twelve years old. Peter Wernick, a banjo player, produced this CD "Stealing Second."

Nickel Creek included Chris Thiele on mandolin, Sara Watkins on fiddle, her brother Sean on guitar, and their dad Scott Watkins, played bass. Chris and Sean had the same mandolin teacher, John Moore while Dennis Caplinger and I worked with Sara on her fiddling. They took the name of their young band from the song I wrote called "Nickel Creek." They played for the first time as a band at the Pizza Place with John Moore and me. They came to other places we played, like Norco and I got to know them. I jammed with them and their parents were so appreciative.

May 17 did a G. Lawton session.

May 19-21 Doo Wah Riders played Bronco Billy.

May 22 Doo Wah Riders played Topanga Canyon.

May 23 played somewhere with Dale Watson.

May 31-June 5 played the Neon Armadillo on Pleasure Island at Disneyworld, Orlando, Florida with the Doo Wah Riders. John

Phillips asked me to do another recording session for Full Sail Film School.

June 9 did a Matthew Sweet session.

June 13-16 California played the Telluride Bluegrass Festival in Colorado. I did a pre-festival Super Strings Workshop with Dan Cray and John Hickman.

June 18, 19 California played the Grass Valley Festival. Rose Maddox was on the show and we began making plans to record her next album.

June 22-26 California toured West Virginia and Washington, D.C.

June 30 did a Will Ray session and one for Chad Watson.

July 1 played the Eclectic Café with the Laurel Canyon Ramblers.

Bette and I made up our minds to move to Guthrie, Oklahoma, but we did not know exactly when. One day Herb Pedersen called and said, "Hey, you want to get together and play some good old bluegrass and stuff?"

I said, "Yeah." It sounded good to me.

He invited Kenny Blackwell a mandolin player, Bill Bryson on bass, and I played fiddle. Herb did not know whom he wanted on guitar and considered Billy Ray Latham…a good singer.

I said, "Okay with me."

This was to be a jam session, but Herb had something else in mind. He intended to make this a new band.

Reaching this conclusion, I said, "Hey, I'm leaving."

He was disappointed when he found out Bette and I intended to move to Guthrie. I did get to go on tour with the Laurel Canyon Ramblers to Japan, where we played the huge Gold Country Music Festival. Gabe Wicher eventually replaced me and Roger Reed replaced Billy Ray. I do not think the band plays too much anymore.

July 2 I did a Lanny Cordola session and the Laurel Canyon Ramblers played Eddie Montana's "Montana and Lace" music store.

Monday, July 4 Doo Wah Riders played Pierce College and they had a big Fourth of July fireworks display.

Wednesday, July 6 Doo Wah Riders played the Alpine Inn. This was an unusual booking because we never played the Alpine

Inn on Wednesdays. This gig was booked on my birthday and as I really did not have other plans, I told the band I would buy them all a steak dinner to celebrate. Because it was my birthday, Bette decided to go. We got to the Alpine Inn and all my brothers and sisters were there, Kenny Glasgow, my nephew Barry Patton and Nickel Creek. They prepared a dinner for all of us. Bette sure surprised me that time. What a neat deal. Here is how she did it.

Bette: Because the Doo Wah Riders did not play on Wednesday nights at the Alpine Inn and Byron's birthday fell on that day, I called Kenny Liebenson of the Doo Wahs and asked if it would be possible to get the band booked on that night. He took care of the booking...arranged it and everything. I contacted Byron's family and friends, then we all made arrangements to be at the Alpine Inn on Wednesday, July 6 and Byron really was surprised.

July 10, 14 Doo Wah Riders played a Fair.

July 15, 16 Doo Wah Riders played Santa Anita.

July 17 Doo Wah Riders played the Polliwog Park.

July 18-22 did a Rose Maddox session. I produced her last album, "Rose Maddox, $35 And a Dream." I picked out all the songs, including Gram Parson's "Sin City." I was proud when it received a Grammy nomination. The band behind her is quite incredible. It includes all the players from the Desert Rose band, minus Chris Hillman, with John Jorgenson on guitar and mandolin, Herb Pedersen on rhythm guitar, Bill Bryson on bass, Steve Duncan on drums, I played fiddle and mandolin with added vocals by Herb, John, Bill and Rick Cunha. Rose recorded one of Rick Cunha's songs, "The Place where Love comes from." I cannot convey how much I enjoyed making that album and working with Rose, she was a real pro. There just are not any more like her.

July 20 did a Walden session.

July 20 did a session for Crabb, a cowboy singer.

July 23 played a ranch at Santa Ynez and I asked the Laurel Canyon Ramblers to go with me. This gig was a big, private party held at a ranch near where they had the California Trail Ride. This area is famous for its ranchers such as Michael Jackson and President Ronald Reagan. The party's host, famous movie director Adam Green booked a country band and then wanted a bluegrass band to play. There were two-hundred Hollywood actors at this party. Adam had a woman entertainment coordinator for the party and he absolutely wanted no down time between acts. He wanted the country band to play and then, immediately, the bluegrass band. I tried to explain there had to be a little time before we played in order to set up. I remember that he really chewed out the entertainment coordinator over that. During our set, Steve Martin comedian and banjo player, walked up to the stage and asked quite seriously, "Could you play "Back up and Push?" which is an old, traditional, fiddle tune. Herb Pedersen and I both knew Steve from recording sessions.

I leaned over and said, "Sir, don't bother us…we're trying to do a show here."

Steve just walked away.

"Herb," I said. "He acted like he didn't know us."

After the set, we talked with him, got him up on stage to play with us and we did Foggy Mountain Breakdown. I wonder if he remembers that night.

July 25 played the Sweetwater club.

July 27 did a Keith Taylor session. He had a studio at his home and I did several recording sessions there. Keith had a man working for him and this man could imitate anybody…any accent. He was one of the first to do "Roy D. Mercer" types of prank call tapes. Someone would have him call a friend of theirs or business associate and Keith pretended to be a customer or whatever. He made up wild stories and the person on the other end of the phone thought the gag was for real.

July 27 Doo Wah Riders played the Crazy Horse Saloon.

July 28 Doo Wah Riders played a big party in Sedona, Arizona.

July 29, 30 Doo Wah Riders played the Crazy Horse Saloon.

July 31 Doo Wah Riders played Monrovia, California.

August 12, 13 California played the Washington State Festival.

August 15 did a Karen Mallully session.

August 16-28 Doo Wah Riders played Disneyworld, Orlando Florida.

September 2, 3 California played Escoheague, Rhode Island.

September 4, 5 California played Yucaipa, California.

September 9 did a Tom Berger session.

September 12-14 played the Texas Trail Ride.

September 15-17 played Winfield, Kansas Walnut Valley Festival.

It was not hard to leave California and come home to Oklahoma, but it was difficult to leave all the people we had known over the twenty-six years we lived there. Some of them really threw a fit, but we told them we would come back to visit and we do.

We bought the building that would become the Doublestop Fiddle Shop in down town Guthrie, Oklahoma. As with most buildings in Guthrie, this one is historic and is the old Masonic Lodge. Production company's film many movies in Guthrie because of the historic nature of the downtown. They shot "Rainman," with Dustin Hoffman and Tom Cruise, all along Oklahoma Avenue, where the Doublestop Fiddle Shop is located at 121 E. Oklahoma Avenue and you can recognize parts of it in many movies. When you exit off of interstate I-35 and drive into town, you feel like you have stepped back in time. Guthrie is a very interesting place to visit, a wonderful place to live and we were getting anxious to move.

September 19 Doo Wah Riders played Disneyland in California.

September 20 did a G. Stockdale session.

September 20-21 Doo Wah Riders played the Alpine Village.

September did a Lisa Haley session.

September 22 in Owensboro, Kentucky, I.B.M.A presented our band, "California," with the 1994 Award, "Instrumental Group of The Year."

September 23, 24 played Cal Poly (California State Polytechnic University) at San Luis Obispo. Mike Krukow pitched for the San Francisco Giants and he never forgot his Alma matre, Cal Poly or their baseball team, Cal Poly Mustangs, of which he was a team member. Mike pitched for the giants during the 1989 San Francisco earthquake. It happened October 17, during the warm-up practice for the third game of the 1989 World Series, between the Oakland Athletics and the San Francisco Giants. He retired in March of 1990 and became a sports announcer. Mike had a fundraiser golf tournament for the Cal Poly Mustangs baseball team and he asked John Hickman and me to play music and participate in the tournament. He sent me a baseball from the 1989 World Series with the signatures of all the players on it. You never know who is listening to your music.

Mike Krukow told me that his friend, Will Clark liked my music. Will Clark was first baseman for the Cardinals and he said the Cardinals played my records in their locker room.

Senator Robert Bird, from West Virginia, was also a fiddler and apparently, liked my music enough to call Barry Poss, President of Sugar Hill records because he wanted me to make a special tape for him, which I did and included the tunes he requested. He played the tape in his limo every day on his way to work. Again, you just never know who is listening.

September 30-October 3 California played Escondido, California, Running Springs, and Bakersfield.

October 4 did John McEuen "Good Ole Boys" movie.

October 5 did a Dusty Wakeman session and a Randy Rice session.

October 6-9 California did a four cities Texas tour.

November 8 did sessions in Nashville for my "Fiddle and a Song" album. One of my favorite fiddle tunes is "Sally Goodin'" and I did a special arrangement of it for this recording session.

After leaving Bill Monroe's band, he and I stayed friends through the years and I always enjoyed the rare opportunities we had to visit and sometimes play together. Whenever Earl Scruggs came to Los Angeles and needed a fiddler, he always called me. We did the Beverly Hillbillies Reunion and other things. I always told him that one day I would call him and would ask, "Would you play on a project of mine if I call?"

He said, "Oh, yes."

I got this idea to do an album called "Fiddle and Song" and wanted to get people to play and sing on it with me. My solo albums had always been instrumentals, but his time I wanted to have some singers. I asked Bill Monroe and Earl Scruggs to record on it with me...at the same time. They had not recorded together since 1944, which is the year I was born...they had not recorded together in over fifty years. People, especially in Nashville, could not believe I got the two of them together. It was the talk of the town. I just called them up!

I said, "Bill, we're going to have Earl there." I told Earl, " Bill's going to be playin' mandolin." I talked to them about it... it was not a shock when they both showed up at the recording studio. When the day came to record, Earl came in a little late and was upset. He could not find the place and did not know where to park and I do not know what all happened.

Earl said, "I hate it I'm late...."

I told him, "No, no, don't worry about it."

Earl said, "Who you got over there playing mandolin?"

Bill said, "Bring any picks with you? Did you bring any picks with you to play the banjo?"

I said to Bill, "No, he had to go to K-Mart to buy some. That's why he's late."

I am sorry you readers cannot see this because I am doing my best Earl Scruggs and Bill Monroe imitations.

Bringing Earl Scruggs and Bill Monroe together after so many years is musical history. I knew that at the time and so did local television and TNN, in Nashville. The media covered it as major news in country music. The press wanted interviews and they came in to film the event. I am so glad I had the opportunity to be a part of it. I was aware of how important that session was and I wanted it documented.

Here is another interesting thing about that recording session. Earl played banjo on it with his son Randy, on guitar, Bill played mandolin and sang on it, with his son James on bass and I played fiddle on it while my nephew Barry Patton videotaped it. That session is a wonderful memory I will carry with me a long time.

November 11 did a John McEuen movie session.

November 12 did a Will Ray session.

November 13 played Montana and Lace with the Laurel Canyon Ramblers.

November 14-16 did a Laurel Canyon Ramblers session for their album.

November 17 did a Cliffie Stone session. Cliffie's son played bass with Jack Daniels on guitar.

November 18 did a Chris Beck session.

November 22 did a session with Willie Nelson who booked me to do a recording session on "Peach Pickin' Time down in Georgia," which was to be on the tribute album, "The Songs of Jimmie Rodgers." We did this Jimmie Rodgers song and I was quite impressed with how he approached it. Willie had us listen to the original tape. We had it all done in one or two takes, all at one time with no overdubbing. Willie played and sang with us. I remember Mickey Raphael played harmonica. It sounded wonderful and Willie was such a professional...what a pleasure to work with him.

November 25, 26 Doo Wah Riders played the Flying "J."

The Doo Wah Riders played the National Rodeo Finals in Las Vegas at the MGM Hotel. During the Finals, there is a country act in every hotel in Vegas...Reba McIntyre, Merle Haggard, all of the big names.

Bette and I had a young friend from Italy visiting us when the Doo Wah Riders were booked for Vegas and our young friend came with me.

The rodeo runs all day and into the night, so it is late before the rodeo is over each day and our first show at the MGM Hotel did not go on until midnight. Our leader, Kenny Lee Benson, got

1994 Nashville recording session for the CD FIDDLE & A SONG. l to r; James Monroe, Bill Monroe, Byron Berline, Earl Scruggs, Randy Scruggs.

excited and worried that everything had to go just right. We had on long coats and looked the cowboy part. The curtains remained closed until it was time for us to go on. There was a big introduction and the curtains opened. The only one in the audience was our young friend from Italy and I burst out laughing!

It took people a while to get there after the rodeo finished. Finally, people came in...mostly musicians. The rodeo finals ran for several days and the band stayed for the whole thing, but I had to leave early to get to my next gig.

November 12-December 6 did a Will Ray session.

December 8 Doo Wah Riders played the Beverly Hilton.

December 13 did a Jean Paralone session.

December 14 did a session with the Doo Wah Riders for County Star at Universal Studios.

December 15 played Academy of Country Music Christmas party with the Doo Wah Riders, in conjunction with the Universal Studios gig.

December 17, 19, 20 Doo Wah Riders played Disneyland, Los Angeles, and New Year's Eve.

Journal Entry 1995
Moving to Guthrie – Chiggers

January 4-7 California played the Crazy Horse Saloon.

January 9 did a "Fiddle and a Song" session. We recorded at Rick Cunha's "Rainbow Garage" studio in Van Nuys, California and Rick engineered the session. We featured California on "Faded Love," with Steve Spurgin, John Moore, Dan Crary, Jay Dee Maness, and me. We also recorded "Fiddle Faddle," with Dennis Caplinger on banjo.

January 12 did another "Fiddle and a Song" session. Mason Williams and I have been good friends and have been playing together since our days at OU and he wrote a song about me called, "Skippin' along on Top." We got together at Don Ross' Studio in Eugene, Oregon, Don engineering the session. Mason sang and Rick Cunha, Doug Haywood, John Hickman, Jerry Mills, Hal Blaine, and I, all played on it. Rick, Doug, and I sang backup vocals.

That night I went to Yosemite with the Doo Wah Riders for a two-night gig. I remember we played at a big lodge and they paid us well.

January 16, 17 Doo Wah Riders played Palm Springs, California and Phoenix, Arizona.

January 19 did a Rich Fox session and played with Dave Agualla.

January 23 did another "Fiddle and a Song" session. We recorded "Second Fiddle" and featured Jann Brown as lead vocalist. We had quite a group backing her up with John Moore, Ken Liebenson, Lindy Rasmussen, Ken Lynard, Ed Eblin, Rick Cunha, and me. We also recorded "Cajun Medley" featuring "The Doo Wah Riders" with Ken Liebenson, Ken Lynard, Ed Eblin, Rick Cunha, and me. We recorded a third cut that day, "Roly Poly," also featuring the Doo Wah Riders with Jay Dee Maness on steel guitar. We did the recording at Rick Cunha's studio and he engineered the session.

January 26 did a recording session with the Laurel Canyon Ramblers and played the Alpine Village with the Doo Wah Riders.

January 27 did a "Fiddle and a Song" session at Rick Cunha's studio with Rick engineering.

When Bette and I moved to California, we joined the Sherman Oaks Presbyterian Church, where we remained active members for twenty-five years. Jack Halloran, well known for his vocal arrangements, directed the choir. His wife Ella Rose played the church's organ. I was taken with his arrangement of "Were You there" and decided to include it on my "Fiddle and a Song" CD. "Were You There" features the Sherman Oaks Presbyterian Church Quartet," Donna Falco, Ellie Doud, Frank Heckadon and Bette Berline. Bette also played piano, as did Ella Rose Halloran, and I played fiddle.

A special thank you to my dear wife Bette, for all her hard work on this song...it came out better than I ever imagined.

February 2 did something with Jeff Wilson.

February 6 did another "Fiddle and a Song" session at Rick Cunha's studio with Rick engineering. We recorded Bill Monroe's "Rose of Old Kentucky" featuring Vince Gill...he also played guitar. We had Ken Lynard, John Moore, Dennis Caplinger, Bill Bryson, and me. We also recorded "Sweet Memory Waltz," a tune I wrote, with Jack Skinner and featured Vince Gill on vocals. Vince also played guitar on this and Jann Brown did back-up vocals. John Moore, Dennis Caplinger, Bill Bryson, Bette, and I played. We also got a third recording that day, "My Dixie Darling" featuring Rick Cunha on vocals and guitar. Ken Lynard and I did back-up vocals. John Moore, Dennis Caplinger, Bill Bryson, and I played.

February 7 did Chad Watson and Sarah Montes sessions and played Santa Barbara.

February 8-13 played Mason Williams' Bluegrass Symphony Concert with the Eugene Symphony at Silva Hall Hult Center in Eugene, Oregon.

February 15-March 4 Doo Wah Riders played Disneyworld in Orlando, Florida.

February 13 did a session for David Hamilton who did a lot of movie scores.

March 13 the Doo Wah Riders played a Warner Brothers party.

March 15-19 played the Country Gazette Reunion in Michigan or Wisconsin. We taped it and I remember Joe Carr was there.

March 20 did a Will Ray session.

March 22-27 California played an east coast tour.

All the while, the Berlines were getting anxious to move home to Oklahoma. I always liked Guthrie and we visited here a lot during those twenty-six years. I liked all the golf courses out west of town, which is real convenient. Golf is plentiful, so that was good. Becca had already graduated from college and was working, so we let her stay in the house until it sold and she rented out part of it when we moved to Guthrie. At the time, we did not want to sell the house and pay all that capital gains tax. One of us had to be fifty-five; that is the law...I was only fifty. We made the move on April 1, 1995. Bette and Becca drove the van. My nephew Barry Patton came out and we drove the big truck and towed a car.

John Hickman asked me, "You suppose you might need a Luthier in your fiddle shop?" John moved to Guthrie with me. He sold out where he was in the Redding, California, Shasta area, bought a house here in Guthrie, and helped me work on the fiddle shop building. I opened up the front part of the fiddle shop in May of 1995. We had not yet fixed up the back or put in the Music Hall. John put his workshop upstairs, above the fiddle shop. He has never been without instruments to repair since we opened our doors. Not one day...he has always had something to work on. That is amazing.

John and I immediately began looking around for musicians. When I first got here, I did a recording session with a man and woman. While in the studio the woman said, "You know, there is a friend of yours from your home town who's going to retire and he works at Boeing. Larry Rader is his name and we want you to play at a little surprise party for him at noon on Friday in Oklahoma City. I told her I would, but that I would need a guitar player. She said there was a guitar player that I had not met, but who also played on their record. They recorded my track separately so sometimes a musician does not meet everyone that plays on a record. She said his name was Jim Fish and she suggested we get together and maybe work something up for the retirement luncheon. Jim came to my house and we went through some songs. He knew "Huckleberry Hornpipe," a tune I wrote, because he had heard Clarence White play it. Jim played it just great.

"Hm," I thought. "That's interesting."

"You never play with a flat pick?" I asked him.

"No, never do." He said.

We played that little gig and I told him about opening up the Music Hall and trying to get some musicians together.

Jim said, "Well, I play electric guitar too."

Eric Dalton, the drummer that went to Holland with our Flying Burrito Brothers tour in 1972, was now a rolfer and lived in Oklahoma City. I gave him a call and when I invited him to join the band, he said, "Yes."

There was a kid named Greg Kennedy, playing piano at the Blue Belle Saloon in Guthrie where Tom Mix once tended bar and is another historic building in town. Greg had played bass a little bit with Country Gazette and Bill Monroe and I thought, "Oh, he'll be perfect." I got him and that was the Byron Berline Band, then we began rehearsing.

April 24 Dennis Agajanian flew me out to L.A. to do a session for his mail order video.

April 28, 29 California played Merle Fest for the last time.

May 7, 8 played with the Doo Wah Riders in California

May 9-15 played the California Trail Ride, McCabes, Bakersfield, Calico Ghost Town Festival and most of these were with the California band.

May 19-21 California played Fallon, Nevada. It was not nearly as cold this time. Musicians remember these things.

June 20-26 played Mason Williams' Bluegrass Symphony Concert on the 22. We played with the Cascade Music Festival Orchestra at Drake Park Pavilion in Bend, Oregon. I played the Mason Williams and Friends concert on the twenty-fourth at the Aladdin Theater in Portland.

June 28 did a Bob O'Connor session for Bob Wood in Oklahoma City. Bob had a music store in Del City. When we moved to Guthrie, Bob was responsible for getting me some gigs and helped get the sound system for the new Music Hall. Bob and I go way back to my years an OU when we played a lot of music together.

July 3 did something with Debbie/Randy Allen.

July 5-17 California played Barryville and Shinhopple, New York. The day before we left on this tour, Bette and I drove to the farm just outside of Guthrie to pick black berries. I had not done that in years. Then we went to some friend's house to watch the Fourth of July fireworks display. This was our first Fourth of July since moving to Guthrie. The next morning John Hickman and I rented a car to drive to New York. I really wish I had immediately showered after picking those berries the day before. I had a hundred chigger bites...all over me. It was the most miserable trip I have ever taken. Calamine lotion helped a little, but the only thing that really gave relief was a hot bath up to my neck. We did the tour, but it is hard to scratch with a fiddle in one hand and the bow in the other.

One of our stops on this tour included a festival where Chubby Wise was booked. The stage at the top of a hill was fenced to keep fans from entering the back stage area. There was a gate in the fence and through that, you could drive up to the back of the stage and unload instruments and equipment. Somebody forgot to tell Chubby about the gate...it was so very hot that day. I was back stage and saw Chubby walking all the way up that hill. When he finally got to the stage he was exhausted and overheated...I thought he was going to have a heart attack. I told him that he could get his van, drive up the hill and through the gate. I remember that when he was on stage I stood in the wings and watched him perform. I certainly respected all he has done. When it was our turn to go on, I looked to the side of the stage and there was Chubby, watching us perform. I thought, "How neat." Mutual respect...that was nice.

A Mr. Farmer, promoter of this festival, was an older man who held this festival for several years and always wanted to have it the same weekend as Mary Dod's Albany Festival. The area was having a heat wave and it was one hundred degrees... hot, hot, hot. I remember that on the Friday night show we played "Walk in the Irish Rain." Saturday morning I did a fiddle workshop. Afterwards, Farmer and Raymond Fairchild were back stage. Farmer said, "Berline, you guys need to play straight bluegrass, none of that Irish stuff. Last year Tim O'Brien started playing that Irish stuff and people started walking out. If you play that old time stuff you'll get a really good hand."

Raymond said, "You need to play "Sally Goodin'" every set because that's your main song. I play "Buckin' Mule" every set because people expect it."

I said, "I agree with everything you've said. You're right, we will."

I told Crary and Spurgin, "I told Farmer we were going to do some straight bluegrass this set."

They looked at me like, "Whaaaat?" I said, "Don't worry about it; we'll just do our regular set." Our last set Steve and Dan got on stage and I said, "So, which one of you are going to sing "Salty Dog" or "Rollin' in my Sweet Baby's Arms?" These, are songs we never performed. We did our regular show and had three encores and standing ovations.

While we were busy selling CD's after the show, Farmer comes by in his golf cart and says, "I told you if you played that old time music you'd get a good response."

Oh, right.

Dolf Hewitt and I traded some fiddles and I let him know I was interested in other instruments. When I opened the Double-stop Fiddle Shop, I knew I would need to carry other instruments in addition to fiddles and mandolins. Dolf told me about a man from Pennsylvania who had died and his wife had all her husband's instruments, so I arranged to go to her home to see them. John Hickman and I loaded up the rental car with mandolins, guitars, fiddles...you cannot imagine how many instruments we got in that car. We still had one more gig to play before we could drive back to Oklahoma. We finished the tour and made it back to Guthrie and the fiddle shop with all those instruments.

July 20-29 John Hickman, John Moore, Steve Spurgin, and I, played in Montana and at South Plains College in Levelland, Texas.

We released "Fiddle and a Song" in August of 1995 on the Sugar Hill label. In addition to the recordings we made for the CD, I included an additional song, recorded December 3, 1983 at Skyline Studios in Topanga Canyon, California engineered by Brett Bacon. It features "Sundance" on a tune I wrote, called "Fiddler's Dream." The lineup includes Steve Spurgin, Don Whaley, Rick Cunha, Pete Wasner, Skip Conover, and me.

August 12 Mt. St. Helens...strange journal entry, I cannot remember if it blew or we played there.

August 14-28 Doo Wah Riders played Disneyworld Orlando, Florida.

September 7 played Midwest City, Oklahoma.

September 9 California played the Tulsa Chili Cook Off.

September 15, 16 played Winfield, Kansas Walnut Valley Festival.

September 20 did a session for Bob Wood.

September 29 - October 4 played Nashville's Wild Horse Saloon with the Doo Wah Riders and Bill Monroe. When I got to town, I gave Bill a call and asked if he would like to come over to the Wild Horse Saloon. None of the Doo Wah Riders had ever met Bill. We were on stage the very first set and I told the stage managers to let me know when Bill arrived.

I told the Doo Wah Riders, "Now, when Bill grabs your hand to shake, he will pull you to him."

In the middle of our set the manager said, "Bill Monroe is here and wants to know what you want him to do."

I said, "Tell him to get his mandolin out and get up here."

Bill, decked out in an all white suit and white hat, really looked nice and was in a good mood. I introduced him to the audience and he was very well received. We played "Blue Moon of Kentucky" with the Doo Wah Riders and "Uncle Pen," but I cannot remember if he sang, or I did. The Doo Wah Riders sure were excited about meeting and playing with Bill Monroe.

The Wild Horse, a dance type place with a younger audience, is quite large with full size horse replicas hanging upside down from the ceiling. There were some girls in their twenties in the audience and they were screaming.

I told Bill, "They're screaming for you, Bill."

In that high-pitched voice, he said, "Yes, I know they are."

Bill finished his part of our set and went off stage. While we finished the rest of our set, I looked down on the dance floor and there was Bill Monroe, dancing with some of those screaming girls. When we finished our set, we went backstage where Bill met the rest of the band. Lindy Rasmussen had already shaken hands with Bill and gave me a sign to know I was right...Bill tried to pull Lindy to him. I signaled back, "Okay." Just glad I could prepare them. Bill and I took some time to visit. I just did not get to see him much and I really enjoyed it. When I walked him to his car, he pulled out a poster and gave it to me. I think he enjoyed the evening, the audience did, and the Doo Wah Riders are still talking about it. It was such a nice thing for Bill to do.

Sometime during the 1990's President Bill Clinton was to honor Bill Monroe and several other artists for an award at a special White House ceremony. Musicians brought their instruments and were to play later in the evening after the awards ceremony. President Clinton began naming the honorees and when Bill Monroe heard his name, he got up and walked right up to the President.

He said, "Mr. President, I'm gonna play the first song Elvis Presley recorded, "Blue Moon of Kentucky. Now, I'm gonna start this out real slow and then, when I'm through, I want that fiddler over there, to kick off real fast."

That other fiddler, another Presidential honoree, was Itzak Perlman. I might not be able to write an entire book of Bill Monroe stories, but almost. I just cannot repeat all of them.

October 4, 5 did workshops at Mark O'Connor's Fiddle Camp in Nashville.

October 7 California played Austin, Texas.

October 11-16 did a tour of Japan with the Laurel Canyon Ramblers.

October 27 did a session with Bob Wood.

October 29 the new Byron Berline Band's first time out we played a Christian Church party. That band included John Hickman, Jim Fish, Eric Dalton, Greg Kennedy, and me.

November 1 flew to California and Peter Feldman played with me at Lake Casitas.

Will Ray said, "While you're out here, let's get you on something." Two days later on November 6, I did a recording session with him.

November 7-11 the Doo Wah Riders played Virginia River Inn in Mesquite, Nevada.

November 14 did a Don Johnson session in Oklahoma City. Don played piano for Emmylou Harris. He mainly does gospel music.

November 27 did a session for Ike Gauley and Harmon in Enid, Oklahoma.

After living in Guthrie for about nine months, I got a call from Rick Morton who lived in Tulsa, wanting to know if he could come over and look at a fiddle he wanted to buy. It was Sunday morning and we were to have a Sunday afternoon jam at the Music Hall. I stood at the fiddle shop door when Rick arrived.

He got out of his Chevy S-10 pickup, came inside, and began looking at fiddles, which at that time were all upstairs. When it was time to leave he went down the stairs and outside to the street. His truck was gone…stolen. Guthrie is a small town and crime is rather rare, especially the theft of a pickup truck on a main street, on a Sunday morning in broad day light. He called his dad who came and picked him up. Rick eventually got his truck back, but it sure was not in the same condition as when it disappeared. Rick is a good friend, fine fiddler and has been a good mentor for young musicians.

December 3 played Albuquerque, New Mexico.

December 13 did a Don Johnson session.

December 20 did a Bob Wood session in Oklahoma City.

Bette and I in front of my Doublestop Fiddle Shop and Music Hall in Guthrie, Oklahoma.

Journal Entry 1996
Giardiasis Bug — Byron Berline Band — Music Hall Opens

January 7 did a Bob Wood session.

January 12, 13 BBB (Byron Berline Band) played Garland, Texas and I did workshops for the Texas Bluegrass Association.

January 20 did something with S. Tomlin in Santa Monica, CA.

January 28 did a pier concert in California with Don May.

January 29 did something with Dana Walden in CA.

January 30 did something with Tommy Borelli in CA.

Bricktown in Oklahoma City is an entertainment area bordered by the Oklahoma River. Bricktown used to be a major warehouse district with four railroad companies having freight operations east of the Santa Fe tracks. All of the buildings around that area are made of brick some of which date back to 1898. The Depression caused businesses of the area to decline. After World War II, people began moving from downtown to the suburbs. Much of the railway freight began shipping by truck and as a result, Bricktown became an eyesore of empty buildings.

In the early 1990's the Oklahoma City Chamber of Commerce, looking for ways to generate interest in downtown, began redeveloping Bricktown. Today Bricktown has the AT&T Bricktown Ballpark, a mile long canal with water taxis, several sculptures, and other art works. A train runs daily between Oklahoma City's Bricktown old Santa Fe Depot and Fort Worth, Texas. Bricktown really is a neat place to visit. Each year they hold many events and the coming out show for the new Byron Berline Band was one of the very first. One of the earliest businessmen to open in Bricktown is Rocky Gilenwater. He called his place Rocky's and he became a good friend.

Rocky's Grand Opening on February 3, 1996 would also be the Byron Berline Band's Coming Out show. At two degrees below zero and bone chilling, it is one of the coldest nights in Oklahoma I can remember. Jack Ekrote and his band, out of Oklahoma City, opened for us. Rocky's held 400 people and they turned that many away, selling out immediately. Rocky's was rockin'! It was insane. My sisters Eleanor and Janice came... just lots of folks! It was a great night for everyone and the Byron Berline Band continued to play at Rocky's for several years.

February 8 BBB played the student union at OSU in Stillwater.

February 18 BBB played with the Oklahoma Youth Symphony Orchestra and we used many of Mason Williams' charts. This was a very special gig for us. I did not feel well the morning of the concert date, but I rode to the venue with John Hickman and we arrived early. I got out of his van and collapsed. I was so sick and just doubled up the entire time we waited for the show to start. I could not keep anything down, could not rehearse, but somehow got through the show...I do not know how, but I did. When we returned to Guthrie, I saw Dr. Robert Ringrose, Bette's brother, who checked me out and said, "You've got the Giardiasis bug and you are lactose intolerant."

He said, "You can't do this and you can't do that, you can't eat this..."

I could not believe what I was hearing! He gave me something for the bug, but it did nothing.

February 23-26 California played Winter Grass in Spokane, Washington. I was still weak, but tried to get through the schedule.

February 28 did a European Tour with two Dutch musicians, Henry Nuyen and Jon Roelof. This was the last European tour John Hickman and I played with them. I was still sick, surviving on bananas and hard rolls called water bread. The roll was bland and for some reason stayed with me. I could not eat anything fried, no butter, or any dairy products. When a language issue arose, Henry and Jon helped order at restaurants. By the end of the tour, I was down to one hundred-sixty pounds and everyone thought I had Aids or worse. At six feet three inches, I was real skinny. Dr. Robert prescribed six, very large pills. After taking just the first one, I knew it began to work and although it took a while, the medication finally killed that bug.

We thought a long time, trying to figure out how I got that bug and eventually figured it out. Several months before, Bette and I went to Puerta Vallarta, Mexico and stayed at a resort. I wanted to play golf and someone allowed me to borrow his clubs. The golf course was on the edge of town and you could play all day for thirty five dollars, and I did. I did not have a cart so I walked the 18 holes in the morning, stopped to eat lunch, and then walked another 18 holes in the afternoon. The person from whom I borrowed the clubs was to come by and pick me up. When he arrived, he saw some friends and wanted to play a few holes with them, for money and I walked with them. By the time they finished it was getting dark. We went to the clubhouse, stood around talking and I noticed a nearby dripping faucet with a puddle around it. I had on shorts and began getting little bites around my ankles and legs. They were mosquito bites and that is how I got that bug. It is a parasite and you can get it from bad water or though mosquitoes. What an ordeal. I never again, want to get it…I can tell you that!

March 5-7 I did workshops, played at Mountain View, Arkansas and I had a very good time.

March 12 played the Shrine Temple on Portland Avenue in Oklahoma City. Bob Wood was a Shriner and he lined up a lot of shows with Texas Playboys, Leon Rausch, Tommy Morrel, and Bobby Boatwright. It was a lot of fun playing with them. Bob Wood was a great person and an old friend from our college days as OU.

March 19 did a session for Pat Payne guitar player and singer.

March 28 BBB played the Oklahoma City Christian Church.

March 30 I played Bob Wills Day at the Capitol building in Oklahoma City. Joe Hutchison put this together and Barry Patton and Kenny Glasgow did this with me. Senator John Dahl started the Bob Wills Day event, adopted by the Senate the twenty sixth day of February, 1985. "The first Wednesday in February of each year is hereby declared "Bob Wills Day" in Oklahoma." Bob Wills may have been born in Texas, but his career blossomed in Tulsa, Oklahoma…the place he called home and where he is buried. Here is some trivia. Bob Wills' father wrote the tune to "Faded Love" and Bob wrote the words. "Faded Love" is the Official State Song of Oklahoma and the fiddle is the State Instrument.

May 4, 5 did something in Santa Cruz for John Lytle, played the California Trail Ride, and did a Tim Goodman session. Tim and I played a lot of golf together.

May 11 BBB played Fayetteville, Arkansas.

May 17 did a Bob Wood session.

May 18 BBB played a show in Del City, Oklahoma.

June 7 Opened the Music Hall. BBB (Byron Berline Band) included Eric Dalton, Greg Kennedy, John Hickman, Jim Fish, and me.

Before the Music Hall opened upstairs above the fiddle shop, we had a new air conditioning system installed and they did not complete the project until the day of our first show. The drain for the condensation, not properly installed, redirected the water into the Music Hall. What a mess. We got that cleaned up and then, when the show started, I found there was a heckler in the audience. The hall was full and there were a lot of people there I did not know…this man was one of those unknowns. At first, I thought he was a plant; someone just wanted to have fun with me and maybe had him there to be funny. It was no joke…he was rip-roaring drunk. He kept putting his arm on his wife's head and giving her a Dutch rub. I remember a friend of mine, Alan Eyerly, a Highway Patrolman, was there in uniform. I tried to introduce the band and this man yelled out in a slur, "Quit talkin' so much. I paid good money to see the show."

Figuring it was my show, I yelled back, "I own this place and I'll talk if I want to." That shut him up, as Patrolman Eyerly escorted him out of the building. To this day, I have no idea who that fellow was.

June 15 BBB played the Oklahoma City Zoo.

June 16 BBB played Quartz Mountain, Oklahoma

June 17 did a Bob Wood session.

June 21 BBB played the Music Hall.

June 22 BBB played a party at the Lazy E in Guthrie, Oklahoma.

June 23 played the Sunday Jam at the Music Hall. Anyone who wanted, signed up and jammed at the Music Hall from 2 p.m. to somewhere around 5 p.m. and we did this for a couple of years.

The Byron Berline Band played for a few months, but it was not long before we began playing too much. Eric Dalton said, "I just can't play this much." He had a business and needed to be working at it so he quit the band.

Bob Wood had a music store in Del City, Oklahoma. I played music with Bob on the Walker House of Lights TV Show while I was a student at OU. He had shows at a country music place and he invited John Hickman and me to play. That is where I met Steve Short our drummer and Richard Sharp our bass player. They were playing there that night and John Hickman and I played with them. I told John, "That drummer is good." They are both good musicians. Steve Short is the best drummer in Oklahoma. He played for Reba McIntyre for three years and has recorded with everyone.

Greg Kennedy was still around. He was a real piece of work. Greg left and I called Richard Sharp. He came on board right before the first OIBF (Oklahoma International Bluegrass Festival) which was October of 1997. We needed a bass player so we added Richard. We have all been together ever since, except when Jim's wife got a job in Pittsburg, Pennsylvania and he was gone about three years. Brad Benge knew all of us and he replaced Jim fish. Brad was also a young recording engineer.

Jim Fish came back and it just happened that his job opened up, so he got his job back and we got our guitar player. We have cut six albums or so during the time we have been together. It is a lot of fun and we have a good time.

June 25-July 1 John Hickman and I did a tour through Colorado, playing Mason Williams and Friends concerts.

June 27 we played the Manitou City Hall in Manitou Springs.

June 28 we played the Mishawaka at Bellvue.

June 29 we played the Arvada Center for the Arts.

June 30 we played the Beaver Creek Resort.

July 3 did a Craig White session, owner of the White Rose Studio in Logan County Oklahoma.

July 4 BBB played Rocky's hoping to repeat the Grand Opening night. Although it was hot, the show was well attended. I mentioned meeting Mike Clark when he was about 15 years old. By this time, he was grown and he and his wife attended this show. Mike was a CPA, served on our OIBF (Oklahoma International Bluegrass Festival) Board, and helped us in many ways. Budweiser sponsored this event and they had scantily clad girls parading in and out of the building, helping to promote their product. Before the show started, I was sitting on a bench in back and Mike and his wife were there, and they had just gotten a big Coca Cola. One of those Budweiser girls walked by and Mike looked…his wife dumped that big Coca Cola on his head. I am sure he was more shocked than I was.

July 11 did a Don Johnson session.

July 13, 14 BBB played the Music Hall and Sunday Jam.

July 18 did another Bob Wood session.

July 19 BBB played the Music Hall.

July 28 BBB played the Music Hall Jam.

August 1 BBB played Taylorville, Oklahoma, which is near Stillwater. We played in a building used for receptions and different kinds of get-togethers.

August 8-11 John Hickman and I played with Mason Williams at the Big Top Chautauqua at Lake Superior in Bayfield, Wisconsin.

August 31 did workshops at the Music Hall. Everyone in the band did a workshop

You might want to refer back to Oct 20 –Nov 1, 1982, for this story. One time Steve Short was telling members of the BBB about when he worked for the Christian World Studio and how Ken Munds got this band to come in to cut an entire album in one day. I began thinking and following along as Steve told the story. Then it hit me.

"Hey! I said, "That was us!" After all those years and I had never before put it together. Steve was the engineer on that session and now he was in my band! Weirder things have happened, but not often.

September 20 BBB played Winfield, Kansas Walnut Valley Festival.

September 28 BBB played the Cookson Festival at Lake Ten Killer.

September 30 did another Don Johnson session.

October 5 BBB played Nick Noble's wedding. I knew Nick from the California and Texas Trail Rides. The Lloyd Noble Center, named for his grandfather, is at OU in Norman. It opened in 1975 and seats over eleven thousand. Lloyd Noble was an oilman, philanthropist, an OU alumnus, and former member of the OU Board of Regents. He was the first to give OU a $1 million gift to finance the center.

October 10 did a recording session, but I do not know for whom.

October 11 BBB played the Down Town Festival in Mulvane, Kansas.

October 12 I played with Michael Martin Murphy in Stillwater, Oklahoma.

October 24 BBB played OSU.

October 26 BBB played my hometown, Caldwell, Kansas.

November 6 did a Bob Wood session.

November 9 BBB played Austin, Texas.

November 11, 13 Bette and I attended the Violin Society of America in Albuquerque, New Mexico. Every other year they have a competition of makers of violins. Judges play and inspect the instruments. It is a lot of fun and I enjoyed the jam sessions.

November 24 Jana Jae invited BBB to play the Grove, Oklahoma Civic Center. Joe Hutchison was there and Barry Patton came from Winfield to go with us and play his bones. It was a cold, raining, freezing day. I drove our van and picked up Greg Kennedy in Oklahoma City. On the way to Grove, the farther we went the worse the weather got. This was an afternoon gig and when we finished our set, I said, "Boys, we need to go." Jana really wanted us to stick around and said, "Stay around and let's play some twin fiddles."

I knew the weather was getting bad. We took off and vehicles on I-44 were sliding and spinning off the road. I was white knuckled the entire trip home.

November 26 BBB played for Sweet Adelines in Oklahoma City. Bette had joined Sweet Adelines and they performed everywhere. I teamed up with Bette and we did some things as a quartet with Jim and Marsha Massey. Jim played a ukulele and I played fiddle.

December 18 BBB plus Barry Patton played Sedan Kansas.

Journal Entry 1997
Bosco and the Tippy Truck — Oklahoma International Bluegrass Festival - Fiddle Fest

In addition to the following, the BBB (Byron Berline Band) played twenty shows at the Music Hall.

January 4 BBB played Garland, Texas.

January 15 Bette and I attended NAMM (National Association of Musical Merchandisers Show) in Los Angeles.

January 19-25 Bette and I went to Palm Springs for a vacation.

February 4 BBB played the Radisson Inn, Oklahoma City.

February 16 I booked Robin and Linda Williams to do a show at the Music Hall.

February 21, 22 BBB played the Music Hall and I booked Steve Kaufman to do workshops and concerts.

April 4 BBB played Medford and Enid, Oklahoma.

April 12 I booked the Reno Brothers with the BBB and we played the Scottish Rite Temple in Guthrie. The Temple had an event and wanted entertainment, so they called and I put this together. I also booked the Reno Brothers for the first OIBF (Oklahoma International Bluegrass Festival,) in October.

April 22 BBB played the Arts Festival in downtown Oklahoma City.

April 25, 26 BBB participated in the 89'ers Celebration, anniversary of the Oklahoma Land Rush with two shows, Friday and Saturday.

May 2 BBB played Oklahoma, City.

May 6-8 Bette, Barry Patton, and I left for L.A. where Barry and I played the California Trail Ride.

May 10 Barry and I played the Calico Ghost Town Festival and the next day we headed home to Oklahoma.

May 13-15 BBB played Wisconsin.

June 13 BBB played a wedding.

June 21 played the Prairie Home Companion with Billy Joe Foster and Andy Stein. The Prairie Home Companion is a live radio show and we did the show at the Oklahoma City Civic

Center. They called saying they wanted southwest fiddling, whatever that is. I called Billy Joe and asked if he wanted to do this with me. He said, "Yeah, I guess we can do that." Andy Stein was the Prairie Home Companion fiddler and he played some with us. I do not know if we did southwest fiddling, but they seemed to like what we played. That night we had a show at the Music Hall and Andy came up and sat in with the BBB.

June 22 BBB played the Will Rogers Park in Oklahoma City.

June 28 BBB played a couple's Fiftieth Anniversary, private party.

July 18 BBB played Ardmore, Oklahoma.

July 27 BBB played the Music Hall Sunday afternoon jam.

August 3 BBB played Perkins, Oklahoma.

August 8 BBB played the Balloon Fest in Oklahoma City.

August 10 BBB played a Music Hall jam.

August 14 BBB played Caldwell, Kansas Sumner County Fair. The first time I ever performed on stage was at this fair. This year I played with my band. Greg Kennedy, our piano and bass player, rode with Jim Fish and his wife. Jim left immediately after the gig and Greg rode back with Steve Short. Steve had all our equipment and instruments in his car and he had his son along on the trip, so his car was full, but he offered to give Greg a ride. It was crowded, but they made it back and then Greg wanted Steve to take him to pick up his impounded car. Steve did not want to, but he did. Then Greg had to borrow some money from Steve to pay his fine…Steve was not happy. Another time when the band was on tour and at an airport, Greg lost his boarding pass somewhere between the ticket counter and the gate. When we finished our gig and it was time to fly home, he left his plane ticket in his motel room and did not miss it until we got to the airport. We had to call the motel and have someone bring it to us.

August 22 BBB played Arkansas City, Kansas.

September 5 Bette turned fifty five, so we could finally sell our house in California. We flew to L.A. to get the house ready to sell. When it was ready, we listed the house and it sold the same day.

September 10 Bosco and the Tippy Truck is not a show we played, well maybe it is. It all began when Bette flew back to Oklahoma and I rented a moving truck. I loaded everything, including a piano, a tow car behind the truck and in the cab, Becca,

Jade the dog, Becca's cat named Bosco, and me. It was crowded, but we got everything in and headed out to the freeway and on to our home in Oklahoma. We were concerned about Bosco, as cats usually do not travel as well as dogs. In anticipation of problems on our trip, we visited a vet and got a sedative for Bosco. We put the extremely relaxed Bosco in the cat carrier, the dog comfortable in the floorboard under Becca's feet and began our long journey home. We did not get very far before the wheels began to vibrate, first one, then another and the truck began to tip. We were scared the whole truck and the car in tow would turn over. I lowered my speed, carefully and slowly returning to our starting point. I went to the truck rental place and told them of the serious problem we had encountered. They said we over loaded the vehicle…we needed a bigger truck. That meant everything had to be unloaded and the tow car unhooked. I hired a couple of people to help me reload everything into the bigger truck. Because this truck was so much larger, they apparently felt they did not have to load it carefully. You can imagine the scratches and dings resulting from that lack of care. We got everything loaded, including the piano, then hooked up the tow car. We had no more sedative for Bosco and he was more than a little upset about riding in the carrier, inside a truck on the floorboard for the next thirteen hundred miles. The smaller truck had a back seat, which worked very well as a place for Bosco and his carrier. The larger truck, however, did not have the extra room. The dog rode between us with the cat carrier on the floor. Becca's legs were propped over the carrier and that is how she rode all the way to Oklahoma. We got as far as Flagstaff, Arizona, but were so tired we just could not go any farther. We stopped at a motel, but they were not happy about us having a dog, even though I assured them the dog would not bark. We all slept well, including Jade and Bosco. We did finally arrive safely in Guthrie, but what a trip!

September 19, 20 BBB played Winfield, Kansas Walnut Valley Festival.

October 2 BBB played Rocky's.

October 4 BBB played Hafer Park in Edmond, Oklahoma. I had just hired Richard Sharp and this was the first show he played with us. He arrived late and missed the first set.

October 5 BBB played Enid, Oklahoma.

October 9-11 BBB plus Barry Patton played the first OIBF (Oklahoma International Bluegrass Festival) in Guthrie.

The idea for OIBF came from the times I went to Europe, Japan, and other places and heard so many great bluegrass bands. They had never been to the U.S. so the only way they could have learned this stuff was from Earl Scruggs, Bill Monroe, Country Gazette, and others on records. I thought the best place to feature these groups would be in the middle of the country and I just kept these ideas in my mind. When I finally moved back to Oklahoma in 1995, Joe Hutchison, the man that held the bluegrass festival in Langley, Oklahoma, had been elected an Oklahoma State Representative. He decided we should push the international festival idea and make it happen. We eventually got the Oklahoma Department of Tourism interested. I told Joe I wanted to do this, but I wanted the money up front...I would not hire any musicians unless the money was in the bank. We got front money and when the festival began, we held it in down town Guthrie. We did that for about five years and then moved the entire festival to the Cottonwood Flats campground.

When we got the festival started, I called all my old buddies like Vince Gill and Emmylou Harris, Mason Williams, and Willie Nelson. They all came in to play and for essentially nothing. We did not have the money to pay their regular fees. They were great about donating their time. We had quite a lineup that first year with Country Gazette, The Dillards, California, the L.A. Fiddle Band, Dan Crary, Vince Gill, Ricky Skaggs, Blue Highway, Claire Lynch and the Front Porch String Band, Jim and Jesse, The Whites, the Byron Berline Band, and Barry "Bones" Patton. We also had groups from Austria, Belgium, the Czech Republic, Germany, Italy, Japan, the Netherlands, and the United Kingdom.

We used various venues in downtown Guthrie, including the Scottish Rite Temple, upstairs in the Music Hall, in a building across the street from the Doublestop Fiddle Shop, another building kitty-corner to the fiddle shop, the outdoor amphitheater, and even had some concerts at the grade school. Figuring out the logistics that first year was a nightmare in addition to lining up emcee's for each venue. I brought in Skip Conover, who had been with the L.A. Fiddle Band, to emcee. We held the big Saturday night show with Vince Gill, at the High School football field.

The storms and tornados came as only they can in Oklahoma.

One of the sponsors called Voice Stream gave us equipment and cell phones to help keep things organized. We also had a golf tournament with one hundred seventy slated to play and the head of Voice Stream wanted to play with Vince Gill. I called Vince and woke him up that morning.

He said, "Are you really going to play in the rain?"

I informed him we were, so he got dressed and came out to the golf course where it rained a while then quit, rained a while then quit. It was warm but rainy, then the weather changed and it turned into cold rain. Finally, I said, "That's enough for me," but Vince just kept playing. He played in the cold rain...would not give up.

As this is an International Festival, we had bluegrass groups from other nations on the program. On the Wednesday before the festival started, it got dark and the winds began to blow. One musician from Germany looked and pointed, saying, "What's that?"

"Tornado." I said.

On Saturday night of the festival, at the football field, the temperature was warm but with storms constantly threatening. Vince came out on stage in a pair of bib-overalls and carrying his mandolin. He looked at the foreboding sky. He had been listening to weather reports as all of us were doing. He said to the audience, "This has been a pretty funky year...I guess if he's going to take me out, I might as well be playing bluegrass. The weather people tell me we've got about 45 minutes before the storms and/or tornado hit. I think I'll stick around, if you want me to."

That was just what the audience wanted to hear and as they applauded, it began to rain.

"I don't care if the instruments get wet," Vince said. "They're not mine...I borrowed them, from Byron."

Organizing that first festival was a lot of work, but as soon as it was over, we were already preparing for the next year.

November 4, 5, 6 BBB played Country Jazz Fusion at Cameron University in Lawton, Oklahoma. We played with the Community Jazz Band and the University Jazz Band. We also lectured classes for the university's music department.

November 7 BBB played the Cowboy Hall of Fame in Oklahoma City, for Diabetes Awareness.

November 9 BBB played the Music Hall, Sunday Jam.

November 20 BBB played Rocky's.

December 13 BBB played the first Victorian Walk in downtown Guthrie. I booked Bill and Rosie Caswell from Bartlesville to play old time music. Bill and I go back to my college band playing days. Merchants sponsor the Victorian Walk and we all dress in period attire and have live scenes in our storefront windows. The Doublestop Fiddle shop window has a settee and rocking chair, so Bette sits and crochets while I play the fiddle. Sometimes John Hickman comes in and plays some banjo. We have an exterior speaker so the music floats outside as street vendors sell hot peanuts and people can stroll on the sidewalks or ride in horse drawn carriages. It is a lot of fun, especially because downtown Guthrie has changed very little and the buildings look essentially, as they did when it was the first Oklahoma State Capitol.

December 14 BBB played Rocky's.

December 19 BBB played a private party for Chip's Bar-B-Que. Chip brought barbeque up to the Music Hall's dining room and people gathered and had dinner before the shows. He eventually opened his own shop so we no longer had the pre-show dinners.

December 27 I invited a bunch of fiddlers to the Music Hall Show and we all played together which was the first of what became many years of having Fiddle Fest at the Music Hall. I remember Vince Gill and his mom dropped by the show.

Journal Entry 1998
Mae Axton Award

In addition to the following, BBB (Byron Berline Band) played 18 shows at the Music Hall.

January 8 John Hendricks produced commercials in this area and this was one of his sessions. BBB played an event for the Church of the Servant.

January 24 BBB played Rocky's.

January 26, 27 did a Les Gillam session.

February 5-8 this was the first time I played the Saline Fiddlers event Ann Arbor, Michigan.

February 13 BBB played the Farmers Organization in Oklahoma City.

February 21 BBB played Rocky's.

February 22 BBB played a Music Hall Jam.

February 28 BBB played the Ponca City, Oklahoma Poncan Theater.

March 7 BBB played Chip's Bar-B-Que. Instead of chip bringing Bar-B-Que to the Music Hall, we played a show at his place.

March 21 BBB played a Retired Educators Show at the Music Hall and that night we played at Rocky's.

April 11 BBB did workshops in the afternoon and had a show in the Music Hall that night.

April 13 I flew to Kansas City, Kansas and did a session with Michael Parks, the "Bronson" actor.

April 17, 18 BBB played Miami and Claremore, Oklahoma for the Oklahoma Arts Council.

April 19 BBB played a Music Hall Jam.

April 24 BBB played Clinton, Oklahoma. The Oklahoma Arts Council booked us all over the state.

April 25 The Guthrie 89'er Committee booked Red Steagall to play for the Guthrie 89'ers Land Rush Celebration and he asked me to play with him. That night we had a show at the Music hall with the Byron Berline Band and Red came up and played. Red, famous for his western ballads and cowboy poetry, is quite a storyteller.

May 2, 3 went to Santa Cruz, California, did the California Trail Ride, and went to Santa Barbara.

May 9 I played a Calico Ghost Town festival.

May 14 did a Bob Wood session.

May 19 did a session with Dale Pierce a banjo player. He is a big kid, an OSU discus thrower and a super nice person. While attending OSU in Stillwater, he lived in the athletic dorm and hung out with another student there, Garth Brooks. When Garth moved to Nashville, he tried to get Dale to go with him, but Dale was married, had a family, and just could not go.

May 20 Joe Hutchison asked me to play a Wild Life Bar-B-Que.

May 23, 24 played in Grand Junction, Colorado.

May 29 did a Bob Wood session.

May 30 BBB played the Masonic Temple in Guthrie.

June 5, 6 BBB played the Oklahoma City Stockyards.

June 9 BBB played the first, Patsy Montana National Yodeling Championship in Pineville, Missouri. My co-writer, Jane Frost and her husband, Larry, sponsored this event for several years and Jane wrote Patsy Montana's autobiography. I knew and played with Patsy so I was pleased she was being remembered with a festival and yodeling championship in her name. We gave a concert at the festival and played some golf in nearby, Bella Vista, Arkansas. Bill Snow came to the festival and I had not seen him for a number of years…we had a good visit. Katrina Elam also did a couple of songs with us. Bette went with me and we enjoyed the trip.

June 12 BBB played the Meeting of Lt. Governors in Oklahoma City.

June 19, 20 BBB played Cleveland, Oklahoma's first and only bluegrass festival.

June 27 BBB played a Freightliner private party and bar-b-que on the Freightliner lot in Oklahoma City, that night we played Rocky's.

June 28 BBB played the First Presbyterian Church in Tulsa, Oklahoma. This was the first time for this event and we have played it every year since.

July 9 I played a gig in Bowling Green, Kentucky with Eddie and Martha Adcock with Curtis Birch playing Dobro.

July 10 Bette and I attended the NAMM (National Association of Musical Merchandisers) show in Nashville.

July 14-16 BBB played the Oklahoma City Zoo.

July 17 BBB played Chip's Bar-B-Que.

July 20 BBB played the Council on Aging.

July 22-24 Doo Wah Riders had a Reunion at the Crazy Horse Saloon and they flew me to L.A. especially to be a part of it.

July 25 BBB played Rocky's.

July 26 BBB played Rose State College in Midwest City, Oklahoma.

July 30 BBB played a private, surprise birthday party in Tulsa.

August 14 BBB played the Oklahoma Traditional Music Association in Norman, OK.

August 17 did a Todd Barrett session.

August 18 BBB played Mulvane, Kansas.

August 21 BBB played Rocky's.

August 22 BBB with Barry Patton played a bluegrass festival at Serenata Farms in Lecompton, Kansas. This was the second year for this festival and they held it at the Therapeutic Equestrian Academy located at Big Spring. They had two stages and we were their headlining show on stage one. Some of the other groups included the Wilders, Past Tense, Euphoria String Band, Alfred Packer, Kelly and Diane Werts, Blackwolf, Spontaneous Combustion, Linda Tilton, Faris Family, Lost Highway, and the Plaid Family.

August 29, 30 BBB played a bluegrass festival in Santa Fe, New Mexico. While there, I did a recording session with Elliott Rogers and his band. He eventually moved to Austin, Texas and played with Alan Munde.

September 10 BBB played another Freightliner trucking event.

September 12 BBB played a fair in Pawhuska, Oklahoma in the afternoon. We did a Music Hall show, that night.

September 14-16 BBB played the Texas Trail Ride.

September 23 BBB played a private party.

September 26 BBB played Ponca City, Oklahoma.

October 1-3 BBB with Barry Patton played the second OIBF in Guthrie with Emmylou Harris headlining.

October 10 BBB played Remington Park in Oklahoma City. Remington Park is quite a place with the horseracing season opening in March, and there is a casino, restaurants, and live bands playing. They also have special events like New Year's Eve and prizefights.

October 13 BBB played an Environmental Corporate party in Oklahoma City.

October 17 in Ada, Oklahoma, I received the Mae Axton Award at the McSwain Theater.

This was taken at OIBF in Guthrie in 1998; Byron, Emmylou Harris and Bette.

MAE BOREN AXTON AWARD To
Byron Berline
"A CHAMPION IN HIS OWN RIGHTS"

Because of his untiring efforts, his dedication and devotion, and now three times National Champion Fiddle Player, Byron Berline, has become a legend in Country and Blue Grass music. Throughout Oklahoma, the Nation, and many European Countries, he has become a superstar of the highest esteem.

Having been touted as one of the most inventive fiddlers ever, his peers, the press and audiences World Wide have given him great world acclaims.

His skill as a musician, his versatility with musical instruments, his cooperative attitude and personality toward his peers and his fellowman is above reproach.

Byron Berline, a Native Oklahoman, having traveled the World, performing with the greatest of Country and Bluegrass entertainers, has returned to his home state to share, and promote his first love, Country and Bluegrass Music, with all who seek it.

October 24 BBB played Caldwell, Kansas.

October 27 Bette and I played the Epworth Retirement Village in Oklahoma City.

October 30 did a Bob Wood session.

November 21 BBB played Rocky's.

December 14 BBB played Enid, Oklahoma.

December 20 BBB played Shawnee, Oklahoma.

December 31 I played a New Year's Eve gig with Bob Wood.

Journal Entry 1999
Vince Gill and I Induct Each Other Into the Oklahoma Music Hall of Fame

In addition to the following, the Byron Berline Band played fourteen shows and had four Sunday Jams at the Music Hall.

January 9 BBB played Rocky's.

January 19 did a session for Terry Scarberry, one of the top session guitar players in Oklahoma City...he plays all styles and is excellent. Terry played with Richard Sharp and Steve Short who are both in the Byron Berline Band. Terry and his wife run the Rodeo Opry every Saturday night, at the Stockyards in Oklahoma City.

February 10 played the OU Lectures in Norman, Oklahoma, giving talks and demonstrations for classes in the Music Department.

February 12 BBB played the Poncan Theater in Ponca City, Oklahoma.

February 13 BBB played a concert at OU and Billie Joe Foster was on the show with us.

February 23 BBB played a Medical Society party in Oklahoma City.

March 3 BBB played Western Hills, Oklahoma.

March 5 BBB played a corporate party at the Cowboy Hall of Fame in Oklahoma City.

March 10 did a Bob Wood session.

March 14 Jim fish and I played a private backyard party for George Davis in Enid, Oklahoma.

We began recording the Byron Berline Band's Gene Clark/Gram Parson's Tribute CD. I have heard tribute CDs that just left me cold, so I wanted to make sure this one had the feeling of my two friends and musicians. The CD was two years in the making, but very well worth it. It has six songs of Gram's and six of Gene's. Guest artists include Vince Gill, Chris Hillman, Jay Dee Maness, and Al Perkins. It is amazing sometimes, you get to know somebody... they know some other people and it can really get involved. It is like playing seven degrees from Kevin Bacon, only for real. During the time I was playing in Los Angeles, either I played with most everyone or I knew them in one way or another as all the musicians did. Gene Clark's "Full Circle" song is about this. We have a show tonight and we might just do that song. It is just funny how it all intertwines.

April 9 BBB played in Medford, Oklahoma.

April 10 BBB played Cherokee, Oklahoma.

April 27 BBB played an Arts Council gig in Guyman, Oklahoma out in the panhandle.

April 29 I played the Deer Creek Schools.

April 30 BBB played the Duncan, Oklahoma Festival.

May 4-6 I played the California Trail Ride and did a session with David West.

May 7 Barry Patton and I played in Cambria, California with Peter Feldman and Dennis Caplinger.

May 12 BBB played Joe Hutchison's Wildlife Picnic in Oklahoma City.

May 14 BBB played the Guthrie Amphitheater and had Chip's Bar-B-Que there, instead of at the Music Hall.

May 21 BBB played a party at the Lazy E in Guthrie.

May 25-27 BBB played the Oklahoma City Zoo.

May 30 BBB played the Chuck Wagon at Cowboy Hall of Fame, Oklahoma City.

June 5 BBB played a wedding in Winfield, Kansas.

June 6 BBB played a wedding in the Round Barn at Arcadia, Oklahoma.

June 10 BBB played Weatherford, Oklahoma.

June 11 I attended Mike Clark's funeral that afternoon in Oklahoma City and the Baptist Church had over 1,000 people in attendance. That night, BBB played Rocky's.

June 12 BBB played Sulphur Days in Sulphur, Oklahoma.

June 15 BBB played Steigler, Oklahoma.

June 16 did a session for Katrina Elam a singer.

June 17 BBB played Lawton, Oklahoma.

June 26 played Medicine Park, Oklahoma.

July 9 BBB played Rocky's.

July 11-14 Bette and I went to Nova Scotia for Fiddlers of the World, the largest fiddle event I ever attended. Mark O'Connor was there, Natalie McMasters, several Canadian fiddlers and we did workshops and concerts. It was a very big production. They held this in the big arena where they played hockey. They had big dinners…it was quite an affair.

July 16 BBB played Norman, Oklahoma.

July 18 BBB played Enid, Oklahoma

July 23 Bette and I attended the NAMM Show in Nashville and did a session with Stuart Duncan on "Hamilton County Breakdown."

August 5 BBB played a Department of Tourism reception honoring Jane Ann Jayroe who was Miss Oklahoma 1996 and Miss America 1967.

August 20 BBB played an OSU Picnic.

August 21 BBB played Medicine Park, Oklahoma at a restored old dance hall where Bob Wills played.

September 5 played the Oklahoma Arts Festival.

September 7 played the Oklahoma City, Rotary Club, and Petroleum Club. These were opportunities for me to talk about OIBF.

September 8-10 played the Cowboy Hall of Fame for a promotion at the Oklahoma City Airport.

September 17 18 BBB played Winfield, Kansas Walnut Valley Festival.

Sept 30-Oct 1 BBB with Barry Patton played the third OIBF Guthrie.

October 2 played Mason Williams' Bluegrass Symphony for the OIBF with the Oklahoma City Philharmonic at Squires Ballpark, here in Guthrie.

October 4 did a Paul Hendel session.

October 8-10 played Honesdale, Pennsylvania. Steve Kaufman and I did workshops and concerts.

October 14 Vince Gill and I were inducted into the Oklahoma Music Hall of Fame. The Hall of fame is located at 401 South 3rd Street in Muscogee, Oklahoma and is an interesting place to visit because in addition to the Hall of Fame, there is a museum…one of my fiddles is included in an exhibit. Purpose of the Music Hall of Fame is to recognize Oklahomans for their lifetime achievements in music. The ceremony was interesting in that Vince and I introduced and inducted each other. Once the induction ceremony was complete, we played a concert.

October 17 I played a private party and I sat with Roger Mashore and Billy Perry.

October 23 BBB played Rocky's.

December 16 played at a country school west of Oklahoma City for Victor Rook, a bass player.

December 21 Two Pair, Jim and Marsha Masey and Bette and I, played somewhere.

December 31 played Ponca City, Oklahoma on New Year's Eve.

Journal Entryc 2000
Byron Berline Band in Europe — OU National Champions

In addition to the following, the Byron Berline Band played twenty two shows at the Music Hall.

January 3, 4 did a session for Rod Moag a blind mandolin player from Texas who loves bluegrass and western swing. Bob Will's niece is on this album, Alan Munde, and me. We did the recording at Palladium Studios in Oklahoma City.

February 4 BBB played Rocky's.

February 18 BBB played Ponca City.

March 7-23 BBB did a European Tour. The Oklahoma Department of Tourism arranged for us to go to Berlin, Germany for a four or five day junket. We played in a huge department store, among many displays of Oklahoma items, from handmade things, arts and crafts, to food. Some Indian dancers also went with us and performed. We tried to show the people of Germany what Oklahoma is about, the land, its people, and culture.

The rest of the Byron Berline Band had never been to Europe. When our duties for the State of Oklahoma ended, I arranged for a tour on our own, playing many small venues. We toured Germany and Zurik, Switzerland. There is a photo of us on the web, playing a big country show. The group, "Nugget," from Austria, was on the show. Liz Meyer, from Amsterdam, Holland, put this together and she was on the show. They held this in a huge building that seated over a thousand people for dinner and the show. At other times, Tim McDonald, stationed over there in the service, sat in with us. Tim is a very good keyboard player and always plays with us at the OIBF in October, in Guthrie. Tim is out of the service now and lives in Nashville.

When we were on our own, we bought maps, but sometimes we needed to ask directions and it got rather funny. I remember a few times, a man simply getting out of his car, leaving his wife to follow us and then he rode in our vehicle, pointing the way to our destination. What kind, helpful people.

April 1 BBB played Medicine Park.

April 2 BBB played a Christian Church in Oklahoma City.

April 4 BBB played Rocky's.

April 28 BBB played Cedarvale, Kansas.

May 5 BBB played Park City, KS.

May 9-11 I played the California Trail Ride and did a David West session, "Pickin' on Pink Floyd: A Bluegrass Tribute." David takes other genres and performs them bluegrass style.

May 12 played Las Olivos. Peter Feldman set this up.

May 20 BBB played a private party at Nichols Hills.

June 2 BBB played the Oklahoma City Zoo.

June 3 BBB played Durant, Oklahoma.

June 4 BBB played the First Presbyterian Church picnic in Tulsa.

June 8 BBB played in Yucon, OK, at the park.

June 16-18 California played Grass Valley, CA.

June 22 did a Bob Wood session.

July 14 BBB played Tahlequah, OK.

July 20 played the Station Inn in Nashville with Roland White. This was always in conjunction with the NAMM convention. Bette and I went each year and while we were there, Roland set up the Station Inn gig. I remember one time Barry Patton and Kenny Glasgow went too.

August 3 BBB played the Preservation Playhouse in Guthrie.

August 9, 10 John Hickman and I played the Sioux Falls, South Dakota Fair and met the nicest people. Glen Stoops and his son, Rick who runs the Sunset Pawn Shop, is also a fiddler. They were both so kind to us, taking us places and out to eat. They are very special people.

August 19 BBB played Choctaw, OK.

September 2, 3 played Santa Cruz, CA.

September 14-16 BBB played Winfield, Kansas Walnut Valley Festival.

October 5-7 BBB with Barry Patton played the fourth OIBF.

October 13 BBB played the Oklahoma City Zoo.

October 14 BBB played the Bricktown Arts Festival in Oklahoma City and a private party for Billy Perry.

October 19 BBB played a CHFF Benefit.

October 21 BBB played for the Norman, Oklahoma Schools.

October 28 BBB played the Wewoka Festival. I rode with John Hickman to the Festival. Afterward, he dropped me off at the OU stadium. I missed the first half of the game between OU and Nebraska and things were not looking good. Nebraska made the first two touchdowns. OU finally got in the game and the excitement in that stadium was electric! We won the game! People were so wound up they tore down the goal post and you would have thought OU had won the National Championship!

That January, Bette and I along with Bette's brother and his wife, went to Miami, Florida to see the OU vs. Florida State game when OU really did win the National Championship. That was quite a year for OU football.

October 29 BBB played the Texas Cattlemen's Association in Oklahoma City.

November 1, 2 BBB played Cameron College.

November 14 BBB played for Women Executives.

November 18 Kentucky, for the Violin Society

November 30-Dec 2 John Moore hired me to play for a deer hunt in Midland, Texas. This was for Clayton Williams, an oilman who ran for governor against Ann Richards and lost. He held this annual deer hunt mainly for his employees. They hunted during the day and sat by the fire at night and that is when we played. I am not a big hunter, but Moore is, so this was right down his alley.

Journal Entry 2001
Cain's Ballroom

In addition to the following, the Byron Berline Band did twenty two shows at the Music Hall.

January 12 BBB played Ardmore, Oklahoma.

January 19 did a Sarah Getto session.

January 28 BBB played Ardmore, Oklahoma.

February 1-3 BBB played Saline, Michigan. While at the airport, we received the news that Bob Wood had suddenly died from a heart attack. Bob was a wonderful person and everyone loved him.

February 8 BBB played El Reno Community College.

February 9 BBB played a Convention in Oklahoma City.

February 17 BBB played the Marriott in Wichita, Kansas for the Kansas Association of Bluegrass.

March 3 BBB played Bull Shoals, Arkansas.

March 7-9 went to Los Angeles to work on the Disney movie, "The Country Bears," released in 2002. This was through Glen Johns who produced the Rolling Stones and was in charge of the music for "the Country Bears" movie. He put me up in a very nice hotel and personally asked me to do this session.

March 10 BBB played an Ottowa, Kansas Theater Show.

March 11 I played in San Diego.

March 30 BBB played a Motor Coachers show.

March 31 played a benefit for a cancer victim in Medford, Kansas.

April 2-4 I did a session in Nashville, Tennessee, with Katsuyuki, Miyazaki. Katz and his wife, Chiaki, are from Japan.

April 21 BBB played Stillwater, Oklahoma and did a show at the Music Hall.

April 28 BBB played Cedarvale, Kansas.

May 5-12 played the California Trail Ride and some other southern California gigs.

May 18 BBB played a private party at the Music Hall.

May 19 BBB played Tahlequah, Oklahoma.

June 4 BBB played a private party at the Music Hall.

June 10 played the First Presbyterian Church picnic in Tulsa.

June 15, 16 played Lynn County Kansas.

June 18 BBB played the Regents in Medicine Park, Oklahoma.

July 4 BBB played Ponca City with fireworks at the park, sponsored by Conoco.

July 13 BBB played the Oklahoma City Zoo. Jim fish worked at the zoo and arranged this booking.

August 4 BBB played Lawton, Oklahoma and played a Music Hall show that night.

August 5 played an OSU event at the Cowboy Hall of Fame.

August 9 did a Brad Corwin session.

August 11 BBB played a party at the Music Hall.

Aug 25 BBB played a Harrah, Oklahoma Festival.

September 6, 7 BBB played the Oklahoma City Civic Center.

September 13, 15 BBB played Winfield, Kansas Walnut Valley Festival.

September 23 BBB played at the park in Norman, Oklahoma.

October 4-6 BBB and Barry Patton played the fifth OIBF.

October 15, 16 BBB played the Norman, Oklahoma Schools.

November 3, 4 BBB played the Pahrump, Nevada Bluegrass Festival at an RV park out in the desert about 50 or 60 miles from Las Vegas. It was beautifully set up.

November 16 BBB played the Oklahoma City Stockyards.

November 17 played a benefit for the Oklahoma Traditional Music Association. They hold this annually, but in a different town each year.

November 19 did a Debbie Henning session.

December 22 BBB with Barry Patton and the Red Dirt Rangers played Cain's Ballroom, in Tulsa, Oklahoma. This was the first time I played this historic venue. There are old photographs on the walls of all the artists that have played there, particularly Bob Wills. It was a special night and could only have been better had not my camera been stolen.

Journal Entry 2002
Byron Berline Band in New York City — Fiddle Heaven in Italy

In addition to the following, the Byron Berline Band did twenty three shows at the Music Hall.

March 13-18 John Hickman and I did three shows with Mason Williams. We played the Black Rose Acoustic Society at the Black Forest Community Center in Colorado Springs on the fifteenth, the Westminister Art Series at Ranum High School in Westminister on the sixteenth. On the seventeenth, we did a Bluegrass band thing at the Rialto Theater in Loveland.

March 21 The play, "Oklahoma" opened on Broadway in New York City and the Oklahoma Tourism department sent the Byron Berline Band with Barry Patton to New York for the opening. We arrived, got out of the cab and first thing, Richard Sharp's hat blew right down Broadway.

I had been to New York many times with the Flying Burrito Brothers, Country Gazette, etc., but this was different. Barry and I played on Fox News to advertise the opening and Oklahoma's Governor Keating was on with us. The Byron Berline Band with Barry played the wrap party at Fiddlers Green. The cast of the play attended, including all the dancers. We played Orange Blossom Special for at least ten minutes and it was quite a sight, seeing all those professional dancers dance to our music. All of the Oklahoma dignitaries were there, like Barry Switzer, the governor and others. While in New York City we also took the time and opportunity to tour the 9-11 bombing site.

April 5, 6 Barry and I played a Folk Festival in Boonville, Missouri set up by Cathy Barton and Dave Para.

April 24 BBB played a private party at the Music Hall.

In 2002, Disney released "The Country Bears" movie, about a country-rock band that disbands and then tries to get back together. This sounds all too familiar. It really is a good movie, as it should be with a budget of thirty two million dollars.

April 29 BBB played the Oklahoma School of Science and Mathematics, a state sponsored school, which takes eleventh and twelfth grade students who excel in science and mathematics.

May 4 BBB played the Winfield, Kansas Fair Grounds, City of Winfield sponsored this.

May 7 BBB played the Will Rogers Air Port, Oklahoma Department of Tourism.

May 10 BBB played Muskogee, Oklahoma.

May 14 BBB played the Myriad Center in Oklahoma City.

May 29 BBB played an Enid, Oklahoma Christian Church.

May31 BBB played a private party for Dr. Harty.

June 2 BBB played the First Presbyterian Church picnic in Tulsa.

June 5-10 Bette and I vacationed in Europe and this trip was long overdue. I had been all over Europe, several times, but never had the opportunity to really enjoy it and see the sites and that is the reason we are traveling now. We go based on our own desires, not just when we are required to do so. We want to travel now before we get too old or something happens and we cannot.

Bette and I had a blast! We went to Prague, Austria, Vienna, Italy, Germany and just everywhere. While in Prague, Czech Republic, we spent time with Eduard Kristufek and his brother Paul. They have a bluegrass band with Eduard on mandolin and Paul on banjo. I played with them at a local pub our first Saturday night out. We also invited several of their friends up on stage, so I got to pick with several very good Czech musicians. You may remember Eduard makes the wonderful Krishot mandolins, which I sell in the shop and his brother Paul, makes banjos as well as selling banjo parts to the Gibson Company.

I had a great time…there are many fantastic bluegrass musicians in the Czech Republic. Bette and I appreciated the use of Paul's flat while we were in Prague and the guided tours by Eduard. They really took care of us.

While walking the streets seeing the many wonderful sights, we stumbled upon the shop of a fiddle maker named Spidlen. We visited with his son Jan and played some of Jan's instruments. We learned we would see him at the Violin society convention in Cincinnati that November in the U.S.

After stops in St. Wolfgang and Schladming, Austria, we visited Salzburg where we toured Mozart's birth home, his childhood home, and the museum dedicated to his memory. Mozart's favorite fiddle was a Klotz! Remember that name…it will come up again.

Italy was the next country on our itinerary. We stopped in Padua to see Giovanni Lazarro, the fine violin and cello maker I met several years ago. We went to his shop and saw his latest works. I have several of Giovanni's violins for sale in the Fiddle Shop.

The next stop was Cremona, the home of Stradivari, Amati, Guarneri, and countless other fiddle makers through the centuries. What a fiddle paradise! There are currently one-hundred or so makers living and building instruments in Cremona today. I had corresponded with Vittorio Villa, via email for several months, so we visited his shop upon arriving in town and he was very helpful in showing us around and allowing me to play his violins. The Strad Museum was very interesting...it contains several displays of his molds, tools and other assorted memorabilia. There were also many other violins and a short film on violin making in the mid 1700's. While in Cremona, we went to the Municipal Hall and viewed five original violins made by Stradivari, Del Jesu Guarneri and Nicolo Amati. We were fortunate to be there just as they removed the Strad for the short concert of the day. They are each, lovingly played for 10-15 minutes every day by two fellows who are paid for just that purpose. Then one instrument is chosen to be played in a brief concert for those who have reserved a spot...we just got lucky! Cremona violinmakers support an observation room of sorts in a local venue, where they may display some of their instruments. Vittorio told us about it and showed us where to find it. The instruments were available to play and I tried them all.

After walking the town of Florence about forty times, we drove to Genoa. I heard that Paganini's violin was on display, a Del Jesu Guarneri called "the Canon," and a copy of it made some time later by Villaume in France. I thought I had a contact that could arrange for me to see them, but I was not successful in making that connection. Bette and I did not have any information about where they were housed and it turned into quite a scavenger hunt. It took us almost three hours to locate the building and a friendly guard unlocked three doors, and we were finally able to view them. He even allowed me to photograph the violins, something I had not been able to do in Cremona.

Our final fiddle adventure occurred in Mittenwald, Germany,

where there is a wonderful violin-making school and the town established a fantastic museum of violins and various stringed instruments in the very house where Klotz lived and worked. Remember, Mozart's favorite violin was a Klotz. Our good friend, Munich native Wolfgang Kovacs and girlfriend Ricci were perfect hosts and helped us sightsee for the remainder of our trip. He contacted Bruno Theil at the Rattlesnake Saloon who arranged an evening of picking for me on my birthday, July 6. On stage with me were Rudiger Helbig on banjo, Willie Jones (a Connecticut native who lives and works in Heidleburg) on bass and Munich native Ingo Sandhofen, a fantastic guitar picker! We had a great time and it seemed the audience did as well. Not only did we see and play a lot of different instruments, we toured several castles and churches. Florence Italy is an artistic paradise and Austria and Germany have amazing castles.

July 22-27 played and did workshops at Rocky Grass with Dennis Caplinger and John Moore.

August 1-11 BBB did a tour of California.

August 13 did a session for Les Gilliam who is from Ponca City and known as the "Oklahoma Balladeer."

August 15 did a Devon Derrick session.

August 30 BBB played Oklahoma Electric Co-Op in Norman, Oklahoma.

September 12 played the UCO Jazz Lab with Mickey Flats band "Brigade."

September 19 BBB played Tulsa, Oklahoma.

September 20, 21 played Winfield, Kansas Walnut Valley Festival.

September 22 BBB played Norman, Oklahoma Summer Breeze Concerts.

September 27 BBB played the Mid West Trophy Show.

October 3-5 BBB with Barry Patton played the sixth OIBF.

October 9 BBB played Norman Schools.

October 15 BBB played for Governor Frank Keating in Oklahoma City.

October 22 John Hickman and I played for the Quail Springs Bank in Oklahoma City.

November 2 played for the OCTMA, (Oklahoma City Traditional Music Association)

November 13-16 BBB played the Violin Society of America in Cincinnati, Ohio.

Journal Entry 2003
Western Swing Show

In addition to the following, the Byron Berline Band played twenty one shows at the Music Hall.

February 20 BBB played the OCU Jazz Lab, Oklahoma City. The University of Central Oklahoma is in Edmond and OCU offers a Master of Music in Jazz Studies. I sat in with the Brigade band, with Mickey Flats, David and Tina Bonham, and Mike Perry.

March 27 BBB played Blackwell, Oklahoma.

John Hendricks and I began having a weekly radio show in April, called, "Salty Licks," on KOMA, which is one of the oldest radio stations in Oklahoma City. Hendricks previously called California home and had been a DJ out there for many years. We wanted the show to be eclectic with some focus on folk, bluegrass, and country. We played all kinds of records on the show, had interviews and a lot of back and forth banter between us. It was a lot of fun. During the OIBF, John came out to the festival and we got some great interviews; with people like Earl Scruggs, Dan Crary, and Tommy Emmanuel.

April 4 BBB played a private party.

April 6 BBB played the Oklahoma School of Science and Mathematics.

April 9-13 I played with Bluegrass Etc. in Cortez and Durango, Colorado.

May 4 BBB played Winfield, Kansas Spring Concert.

May 7 BBB played a private party at Rocky's in Oklahoma City.

May 17 we played our first Western Swing Show at the Music Hall. While still living in California, but making plans to move to Guthrie, Oklahoma, I knew I wanted to come back and do bluegrass and western swing. I knew the people here liked bluegrass and folks from Oklahoma and Texas love western swing. It is a lot of fun to play. I met Leon Rausch at various events and as he is the last remaining Bob Wills' singer, having joined Bob in 1958, I wanted him to be a part of this. I called and he graciously accepted. Leon still sounds great! I put a band together for him with Johnny Bier on tenor banjo and John Hickman played a 5-string. Smiley Weaver played steel and he too, played with Bob Wills. Dennis Buriski played piano and Suttlemier a jazz player, played guitar. The lineup sometimes changed through the years. Brad Benge played guitar a couple of years. Jim Fish joined the Byron Berline Band and he began playing guitar for the Western Swing Show. Leon is a gentleman and such a pleasure to have here. It is so much fun and we have the Western Swing Show every May here in Guthrie. We later began having this show at the Logan County Fairgrounds.

May 31 BBB played the Roxy in Muskogee.

June 15 BBB played the First Presbyterian Church picnic in Tulsa.

June 17 BBB played a park in Broken Arrow and was one of the first times Brad Binge played with the band. The park is huge and the band sang around one microphone, which we always carried with us. We did a sound check and everything sounded fine. We did the first set and before beginning our second set, the soundman said, "It's not reaching out there. We need to put up some more mics."

We knew the sound was fine, but did not say anything. He put an extra vocal mic next to the existing one and on the second set…no Hickman sound. Steve Short is a sound engineer and plays drums in our band. Steve is also the one who makes sure our sound is good whether performing elsewhere or on our own stage at the Music Hall in Guthrie and he also engineers our recording sessions. Tony Moore, from Tulsa, is a friend of ours and he was standing by the stage. Steve told Tony to go tell the soundman to turn up Hickman's microphone. Tony headed for the sound booth and quickly returned.

"He said he won't take instructions from a drummer." Tony told us.

After the show, we began to put our equipment away and here came the soundman for whom, Steve had several choice words.

June 19 BBB played Pryor, Oklahoma. Pryor is a very small town and we played at the school. Very few people lived around there and it was so nice to play a small town again.

June 26 BBB played Red Oak, Oklahoma.

July 1 John Hickman and I played for the Quail Springs Bank in Oklahoma City. Alan Webb had parties for his customers on special days like July 4 and he hired John and me to play these parties.

July 12 BBB played the Roxy Theater in Muscogee, Oklahoma.

August 2-4 played Salt Lake City, Utah.

August 9, 10 played in Texas.

August 18-24 played in San Diego, California.

September 9 BBB played the Quail Springs Church.

September 12 played the Crossings, a huge Church in Oklahoma City.

September 18 BBB played Lindsey, Oklahoma.

September 19 played for Billy Graham's son, Franklin. He wanted to have a big event, which he held at the University of Tulsa football stadium. I played with Dennis Agajarian (the fastest guitar player alive) from San Diego and he brought his own banjo player. This was the first time I ever used earplug monitors and everything was so clear…it was like being in a studio.

September 21 BBB played the Norman, Oklahoma Park.

October 2-4 BBB with Barry Patton played the seventh OIBF in Guthrie.

October 12-19 played for the Northern California Fiddlers in Santa Cruz.

October 20 BBB played for Oklahoma Rural Water in Oklahoma City.

October 24 BBB played a bar in Denton, Texas. I met the owner of this bar one year while in Winfield, Kansas at their Walnut Valley Festival. He wanted us to play at his place in Denton so we did and it worked out just fine.

November 9 BBB played a Christina Church in Oklahoma City.

November 13, 14 BBB played in southeastern Oklahoma.

December 20 BBB played the Guthrie, Oklahoma Country Club.

December 22 BBB played a private party in Oklahoma City.

Journal Entry 2004
A Byrd and a Fish

In addition to the following, the Byron Berline Band played twenty two shows at the Music Hall.

February 3 BBB played Topeka, Kansas.

February 14 BBB played the Kansas Bluegrass Festival at the Mariott Hotel in Wichita.

February 20 BBB played a private party.

February 21 BBB played Fiddle Fest in The Music Hall.

March 13 I played Cortez, Colorado with Bluegrass Etc.

March 21 BBB played Rocky's in Oklahoma City.

April 2 BBB played Pryor, Oklahoma.

April 15-18 BBB played Tyler, Texas. Frank Deramus, my college roommate at OU, has a brother who lives in Tyler, and he helped put this event together for a wealthy Texan. This person wanted to do a big festival, in-doors, at the big Sports Arena in Tyler. I booked all the acts for him…we had Ricky Skaggs and his band, the Texas Playboys with Leon Rausch, Bluegrass Etc., and the Byron Berline Band…this was a big budget show.

May 4 played the Wildlife Dinner for Joe Hutchison.

May 7 Vince Gill and the Byron Berline Band played the Wichita Falls, Texas, Habitat for Humanity. Dr. Brian Hall is from Wichita Falls and he loves bluegrass music. I helped him put this together by booking Vince Gill and my band.

Poor Vince, when he arrived, he could barely talk. He played guitar with us and lowered the keys of everything he had planned to sing. He managed to get through it okay, but not do what he wanted to do. I really felt for him.

Dr. Hall is a wonderful supporter of OIBF and generously donates to the festival.

May 20-22 BBB played the National Aviary in Pittsburg, Pennsylvania. Jim Fish had to leave BBB because his wife got a job in Pittsburg. While living there, Jim and his wife worked for the National Aviary, America's Bird Zoo. Jim oversaw living programs at the National Aviary and his wife was director of veterinary medicine. Mrs. Fish gave us a very interesting behind-the-scenes tour of the zoo.

This event was a benefit to raise funds for and promote rare bird conservation. Jim wanted to have a special concert at the National Aviary and he booked the Byron Berline Band. He also wanted to have a Byrd on the show and Chris Hillman came in to be with us. As a result, we had a Byrd and a Fish perform at the National Aviary. This story may sound fishy, but it is true. The Byron Berline Band opened the show, then Chris Hillman played solo and then he played with us. It was a good night.

We have shows in the Music Hall twice a month, I do some workshops, I still do a few things on the road, but nothing like I used to. I did not try to get on the bluegrass circuit. It was just too much...on the road all the time. Now, I go out when I want to and Bette and I travel the same way.

May 26 BBB played the Women's NCAA World Series Softball Championship in Oklahoma City. Marita Hynes, one of the directors of this event, had been a softball coach at OU and in 1998 had a ball field at OU named for her, the Marita Hynes Field, home of the OU softball team. Marita liked me and she liked the music I played, which led her to hire the Byron Berline Band to entertain the athletes at the pre-World Series Bar-B-Que. We have also played the National Anthem at the World Series...and we still do. I have really gotten to do some interesting things in my career and this is certainly one of them.

June 13 BBB played the First Presbyterian Church picnic in Tulsa, Oklahoma.

June 18-20 BCH played the Huck Finn's Festival in California. Don Tucker and his family ran the Huck Finn festival for a time and at one time, ran the Calico Ghost Town.

At the first show, no Hickman. John was sick so Dan Crary and I did a duo. We found that Craig Smith was out there with Laurie Lewis. Craig is a good banjo picker and he played with us on the last day.

June 24 BBB played the Quail Creek Bank party.

July 8-11 played Colorado Rocky Grass with Bluegrass Etc.

July 22 played with Roland White at the Station Inn in Nashville. Bette and I were in town for the NAMM show.

August 13 BBB played the Bethany, Oklahoma Balloon Fest.

They held this at Eldon Park and in addition to the Byron Berline Band; they booked Edgar Cruz, Narrow Gate, and Harvey and The Wallbangers. There is something quite beautiful about hot air balloons against an Oklahoma sky.

August 16-20 did a Peter Feldman session in Los Olivos, California, which is in the San Diego area. Dennis Caplinger was on it, Dan Crary, Wayne Shrubsall, Bill Bryson, and me. It was just me and my fiddle, and all those banjos. The name of the CD is "Grey Cat, on the Tennessee Farm" and is a tribute to Uncle Dave Macon an early performer on the Grand Ole Opry in Nashville. We did his songs and had banjos on everything. Peter Feldman referred to us as "The Pea Patch Quintet." Peter and Dennis Caplinger produced it and I had to learn all the songs while we were in the studio. To be honest, this is one of my favorite CD's and we really had a lot of fun doing it.

August 27 BBB played El Reno.

September 15-17 BBB played Winfield, Kansas Walnut Valley Festival. In addition to the festival, I did some pre-festival workshops and I remember Greg Burgess went with me.

September 26 BBB played the Park in Norman, Oklahoma.

Sept 30, Oct 1, 2 BBB with Barry Patton played the eighth OIBF in Guthrie.

October 28 BBB played Altus, Oklahoma.

November 7 BBB played a church picnic in Oklahoma City.

December 4 BBB played a private party at the Lazy E, in Guthrie for Ditch Witch of Perry, Oklahoma.

December 9 BBB played for Oklahoma Women in Oklahoma City.

Journal Entry 2005
Deadwood — Byron Berline Band in China

In addition to the following, the Byron Berline Band played twenty five shows at the Music Hall, including a special one on New Year's Eve.

I released another CD in 2005 called "Flat Broke Fiddler." It has four traditional fiddle tunes on it and the rest are my own compositions.

January 27 Barry "Bones" Patton and I played a pre-OK Mozart promotion in Bartlesville where we went to different homes and played.

January 28 BBB played the Cattleman's Ball in Wichita Falls, Texas. Dr. Hall also hired Asleep at the Wheel.

February 12 played Winfield, Kansas.

March 6-10 Barry Patton and I acted in the "Deadwood" TV series, in Burbank, California. "Deadwood" was an HBO series that ran for two seasons. David Ligon from Nickel Creek, Texas, hired the musicians for the series and in the first season of the show, he played a judge, lawyer, or something. I met David in about 1980 when we played the California Trail Ride. He is a very outgoing character with a very bubbly personality and he loves music, fiddles, and pickin'. When riders at the various trail ride camps spread their bedding on the ground under the oak trees and folks began to pick and sing, David referred to them as "Mattress Jams." He went to each camp at the Trail Ride and got singers and pickers from each camp and brought them together and they all played for about an hour and a half. He had these "mattress jams" at ten in the morning.

For the "Deadwood" episode, Ligon had John Moore, Steve Spurgin, Bill Bryson, Barry Patton, and me. He flew Barry and me to Burbank for this shoot, filmed at Melody Ranch, an amazingly realistic set. The first day we did a session and recorded all the songs they were going to use. They did not know exactly what music they were going to use, so we did some old tunes, like Sally Goodin', Arkansas Traveler, and a waltz, "Over the

Waves." The scene in which we were to act was a big wedding scene. John Moore had to play the wedding march on an old taterbug mandolin and Ligon was in this scene. "Sally Goodin'" ended up being a big number...it must have lasted nine minutes. We were all there, but very little on screen.

The director on this series, David Melch, also participated in the California Trail Rides. On the set, he asked me, "Can you dance?"

I said, "Well, I guess I can do that." He wanted me to lead the wedding party around and play the fiddle, but it never happened because we ran out of time. This whole thing was quite fun...having Barry there and all our friends. We had such a good time. They put us in these 1800's period costumes and we had to look dirty so they put fake dirt on our faces. Barry looked like a stuffed sausage! Everything on him was too small. Well, everything except the stove pipe hat.

March 11-23 BBB went on a southwest tour. We played Cortez, Colorado on our way out west, Salt Lake City, Utah and then on to California.

March 30 played the Norman, Oklahoma, Schools.

April 1 & 2 BBB played Muskogee, Oklahoma.

April 4-19 BBB with Barry Patton went on tour to Bejing, China. I met Mr. Jing Q. Song who also played violin, at the Violin Society of America, and he asked if I would like to go to China and play. He set it all up...we agreed on price and everything. This tour was for the entire band to go, but Brad Benge did not want to...he was afraid to travel in China. I got Mitch Corbin to go with us instead. He lived in Tennessee at this time and came back and forth to Oklahoma to play with the band. Mitch Corbin was instrumental in getting David Bromberg and Suzy Bogus at OIBF.

While touring China, the Byron Berline Band took a tour of the Eastman Company, makers of fiddles, mandolins, guitars, and bass's. I sell their instruments in my Doublestop Fiddle Shop. The U.S. Eastman outlet is in Maryland and their factory is in Bejing. They gave us many opportunities to sightsee and gave us a wonderful tour of their factory. As I carry their instruments in the fiddle shop, I was eager to see how they made them. The factory has no machines, every instrument is handmade...I thought that was amazing. They asked if we would like to play some mandolins. Mitch Corbin and I did so and they were so very pleased at this.

They said, "We've never heard our mandolins played."

There are many violinists in China, but not mandolin players. Their factory employs seven-hundred people, but they allow no one to work in the factory until they have studied for two years.

The female associate of one of the Eastman Company owners did not speak English, but her assistant did and the company associate went to great lengths to see that our tour was pleasant. She went way beyond expectations, taking us, everyone in the band, out to dinner. The food in China is wonderful. We wanted to see Ming's tomb and she took us, the whole band, paying for all our entry fees. Afterwards, she said, "Let's go eat again." Then, she took us to another exceptional restaurant where Barry Patton was in fine form and we laughed so hard. Barry went through this babble that sounded to us like Chinese, but of course, was not. All this went on with the waitress standing there, while Barry had the menu in his hand. When he finally stopped, she just looked him like, "What was that - I don't speak Japanese." We were hysterical.

Mr. Song taught us a Chinese folk song, which we performed with Mr. Song on violin. Another highlight was when Barry played the chopsticks (drum style) on my fiddle strings…that was the best use we made of chopsticks!

We were tourists as well as musicians while in china. We saw the Great Wall, Tienemen Square, the Forbidden City, the Summer Palace, and the many markets where shopping was fun, especially if you like to bargain and what musician does not? The venues we played were fifteen-hundred-seat theaters in Beijing, Shanghai, Hangzhou, and Ningbo. This trip to china was wonderful and the people, so hospitable.

April 22 BBB played a bombing benefit for the ten-year anniversary of the Oklahoma City bombing. This was really a very nice thing. Vince Gill performed, along with Toby Keith, and Katrina Elam. Our bluegrass went over great! We did Uncle Pen and Wheel Hoss. We tore them up! We had one of the best receptions I can ever remember and we were so glad they liked what we were doing.

April 26 BBB played Bob Wills Day in a little theater in Turkey, Texas. All of Bob Will's musicians annually get together for this.

April 28 BBB played in El Reno, Oklahoma.

April 29 BBB played Yucon, Oklahoma.

May 4 BBB played the Oklahoma Opry in Oklahoma City.

May 7 BBB played the annual Western Swing Show in Guthrie.

June 10, 11 BBB played the City of Edmond Arts Council Acusticadia at Lake Acadia to benefit the Edmond school string program. I booked the acts for this event including Ricky Skaggs, the Kruger Brothers, Austin Jug Band, Tom Ball and Kenny Sultan, Steve Spurgin, Mitch Corbin, and the Byron Berline Band.

June 12 BBB played the First Presbyterian Church picnic in Tulsa, Oklahoma.

June 16 BBB played the OK Mozart Festival in Bartlesville, Oklahoma,

June 18 BBB played the Chandler Ice Cream Festival in Chandler, Oklahoma.

July 2 BBB played the Tidal School Vineyards in Drumright, Oklahoma. This was a tribute to Jazz legend Chet Baker to benefit the Oklahoma Jazz Hall of Fame. There were places to play outside and they had all kinds of bands including jazz, bluegrass, rock, and blues. They had jazz all day inside the winery. After playing, we headed right back to Guthrie to play a show at the Music Hall that night.

July 9 BBB played Dr. Hart's retirement party.

July 12 BBB played the Quail Springs Bank party for Alan Webb.

August 6, 7 BBB with Mitch Corbin played the Edgewood Wildlife Festival in New Mexico. We stopped to play a theater in Turkey, Texas on our way out west.

August 14-20 I played the Rocky Mountain Fiddle Camp.

August 26 BBB played El Reno, Oklahoma.

September 5 BBB played the Edmond, Oklahoma, Park.

September 12-15 John Hickman, Richard Sharp, Barry Patton, and I played the Texas Trail Ride making the trip in my pick-up truck. On our return to Oklahoma, we went through Austin, Texas and I thought I was cruising along with the flow of traffic;

probably going seventy...the speed limit was sixty. I looked over at two motorcycle cops with a radar gun on the side of the road.

Barry said, "They just gunned you."

"Really?" I said and sure enough, one came after me and I figured I was toast. I had out of state plates and a big OU receptacle on the trailer hitch. I pulled over and got out my driver's license, proof of insurance and vehicle registration. I looked in the rearview mirror and saw a scruffy black man with a rather scraggly beard approaching. I remember thinking he looked strange for a cop.

He said, "Let me see your driver's license, proof of insurance and vehicle registration."

He looked them over. "Know why I stopped you?" he said in a gruff voice.

I of course told him "no."

"You were going eighty miles an hour." Then he showed on the radar gun where it registered my mph. "And guns don't lie."

"This is going to be my first and only warning of the day." He announced. "And the reason is because I'm on the fence between OU and Texas."

All the worrying about the license plates and OU hitch cover...they are what saved me from getting a ticket. Then he came back.

"Another reason I didn't give you a ticket," he began, "I went to school in Langston (Oklahoma) for a year, but the cows were prettier than the girls."

Langston College is mainly an all black school just about twenty-five miles east of Guthrie.

September 17 & 18 BBB played Winfield, Kansas.

September 25 BBB played Norman, Oklahoma, park.

October BBB with Barry Patton played the ninth OIBF. Great line up with David Bromberg, Bobby Hicks, Fletcher Bright, and Billy Joe Foster.

October 2 BBB played the Water Works in Oklahoma City.

October 11 BBB with Brad Benge and Mitch Corbin played with the Oklahoma Community Orchestra in Oklahoma City, for OCC (Oklahoma Christian College.) We used some of Mason Williams' charts from his Bluegrass Symphony. These events were always fun to do and very different…really enjoyed playing with our bluegrass band and the orchestra.

October 20 BBB played for Stillwater Agriculture in Stillwater, Oklahoma.

October 28 BBB played Dumas, Texas.

December 3 Greg Burgess and I played a Western Swing Christmas event in Cement, Oklahoma. Billy Joe Foster put this together, but then became ill and could not be there. Greg and I teamed up with some other musicians for this gig.

November 12 played the Grand National Quail Hunt in Enid, Oklahoma. This was the first year I went to this event, which is attended by many celebrities. The first day I hunted and shot two quail, not getting my limit, but that was okay. That night we went to a stag dinner for all the men on the hunt. John D. Groendyke is one of the sponsors of this event and he built the Groendyke Hunting Lodge on Lake Hellums, which is where they held the dinner. They served up the most beautiful prime rib I had ever seen. I took one bite and it lodged in my esophagus. I could still breathe, but I could not swallow. I returned to Guthrie and Dr. Robert, my brother-in-law who specializes in gastrointerintology. He did a scope and got that out of there. I waited a few days, and then he went back in and stretched my esophagus. Acid reflux can cause the esophagus to shrink and that is exactly what happened. The Quail Hunt ended and of all things, our team won the Grand National Quail Hunt! I have this big trophy/plaque at home. I could not imagine my two birds helping our team's score. The rest of the team must have been some kind of shots!

December 12 BBB played the Enid Country Club in Enid, Oklahoma.

Journal Entry 2006
The Red Diamond Stradivarius

In addition to the following, the Byron Berline Band did twenty one shows at the Music Hall in Guthrie.

January 17 John Hickman and I played Newkirk, Oklahoma.

February 2 played a Pre-Oklahoma Mozart in Bartlesville to help promote the event.

February 5-11 BBB with Barry Patton played a Cruise. We sailed out of Galveston Island, Texas and cruised to Cozumel and Progresso, Mexico, but hurricanes in the area cut short our trip. This was a working vacation and our spouses and families came too, including my sister Eleanor and some cousins from Texas. About fifty people went along with us and other musicians joined our jams and workshops.

This trip came about in a rather unusual way. When I was with the Doo Wah Riders in California, we played the Alpine Village many times. A man by the name of John Riddle taught line dancing there and we became friends. After we moved to Guthrie and opened the Fiddle Shop, one day while walking down the street I ran into John Riddle. He too, moved to Guthrie and he booked cruises. He suggested the Byron Berline Band go on a cruise and that is just what we did.

February 17, 18 BBB played Farmerville and Linden, Texas. Richard Bowden lived there and he converted a big building into a venue for music shows and other events. Richard had Don Henley of the Eagles, came in and did a fundraiser to help with the conversion costs. Don is from Gilmer, Texas, about forty-five miles from Linden.

Richard is so funny, just hilarious and he sings funny songs. While living in California he played with lots of people, such as Linda Ronstadt. Richard and I had a mutual friend, Fred Walecki and Richard had Fred fly to Texas from California, to surprise me. He did and so did the snow. I did not expect either one.

Fred Walecki is my age and he helped me a lot when I moved to L.A. His father Herman Walecki opened a violin shop in 1947 as a source for rare violins, harps, and other orchestral instruments and after he passed away, Fred kept the shop open. He repaired instruments, sold strings, etc.

I was always looking for a place to get bows re-haired or buy new strings...things like that. Steve Stevenson a bluegrass musician, who played with Don Parmley of the Bluegrass Cardinals, lived in the San Fernando Valley. Steve said he knew Fred Walecki, who could help with instruments. We went to Fred's violin shop in Westwood and Steve introduced us...it was an immediate friendship. He is such a nice person.

Growing up in his father's violin shop, Fred knew violins well and could work on them. I remember one time we spent two full days getting a sound post just the way I wanted it. He was so patient...I could not believe he did that. I spent a lot of time in his shop.

Fred liked to hang around musicians. I introduced him to Emmylou Harris, Gram Nash, Bernie Leadon, everyone I could, and as a result, he sold a lot of instruments. He got into carrying other instruments such as guitars, mandolins, banjos...not just violins. He also began selling some sound equipment.

One night he picked me up in his brand new Porsche. We went to the Troubadour Club, had a few drinks and when it came time to go home he said, "You drive."

I said, "Are you sure?"

It had a 5-speed transmission and I had never driven a car that had one. I got behind the wheel and Fred said, "Put your foot on the foot feet and don't let up."

I went from first gear into second with no problem...from second to third gear, no problem and third to fourth gear, but when I thought I was shifting straight down into fifth gear it moved a little to the left...into second. You cannot imagine how that engine sounded! We were ten or fifteen miles from my house, but somehow we made it home then I had to take Fred home. I blew the engine in his brand knew Porsche. I felt so bad...unimaginable.

As long as we are talking about Fred Walecki, I would like to tell you a true story. First, I learned a lot about violins from Fred and he still has all his father's violins. Someday I hope to see them if he ever remembers how to open the safe.

You may not know this...every Stradivarius violin has a

name. Fred Walecki's father had the "Red Diamond" in his shop, on consignment. A concert violinist came into his shop one day and asked if he might borrow the Strad to play at a Sunday afternoon stringed quintet affair. This is a rather common occurrence as most concert violinists are without Stradivarius violins and often borrow one for special performances. Herman Walecki complied with the request and the violinist left the shop, driving away in his car with the Strad safely in its case. The weather was terrible that day with torrents of rain coming down, flooding the city streets and gutters. The violinist picked up the violin case with the precious Strad inside then got out of the car and into the rushing water. The violin immediately fell from his hands and quickly floated down the flooded street, into a drain, and finally out to sea.

Herman Walecki placed an ad in the newspaper without mentioning that the missing violin was a Stradivarius. The ad simply read, "Violin lost at sea." followed by the shop's phone number. Time passed and one day a man called the shop and said, "I found a violin in its case, washed up on the beach. Do you think it could be yours?"

He brought the violin to Walecki's shop and it was indeed, the Red Diamond. The Strad was in pieces, but each piece was there and all warped out of shape after being waterlogged in salt water. With Herman Walecki's knowledge and skill and with the help of Hans Weisshaar, they began restoring the Red Diamond. Hans Weisshaar is the master of violin restoration and he has a violin shop in Los Angeles. Hans Weisshaar has published an extensive book on Violin Restoration. I have a copy of this book and it is an excellent resource.

They cleaned the pieces then made counter-forms of sand bags to reshape them. It took them a year to restore it and today, someone, somewhere is playing the Red Diamond Stradivarius. I have played seven Strads and one of them is truly the finest instrument I have ever played. While the others were quite nice, they were nothing like that one.

February 19-26 played Winter Grass in Washington and played some with Bluegrass Etc.

March 11 played Cortez, Colorado with Bluegrass Etc.

March 18 played the San Diego Acoustic Music Series.

March 24 BBB played Elk City, OK.

March 27-28 did a Nashville session that may have been done in Guthrie.

April 7-10 played the Saw Grass Fiddle Contest in Gainesville, Florida at Payne's Prairie State Preserve. Annemieke Pronker-Coron, a violinist from Holland, lived in Florida and I met her while playing with the Doo Wah Riders. She booked Mitch Corbin and me to judge and to do workshops.

May 12-15 I played the California Trail Ride.

May 20 played the Western Swing Show and Dance at the Fairgrounds in Guthrie.

June 8 BBB played a Quail Springs Bank party.

June 9-10 BBB played Acousticadia, which was the last one they had. I was not responsible for booking all the acts that year which included Michael Martin Murphy and the Byron Berline Band with Mitch Corbin flying out to do this with us.

June 11 Mitch Corbin with BBB played the First Presbyterian Church picnic in Tulsa.

June 15 Mitch Corbin played with BBB in Bartlesville for Oklahoma Mozart.

June 17 BBB played the Chandler Ice Cream Festival in Chandler, Oklahoma and this was Jim fish's first gig back with the band.

June 24 BBB played the Skiatook Bluegrass Festival.

July 7-9 BBB toured Texas and New Mexico. We played at Turkey, Texas on the way to New Mexico where we played a bluegrass festival at a wildlife refuge in Moriarity.

July 19 we did an "Oklahoma Rising" session. Ackerman McQueen is an advertising company in Oklahoma City and they filmed many different people in many different styles, performing a new state anthem called "Oklahoma Rising, written by Vince Gill and Jimmy Webb. This was to promote the Oklahoma Centennial in 2007. Kyle Dillingham and Brad Benge of Horse Shoe Road recorded it and they had a jazz version recorded as well as The Byron Berline Band with Mitch Corbin.

August 6-12 I taught at the Rocky Mountain Fiddle Camp.

August 2-26 California got together to play and do workshops at the Summer Grass Festival.

September 2-4 Bette and I went to Clippermills, California where I played Steven Plazzo's birthday party.

September 8 BBB played the park in Mustang, Oklahoma.

September 11-14 played the Texas Trail Ride, Tejas Vaqueros, with John Hickman on banjo, Richard Sharp on bass, Barry "bones" Patton, John Moore on guitar and I played fiddle.

September 15, 16 BBB played Winfield, Kansas Walnut Valley Festival.

September 21-24 BBB played Edmond, Choctaw, and Norman, Oklahoma.

October 5-7 BBB with Barry Patton played the tenth OIBF in Guthrie. We had a California band reunion with Dan Crary, Steve Spurgin, John Moore, John Hickman, and Byron Berline. The lineup included Claire Lynch Band and Rhonda Vincent and her band, John Jorgenson's band, Asleep at the Wheel, Alasdair Fraser and Natalie Hass from Scotland, April Verch from Canada, Blue Railroad Train from France and the Kruger Brothers from Switzerland. Oklahoma folks included High Ground, Cedar Ridge, Neverly Hillbillies, Common Tyme, Brigade, and III Generation.

Journal Entry 2007
Oklahoma Centennial — Getting to Stage 5

In addition to the following, the Byron Berline Band played nineteen shows at the Music Hall.

February 9 BBB played the new OU Weather Center opening in Norman. OU has the largest weather communications school in the world. The new Weather Center is quite something and what better place for weather monitoring than Oklahoma, the severe weather capital?

February 8-21 BBB toured California.

April 14 BBB played a private party for the Optometrist's National Convention. Dr. Bennett of Guthrie, president of this national organization, had his office right around the corner from the Doublestop Fiddle Shop and he hired us to play.

April 17 BBB did a recording session at OCC (Oklahoma Christian College.)

April 24, 26 BBB played for employees during their lunch hour at Integris Hospital.

April 20 BBB played Chickasha, Oklahoma.

April 27-30 played with Bluegrass Etc.

May 5 BBB played a private wedding.

May 12 BBB played the Western Swing Show at the Logan County Fair Grounds.

June 10 Mason Williams played with the Byron Berline Band at the First Presbyterian Church picnic in Tulsa.

June 12 BBB played a Norman, OSU function at the Cowboy Hall of Fame in Oklahoma City.

June 14 Mason Williams played with the Byron Berline Band at the OK Mozart Festival in Bartlesville, Oklahoma while a filming crew followed us around shooting footage for a documentary they were doing on Mason. They also came to our next gig.

June 16 Mason Williams played with the Byron Berline Band in Chandler, Oklahoma at their Ice Cream Festival and that night we headed back to Guthrie for a show at the Music Hall. Mason played with us and they did more filming.

June 20-22 BCH played the Legends Concert in Owensboro,

Kentucky. Fred Bartenstein hosted this and asked questions as they did a lot of interviews at the museum.

June 23 BBB played the Skiatook Bluegrass Festival.

June 30 Vince Gill played with the Byron Berline Band at the Music Hall in Guthrie. While in Oklahoma visiting family Vince saw the music Hall show schedule and decided to stop by, bringing his mother Jerene, Benny Garcia and a couple of other friends…everything except his mandolin…he played mine. He played the whole show, both sets. He enjoyed the Hunt Brothers Jonathan and Andrew and after hearing them play Vince said, "I want to be a Hunt Boy."

The Byron Berline Band enjoyed playing with Vince and he seemed to have a good time. I remember writing about that night on our web page, doublestop.com. I still feel the same, "Vince is a very giving person with his time, talents, and friendship. Success has not spoiled this young man at all. Thanks Vince, for your continued friendship and your willingness to share your talents."

July 6 BBB played Mass Street Music in Lawrence, Kansas. We did this on my birthday and afterward we had a family reunion at a little town just north of Lawrence.

July 28 played the Cactus Café.

August 6-12 played the Rocky Mountain Fiddle Camp.

September 2-4 played Steve Plazzo's birthday party in Clipper Mills, California.

September 10-12 Richard Sharp, John Hickman, and I played the Texas Trail Ride.

September 14 BBB played Choteau, Oklahoma.

September 15 I played with the Enid Symphony Orchestra in the Celebration with Oklahoma Centennial Sounds. Jimmy Webb, Edgar Cruz, Susan Powell, David Hooten, Leona Mitchell, and others were on this show. They also had a very interesting Indian flute player named Bill Miller and he too, recorded the song, "Oklahoma Rising," for the Centennial. His Native American flute gives a special feeling to the Oklahoma centennial song. They charted a couple of songs I wrote and I played them with the Symphony Orchestra. One song I thought fitting, was "Cherokee Bell." To be a part of this was quite a special thing.

The Walnut Valley Festival was going on at this time in Winfield, Kansas and although I was not booked for that festival, my nephew Barry Patton, wanted me to come to Winfield and pick with him on Stage 5. After the Enid, Oklahoma Symphony, I headed for Winfield to play bluegrass. It was late, but picking at Winfield goes on all night.

A highway patrol officer pulled me over. At that time of night, they were usually looking for drunks.

I told him I had just done a gig in Enid and was on my way to Winfield to play.

"This late?" he questioned.

"Yes." I said. My instruments were visible in the back seat and although I had been doing 70 mph in a 60 mph zone, he let me go with a warning. I got to Arkansas City, Kansas, about eight miles from Winfield and another cop pulled me over. After the earlier warning I shadowed the speed limit...I was extremely careful.

"You were speeding." He said.

This was right in front of the speed sign and I said, pointing, "It says 45, right there on the sign."

"You start 45 there," he said pointing to the sign; "...**this** is 35."

Oh, brother! He let me go with another warning and I played on stage 5 with Barry.

September 18 BBB played Chickasha, Oklahoma.

September 20 BBB played the Oklahoma City Heritage Foundation.

September 23 BBB played Norman, Oklahoma Parks.

September 27 BBB played the theater in Gilmer, Texas, again, Don Henley's hometown.

October 4-6 BBB with Barry Patton played the eleventh OIBF in Guthrie.

October 14 Oklahoma City had a big Centennial Parade and the Byron Berline Band played on a float. They decided that rather than play live they would record the band playing the appropriately titled, "Oklahoma Stomp," edit it down, then play it along the parade route while the band pretended to play. There were a couple of glitches. First, Steve Short our drummer could not be there. I called Barry Patton and although he is not a drummer, he could certainly pretend to be one. Barry sat on his drum stool, Richard Sharp had his bass, Jim Fish had his guitar, Greg Burgess had his mandolin and I had my fiddle...we were ready.

As the parade began to move we waited for the signal to begin pretend playing with the music, but the signal never came. We waved to the thousands of excited spectators that lined the parade route. When we got to the point where the cameras were rolling…unannounced, the music started playing and none of us was in position to play. Our instruments were everywhere except how they are supposed be played. The music continued and we finally caught up with it. At one point, Jim Fish while pretending to play his guitar, stepped off the float and almost did not make it back on. Barry Patton is a great air drum player and you can quote me on that.

October 27 Greg Burgess, John Hickman, and I played Remington Park.

November 5 did a session with C. Shelton.

November 11 Mason Williams played with the Byron Berline Band for Boots and Ties at the Untitled Artspace Gallery in Oklahoma City.

November 15 BBB played the Dell Corporation in Oklahoma City. Dell has a huge plant there. That night we had a gig in Ponca City at the Poncan Theater.

November 16 I played the Oklahoma Centennial Show production at the Ford Center in Oklahoma City. This was a huge televised production, celebrating Oklahoma's Centennial and it was an amazing show. They had a full orchestra and all the big Okies were there including Vince Gill, Reba McIntyre, Toby Keith, and Flaming Lips an Oklahoma rock group. I played with Vince and Reba when they did their duet, "Oklahoma Swing." Meanwhile, Guthrie, location of Oklahoma's first state capitol, was having their big Centennial Celebration with a parade and everything and I missed it completely because the filming of the Centennial Production in Oklahoma City took all day. I regret missing Guthrie Day, but I really enjoyed being part of the Oklahoma Centennial Show. Unfortunately, we cannot do everything and sometimes must make difficult decisions.

Journal Entry 2008
Record Disks to CD's

In addition to the following, the Byron Berline Band played twenty one shows in the Music Hall.

February 20 did a session with Lewsader.

February 18 BBB played a private party in Oklahoma City.

February 22 BBB played a School Concert in Glencoe, Oklahoma.

March 5 Mel Durham a musician and friend, passed away at the age of 93.

March 7 did a commercial session.

March 8 BBB played a Habitat for Humanity show in Wichita Falls, Texas and Amy Grant was on the show.

May 10 BBB played the Western Swing Show at the Logan County Fairgrounds in Guthrie.

May 18-23 did an Andy Statman session in New York City. Andy is an orthodox Jew and an incredible clarinet and mandolin player. He is truly an amazing musician and I felt honored when he asked me to play on this. He used his bass player, drummer, and guitar player. I thoroughly enjoyed this session and we recorded an entire album.

May 24-25 BBB played Cowboy Days at the Cowboy Hall of Fame in Oklahoma City.

June 13-16 California played Huck Finn's Festival in California. Don Tucker has promoted many bluegrass shows in the L.A. area and this was his deal. The Nitty Gritty Dirt Band was on the show and they asked me to come up and join them for "Will the Circle Be Unbroken" then went right into "Take a Load Off, Annie." John McEuen said, "I've been a fan of Byron's since he played with the Dillards. Remember Byron from the old days... stuff on the Charlie's album...to be able to play the way he did..."Mandolin Rag" he just fried it. We've known each other for thirty years and were friends the first two."

June 29 BBB played the First Presbyterian Church picnic in Tulsa.

July 7 my brother Leonard and I played a Pistol Pete Reunion at the Music Hall in Guthrie. Pete's granddaughter Yandell Gardner put this together and I let them use the Dining Hall upstairs. Leonard played guitar and I played fiddle, just as we did back in the old days…wonderful memories of Pistol Pete.

June 22 BBB played the Convention Center in Tulsa for the Farm Bureau.

June 29 BBB played the First Presbyterian Church picnic in Tulsa.

July 10-12 BBB played in Wyoming. Bret Jones City Manager of Gillette, Wyoming was formerly the Guthrie, Oklahoma City Manager. I called, telling him the Byron Berline Band was coming his way and wondered if he knew of a place we could play while there. As a result, the City of Gillette had us do a concert. After that show, we went on to Buffalo, Wyoming for a small festival.

August 1 BBB played the Country Barn Steak House in Amarillo, Texas.

August 8 BBB with Barry Patton played Caldwell, Kansas my hometown, at the Sumner County Fairgrounds. This is always fun to play, seeing old friends and my family.

September 8-11 played the Texas Trail Ride.

September 19, 20 BBB played Winfield, Kansas Walnut Valley Festival.

September 21 BBB played the Summer Breeze Concert in Norman, Oklahoma.

September 26 BBB played Tonkawa, Oklahoma.

September 28 BBB played in Caldwell for Leonard's 75th Birthday. This was a surprise party for my brother…all the family came and several members of the Byron Berline Band.

When we were kids and growing up on the farm, dad bought a Wilcox record making machine. Dad made disks of all of us kids playing whatever we played; piano, trombone, fiddle, etc. My sister Janice thought those recorded disks, made so many decades ago were lost forever, but I found them and with help from Richard Sharp and Steve Short we digitized the music and made CD's. I gave each of my siblings a CD and the tears flowed…a piece of our childhood carefully preserved by our dad, right there in our hands. I am so glad he made those recordings… what wonderful memories of growing up on the Berline farm.

October 2-4 BBB with Barry Patton played the twelfth OIBF in

Guthrie. The lineup also included David Munnelly's Irish band, Red Wine band from Italy, Gibson Brothers, Frenchie Burke on Cajun tunes, Claire Lynch's Band, California reunion with Dan Crary, Steve Spurgin, John Moore, John Hickman, and Byron Berline, Mason Williams, John McEuen, Edgar Cruz, Red Dirt Rangers, High Ground, Cedar Ridge, Brigade, Neverly Hillbillies and Jim Garling. Mason Williams played with the Byron Berline Band on the fourth.

November 6 BBB played a Baker Hughes Party at the Aquarium in Jenks, Oklahoma. This was an Employee Appreciation Party arranged by my friend Tony Moore.

November 11-14 played Enid, Oklahoma's Grand National Quail Hunt.

When we began having Fiddle Fest at the Music Hall my friend Frank Kinard, the one who taught me, when I was thirteen, to retune my fiddle so I could play Black Mountain Rag, came to Fiddle Fest for several years and we played Black Mountain Rag together.

One day he called and said, "I've got our 50th Anniversary song picked out to play."

"What are you talking about?" I asked him.

"It was 1958 when we met," he explained, "and you wanted to play black Mountain Rag."

Indeed, it had been fifty years. Unfortunately, he passed away and we never had the opportunity to play that anniversary song. I remember some books he wrote, one in particular, "Tougher than a Boot." He was a good friend.

Journal Entry 2009
Earl Scruggs at the Banjo Museum - Texas Shorty

In addition to the following, the Byron Berline Band played twenty two shows at the Music Hall.

January 26 played the All Star Bluegrass Jam in Stillwater, Oklahoma. The best bluegrass players played this and most were from the east, like Nashville, Kentucky and the Carolinas, and included players like Rob Ickes, Terry Baucom, Alan Bibey, and Tim Crouch. Rob Ickes is a Dobro player from Nashville, Alan Bibey a mandolin player, grew up in Walnut Cove, North Carolina and Tim Crouch is a fine Arkansas fiddler. This is only a sampling of the great musicians playing the All Star Bluegrass Jam and they all come a long way to be there. Each artist is given a song and must pick his band members right there at the jam. I played on some other bands and I had my own song and band to put together. For one thing, this is just a whole lot of fun and the result is some of the best bluegrass playing anywhere.

April 9-13 did a workshop at a bluegrass and Folk Festival in the Louhans of France with Alan Munde on banjo, Jim Hurst on guitar, and I played fiddle. This was a two-day workshop with a concert in the evening held out in the country at "LaGrange Rouge," (which means the red barn, in English) and I remember selling a fiddle while I was there.

April 22-27 I played with Bluegrass Etc. at Salt Lake City Utah and at the Omtras, Colorado Festival.

April 29 Rick Morton, Jana Jae, and I played the Fiddlers Hall of Fame in Tulsa. They inducted Vassar Clements into the Fiddlers Hall of Fame and this show was a tribute to him. Rick, Jana, and I played tunes for which Vassar is well known.

April 30 BBB played the Norman Schools.

May 4-11 Barry Patton and I played the California Trail Ride with Bluegrass Etc. We also played the Calico Ghost Town, Mc-Cabes, and San Diego.

May 15 I sat in with Jim Blair's band at the Hankerin' for Hank Show in Stillwater.

May 16 BBB played the Western Swing Show at the Logan County Fairgrounds in Guthrie.

May 18 did a session with someone named Jones recording cowboy music engineered by Steve Short.

May 21 did a session with Sue Ogden engineered by Steve Short.

May 29 BBB played Durant, Oklahoma.

June 5-7 BBB played a bluegrass festival in Greenfield, Illinois.

June 14 BBB played the First Presbyterian Church picnic in Tulsa.

June 18 BBB played an OSU function in Oklahoma City at the Cowboy Hall of Fame.

June 25 BBB played an OSU function at their Student Union.

July 20-25 California had a reunion with John Hickman, Dan Crary, Steve Spurgin, John Moore, and me when we played concerts and did workshops at Rocky Grass in Lyons, Colorado.

August 6 BBB played the Yukon, Oklahoma City Park.

August 25-28 BCH played a PBS show in San Antonio, Texas produced by Bill Millet. Bill played banjo with Bluegrass Alliance in the 1970's and he does a lot of production work. This was a very unique show and I enjoyed doing it. It was a Texas Tornado's type of music…Timex with Flaco Jimenez the accordion player and Augie Meyers, who had played keyboards with the Beatles. The venue, a big country music place, had probably a thousand people there. We cut some tracks for an album but I do not think they released it; however, there is a DVD of the show called "Texas Music Extravaganza, the San Antonio Sound.

September 6-8 I played Steve Plazzo's birthday in Clipper Mills, California. David Grier, Lamar's son played guitar. Lamar played banjo with Bill Monroe when I was in the band back in 1967 and David was just a little ole kid. He grew up listening to Clarence White…Clarence was his influence. It sure is fun to sit and jam with him!

September 10 Earl Scruggs and the Byron Berline Band played the Opening of the Banjo Museum, in Oklahoma City. The Museum was originally in Guthrie, Oklahoma, right across the street from my Doublestop Fiddle shop. They purchased a building in Oklahoma City and spent a ton of money renovating it. They scheduled a Grand Opening of the new museum, booked the Byron Berline Band and asked if I thought they could get Earl Scruggs. They said he did not even have to play if he did not want to…they really wanted him to be there, but did not know if they could afford him. I called Earl about six months before the opening and asked if he would go. He kind of said he would, but with no mention of price or anything. I played Rocky Grass and Earl was on the show and back stage in the dressing room I again approached him about the museum opening.

I said, "Earl, they really do want you to be there and they don't mind if you don't want to play…just being there would mean a lot. They're not sure they can afford you."

Earl said, waving his hand, "Byron, I charge as much to wave as I do for an hour concert."

I still laugh about that. His son Gary, said, "Byron, just call me…I handle all that." Earl asked for two extra plane tickets. That was it. He charged them nothing for playing or waving. Earl Scruggs, what a gem.

September 16 BBB played an OSU show at the Cowboy Hall of Fame in Oklahoma City.

September 17 BBB played at the Petroleum Club for an OU event, Doctors of Neuroscience.

September 25 BBB played Ada, Oklahoma at the McSwain Theater.

October 1-3 BBB with Barry Patton played the thirteenth OIBF. The lineup also included Rockin' Acoustic Circus, the Hunt Family, Richard Smith and Chris Jones, Alaskan String Band, Mark O'Connor and his Appalachian Waltz Trio, Peter Feldman, Wayne Shrubsall and Bruce Thompson, Alan Munde's group, the Gibson Brothers, Red Dirt Rangers, Mountain Smoke, Cedar Ridge, Brigade, Edgar Cruz, Frenchie Burke and Jim Blair's Hankerin' for Hank Show.

October 8-10 I played Ruidoso, New Mexico with Texas Shorty. We had a great time playing together and catching up. We have known each other since I was a teenager. Shorty informed the audience that this was a forty-seven year reunion and it was. We had not played together in all those years, since competing against each other in fiddle contests. What a great time we had.

November 17 BBB played Alva, Oklahoma.

November 18-20 I played Enid, Oklahoma's Grand National Quail Hunt.

Journal Entry 2010
Happy Birthday Contest Tune – Hole in One – Ambassador of Creativity

In addition to the following, the Byron Berline Band played twenty shows at the Music Hall.

January 23 played the Stillwater, Oklahoma All Star Bluegrass Jam.

February 20 BBB Played Woodward, Oklahoma.

March 14 my fist grandchild, Brighton Drake Berline O'Conner was born.

March 20 we cancelled the Music Hall Show due to snow.

March 27-29 Alan Munde and I did workshops and concerts at the Fischer, Texas Ricegrass Bluegrass Festival. Fischer is just south of Austin and Alan does not have as far to travel as I do because he lives there. They held the event on the grounds of the Fischer Haus B&B and set the stage in the Cantina. This was the first year for this event.

May 8 BBB played the Western Swing Show at the Logan County Fairgrounds.

May 26 BBB played in Oklahoma City at the Cowboy Hall of Fame for an event sponsored by the Topeka Bank and Trust.

June 12, 13 BBB played Sperry, Oklahoma, (near Tulsa) downtown under the gazebo. Larry Briggs does guitar shows and he put this together. He also hired the Tommy Alsop band for this event. It was a long drive to Guthrie from Sperry, just to have to get up and drive back to Tulsa the next morning, so I spent the night with Tony Moore in Tulsa. We played golf in the morning and did the Picnic in the afternoon.

June 13 I have been playing golf for thirty seven years and a golfer's most coveted prize has always eluded me. No way did I expect this to be my day! Tony Moore and I were on the fifth tee, a 120-yard par three. I felt particularly stiff, so I took a few stretches before approaching my ball, then I took my pitching wedge, lined up my shot and swung. It felt good and solid when I hit it…I knew it was a good shot. Tony and I watched the ball fly, land on the green and then roll away. I remember asking

Tony, joking of course, if he thought it went into the cup. He actually thought it rolled off the backside of the green. When we reached the green, we found the ball in the cup! Oh, my gosh! What a thrill! The rest of the round was a blur…I had gotten MY HOLE IN ONE!

June 14 BBB played the First Presbyterian Church picnic in Tulsa.

June 18 BBB with Barry Patton played in Miami, Oklahoma for the Free Wheel Bicycle Ride whose members ride all over the state then stop somewhere. I figured the appropriate song to do was "Free Wheelin'" and it must have been because we had CD's with us, "One Eyed Jack" with the song "Free Wheelin'" on it and we sold out!

June 20-July 6 Greg Burgess and I went to Weiser Idaho, for the National Old Time Fiddlers Contest. This was the first time I had been to Weiser in 40 years and I had not entered the contest since 1970. They asked Greg and me to judge the contest and Bette

Byron Berline Band in 2010, Byron center front, l to r, Greg Burgess, Steve Short, John Hickman, Jim Fish, Richard Sharp.

and Greg's family went along. They put Greg and his family in a motor home while Bette and I stayed in someone's home. It was good to see old friends again and it was fun to hang out and jam.

At the end of the contest, they have a Round Robin. They place all five finalists on the stage and the judges tell the contestants what songs they must play. The contestants then draw for the order of each song. We had them play a hoedown for the first song and they all did well. For the second number we had them play a simple, old time tune then improvise on it. The third round I suggested we have everybody play the same song…"Happy Birthday" in any way they wanted to play it. This way there was

I made a hole-in-one in 2010 and had a witness and photograph to prove it!

no opportunity for them to practice it…they had to be creative on the spot. As we walked through the campground that night, we heard Happy Birthday coming from every camp.

June 27 Bette and I left Weiser, went to McCall, Idaho a town north of Weiser, to visit with Rick Youngblood, someone I knew when he was a kid. From there we went on to Salt Lake City, Utah. I bought two guitars while there and one is the guitar Greg Burgess now plays.

July 4 I played with Bluegrass Etc. in Dove Creek, Colorado

John Hickman and I enjoying the OIBF festivities in 2011. Courtesy of Tom Dunning.

where John Moore lives. This is a real small town and the night before, we played for a dance held on the tennis courts. For the fourth celebration, we played in a field and it was the blowing, coldest Independence Day Celebration I can remember. Bluegrass Etc. played and Steve Spurgin played drums, Bill Bryson played bass and I played fiddle with them. The fireworks began and we played a song that must have lasted twenty minutes because we looked into the sky and just kept playing while watching the fireworks.

July 25-30 I taught every day and did a show in New York City at Mark O'Connor's Fiddle Camp.

While on the Byron Berline Cruise in the Gulf of Mexico, I met Lukas Wronski a young violinmaker from Poland. He was thirty one years old and had not yet decided where to settle in the United States. I suggested that Guthrie, Oklahoma would be a good place for him. Lukas moved to Guthrie and set up shop. I do not know how many violins he made while he was here in addition to taking care of all my instruments. He stayed in Guthrie for about a year and then decided he needed to be in a larger city so he moved to New York. While I was in New York at Mark's fiddle camp, I got together with Lukas. He introduced me to his friends and I got to play a Strad and an Amati while I was there.

July 31 I played Poughkeepsie, New York. I met Fred Robbins when I was in the army at Fort Polk, Louisiana. Fred booked this show in Poughkeepsie and got a good band for me. They filmed it and it is available on Fred's website.

September 5, 7 David Grier and I played in Clipper Mills, California for Steve Plazzo's birthday party.

September 30-October 2 BBB with Barry Patton played the fourteenth OIBF in Guthrie.

September 8, 9 BBB played the Cowboy Symposium in Ruidoso, New Mexico. John Hickman was sick and could not be there, however the show went over well.

September 14 gave a luncheon talk in Oklahoma City at the Church of the Servant.

November 3 BBB played in Jenks, Oklahoma for a Baker Hughes party at the Aquarium.

November 9-11 BBB played Cameron University at their Country Jazz Fusion Festival.

November 16 this was my Creativity Ambassador Induction at the Oklahoma Country Hall of Fame. This event, attended by people from all over the world, is not just for music, it is for all things creative. These ambassadors, chosen for their national and international creative accomplishments, agree to serve as representatives for the state of Oklahoma. They ask us to share our ideas and expertise on how to best advance the state using new approaches that can change perceptions about Oklahoma.

Other inductees included Benjamin Harjo, Jr. an American Indian artist, Allan Vest composer and producer, David Boren President of OU and former Governor of Oklahoma, Dayna Dunbar author, and many other successful, creative Oklahomans.

This was quite an event and included Sandi Patty, the Hansons, Kyle Dillingham, and Junie Lowry-Johnson casting director for "Deadwood." That was the HBO series that I got to be in and

During Guthrie's holiday Victorian Walk in 2011, Bette and I dressed in period costumes and it became a live store window at the Fiddle Shop with our grandson, the wee fiddler, Brighton Drake Berline O'Connor.

did the music for it. There were many more Creativity Ambassadors inducted that night.

December 31 Bette and I will be going to Greg Burgess' house for a New Year's Eve celebration, but first, I think we will go to a local restaurant and unknowingly have lunch with Jane and Larry Frost…at different tables…and we did. Happy New Year 2011!

THE FIDDLE LESSON. Byron and grandson Brighton Drake Berline
O'Connor, 2012.

Epilogue

It was an honor to be inducted into the National Fiddler's Hall of Fame in Tulsa, Oklahoma, on February 6, 2013. We are still doing about 20 Shows a year at The Music Hall, the Byron Berline Band is doing recording sessions, OIBF continues, I am touring occasionally and Bette and I have a new granddaughter, Coralie Pearl O'Connor, born September 29, 2011. I have written some new tunes, an Irish song inspired by our many trips to Ireland, Brighton's Breakdown for our grandson and Coralie's Waltz for our granddaughter. They have been recorded and are includeed on my CD, Jammin' with Byron. Brighton and I are on the cover. I will again, enjoy writing a new tune for my newest granddaughter, Ginger Grace O'Connor, born February 20, 2013.

My co-writer, Jane Frost, asked me how long I will continue to play the fiddle. I will tell you my answer. I once asked Bill Monroe the same question and he said as long as people wanted him to play and his voice held out he would perform. I feel the same way. No one cared if Jack Nicklaus won a tournament... they just wanted to watch him play.

Bette and I have enjoyed reliving memories while working on this book. It is hard to believe sometimes...so many years. Music has been a good life and I would not change it if I could. I have been blest with a wonderful family and many, many friends. I consider every show an opportunity to make people smile and I continue to pass on the music.

The End

Epigraph

"Mighty fine, Barn, mighty fine."
Bill Monroe

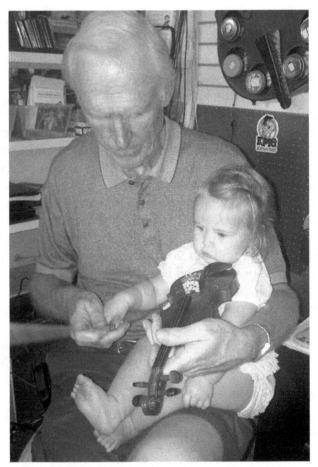

Granddaughter Coralie, getting an early fiddle
lesson from grandpa at the fiddle shop in 2012.

Index

101 Ranch 12, 20
25 Year Retrospective Concerts 232
47 Straight, (book) 49

A

A & M Records 88, 94, 100, 122, 125, 127, 146, 176
ABC (American Broadcasting Company) 83, 99, 104, 108, 127, 128, 131, 151, 153, 160. 174, 186, 296
Absorbine Senior 4
Academy of Country Music 269, 273, 278, 293, 306
Ackerman McQueen Advertising 363
Acousticadia (event) 357, 363
Acuff, Roy 55, 56, 71, 74, 84, 103, 219, 220
Adcock, Eddie 293, 330
Adcock, Martha 330
Africa iv, 218, 224, 225
Agajanian, Dennis 282, 284, 310, 350
Agualla, Dave 307
Ahearn, Brian 155, 168, 191, 235, 264
Aladdin Theater 310
Alaskan String Band 374
Albany Festival (event) 311
Aldridge, Dee 16
Alford, Gene 77
All Star Bluegrass Jam 372, 375
All the Good Times (song) 203
Allen, Debbie 310
Allen, Randy 310
Allen, Rex 211
Allison, J.I. 178
Along came Bronson (movie) 181, 329

Alpine Village (venue) 237, 248, 276, 277, 279, 282, 283, 287, 288, 294, 295, 296, 297, 298, 299, 300, 302, 307, 360
Alsop, Peter 206
Alsop, Tommy 221, 375
Alvin and the Chipmunks (group) 288
Amati, Nicolo 345, 379
Amazing Grace (song) 130
Ambassador Auditorium (venue) 280, 293
Ambassador of Creativity v, 375, 380, 381
American Music Shop (TV show) 295
Amistad (movie) 88
Anaheim Convention Center (venue) 151, 227
Anchuts, Phil 256, 258
Anderle David 258, 177
Anderson, Evan 245
Anderson, Mike 197
Anderson, Pete 252
Andrew Jackson (hotel) 56
Andrew Sisters 3
Angela's Ashes (movie) 88
Anglund, Jack 62
Antilles Records 160
Any Which Way You Can (movie) 221
Appalachian Waltz Trio (band) 374
Apple Blossom (song) 38
Aquarium at Jenks, Oklahoma (venue) 371, 379
Ariola Records 124, 126, 160
Arkansas Traveler (song) 185, 354
Armstrong, R. G.165
Arnold, Jack 256
Arnold, Lee 153
Arnold, Taf 106
Arvada Performing Arts Center (venue) 232, 251, 253, 285, 320, 251

Ash Grove, The, (venue) 63, 64, 95, 97, 99, 114, 138, 139, 151
Asher, Peter 181
Asher, Terry 166, 167
Asleep at the Wheel (band) 124, 153, 354, 364
Aspen Inn (venue) 109
Asylum Records 172
Atkins, Chet 96, 103
Atkins, Susan 98
Atlantic Records 120, 121, 125, 145
Atwell, Doug 221
Auldridge, Mike 96
Aunt Dinah's Quilting Party (band) 97
Austin City Limits (TV show) 192
Austin Jug Band (band) 357
Australia iv, 224, 232, 236
Axton, Hoyt 31, 96, 101, 122, 184, 186, 206

B

B & B Rag (song) 185
Baby Boy (song) 177
Baby Elephant Walk (movie) 111
Back to the Future (movie) 269, 297
Bacon, Brett 312
Bacon, Kevin 334
Baez, Joan 30, 31, 46
Bailey, Bill 77
Baird, Dan 280
Baja 1000 (event) 233
Baker Hughes Party (event) 371, 379
Baker, Chet 357
Baker, Joe Don 124, 128
Baker, Kenny 78, 82, 116, 201, 293
Balcher Folk Festival (event) 259
Ball, Tom 237, 252, 275, 357

Ballad of Easy Rider,
(album) 87, 88, 93
Balloon Fest (event) 324,
352, 353
Band of Angels (song) 283
Bandstand (venue) 241,
250, 270, 272, 273, 274,
275, 277, 281
Banjo Band Contest
(event) 158
Banjo Café (venue) 196,
197, 206, 207, 209, 211,
215, 217, 218, 221, 222,
223, 224, 227, 228, 229,
230, 231, 232, 247
Banjo Museum (venue) v,
372, 373
Barbara, John 153
Barn, The (venue) 176,
210, 213, 214
Barnard, R. W. 29
Barndance (song) 201
Barrett, Todd 331
Bartenstein, Fred 366
Bartlett, Helen 270, 271,
273
Barton, Cathy 343
Basehart, Richard 127
Basic Instinct (movie) iv,
275, 277, 283
Battin, Skip 142, 144, 145,
146
Baucom, Terry 372
Baxter, Bob ix, 138, 158,
172
Baxter, Taylor 31
BCH, (Berline, Crary,
Hickman) 192, 193,
195, 196, 197, 199, 200,
206, 207, 210, 211, 212,
213, 215, 217, 218, 220,
221, 222, 223, 224, 227,
228, 230, 231, 232, 233,
236, 237, 238, 239, 241,
242, 243, 244, 245, 247,
248, 249, 250, 253, 256,
258, 259, 260, 262, 264,
270, 352, 365, 373
Beach Boys (band) 87,
103, 210
Bean Blossom Festival,
(venue) 65, 66
Bean, Buck 272, 273
Bear Country (TV show)
160

Bear Country Jamboree
(venue) 126, 231, 247,
252
Bear Valley Lodge (venue)
248
Bear, Gene 160
Beasley, Jack 44
Beatles (band) 176, 205,
373
Beatty, Ned 247
Beaver Creek Resort
(venue) 320
Beavers, The, (venue) 84
Beck, Chris 304
Beck, Don 93, 122, 134
Bee, Kathy 220
Beefeaters (band) 39
Behind Closed Doors (song)
283
Bel-Air Bay Club (venue)
210, 220
Bell, Delia 224
Belling, Andy 133
Belly Up Bar (venue) 218,
223, 224
Benge, Brad 320, 349, 355,
358, 363
Benno, Mark 126
Berger, Tom 301
Bergholz, Betty 109
Bergman, Alan 87
Bergman, Marilyn 87
Berline, Ann Elizabeth
Jackson (Mom) vi, 2, 3,
8, 9, 10, 12, 13, 16, 17,
18, 19, 22, 28, 35, 44,
46, 51, 53, 61, 66, 74,
90, 110
Berline, Becca Diane xv,
132, 138, 148, 151, 160,
171, 181, 183, 186, 188,
189, 192, 193, 199, 205,
211, 213, 223, 227, 229,
233, 240, 244, 250, 255,
265, 273,281, 289, 290,
295, 297, 309, 324, 325
Berline, Bette (Ringrose)
vii, viii, xv, 51, 53, 50,
51, 53, 55, 56, 60, 66,
71, 74, 76, 77, 81, 82, 84,
85, 86, 87, 89, 90, 93, 94,
97, 98, 99, 101, 102, 105,
106, 107, 109, 110, 112,
113, 125, 127, 131, 132,

138, 143, 145, 148, 157,
166, 175, 180, 182, 183,
185, 186, 189, 190, 192,
211, 212, 218, 223, 224,
227, 232, 247, 258, 262,
283, 290, 295, 299, 300,
305, 308, 309, 310, 315,
317, 322, 323, 324, 328,
330, 331, 332, 333, 335,
336, 337, 339, 340, 344,
345, 352, 363, 376, 377,
378, 380, 381, 383
Berline, Beverly 12
Berline, Bob 6
Berline, Eleanor 2, 6, 8, 9,
10, 13, 15, 16, 20, 110,
128, 156, 209, 317, 360
Berline, Henry 2, 4, 6, 9,
10, 15, 20, 24, 66, 209,
Berline, Henry Sr. 1,
Berline, Janice 2, 6, 8, 9, 10,
13, 15, 16, 20, 21, 156,
209, 317, 370
Berline, Lee 6
Berline, Leonard 2, 4, 6, 9,
10, 12, 13, 15, 16, 20, 21,
84, 101, 156, 157, 196,
220, 223, 369, 370
Berline, Lue George (Dad)
vi, x, 1, 2, 3, 4, 5, 6, 7,
8, 9, 10, 11, 12, 13, 16,
17, 18, 19, 20, 22, 24, 27,
28, 33, 35, 36, 39, 44, 46,
48, 51, 52, 53, 61, 74, 82,
101, 102, 110, 129, 140,
182, 185, 196, 197, 201,
280, 284, 370
Berline, Luzetta Wood 1
Beverly Hillbillies 210,
292, 298, 303
Beverly Hilton Hotel
(venue) 93, 306
Bibey, Alan 372
Bier, Johnny 349
Big 8 Track Meet 27, 49
Big Bear Festival (event)
189
Big Country (band) 221
Big Dog (song) 258
Big Top Chautauqua at
Lake Superior (event)
321
Bikales, Eric (Bikela) 273,
293
Bill Cheatham (song) 35

Bill, Tony 270, 271
Billboard (magazine) 154
Billingsley, Jennifer 128
Billy Graham Crusades 282
Bird, Senator Robert 303
Bitter End (venue) 116,
Bitter End West (venue) 111, 112
Black Forest Community Center (venue) 343
Black Hills Festival (event) 248
Black Mountain Rag (song) 12, 13, 38, 50, 168, 371
Black Rose Acoustic Society (event) 343
Blackberry Blossom (song) 243
Blackwell, Kenny 262, 299
Blaine, Hal 307
Blair, Jim 372, 374
Blair, Marty 268
Blake, Nancy 96, 130
Blake, Norman 129, 130, 167, 197, 219, 220
Blaze (movie) 262, 263, 264, 265
Blazing Saddles (movie) 297
Blitz Bluegrass Festival (event) 184, 197
Block, Billy 293
Bloemendaal, Wim 138
Blue Bayou (venue) 256
Blue Belle Saloon 310
Blue Day (song) 160
Blue Grass (song) 145
Blue Highway (band) 326
Blue Kentucky Girl (song) 204
Blue Moon of Kentucky (song) 47, 313, 314
Blue Railroad Train (band) 364
Blue Stem Boys (band) 41, 42
Bluebird Café (venue) 158, 166, 168, 195, 278, 287, 290, 291, 292
Bluebird Records 63
Bluebonnet Bowl 21
Bluegrass Alliance 147, 159, 179, 373

Bluegrass Boys (band) xiv, xv, 15, 47, 57, 65, 66
Bluegrass Breakdown (song) 47, 81
Bluegrass Canada (event) 155, 167, 197,
Bluegrass Cardinals (band) 96, 146, 232, 361
Bluegrass Country Boys (band) 129
Bluegrass Etc. (band) 96, 348, 351, 352, 362, 365, 372, 378, 379
Bluegrass Expo (event) 249
Bluegrass Hall of Fame 62
Bluegrass Revue (band) 156
Bluegrass Unlimited (magazine) 131
Bluer Rdge Pickin' Parlor (venue) 189, 251, 229
Boarding House, The (venue) 153, 175
Boatman, Bob 237
Boatman, Brad 237
Boatwright, Bobby 318
Boatwright, Grant 141
Bobby Simpson Party (event) 278
Boddy, Jan 135
Boddy, Nicky 123, 134, 135, 136
Boddy, Nicolette 135, 136
Boddy, Patricia 136
Boddy, Ted 123, 135, 150
Boddy's Music Inn (venue) 135
Body and Soul (song) 63
Boettcher Hall (venue) 242, 269
Bogdanovich, Peter 291
Bogguss, Suzy 198
Boil the Cabbage Down (song) 5
Bon Bon (band) 268
Bonaparte's Retreat (song) 103
Bonham, David 348
Bonham, Tina 348
Boom, Darrell 159
Boonville Folk Festival (event) 343
Boot Scootin' Boogie (song) 288

Boots and Ties (event) 368
Borelli, Tommy 316
Boren, David 380
Bosco the cat 323, 324, 325,
Bossier Press 155
Boston Pops Symphony Orchestra 88
Bound for Glory (movie) 170
Bounty Hunter/ The Bounty Man (movie) 127, 131
Bourgoise, Dan 124
Boutwell Studio 202, 243
Boutwell, Ed 202
Bowden, Richard 139, 360
Bowen, Jimmy 104, 278,
Bowen, Richard 293
Bowers, Bryan 96, 167
Bowman, Paul 238, 241, 242, 254
Box, B. Bill 212
Boy Howdy (band) 271
Boylan, John 82, 288
Boys From Indiana (band) 197
Braff, Brian 293
Brainard, Pop 31
Brainard, Steve 31
Bramble and the Rose, The (song) 163
Bramlett, Bonnie 91, 92
Brand, Oscar 96
Branding Iron (venue) 230
Breakfast at Tiffany's (movie) 111
Breckenridge Music Institute Tent (venue) 286
Brewer and Shipley (band) 96, 153, 162
Bricktown 316, 339
Bridges, Jeff 163, 164
Brigade (band) 346, 348, 364, 371, 374
Briggs, Larry 375
Bright, Fletcher 253, 358
Bright, Gary 269
Brighton's Breakdown (song) 383
Brisco, Jim 77
Britt Music Festival (event) 285
Brock, Jim 128
Broken Chord (movie) 282

Bromberg, David 95, 355, 358
Bronco Billy (venue) 296, 298
Brooks, Garth 330
Brooks, Karen 217
Broughton, J.C. 102, 156
Brown County Breakdown (song) 203
Brown, Albert 44
Brown, Gate Mouth 206
Brown, Jann 207, 208, 250, 251, 252, 254, 255, 256, 257, 258, 262, 264, 283, 293, 307, 308
Browne, Jackson 126
Bruce, Lenny 96
Bruno, Al 182, 190, 213, 251, 256
Brush Arbor (band/album) 128, 131, 136, 139, 189, 222, 248
Bryant, Boudleaux 221
Bryant, Felice 221
Bryson, Bill 197, 242, 291, 299, 300, 308, 353, 354, 379
Buckin' Mule (song) 311
Buckingham, Jan 283
Bucknell University (venue) 118
Bud Girls (commercial) 233
Buddhi, (venue) 31, 33
Buffalo Springfield (band) 93
Bulene, Herb 8
Bull Durham (band) 252, 265
Bullitt, (movie) 88
Bunch, Steve MarChris 113
Burbank Juniper Studio 258
Burch, Curtis 129, 197, 330
Burgan, Jerry xi, 100
Buriski, Dennis 349
Burke, Frenchie 371, 374
Burnett, Dorsey 138, 151
Burnett, T-Bone 96, 166, 242, 244
Burns, Jethro 96, 198, 210, 228
Burnstein, Corbin 254, 255

Burrito Deluxe (album) 94, 96, 97, 100
Burton, James 128, 154, 186, 205, 206, 263
Busey, Gary 177
Bush, Billy Green 128
Bush, Roger 1, 37, 95, 96, 103, 104, 107, 108, 109, 111, 112, 114, 115, 116, 119, 120, 122, 124, 125, 126, 127, 129, 134, 135, 137, 138, 139, 141, 142, 143, 145, 151, 158, 160, 162, 179, 221, 228
Bush, Sam ix, 46, 129, 130, 141, 175, 179, 197, 221, 223, 284
Bush, Yvonne 143
Buttram, Pat 265
Byrd and a Fish (event) 351, 352
Byrd Watcher (website) 88
Byrds (band) 39, 87, 88, 93, 94, 96, 97, 99, 101, 104, 111, 138, 139, 141, 142, 145, 176, 352
Byron Berline and Sundance (album) 175
Byron's Barn (song) 201

C

Cabelas (venue) 217, 223
Cactus Café (venue) 366
Cactus Corral (venue) 269, 283
Cain's Ballroom, Tulsa, OK (venue) v, 341, 342
Cajun Medley (song) 307
Cajun Waltz (song) 243
Cal Poly (California State Polytechnic University) (venue) 302
Cal Poly Mustangs 302
Cal State Long Beach (venue) 141, 153, 197, 210, 221, 232, 237, 253, 271
Cal State, Fullerton (venue) 138, 190, 210
Calamitys (venue) 218
Caldwell, Kansas x, 1, 2, 3, 6, 8, 9, 15, 17, 20, 21, 22, 23, 29, 44, 50, 51, 52, 56,

90, 140, 225, 254, 294, 322, 324, 333, 370
Calico Ghost Town (venue/event) 241, 258, 270, 278, 284, 292, 298, 310, 323, 330, 352, 372
Calico Saloon (venue) 269
California (band) iv, 270, 271, 272, 277, 278, 279, 280, 281, 282, 283, 284, 285, 286, 292, 293, 294, 295, 298, 299, 301, 302, 303, 307, 309, 310, 313, 314, 317, 339, 363, 364, 369, 373
California State Fair (event) 249
California State Fiddler's Contest (event) 139
California Trail Ride (event) 236, 241, 252, 254, 258, 269, 272, 278, 284, 298, 300, 310, 318, 323, 330, 335, 339, 341, 354, 355, 363, 372
California's Traveler (Album) 282, 283
Calvin, Jim 275
Cameron University 327, 340, 379
Cameron, Colin 133
Campbell, Glen 89
Campbell, Royce 30, 41, 44, 46
Can Ellen be Saved? (movie) 151, 153, 181
Canada iv, 155, 159, 167, 182, 184, 189, 197, 199, 211, 224, 228, 232, 236, 241, 242, 249, 264, 272, 279, 281, 298, 364
Canadian Driftwood (album) 168, 170
Canned Heat (band) 96
Cannon, Dyan 280
Cannon, Katherine 151
Canyon Country (venue) 264, 294
Capitol Records 95, 103, 128, 131, 136, 145, 170, 214, 224, 252, 278, 291
Capp, F. 273
Caradine, David 170, 199
Caradine, Keith 181, 199

Cardinals, St. Louis 303
Carlsbad Pizza Place
  (venue) 218, 224
Carr, Joe 131, 197, 308
Carrol, Bill 27, 28
Carroll County Blues (song)
  64
Carroll, Terry 242, 246
Carter, Russell 296
Cascade Music Festival
  (event) 310
Casey Kasem 254
Cash, Roseanne 96
Cassidy, Mike 198, 199
Castle Creek (venue) 146
Castle Peak Inn (venue)
  215
Caswell, Bill 30, 31, 32, 41,
  96, 212, 216, 220, 328
Caswell, Rosie 328
Cat Ballou (venue) 273
Catch the Wind (album)
  xi, 100, 104,
Cattleman's Ball (event)
  354
CBS (Columbia Broadcast-
  ing System) 87, 125,
  128, 138, 139, 176, 192,
  207, 236, 268
Cedar Ridge (band) 364,
  371, 374
Cellar Door (venue) 117,
  118, 179
Chad and Jeremy 99
Chancellor, James (see-
  Texas Shorty) 19
Chandler Ice Cream
  Festival (event) 357,
  363, 381
Charles River Valley Boys,
  (band) 46
Chase, Jerry 233
Cheech and Chong 93, 116
Cher (Las Vegas show)
  211
Cherokee Bell (song) 366
Cherokee Waltz (song) 101
CHFF Benefit (event) 339
China iv, v, 224, 227, 354,
  355, 356
Chino Festival (event) 192,
  211, 213, 220
Chip's Bar-B-Que 328,
  329, 331, 335

Christian World Studio
  222, 321
Christmas in Connecticut
  (movie) iv, 275, 280,
  288
Chuck E. Cheese 126
Church of the Servant
  (event/venue) 329, 395
Cinderella (song) iv, 241,
  244
City Limits (venue) 258,
  262, 264, 268, 269, 272
City Recorders studio 276
Civic Center Music Hall
  (venue) 173, 292, 322,
  323, 342
Claire, Lynch 326, 364, 371
Clark Music Hall (venue)
  116
Clark, Charlie 41, 42
Clark, Chris 287
Clark, Dick 281, 282
Clark, Gene 39, 82, 84,
  85, 87, 93, 125, 126,
  153, 175, 182, 183, 278,
  334, 335
Clark, Glen 265
Clark, Jackie 152
Clark, Mike 41, 173, 320,
  335
Clark, Patsy 243
Clark, Roy 107, 219, 220,
  292
Clark, Sandy 217
Clark, Will 303
Clarke, Michael 94, 101,
  115, 117
Classical Gas (song) 172
Clements, Vassar 141, 153,
  189, 192, 285, 372
Cleveland County Ram-
  blers (band) 30, 31,
  33, 34
Clinton, George 268
Clinton, Governor Bill
  224, 314
Close Encounters of the
  Third Kind (movie) 88
Cloud, Pat 112
Clouds (song) 106
Club Med Playa Blanca
  (venue) 190
Clyde, Jeremy 99
Cocker, Joe 88, 93

Cohen, Marc 179, 187
Collins, Charlie 55
Collins, Judy 31
Collins, Larry 221
Colton Festival (event)
  213
Columbia Records 87, 104,
  177, 283
Coming from Denver (song)
  185
Coming Home (song) 201
Commander Cody (band)
  153
Common Tyme (band)
  364
Compton, Richard 128
Concert for Bluegrass
  Band and Orchestra/
  Bluegrass Symphony
  (event) xvi, 172, 173,
  175, 176, 177, 181, 184,
  189, 192, 197, 199, 202,
  203, 207, 208, 217, 220,
  224, 225, 232, 233, 235,
  242, 249, 262, 268, 269,
  273, 286, 289, 290, 292,
  308, 310, 336, 358
Concertgebouw (venue)
  134
Connors, Chuck 226
Conoco Ponca City Fire-
  works (event) 342
Conover, Skip 145, 160,
  168, 175, 178, 197, 200,
  201, 203, 206, 216, 222,
  312, 326
Conrad, John 128
Constable, Billy 197
Convention Center Music
  Hall (venue) 203
Cooder, Ry 96, 122, 138,
  139, 153
Cook, Wayne 289
Cookson Festival (event)
  321
Cool Hand Luke (movie)
  82, 88
Cooley, Spade 194
Coolidge, Rita 145
Cooper, Stoney 57
Cooper, Wilma Lee 57
Copperfields, (album) 82
Coralie's Waltz (song) 383

Corbin, Mitch 77, 198, 355, 356, 357, 358, 363
Corbin, Red 77, 198
Cordola, Lanny 297, 299
Corn Bred (band) 159
Corneal, John 84, 85, 87
Cornet, John 273
Corral, Topanga (venue) 177
Corwin, Brad 342
Costner, Kevin iv, 251
Cotati (venue) 186
Cotton Patch Rag (song) 38, 101, 243
Cotton, Elizabeth 192
Coulter, Joe 30
Coulter, Tim 30
Council on Aging (event) 331
Country Barn Steak House (venue) 370
Country Bears, The (movie) 341, 343
Country Boys (White brothers) (band) 108
Country Fest (event) 190, 252, 298
Country Gazette, (band) iii, 39, 47, 112, 114, 115, 120, 122, 123, 124, 125, 126, 127, 128, 129, 130, 131, 133, 134, 135, 136, 138, 139, 140, 141, 142, 146, 147, 148, 149, 150, 153, 154, 155, 157, 158, 159, 160, 162, 163, 166, 167, 171, 179, 183, 192, 197, 221, 228, 235, 236, 308, 310, 326, 343
Country Gentlemen (band) 167
Country Honk (song) 91
Country Jazz Fusion (event) 327, 379
Country Music Disc Jockey Hall of Fame 21
Country Rock Tour (event) 141, 142, 143, 144, 147
Country Store (band) 167
County Star 306
Coushatta Festival (event) 151, 252
Cousin Emmy 46

Cowan, John 197
Cowboy Boogie (venue) 282, 288, 289, 292, 293
Cowboy Club (venue) 208, 209, 211, 213
Cowboy Days (event) 369
Cowboy Hall of Fame (venue) 328, 334, 335, 336, 342, 365, 369, 373, 374, 375
Cowboy Maynard 97, 100, 127, 196, 215
Cowboy Symposium (event) 379
Crabgrass (band) xvi
Cramer, Floyd 103
Crary, Dan 129, 130, 141, 155, 166, 168, 169, 175, 178, 179, 189, 190, 192, 193, 196, 201, 202, 207, 210, 212, 218, 221, 222, 228, 238, 258, 259, 261, 263, 276, 278, 286, 287, 307, 312, 326, 348, 352, 353, 364, 371, 373
Crazy Creek (song) 38, 48
Crazy Horse Bluegrass Festival (event) 223
Crazy Horse Saloon (venue) 208, 212, 213, 215, 222, 235, 236, 237, 241, 251, 252, 254, 256, 257, 268, 270, 271, 273, 275, 277, 278, 279, 280, 281, 282, 283, 289, 291, 295, 296, 301, 307, 331
Creativity Ambassador (event) v, 375, 380, 381
Crescendo (venue) 199
Crestline Festival (event) 279, 294
Creston, California Festival (event) 280
Crickets (band) 178
Cripple Creek (song) 30
Cripple Creek Trio (band) 30
Criteria Records 119
Croft, Lonnie 71, 81
Crosby, Bing 3
Crosby, David 39, 95, 114, 126, 151
Crosby, Stills and Nash (band) 114, 151

Cross, Leon 23
Crossings Church (venue) 350
Crouch, Tim 372
Crow, J.D. 142
Crowell, Rodney 154, 168, 175, 188, 191
Cruise from Galveston (event) 360
Cruise, Tom 302
Crumpton, Frank 165, 166
Cruz, Edgar 353, 366, 371, 374
Cudney, Larry 209
Culpeper-Warrenton, VA Bluegrass Festival (venue) 141
Cunha, Rick 172, 173, 206, 207, 211, 213, 216, 239
Curb Records 258, 277
Curtis, Sonny 178
Cushman, Charlie 215

D

Dad's Favorites (album) iv, 19, 182, 185, 196, 197
Dahl, Senator John 318
Daily Titan (paper) 210
Dallas (TV show) 250
Dallas Cowboys 28
Dalton, Eric 122, 134, 137, 310, 314, 319
Dana Point Inn (venue) 272
Dance Party (venue) 279
Danhoff, Bill 138
Danhoff, Taffy Nivert 138
Daniels, Jack 231, 232, 233, 241, 304
Danko, Rick 168
Danny Gatton Band (band) 198
Darling, Eric 31
Darlins (Darlings) family 37
Dartmouth College (venue) 118
David Munnelly's Irish Band 371
Davidovich, Lolita 263
Davies, Gail 176
Davis, Bob 169

Davis, Danny 105, 106,
Davis, Duke 245, 252, 269
Davis, Ed 192
Davis, George (event) 334
Dawes, Bob 103
Day, Doris 99
Days of Wine and Roses
    (movie) 111
Deadwood (TV show) v,
    354, 380
Dean, Jimmy 128
Dean, Larry 251
Dear Old Dixie (song) 64
Decca Records 70, 188
Deer Hunt (event) 340
Deer, Monty 23
Dell Corporation (event)
    368
Denny, Martin 106
Denver, John 138, 167,
    174, 186, 206
Deputy Dalton (song) 133
Deramus, Frank 41, 42, 43,
    49, 351
Derrick, Devon 346
Desert Rose Band 163,
    253, 300
Detroit Bluegrass Festival
    (event) 212
Devil Went Down to Geor-
    gia (song) 211
Devil's Dream (song) 47
DeVito, Hank 154
Diabetes Awareness
    (event) 328
Diamond, Neil 93
Diaz, Dave 228
Dickson, Jim 39, 115, 117,
    122, 124, 125, 139, 141,
    160, 195, 196
Dillard and Clark Expedi-
    tion iii, 81, 82, 83, 84,
    85, 86, 87, 88, 93, 232,
    271
Dillard and Meader (al-
    bum) 172
Dillard Expedition iii, 93,
    94, 95, 96, 97, 99, 100,
    101, 103, 104, 105, 106,
    107, 108, 109, 111
Dillard, Douglas Flint xi,
    xii, 32, 37, 38, 39, 40,
    64, 81, 82, 83, 84, 85, 86,
    87, 88, 89, 92, 93, 94, 95,

96, 100, 104, 105, 107,
108, 109, 111, 122, 133,
136, 142, 143, 145, 170,
172, 176, 190, 191, 193,
195, 196, 197, 198, 253
Dillard, Rodney 32, 92,
    133, 190, 191
Dillards, The (band) iii, x,
    xii, xv, 25, 31, 32, 33,
    37, 38, 39, 46, 63, 64, 82,
    85, 86, 93, 108, 139, 221,
    269, 326, 369
Dillingham, Kyle 363, 380
Dinah Shore Golf Club
    267
Dirt Band, The (see Nitty
    Gritty Dirt Band)
Dirty Harry, (movie) 88
Dismembered Tennesse-
    ans (band) 253
Disney 124, 126, 181, 231,
    236, 244, 256, 258, 264,
    265, 278, 280, 282, 283,
    341, 343
Disneyland 124, 125, 126,
    127, 139, 302, 306
Disneyworld 265, 276,
    278, 282, 292, 293, 295,
    296, 298, 301, 308, 312
Dixie Dynamite (movie)
    174
Dixie Hoedown (song) 203
DKPI 153
Docker Hill Boys (band)
    153
Doctors of Neuroscience
    (event) 374
Dod, Mary 311
Dodge Challenger 104
Don Ross Studio 307
Don't Fence Me In (al-
    bum) 206
Don't Give Up Your Day
    Job (album) 133, 138,
    139, 141
Don't Put It Away (song)
    201, 203
Donahue, Jerry 260
Donner, Richard 298
Doo Wah Riders (band)
    232, 248, 251, 252, 256,
    257, 258, 262, 264, 265,
    267, 268, 269, 270, 271,
    272, 273, 274, 275, 276,

277, 278, 279, 280, 281,
282, 283, 284, 287, 288,
289, 290, 291, 292, 293,
294, 295, 296, 297, 298,
299, 300, 301, 302, 305,
306, 307, 308, 310, 312,
313, 314, 331, 360, 363
Doobie Brothers (band)
    192
Doors, The (band) 91
Dorman, Greg 295
Double Trouble (album)
    241, 243
Double Trouble (song) iv,
    243
Doublestop Fiddle Shop
    vii, 61, 247, 287, 302,
    312, 315, 326, 328, 355,
    365, 366, 373
Doud, Ellie 308
Douglas, Jerry 210, 295
Douglas, Michael 277
Dove Creek (venue) 378
Down Home Pickin' Par-
    lor (venue) 249, 280
Down in the Bluegrass
    (song) 47, 160
Down the Road (song) 153
Downing, George 20
Downtown Mulvane
    Festival (event) 322
Dr. Hook and the Medi-
    cine Show (band) 153
Dr. John 263, 264
Drake Park Pavilion
    (venue) 310
Drifting Cowboys (band)
    79
Driftwood, Jimmy 129
Drunken Billy Goat (song)
    38, 39
Duelin' Banjo (album)
    133, 143
Duffy, Chris 236
Dukes of Hazard (TV
    show) 297
Dunbar, Dayna 380
Dunbar, Eddie 248, 251,
    252, 257, 258, 288, 290
Duncan, Glen 221
Duncan, Oklahoma Festi-
    val (event) 335
Duncan, Steve 230, 241,
    242, 244, 281, 300

Duncan, Stuart 191, 251, 336
Dunn, Clancy 294
Durang's Hornpipe (song) 38
Durham, Bill 29, 36
Durham, Buddy 29, 36
Durham, David 252, 265, 270
Durham, James 129
Durham, Mel 97, 192, 239, 369
Durham's Reel (song) 109
Dusty Miller (song) 48
Dylan, Bob 39, 46, 93, 95, 192

E

E.T. the Extra-Terrestrial (movie) 88
Eagles (band) 135, 139, 149, 150, 188, 360
Earthquake 2/9/1971 108
Eastman Company 355, 356
Eastwood, Clint 191, 194, 221,
Eaton, Frank (see Pistol Pete)
Ebbets Field (venue) 153
Eblin, Ed 307
Eddy, Duane 107
Edgewood Wildlife Festival (event) 357, 363
Edmond Arts Council 357
Edmonton Folk Festival (event) 228
Edward, J. 174
Edwards, Ralph 8
Ekrote, Jack 316
El Reno Community College (venue) 341
Elam, Katrina 330, 335, 356
Electra Records 37, 82, 91, 181
Electric Café 299
Elk-B Park (venue) 281
Elliott, Ramblin' Jack 95
Elmore, Randy 19
Emmanuel, Tommy 348
Emmerich, Roland 284
Emmons, Buddy 128, 133, 198

Empire of the Sun (movie) 88
Emporia State University 21
English, Johnny 49
Enid Christian Church (venue) 344
Enid Country Club (venue) 359
Enter The Dragon (movie) 88
Environmental Corporate party (event) 332
Epworth Retirement Village (venue) 333
Ericson, John 127
Ertegun, Ahmet 120
Eskridge, Art 129
Ethridge, Chris 122, 142, 143, 145, 153
Euphoria String Band 331
Evans, Dave 237
Evans, Marc 276
Eve of Destruction (song) 101
Evening Shade (TV show) 296, 297
Every Which Way but Loose (movie) 191, 194
Eyerly, Alan 319

F

Faded Love (song) 307, 318
Fairchild, Raymond 311
Falco, Donna 308
Fall Creek (song) 201
Fallen Eagle (song) 119
Fame (movie) 233, 295
Family Jams (album) 98, 99
Far and Away (movie) 88
Faris Family (band) 331
Farm Bureau (event) 370
Farmer's Son (song) 283
Farmers Organization (event) 329
Farther Along (song) 125, 145
Feldman, Peter xv, 241, 248, 252, 264, 270, 277, 282, 298, 314, 335, 339, 353, 374
Feldman, Rudy 22, 23

Ferguson, Dave 192, 269
Fernwood Tonight (TV show) 177
Fetchet, Dennis 170, 189, 190, 206, 242, 258
Fiddle Faddle (song) 307
Fiddle Fest (event) 3iv, 23, 328, 351, 371
Fiddler on the Roof (movie) 88
Fiddler's Dream (song) 312
Fiddler's Park (venue) 285
Fiddlers Green (venue) 343
Fiddlers of the World in Nova Scotia (event) 335
Fiddling Thru the Years (song book) 5
Fiedler, Arthur 88
Field, Sally 163, 164, 165, 166, 183
Fifty Cents (song) 4
Findelle, Stann 114
Firks, Robert 122
First Family, The (song) 172
First Presbyterian Church picnic (event) 330, 339, 342, 344, 349, 352, 353, 357, 363, 365, 369, 370, 373, 375, 376
Fischel, Steve 244
Fischer Haus B & B (venue) 375
Fish, Jim 309, 310, 314, 319, 320, 324, 334, 342, 349, 351, 352, 363, 367, 368, 376
Fisher, Chris 179
Fisher's Hornpipe (song) 38, 208
Five Days Home (see Welcome Home Soldier Boys) (movie) 125, 128
Flaming Lips (band) 368
Flapper McGee's (venue) 204
Flat Broke Fiddler (album) 354
Flats, Mickey 346, 348
Flatt and Scruggs (band) xii, 5, 16, 55, 96, 119
Flatt, Lester 5, 55, 128, 138, 147, 159, 197

Fletcher, Louise 151
Flores, Rosie 244
Florida Prairie State Preserve 363
Florida State (University) 69
Flying Burrito Brothers, The, FBB, (band) iii, 39, 84, 87, 90, 94, 96, 97, 100, 106, 112, 115, 116, 117, 118, 119, 120, 121, 122, 123, 124, 125, 126, 135, 136, 141, 142, 143, 148, 310
Flying Fish Records 201, 204
Fogelberg, Dan 153
Foggy Mountain Breakdown (song) 104, 112, 113, 115, 301
Folger, Joe 240
Follows Camp Bluegrass Festival (event) 243, 248, 252, 270, 287
Fonda, Henry 111
Fonda, Jane 96
Footprints in the Snow (song) 64
Ford Center 368
Ford, Tennessee Ernie 9
Forrestburg, Chris 92
Forrester, Howdy 20, 56
Fort Hood, Texas 76
Fort Polk Louisiana 69, 74, 77, 78, 79, 379
Fortina, Carl 89
Fosman, Barry 295
Foster, Billy Joe 323, 334, 358, 359
Foster, Jodie 297
Foster, Wayne 271
Fox Theater (venue) 124
Fox, Rich 307
Frampton, Peter 153
Francis, Archie 257
Frank, Randy 257
Frankie and Johnny (song) 107, 145
Franklin, Larry 19
Franklin, Louis x, 19, 66
Franklin, Major x, 19
Fraser, Alasdair 364
Free Wheel Bicycle Ride (event) 376

Free Wheelin' (song) 376
Freedom (movie) 206
Freedom/Holiday Bowl (event) 233
Freeman, Ed 247
Freight and Salvage (venue) 95
Freight Train (song) 192
Freightliner (event) 330, 331
Fremont Hotel (venue) 96, 103, 104
Fret House Music Store (venue) 250, 255, 264, 289
Frey, Glen 135, 139
Friday at Four (event) 30, 31
Frizzell, David 186, 221
Fromm, Lynette "Squeaky" 98
Front Porch String Band (band) 326
Frost, David (TV show) 118
Frost, Jane I, vi, vii, viii, xv, 285, 330, 383
Frost, Larry 130, 131, 381
Frost, Lee 174
Frost, Ronnie 26
Full Circle (song) 335
Full Sail Film School 296, 299
Fuller, Jerry 232, 288, 290
Fullerton Chili Cook Off (event) 196
Funicello, Annette 235
Funky Chicken (song) 243
Funky Deer (song) 201

G

Gabriel's Fire (movie) 273
Gadette, Katy 258, 269
Gainer, Garland 19
Gallagher 103
Gambaccini, Peter 118
Garcia, Benny 366
Gardner, Yandell 370
Garling, Jim 371
Garner, James 199, 297, 298
Garrets House of Furniture 41, 42

Garrett, Snuff 191, 194, 221
Gary, Russ 245, 251
Gatton, Danny 198
Gauley, Ike 314
Gautier, Armand 194
GEB, Great Empire Broadcasting 20
Gene Autry Museum of Western Heritage (venue) 256, 270, 272, 273, 283, 295
George, Christopher 174
George, Lowell 152
Getto, Sarah 341
Giardiasis iv, 316, 317
Gibson Brothers (band) 371, 374
Gibson, Bob 115
Gibson, Mel 248, 297, 298
Gilded Palace of Sin (album) 94
Gilenwater, Rocky 316
Gilkenson, Jeff 133
Gill, Jerene 366
Gill, Stan 180
Gill, Vince iv, xiii, 156, 172, 174, 179, 180, 181, 182, 185, 187, 189, 190, 196, 200, 201, 207, 224, 244, 298, 308, 326, 327, 328, 334, 336, 351, 356, 363, 366, 368
Gillette, Corine 213
Gillette, Steve 213
Gilliam, Burton 297
Gilliam, Les 346
Gimble, Johnny 250
Glasgow, Kenny 300, 318, 339
Glencoe School Concert 369
Glendale Community College (venue) 208, 213, 217, 222, 225, 230, 235, 241, 250, 252, 257, 269, 284, 292
Glodell, M. 245
Goalby, Becky 210
Godfrey, Arthur 9
Gold Country Music Festival (event) 299
Gold Hill Inn (venue) 279, 286

Gold Rush (song/album) ix, x, 66, 81, 95, 141, 287, 295
Golden Bear (venue) 174
Golden West (venue) 190
Goldstein, Sam 128
Good Ole Boys (movie) 303
Good Time Hour (TV show) 89
Good Times Canada (event) 211
Goodman, Steve 231
Goodman, Tim 292, 318
Goodnight, Rollie 12
Goof 227
Gordy, Emory 154, 168, 188
Goux, John 282
GP (album) 127, 128
Grace King High School (venue) 197
Grace, Simon 228
Graf, John 245, 246
Graham, Billy 282, 350
Graham, Franklin 350
Grammer Guitar Factory 60
Grand Masters Fiddle Contest (event) 220
Grand National Quail Hunt (event) 359, 371, 374
Grand Ole Opry 8, 9, 43, 44, 55, 56, 57, 59, 66, 74, 353
Grand Ole Opry of England 8, 149
Grant, Amy 369
Grant, Bill 66
Grappelli, Stephane x
Grass Valley Bluegrass Festival (event) 221, 236, 249, 261, 262, 299, 339
Graves, Josh 167, 293
Graves, Peter 152
Great American Music Hall (venue) 223
Great Northern Opry (venue) 197
Great Speckled Bird, The (song) 74
Grech, Ric 128

Green Back Dollar (song) 101
Green Berets 128
Green Mile, The (movie) 82
Green, Adam 300
Green, Doug (Ranger) xv, 63, 65
Green, Ed 139
Green, Green (song) 101
Green, John 258
Green, Richard ix, 58, 59, 252
Greenbrier Boys (band) 39
Greene, Richard 56, 58
Grey Cat on the Tennessee Farm (album) 353
Grey Eagle (song) 61, 101, 156, 185
Grier, David 373, 379
Grier, Lamar 56, 57, 58, 59, 62, 63, 373
Grievous Angel (song/album) 142, 146
Griffith, Andy (TV show) 15, 37
Griffith, Nanci 236
Grisman, David 95, 115, 141, 283
Groendyke, John D. 359
Gruhn's 119
Guadalcanal 260
Guarneri, Del Jesu 345
Guerin, John 128
Guilbeau, Gib 144
Guitar Workshop (TV show) 138, 172
Guthrie Country Club (venue/event) 350
Guthrie Land Rush Celebration (event) 257
Guthrie, Arlo 122, 151, 207
Guthrie, Oklahoma 89'er Day 100th Land Rush Anniversary (event)
Guthrie, Woody 170

H

Haas, Natalie 364
Habitat for Humanity 351, 369
Hackett, Buddy 205
Hafer Park (venue) 325
Haggard, Merle 305

Haggers, Loretta 188
Hair (play) 101
Haley, Lisa 302
Half Moon Bay (venue) 294
Hall, Dr. Brian 351, 354
Hall, Ralph 231
Hall, Tom T. 215
Hallelujah Harry (song) 259
Halloran, Ella Rose 211, 308
Halloran, Jack 308
Halloran, Molly 211
Hambly, Scott 147
Hamilton County Breakdown (song) xii, 32, 38, 336
Hamilton Place (venue) 189
Hamilton, David 289, 295, 308
Haness, Abigale 152
Hangin' On (movie) 211
Hankerin' for Hank (show) 372, 374
Hansons, The 380
Happy Birthday (song) v, 375, 377, 378
Hard Hearted (song) 138
Hard Hearted Hannah (song) 106
Hardin, Glen D. 128, 154, 195, 230
Harding, Charles 196, 213
Harding, May 196
Harjo, Benjamin Jr. 380
Harker, Mel 292
Harrah Festival (event) 342
Harrah's Hotel (venue) 103
Harris, Doc 56, 60
Harris, Emmylou 118, 128, 141, 146, 147, 153, 154, 155, 162, 163, 168, 170, 171, 174, 180, 181, 193, 194, 196, 204, 205, 210, 224, 231, 244, 314, 326, 331, 361
Harris, Fred 33, 34, 52, 53
Harris, Jim 15
Hart, Harvey 151

Hartford, John ix, 96, 158, 159, 170, 181, 186, 189, 219, 220, 253, 271
Harwood 168
Hatchet, Molly (band) 197
Hatfield, Bobby 277
Hawkins, Walter 41, 42, 44
Hayes, Cherie 295
Haywood, Doug 307
Hazelwood, Carl 18, 19
Hazlewood, Lee 107, 208, 217
Heard, Hubie 152
Heard, Marvin 275
Hearn, Don 117
Heartbreak Hotel 33
Heartland (album) 269
Hearts of the West 295
Heckadon, Frank 308
Hee Haw (TV show) 89, 93, 94, 107, 217, 219, 220, 237
Hefner, Hugh 100
Helbig, Rudiger 346
Hellecasters (band) 260
Helm, Don 79
Helm, Levon 168, 174
Hendel, Paul 336
Henderson, Florence 247
Hendricks, John 329, 348
Henley, Don 126, 135, 139, 360, 367
Henning, Debbie 342
Herd, Mark 265
Heroes (album) ix
Heroes (venue) 252
Hersh, Al 145
Hershey, Louis B. 52, 53
Hewitt, Dolf 312
Hiatt, Bernice 8
Hiatt, Cecil iv, 7, 8, 129
Hiatt, Claude 8
Hiatt, Foy 8
Hickman Brothers (band) 146, 147
Hickman, George 159, 200
Hickman, John iv, viii, 147, 159, 160, 161, 166, 167, 169, 170, 173, 175, 182, 192, 193, 200, 201, 202, 204, 205, 207, 210, 212, 218, 219, 221, 222, 224, 225, 226, 228, 230, 233, 237, 238, 240, 241,
243, 245, 247, 249, 251, 252, 253, 258, 259, 260, 262, 263, 271, 272, 276, 278, 279, 280, 286, 287, 288, 290, 291, 299, 300, 302, 307, 309, 311, 312, 314, 317, 319, 320, 321, 328, 339, 343, 346, 349, 350, 352, 357, 360, 364, 366, 368, 371, 373, 376, 378, 379
Hickory Holler (song) 93
Hicks, Bobby 358
Hicks, Lonesome Dan 154
High Ground (band) 364, 371
High Sierra Festival 228
Highfill, George 229, 247
Highway 101 (band) 231
Hill, Joel Scott 153
Hill, W.E. 168
Hillman, Chris 39, 94, 101, 112, 115, 117, 118, 119, 120, 121, 123, 126, 172, 184, 215, 217, 227, 242, 283, 300, 334, 352
Hobbs, John 170, 188, 201, 205, 252, 257, 281, 291
Hobo's Lullaby (album) 122
Hodges, Lee 295
Hoffman, Dustin 99, 247, 302
Hoffner Beatle 178
Hokom, Suzi Jane 107
Holdridge, Lee 206
Holland Holiday (song) 160
Hollister Festival (event) 270
Holly, Buddy 177, 178
Hollywood Bowl (venue) 127
Honeymoon Waltz (song) 276, 280
Honk (band) 154
Honky Cat (song) 153
Hooker, Liz 284
Hoot Night (event) 93
Hooten, David 366
Hootenanny 30
Hord, Eric 101
Horn, The (venue) 213
Hornet Stadium CSUS Sacramento (venue) 262
Horse Shoe Road (band) 363
Hospitality Point (venue) 271
Hot Band (band) 154, 204
Hot Burrito Breakdown (song) 116, 117, 124, 126
Hot Burrito Revue (event) 134, 136
Hot Burritos, The True Story of the Flying Burrito Brothers (book) 120
Hot Country Nights (TV show) 281, 282
Hot Rize (band) 221, 232, 237, 280
Hotel Wiechmann 123, 134, 135, 149
Hotmud Family (band) 197
Houndog Ramble (album) xiii
House of the Rising Sun (venue) 96, 97, 100, 104, 108, 111
Howard, Howie 119
Howard, Ron 119
Huckleberry Hornpipe (song) iii, 95, 133, 259, 309
Hudson, Garth 168, 230
Hughes, Baker 371, 379
Hughes, Howard 209, 254
Hugo Bluegrass Festival (event) 146, 159
Hui Concert (event) 220
Hult Center's Silva Hall (venue) 289, 308
Humbolt State (venue) 182, 247
Humphrey, Greg 210
Hungry Farmer (venue) 186
Hunt Brothers (band) viii, 366
Hunt Family (band) 374
Hunt, Andrew 366
Hunt, Jonathan 366
Hurst, Jim 372
Hutchens, Doug 221

Hutchison, Joe 156, 167, 242, 259, 318, 322, 326, 330, 335, 351
Hynes, Marita 352

I

I am the Black Sheep of the Family (song) 236
I can Help (song) 273
I Can Still Hear You Calling 81
I Can't Stop Loving You (song) 106
I Don't Love Nobody (song) 243
I Fall to Pieces (song) 114
I Fought the Law (song) 178
I Guess He'd Rather be in Colorado (song) 138
I Live in the Past (song) 63
I Wonder Where You are Tonight (song) 81
I'll Dry Every Tear That Falls (song) 283
I'll Just Stay Around (song) 203
I'll Live my Lonely Life Alone (song) 81
I'm No Stranger to the Rain (song) 178
Ian, Janis 207
IBMA International Bluegrass Music Association 280, 294
Ice House (venue) 103, 108, 109, 207
Ickes, Rob 372
If I be Lifted up (song) 138
If I Could Only Win Your Love (song) 155
If You Don't Leave Me Alone, I'll Find Somebody Who Will (song) 256
If You're Ever Gonna Love Me (song) 138
III Generation (band) 364
Indian See Saw (song) 243
Indianola Festival (event) 228
Ireland iv, 206, 212, 259, 260, 383
Iron Horse Agency 148, 149

Irvine Festival (event) 193, 215
It's So Hard to be a Woman (song) 207
Italy v, 203, 305, 306, 326, 343, 344, 345, 346, 371

J

Jack Rabbit (album, song) 197, 201, 203
Jackson, Bill 257
Jackson, David 84, 85, 271
Jackson, Grandpa Jesse 10
Jackson, Michael 300
Jackson, Tommy 20, 32, 38
Jade the dog 325
Jae, Jana 322, 372
Jagger, Dean 104
Jagger, Mick 91, 94
Jam Sessions (album) 35
Jammin' with Byron (album) 383
Japan 10, 160, 192, 197, 202, 204, 231, 236, 251, 60, 294, 295, 299, 314, 326, 341, 356
Japanese Village (venue) 138, 158
Jason, Robert 294
Jaws (movie) 88
Jayne, Mitch 32
Jayroe, Jane Ann 336
Jazz Bow Rag (song) 38
Jeans, Jimmy 75, 76
Jefferson County Civic Center (venue) 233
Jefferson House 34, 41, 42, 49, 50
Jefferson, Thomas xiv
Jenkins, Buster (see Kinard, Frank)
Jennings, Waylon 31, 175
Jimenez, Flaco 373
Jimmie Rodgers 304
Joe Cocker! (album) 88, 93
Joffe, Ken 29
John Denver 138, 167, 174, 186, 206
John Hardy (song) 64
John Henry (song) 81, 138
John, Elton 253
John, Olivia Newton 184
Johns, Glen (Glyn) 91, 341

Johnson Mountain Boys (band) 233, 237
Johnson, Al 264
Johnson, Ben 124
Johnson, Bruce 170, 203, 210, 242
Johnson, Carel 128, 129
Johnson, Courtney 129, 197
Johnson, Don 314, 315, 321
Johnson, Johnny 128
Jones, Bret 370
Jones, Chris 374
Jones, Douglas 112
Jones, George 93, 259
Jones, Gomer 33
Jones, Mickey 297
Jones, Willie 346
Joplin, Janis 104
Jordan, Vic 66, 128
Jorgenson, John 233, 242, 260, 281, 300, 364
Joyland Park 20
Jubilee Auditorium (venue) 184
Judy and Janet (twins) 249, 287, 292
Jumpin' the Strings (album) 248, 287
Junior Bonner (movie) 124, 127

K

Kaiser, Hans 196
Kansas Association of Bluegrass (event) 341
Kansas City Philharmonic (band) 199, 220
Kassel, Joan 250
Kathy, Camal 73, 78, 79
Kaufman, Phil 90, 91, 93, 98, 99, 145, 147
Kaufman, Steve 323, 336
Kay Starr Country (album) 145
Kay, Jack 79
Keaton's Cop (TV show) 264
Keep On Pushin' (song) 126, 134
Keith, Ben 154
Keith, Bill 46, 47, 48, 141
Keith, Harold 49

Keith, Johnny 49, 50
Keith, Toby 356, 368
Kennedy, Greg 310, 314, 319, 320, 322, 324
Kennedy, President John F. 31, 172
Kenner, Bill 141
Kenny Rogers Second Edition (band) 297
Kentucky Colonels (band) 37, 63, 64, 96, 103, 108, 138, 139, 140, 141, 170
Kentucky Fried Chicken (event) 221, 237
Kentucky Grass (band) 167
Kerrville Country Fair (event) 204
Kerrville Folk Festival 232
Keuhl, Tom 96, 100, 127
KFDI 20
KFML 153
Kickers Club (venue) 213, 214, 215
Kidder, Margot 127
Kienzle, Rich 204
Kimberlys, The, (group) 30, 31
Kimmel, Bobby 168
Kinard, Frank (see Buster Jenkins) 12, 13, 371
King of Morroco 225
King of Tonga 260
King, Larry 272
King, Pee Wee 44
Kingdom of Tonga 260
Kingston Trio (band) 30
KITO 5
Kleinow, Sneaky Pete 94, 101, 114, 134, 137, 139, 142, 143, 230
Klink, Mike 277
Klotz 344, 346
KLPR 44
KMET-LA 115
KMPC L.A. Country Show (event) 265
Knoll, Jeff 276
Knopf, Bill 191
Knott's Berry Farm (venue/event) 126, 190, 196, 198, 217, 218, 222, 232, 235, 241, 252, 257, 277, 292, 293

Knotts Landing (TV show) 236
Knotts, Don 15
Kochs, Dan 129
KOCO TV 41
Kodak 1955 (song) 259
Kolchak: The Night Stalker (TV show) 160
KOMA 348
Kootch, Danny 152
Korean War 10
Koslo, Paul 128
Kovacs, Wolfgang 346
KPFK 196, 222, 264
Krauss, Alison 95
Krenwinkel, Patricia 98
Kristofferson, Kris iv, 93, 145, 172, 176, 177, 199, 244, 258, 280
Kristufek, Eduard 344
Kristufek, Paul 344
Kruger Brothers 357, 364
Krukow, Mike 302, 303

L

L. A. Country Scene (event) 247
L.A. Fiddle Band (band, album) iii, 162, 170, 171, 193, 200, 203, 206, 209, 213, 217, 225, 230, 232, 235, 236, 237, 241, 242, 247, 248, 250, 252, 253, 259, 271, 279, 284, 326
L.A. Law (TV show) 255
L.A. Street Scene (event) 233, 238
La Bianca murders 87
La Grange Rouge (red barn) (venue) 372
Laguna Nigel (venue) 269
Lala, Joe 120, 126, 152
Lamb, Bill 50
Land, Bosco 71
Land, Mitchell 44, 45, 64, 71, 72, 79, 81, 129, 288
Land, Peter 197
Landmark Hotel (venue) 105, 106
Lane County Fair (event) 181, 184, 197, 204, 208, 217
Langford, Steve 242

Langhorn, Bruce 182
Langley Oklahoma Festival (event) ix, 156, 167, 200, 236, 242, 248, 259, 326
Langston College 358
Las Vegas Bluegrass Festival 279
Last Kansas Exit (band) 232
Last of the Red Hot Burritos (album) 117, 118, 121, 125
Latham, Billy Ray 96, 103, 104, 107, 108, 115, 133, 228, 299
Laughing Guitar (song) 160
Laurel Canyon Ramblers 299, 300, 304, 307, 314
Lawson, Doyle 232
Lawson, Michael T. 153
Lawton Community Jazz Band (band) 328
Lawton, G. 298
Lazy E (venue) 319, 335, 353
Lazzarro, Giovanni 345
Leadon, Bernie 84, 94, 100, 101, 115, 121, 126, 135, 139, 145, 149, 197, 251, 361
Leave Me the Way I Am (song) 259
Leavin' Louisiana in the Broad Day Light (song) 191
Ledbetter's (venue) 40, 107
Lee, Albert 180, 181, 205, 230
Lee, Arthur 295
Legends Concert 365
Leonard's 75th Birthday Party (event) 370
Lesley, Jim 272
Let it Bleed (album) 91, 92, 93
Let Me Love You Tonight (song) 200
Levin, Geoff 179
Lewis Family (band) 129, 222
Lewis, Laurie 352
Liberty (song) 243
LIE (album) 99

Liebenson, Kenny (Kenny Lee Benson) 265, 268, 276, 300, 305, 307
Liebert, Billy 145
LIFE Magazine 99
Light, Chris 252
Lightfoot, Gordon 93
Lighthouse, The (venue) 170, 175, 256
Ligon, David 354, 355
Lilly, Everett D. 46
Limelighters (group) 233
Limerock (song) ix, 185, 259
Lincoln Center (venue) 221
Lineberger, Don 47
Little Bear (venue) 184
Little Rascals (movies) 49
Little, Cleavon 104
Litton corporate party (event) 273
Live Almost (album) 37
Live and Let Live (song) 41, 64
Live at McCabes (album) 160
Live in Amsterdam (album) 126, 134, 136
Live in Sweden (album) 140
Lloyd Noble Center 321
Lloyd, Mike 265, 277
Logan County Fairgrounds 349, 365, 369, 373, 375
Logan, Tex 46, 47
Lomax, Alan 39
Lone Star Saloon (venue) 206, 208, 213, 217
Lonesome Blues Tonight (song) 153
Lonesome Road (song) 160
Lonesome Road Blues (song) 30, 64
Longhorn Saloon (venue) 217, 222, 235, 245, 247, 248, 268, 269, 270, 271, 273, 275, 278, 279, 282, 284, 289, 291
Los Angeles Free Press (paper) 114
Los Angeles Times 97
Lost Between the Falling Snow (song) 81

Lost Highway (band) 331
Lost Indian (song) 146
Louhans, France Folk Festival (event) 372
Louisiana (song) 81
Louisiana Man (song) 188
Louisiana, Fort Polk 69, 74
Louisiana, I Can Still Hear You Calling (song) 81
Louisville Gardens (venue) 202
Love Another Man (song) 81
Love Has Got Me (song) 126
Lowinger, Gene 47
Lowry-Johnson, Junie 380
Lucas, Dennis 77
Lucas, George 291
Lundgren, Dolph 284
Lupino, Ida 124
Lynard, Ken 307, 308
Lynch, Claire 326, 364, 371
Lytle, John 287, 294, 318

M

M.A.S.H. (TV show) 199
Mack, Ronnie 293
Macon, Uncle Dave 353
Maddox, Rose 96, 177, 183, 207, 252, 254, 299, 300
Mae Axton Award (event) iv, 329, 332, 333
Magic Mountain (venue) 187, 192
Mallully, Karen 301
Mamas and Papas (band) 101
Manassas (album) 119, 120, 121, 125
Mancini, Henry 111
Mandolin Rag (song) 369
Manhattan Transfer (band) 175
Manitou Spring City Hall (venue) 286, 320
Manners, Zeke 103
Mansfield, Ken 172, 175
Manson, Charles iii, 87, 95, 98, 99, 101
Manuel, Richard 168
Maphis, Joe 96
Maphis, Roselee 96

Marathon (events) 174, 213
Marcellino, Jerry 251
Margolin, Stuart 199
Mariners Church Social (event) 218
Mark O'Connor xi, 156, 167, 175, 196, 244, 287, 295, 314, 335, 374, 379
Market Place, The (venue) 221, 228, 237, 242
Marks, Groucho 205
Marshall, Jim 92
Martin, Gene 60
Martin, George 176
Martin, J.D. 49, 241, 247
Martin, Jack 128
Martin, Jimmy 66
Martin, John "Moon" 122
Martin, Pete 270
Martin, Steve 113, 114, 155, 301
Mary Hartman, Mary Hartman (TV show) 188
Mary Tyler Moore (TV show) 199
Mashore, Roger 336
Mass Street Music (venue) 366
Massey, Jim 322
Massey, Marsha 322
Masters, Art 208
Masters, The (band) 293
Mathis, Samantha 291
Mattress Jams 354
Maverick (movie) 297, 298
Maxwell House (venue) 273
May, Don 316
Mazda (commercial) 133, 213
MCA Records 162, 169, 175, 177, 180, 184, 203, 242
McAuliffe, Leon 252
McCabes (venue) 96, 101, 104, 122, 125, 128, 131, 136, 141, 153, 154, 159, 160, 166, 168, 174, 175, 183, 186, 190, 193, 196, 202, 208, 217, 241, 242, 245, 248, 250, 253, 258, 270, 272, 294, 298, 310

McClain Family (band)
159
McClellan, Mike 23
McCloud, Murray 83, 104,
151, 158, 190, 196, 199,
296
McCormick, Haskell 128
McCrae, George152
McCrae, Gwen 152
McCrory, Del 222
McDonald, Tim 338
McElvey, David 247, 248,
250, 256
McEuen, Bill 113
McEuen, John xiii, 95, 113,
152, 186, 192, 287, 293,
296, 303, 304, 369, 371
McFarland, Spanky
(George) 49
McGee, Kirk 46
McGee, Sam 46, 167
McGraw, Frank 8
McGuinn, Jim 39
McGuinn, Roger 87, 139,
176
McGuire and the Doctor
(album) 101, 106
McGuire, Barry 100, 101,
106
McIntyre, Reba 222, 298,
305, 320, 368
McMasters, Natalie 335
McNeely, Larry 55, 56,
179, 189, 198
McNees, LeRoy Mack xiv,
108, 169, 190
McQuarter, Ed 26
McQueen, Steve 87, 124,
127
McReynolds, Jesse 128,
293
McReynolds, Jim 128
McSwain Theater (venue)
332, 374
Mead, Gene 35
Meader, Vaughn 172
Mecca, The, (venue) 37
Medica, Leon 188
Medical Society Party
(event) 334
Medly, Bill 277
Meeting of Lt. Governors
in Oklahoma City
(event) 330

Meisner, Randy 126, 135,
188
Melbourne Jazz Club
(venue) 236
Melch, David 355
Melcher, Terry 87, 88, 99,
167, 169, 176,
Melodrama at Bakersfield
(event) 229, 235, 269,
278, 279, 284, 287, 292,
293
Melodrama at Oceana
(event) 192, 196, 197
Melody Ranch (movie
set) 354
Mercer, Roy D. 301
Merle Fest (event) 292, 310
Messenger, David 298
Messina, Jim 191
Meyer, Liz 338
Meyer, Park 254
Meyers, Augie 373
MGM (Metro Goldwyn
Maher) 20, 124, 127,
165, 233
MGM Hotel (venue) 305
Michaels, D. 294
Mickey Mouse 181
Mid West Trophy Show
(event) 346
Midler, Bett iv, 189, 190
Miles, Heather 254
Milk Cow Blues (song) xi,
100
Miller, Bill 366
Miller, Roger (TV show)
172
Miller, Steve 150, 151
Miller's Reel (song) 185
Millet, Bill 373
Million Dollar Band 219,
220
Mills, Donna 128
Mills, Jerry 307
Milwaukee Festival
(event) 157
Minnesota Bluegrass
Festival (event) 285
Mish, Michael 271
Mishawaka (venue) 320
Mission Impossible
(movie) 88
Mississippi Sawyer (song) 5
Mitchell, Frank 7, 8, 9, 12

Mitchell, Jack 21
Mitchell, Joni 93
Mitchell, Leona 366
Mitchell, Mike 8
Mix, Tom 310
Miyazaki, Chiaki 341
Miyazaki, Katsuyuki 341
Moag, Rod 338
Mojave Narrows (venue)
269, 284
Mole Lake Indian Reser-
vation Festival (event)
253
Monkees, The (band) 147
Monkey Grip (song) 151
Monroe, Bill iii, ix, x,
xiv, xv, 39, 46, 47, 55,
56, 57, 58, 59, 60, 61, 62,
63, 65, 66, 78, 79, 81, 82,
84, 86, 95, 96, 116, 141,
146, 147, 151, 159, 167,
201, 221, 252, 259, 283,
287, 295, 296, 303, 304,
305, 308, 310, 313, 314,
326, 373, 383, 384
Monroe, Charlie 63
Monroe, James 47, 57, 58,
59, 62, 63, 64, 65, 66,
159, 305
Monroe's Hornpipe (song)
57
Montana and Lace 299,
304
Montana, Eddie 294, 299
Montana, Patsy vii, 177,
330,
Montes, Sarah 308
Montgomery Ward 2
Moonlight Motor Inn
(song) 258
Moore Burger 50
Moore, Dudley 271
Moore, John 207, 233, 245,
254, 255, 257, 268, 269,
270, 271, 272, 273, 278,
280, 286, 288, 292, 297,
298, 307, 308, 312, 340,
346, 354, 355, 364, 371,
373, 379
Moore, Julie 245
Moore, Mary Tyler (TV
show) 199
Moore, Minnie 129, 159
Moore, Tony 349, 371, 375

Moorhead, Agnes 128
More Than I Can Say
   (song) 178
Morgan, Tommy 255
Morrel, Tommy 318
Morton, Rick 314, 372
Mosebacke Establissement
   (venue) 162
Mosher, Becka 293
Mossman Guitars 129,
   130, 168, 179
Mossman, Martha 193
Mossman, Stuart 129, 130,
   131, 168, 179, 182, 193,
   199
Motor Coachers Show
   (event) 341
Mountain Smoke (band)
   374
Movie of the Week, (TV
   show) 83, 88, 99, 104,
   128, 131, 153, 296
Mowery, Glen 41, 44
Mozart 344, 346, 354, 357,
   360, 363, 365
Mr. Tambourine Man
   (song) 39
Muldaur, Maria 126
Mule Lip Saloon (venue)
   236, 241
Mule Skinner Blues (song)
   47, 58, 64
Mulroney, Ermot 291
Munde, Alan 43, 44, 71,
   72, 122, 123, 124, 125,
   128, 129, 134, 135, 137,
   138, 139, 140, 141, 142,
   145, 147, 151, 158, 160,
   161, 162, 197, 221, 224,
   228, 259, 269, 288, 331,
   338, 372, 374, 375
Munds, Ken 222, 321
Mundy, C.W. 190
Murcia, Joey 152
Murphy, Deanie 159
Murphy, Dudley 159
Murphy, M. 214, 224
Murphy, Michael 192
Murphy, Michael Martin
   192, 202, 322, 363
Murray, Ann 155, 285
Music From Bear Valley
   (event) 248

Music Hall Jam (event)
   314, 319, 321, 324, 328,
   329, 334
Mustang Club (venue) 212
My Baby's Gone (song) 160
My Dixie Darling (song)
   308
My Little Georgia Rose
   (song) 58
My Oklahoma (song) 153
My Sweet Blue-Eyed Darlin'
   (song) 283

N

Nacogdoches Festival
   (event) 242, 248
Nader, Ralph 46
NAMM (National As-
   sociation of Musical
   Merchandisers) 182,
   323, 331, 336, 339, 352
Napa Clarion Inn (venue)
   242
Napa Country Arts Coun-
   cil 242
Narrow Gate (band) 353
Nash, Gram 361
Nashville Banner, The
   (paper) 59, 60, 61
Nashville Brass (band)
   105, 106
Nashville Grass (band)
   128, 197
Nashville Rooms Concert
   (event) 148, 149
Nashville Symphony
   Quartet 59
Nashville West (venue)
   143
National Aviary 351, 352
National Cash Register
   Company 44
National Fiddlers Hall of
   Fame 383
National Flat-Picking
   Championship (event)
   198
National Indoor Track
   Meet (event) 241
National Old Time Fiddle
   Championship (Mis-
   soula, Montana) 35, 36

National Old Time Fiddle
   Championship
   (Weiser, Idaho) ix, x,
   24, 28, 29, 35, 36, 46,
   49, 82, 101, 102, 175,
   212, 376
National Rodeo Finals
   (event) 305
NBC (National Broadcast-
   ing Company) 29, 281,
   282
Neely, Ralph 27, 28
Nelson, Willie 153, 304,
   305, 326
Neon Armadillo (venue)
   265, 276, 278, 282, 295,
   296, 298
Nesmith, Michael 132,
   133, 146, 147, 155
Never Ending Love (song)
   160
Never Going Back (song)
   100
Neverly Hillbillies (band)
   364, 371
New Broom (song) 48, 185
New Christy Minstrels
   (group) 101
New Grass Revival (band)
   129, 197, 237
New Port Park (venue)
   271
New Riders of the Purple
   Sage (band) 124
Newkirk, El 213
Newman, Barry 104, 110,
Newman, Jimmy C. 76
Newman, Paul 111, 262
Newman, Randy 298
Newport Beach (venue)
   210
Newport Folk Festival
   (event) iii, x, 39, 41, 46,
   47, 55, 130
Newton, Juice 174
Nickel Creek (band) iv,
   95, 218, 296, 298, 300
Nickel Creek (song) 298
Nielsen, Leslie 151
Night Stalker (movie) 160
Night Strangler (movie)
   160
Nikas, Sue 284
Nitsik, Bob 271, 283

Nitty Gritty Dirt Band (Dirt Band) iii, xii, xiii, 95, 96, 113, 115, 155, 178, 186, 258, 369
No Hats Show 58
Noble, Lloyd 321
Noble, Nick 321
Norco Prado Park (venue) 242
North, Sheree 128
Northern Exposure (TV show) 199, 287, 288, 289, 291, 294, 297
Northwest Charity Horse Show (event) 204
Now We Are Four (album) 258, 263
Nu Gnu, The (venue) 186
Nugget (band) 338
Nutt, Word 155
Nuyen, Henry 317

O

O'Brien, Tim 237, 280, 311
O'Connor, Bob 283, 310
O'Connor, Brighton Drake Berline 375, 380, 382
O'Connor, Coralie Pearl 384, 383
O'Connor, Ginger Grace 383
O'Connor, Mark xi, 156, 167, 175, 196, 244, 287, 295, 314, 335, 374, 379
O'Neal, Jim 127
Oak Street Bar (venue) 167, 180
Oakland A's 302
Oakland Tribune 204
Oates, Warren 174
Oatman, Mike 20, 21,
OCU Oklahoma Central University (venue) 348
Odds and Ends (song) 145
Ode Records 101, 106
Odetta 95
Ogden, Sue 373
Oklahoma (play) 343
Oklahoma Arts Council 329
Oklahoma Arts Festival (event) 336
Oklahoma Centennial Parade 367

Oklahoma Centennial Show 368
Oklahoma Centennial Sounds Celebration 366
Oklahoma Centennial v, 363, 365
Oklahoma Christian College (event) 358, 365
Oklahoma City Arts Festival (event) 323, 336
Oklahoma City Bombing 356
Oklahoma City Christian Church 318, 338
Oklahoma City Civic Center Music Hall (venue) 173, 292, 323, 342,
Oklahoma City Heritage Foundation (event) 367
Oklahoma City Myriad Center (venue) 344
Oklahoma City Philharmonic 292, 336,
Oklahoma City Stockyards (venue) 330, 334, 342
Oklahoma City Will Rogers Park (venue) 324
Oklahoma City Zoo 319, 331, 335, 339, 342
Oklahoma Community Orchestra 358
Oklahoma Country Hall of Fame 380
Oklahoma Daily (OU paper) 33
Oklahoma Department of Tourism 326, 336, 338, 343, 344
Oklahoma Electric Co-Op (event) 346
Oklahoma Friendship Force 227
Oklahoma Governor Keating 343, 346
Oklahoma Hills (song) 23, 145
Oklahoma Historical Society 2
Oklahoma International Bluegrass Festival, (O.I.B.F.) iv, vii, 61, 209, 275, 320, 323, 326,

331, 332, 336, 338, 339, 342, 346, 348, 350, 351, 353, 355, 358, 364, 367, 370, 374, 378, 379, 383
Oklahoma Jamboree 41, 42, 43
Oklahoma Jazz Hall of Fame 357
Oklahoma Land Rush 1, 11, 257, 323, 329
Oklahoma Music Hall of Fame iv, 334, 336
Oklahoma Opry (venue) 357
Oklahoma Rising (song) 363, 366
Oklahoma Rural Water (event) 350
Oklahoma School of Science and Mathematics (event) 343, 348
Oklahoma State Song 318
Oklahoma State University (OSU) 11, 21, 22, 23, 25, 49, 69, 317, 322, 330, 336, 342, 365, 373, 374
Oklahoma Stomp (song) 201, 367
Oklahoma Swing (song) 368
Oklahoma Symphony Orchestra 172, 173
Oklahoma Territory 1, 11
Oklahoma Traditional Music Association (event) 331, 342, 347
Oklahoma Women (event) 353
Oklahoma Youth Symphony Orchestra 317
Old Logan (song) 48
Old Rugged Cross, The (song) 243
Old South Jamboree, (event) 81
Old Time Café (venue) 222, 224, 227, 228, 233, 235, 237, 241, 242, 244, 245, 249, 250
Old Time Music (magazine) 204
Olin, Ken 282
On and On (song) 203
One Cup Of Coffee (movie) 273

One Eyed Jack (song) 376
One Tear (song) 115
Onjes, Sam 130
Only Way Home (song) 160
Optometrists National
    Convention (event)
    365
Orange Blossom Special
    (song) 72, 79, 104, 109,
    146, 163, 182, 343
Orange Country Fair
    (event) 293, 298
Orange Country Festival
    (event) 169
Orick, Ken 251
Orlis, Will (RIP) 265
Osborne Brothers, (group)
    55
Other Woman's Child
    (play) 223, 224
Otis, Brooks 36
Outlaw Blues (album) 182
Outrageous (album) iv,
    201, 204
Over The Waves (song)
    354, 355
Owens, Buck 93, 162
Oxford Hotel (venue) 168,
    185
Ozark Jubilee 9
Ozark Mountain Daredev-
    ils (band) 153

P

Packer, Alfred 331
Paddy on the Turnpike
    (song) 38
Pahrump Bluegrass Festi-
    val (event) 342
Pain Down Deep (song) 145
Palace Hotel (venue) 35
Palladium Studio 338
Palmdale H. Saloon
    (venue) 269
Palomino (venue) iv, 136,
    147, 151, 160, 171, 174,
    175, 177, 181, 182, 184,
    185, 188, 189, 192, 193,
    194, 195, 196, 198, 199,
    206, 218, 232, 233, 242,
    245, 254, 255, 257, 262,
    265, 280, 282, 293
Palos Verdes City Hall
    (venue) 237

Panhandle Country (song)
    64
Para, Dave 343
Paralone, Jean 306
Park City, Utah Festival
    (event) 294
Park, Cary 271
Park, Larry 204, 265, 271
Parks, Michael 151, 181,
    329
Park, Ray 197, 204, 236,
    239, 265
Parker, Judge Isaac 11
Parmley, Don 146, 361
Parsons, Gene 87, 142, 153
Parsons, Gram iii, 90, 92,
    94, 96, 98, 100, 118, 122,
    127, 128, 133, 141, 142,
    145, 146, 147, 154, 163,
    300, 334
Parton, Dolly 180
Passin' By (song) 201
Past Tense (band) 331
Patsy Montana vii, 177,
    330
Patton, Barry 8, 129, 173,
    202, 208, 257, 294, 300,
    304, 309, 318, 322, 323,
    326, 331, 335, 336, 339,
    342, 343, 346, 350, 353,
    354, 355, 356, 357, 358,
    360, 364, 367, 368, 370,
    372, 374, 376, 379
Patton, Irvin 156
Patty, Sandi 380
Paul, Woody iv, 245, 249
Paulson, Pat 172
Pawhuska Fair (event) 331
Paxton, Tom 31, 95
Payne, Pat 318
Payne's Prairies State
    Preserve (venue) 363
Payton, Joe 129
PBS Public Broadcasting
    System 373
Pea Patch Quintet (band)
    353
Peach Pickin' Time Down in
    Georgia (song) 304
Pearlman, Dave (David)
    273, 281
Peckinpah, Sam 124
Pedersen, Herb xv, 108,
    112, 124, 138, 139, 140,

145, 154, 159, 242, 283,
    291, 298, 299, 300, 301
Peebles, Hap 44
Peninsula Music Fair
    (event) 199, 250
Penn, John Malcolm 283
Pennsylvania Polka (song)
    103
Penny, Hank 194
Perkins, Al 115, 116, 117,
    119, 120, 121, 125, 126,
    128, 145, 166, 235, 247,
    334
Perlman, Itzak 314
Perry, Billy 336, 339
Perry, Mike 348
Peter Britt Amphitheater
    (venue) 285
Peter, Paul and Mary
    (band) 30, 46
Petroleum Club (venue)
    336, 374
Philadelphia Folk Festival
    (event) 116
Phillips Academy (venue)
    119
Phillips, Jamie Lewis 129
Phillips, John 298, 299
Phoenix, River 291
Picket Fences (TV show)
    294
Pickin' n' Fiddlin' (album)
    x, xv, 33, 37, 38, 39, 46
Pickin' on Pink Floyd:
    A Bluegrass Tribute
    (album) 339
Pickins, Slim 187, 188
Pico Rivera Festival
    (event) 211
Pierce College (venue)
    270, 299
Pierce, Dale 330
Pierce, John 250, 262
Pierce, Lonnie 179
Pierce, Webb 79
Pikes Peak Center (venue)
    269
Pines Club (venue) 75
Pink Panther (movie) 111
Pinkard, Sandy 221
Pinnacle Boys (band) 197
Pistol Pete (Frank Eaton)
    11, 12, 199, 369, 370

Pittsburg State University 21
Place Where Love Comes From, The (song) 300
Place, Mary Kay iv, 177, 182, 187, 188
Plaid Family (band) 331
Plata, John 245, 246
Playboy After Dark (TV Show) 100
Plazzo's, Steven Birthday Party (event) 363, 366, 373, 379
Please Pass the Biscuits (song) 41, 42
Plotkin, Charles 126
Plumber, Kenny 13
Poco (band) 93
Podler, Richie 268
Point, The (movie) 99, 100, 108
Pointer, Sergeant John 70
Polansky, Roman 87
Polland, Pam 88
Polliwog Park (venue) 232, 252, 271, 279, 284, 294, 300
Poncan Theater (venue) 329, 334, 368
Pop Goes the Weasel (song) 10
Porterville Festival (event) 248
Poss, Barry 303
Post, Mike 159
Potter, Dale 9
Powder Horn Park Festival (event) 156
Powell, Susan 366
Prairie Home Companion (event) 323, 324
Preservation Playhouse (venue) 339
Presley, Elvis iv, 144, 154, 182, 186, 205, 314
Preston, Robert 124
Pretty Much Your Standard Ranch Stash (album) 132
Price, C. 269
Price, Gary 41, 42
Prince Charles 236
Prisoner's Song (song) 64
Pronker-Coron, Annemieke 363

Pryor, Richard 93
Puma, Tom 18, 34
Pumpkin Festival (event) 168, 169, 287
Pure Prairie League (band) 153, 174, 200, 220
Put my Rubber Doll Away (song) 64

Q

Quail Springs Bank (event) 346, 350, 352, 357, 363
Quantrill's Raiders 11
Quartz Mountain (venue) 319
Queen Mary Ship (venue) 273
Quicksilver (band) 232

R

R.F.D. Boys (band) 167, 197
Rader, Larry 309
Radisson Inn (venue) 323
Rafelson, Bob 163, 165
Ragtime Annie (song) 5, 20, 185, 280
Rainbow Garage Studio 307
Raindrops Keep Falling on My Head (song) 106
Rainman (movie) 302
Rains, Roger 21
Rampling, Charlotte 110
Rand, Joey 252
Randolph, Boots 103
Randy Lynn Rag (song) xii
Ranger Doug xv, 63
Rangers Waltz (song) 145
Raphael, Mickey 305
Rapid City Festival (event) 227
Rasmussen, Lindy 268, 307, 313
Rattlesnake Saloon (venue) 346
Rausch, Leon 318, 348, 351
Rawhide (song) 64, 72, 146
Rawhide (venue) 207, 208, 213, 255, 256
Ray, Bill 109

Ray, Will 260, 264, 269, 271, 273, 279, 280, 292, 294, 296, 297, 299, 304, 306, 308, 314
Raye, Susan 264
RCA, Radio Corporation of America 19, 132, 138, 162, 167, 169, 171, 244
Reagan, President Ronald 300
Rebannack, Mac 152
Rebel Rouser (song) 107
Record Plant (studio) 115
Rector, Bill 228
Recycler, The (paper) 275
Red Diamond Stradivarius v, 360, 362
Red Dirt Rangers (band) 342, 371, 374
Red Haired Boy (song) 203
Red Horse Inn (venue) 79, 81
Red Knuckles and the Trailblazers (band) 237
Red Rocking Chair (song) 174
Red Rocks Amphitheater (venue) 172
Red Wine (band) 371
Red, White and Bluegrass (band) 153, 155, 163
Redbird (song) 185
Redding Fiddle Contest (event) 233
Redford, Bob 130
Redondo Frontier (venue) 269
Red-White Alumni OU football game (event) 247
Reed, Ambassador 226
Reed, Colonel 71, 72, 73
Reed, Dennis 200
Reed, Jerry 96
Reed, M. 283
Reed, Roger 200, 220, 225, 226, 258, 299
Regents in Medicine Park, OK (venue) 335, 336, 338, 342
Reishman, John 280
Reivers, The, (movie) 87, 88, 190

Remick, Lee 111
Remington Park (venue) 331, 368
Reno Brothers (band) 323
Reno, Don 66, 212, 228, 230
Reprise Records 128
Retired Educator's Show (event) 329
Reynolds, Burt iv, 83, 183, 296
RFD (TV Network) 93
Rhode Island Cajun-Bluegrass Festival (event) 280
Rhodes, Red 146, 147, 155, 194
Rib Rack (venue) 217
Rice, Randy 303
Rice, Tony 142, 179, 186, 200, 228
Ricegrass Bluegrass Festival 375
Rich, Alan 283
Rich, Charlie 283
Richard, Frank 231
Richards, Ann 340
Richards, Jason 233, 242, 244, 248, 251, 252, 257, 258, 264, 292
Richards, Jenny 257, 272, 292
Richards, Keith 90, 91, 94
Richards, Rusty 233, 257, 258, 264
Riddle, John 360
Riders in the Sky (band) xv, 63, 236, 249
Rifleman (TV show) 226
Rifles for Watie (book) 49
Righteous Brothers (band) 277
Ringrose, Dr. Robert 258, 317
Rinzler, Ralph 39, 46, 95
Riopellle, Jerry 162
Rising Sun Records 122
Riverbend (band) 237
Riverfest (event) 225
Rivers, Jerry 79
Rivers, Johnny 139, 140, 174
Riverside Western Convention (event) 269

Riviera Hotel 103
Road Mangler Deluxe (book) 147
Roadmaster (album) 125
Roanoke (song) 203
Robbins, Butch 66
Robbins, Fred 81, 141, 379
Roberts, Rick 115, 117, 121, 122, 126, 127, 134, 137, 147, 150
Robertson, Eck x, 8, 19, 24, 46
Robertson, Robbie 168
Robinson Music Hall (venue) 224
Robinson, Judy (twin) 249
Roche, Louis 272
Rock and Roll Waltz (song) 103
Rockford Files (TV show) 199
Rockin' Acoustic Circus (band) 374
Rocky Mountain Bluegrass Festival (event) 147, 159, 221, 228, 232, 237, 352
Rocky Mountain Fiddle Camp (event) 357, 363, 366
Rocky Mountain Opera (venue) 211
Rocky Top (song) 81, 221
Rockys (venue) 316, 317, 320, 325, 328, 329, 330, 331, 333, 334, 335, 337, 338, 339, 348, 351
Rodeo Opry (venue) 334
Roelof, Jon 317
Rogers, Elliott 331
Rogers, Kenny and the Second Edition (band) 297
Rollin' in my Sweet Baby's Arms (song) 93, 312
Rolling Man (movie) 128, 131
Rolling Stones, The (band) iii, 81, 90, 91, 92, 93, 94, 151, 192, 341
Roly Poly (song) 307
Ronstadt, Linda 93, 96, 100, 112, 113, 114, 115, 122, 125, 126, 136, 138,

139, 154, 168, 288, 291, 360
Rook, Victor 337
Rookies, The (movie) 158, 159
Rooney, Jim 46, 48
Rose Maddox, $35 And a Dream (album) 300
Rose of Old Kentucky (song) 308
Rose State College (venue) 331
Rose, The (movie) iv, 189, 190
Rosemont School (event) 235
Roses for a Sunday Morning (song) 160
Rosmini, Dick 133
Rough, Jeff 255
Round Barn (venue) 335
Round Barn wedding (event) 335
Rounder Records 37, 140, 185
Roving Boy (band) 251
Rowan, Peter 47, 55, 56, 208
Roxy (venue) 177, 257, 349, 350
Royal Hawaiian Hotel 106
Run Simon Run, (movie) 83, 88, 104, 296
Runaway Country (song) 104, 278
Rural Rhythm Records 127
Russell, Leon 91, 152
Ryan, Terry 167
Rydell, Mark 88, 190, 191
Ryman Auditorium 55, 56

S

Sacramento Community Center Theater (venue) 173, 235
Sacramento Symphony 173, 192, 235, 262
Sad and Lonesome Day (song) 64
Saddle Bronc Club (venue) 206
Sailor's Hornpipe (song) 47
Sainte-Marie, Buffy 30

Saline Fiddlers (event) 292, 329

Sally Goodin' (song) xiv, 8, 19, 66, 113, 146, 160, 209, 311, 354

Sally Goodwin (song) ix

Sally Johnson (song) 39

Salty Dog (song) 312

Salty Licks (radio show) 348

Sammy Davis Festival Plaza (venue) 293

San Diego Acoustic Music Series (event) 362

San Diego Folk Festival (event) 197

San Diego Harvest Festival (event) 239

San Diego Rodeo (event) 270

San Fernando Valley xiii, 3, 90, 108, 168, 217, 270, 361

San Francisco Giants 302

San Jose Old Fiddlers (venue/event) 303

San Luis Obispo Festival (event) 264

San Mateo Fair (event) 114

Sandhofen, Ingo 346

Sands Hotel 103

Santa Ana (song) 259

Santa Anita Racetrack (venue) 138

Santa Barbara Live Oak Festival (event) 272

Santa Barbara Zoo (venue) 270

Santa Fe Bluegrass Festival 331

Santa Margarita Rodeo (event) 278

Santa Monica Hall (venue) 279

Santa Monica Jazz and Folk Festival (event) 279

Sarafian, Richard C. 104

Sasquatch (song) 283

Saturday Night (song) 145

Saw Grass Fiddle Contest (event) 363

Sawtelle, Charles 280

Scarberry, Terry 334

Schneider, Harold 163

Scholoker, John 256

Schuwer, Sari Martin 163

Schwartz, David 287

Schwarzenegger, Arnold iii, 162, 163, 166, 182, 189, 190, 280, 288

Scissors, Paper & Stone (song) 283

Scotland iv, 206, 212, 364

Scott, Jim 271

Scottish Rite Temple (venue) 323, 326

Scottsville Squirrel Barkers (band) 112

Scruggs, Earl iv, v, 5, 16, 55, 96, 112, 119, 210, 215, 219, 220, 292, 296, 303, 304, 305, 326, 348, 372, 373, 374

Scruggs, Gary 112

Scruggs, Randy 112, 304, 305

Scruggs, Steve 112, 215

Sears and Roebuck 2

Second Fiddle (song) 208, 307

Seeger, Mike 46, 236

Seeger, Pete 30, 31, 46, 95

Segal, Lloyd 168

Seldom Scene (band) 167, 232, 233

Serenata Farms Bluegrass Festival (event) 331

Seven Stories (movie) 268

Shannon, Del 122

Shannon, Harry 213, 228, 241, 268, 270, 276, 277, 284

Share, Catherine "Gypsy" 98, 99

Sharp, Richard 320, 325, 334, 343, 357, 364, 366, 367, 370, 376

Sheffield Direct to Disk v, 179, 187, 369

Shelton, Alan 81

Shelton, C. 368

Shelton, Ed 42, 43, 44, 45, 81, 129, 288

Sherman Oaks Presbyterian Church 90, 211, 218, 308

Sherman Oaks Presbyterian Church Quartet 308

Sherman, Michael 97

Shetland Islands Fiddle Festival (event) 247

Shiffrin, Lalo 88

Shindler's List (movie) 88

Shocked, Michelle 281

Short, Steve 222, 320, 321, 324, 334, 349, 367, 370, 373, 376

Show Biz Pizza Place 126

Shrine Auditorium (venue) 189

Shrine Temple (venue) 318

Sifra, Jody 159

Siggins, Bob 46

Silver Bullet (venue) 265, 268, 269, 270, 271, 272, 273, 274, 275, 277, 278, 280, 281, 282, 283, 284, 287, 289, 290, 292, 293

Silver Saddle (venue) 217

Silver Threads with Golden Needles (song) 113

Silverman, Jay 256, 289

Simple Truth (song/album) 251

Sin City (song) 300

Sinatra, Nancy 107

Sing Out (magazine) 39

Sioux City Sue (song) 4

Sioux Falls, S.D. Fair (event) 339

Sitting on Top of the World (song) 203

Six Days on the Road (song) 118

Skaggs, Ricky 201, 202, 204, 210, 326, 351, 357

Skiatook Bluegrass Festival 363, 366

Skinner, Jack 167, 169, 173, 175, 176, 177, 178, 189, 308

Skippin' Along on Top (song) 307

Skippin' Around (song) 201

Sklar, Leland 125, 126, 139, 177, 205, 291

Skyline Studios 312

Skywalker Ranch/ Sound 291

Sleepin' at the Foot of the Bed (song) 42

Sloan, Bruce 156
Smiling Dog Saloon
  (venue) 147
Smith, Arthur 46
Smith, Craig 190, 352
Smith, Duane 152
Smith, Richard 374
Smith, Ted 204
Smith, William 152
Smits, Jimmy 282
Smoak, Jim 79
Smoke Eye (venue) 230
Smoke, Smoke, Smoke That
  Cigarette (song) 209
Smokey and the Bandit
  (movie) 183, 296
Smothers Brothers 31, 103,
  111, 160, 161, 172, 173,
  228, 251
Smothers, Dick 172
Smothers, Tommy 172
Snow, Bill 41, 42, 43, 330
Snowbird (song) 155, 285
Snyder, D.C. 264
Sod House Museum 2
Solomon, Mike 20
Solomon, Norman x, 19
Solomon, Rickie 20
Solomon, Vernon x, 19
Solvang (event) 284
Some Velvet Morning
  (song) 107
Somebody Touched Me
  (song) 47
Something's Missing (song)
  145
Sometimes a Great Notion
  (movie) 111
Song, Jing Q. 355
Sonje, Jo El' iv, 210, 229,
  230, 231, 233, 235
Sonoma-Marin Fair 40
Sons of the Pioneers
  (band) 233
Sooner Scandals, (event)
  33
Soppin' the Gravy (song) 39
Sousaphone 16, 17, 70, 231
South Plains College 224,
  265, 312
Southern Bluegrass Boys
  (band) 77, 78,198
Southern Pacific Railroad
  258, 278, 279

Southern, Hal 210
Southwest Bluegrass Club
  269
Spark's Nugget Inn
  (venue) 109
Speak Softly You're Talking
  to My Heart (song) 259
Spicer, Buddy 253
Spidien, Jan 344
Spokane Opera House
  (venue) 208, 235
Spontaneous Combustion
  (band) 331
Spree '77 Park Concert
  (event) 185
Spreen, Glen 284
Spurgin, Steve xiii, 202,
  203, 206, 210, 211, 257,
  258, 259, 260, 261, 262,
  263, 264, 270, 271, 272,
  273, 278, 283, 286, 307,
  312, 354, 357, 364, 371,
  373, 379
Spurs (song) 283
Stage 5 (venue) v, 365, 367
Stallone, Frank 273
Stallone, Sylvester 273
Stampede (song) 201
Stampeders (band) 135
Stane, Bob 103, 108
Stanley, Ralph 95, 159, 213
Stanton, Harry Dean 82,
  86, 89, 190, 191
Stanton, Michael 230, 233,
  243, 272, 277, 279, 280,
  284
Stanwick, Barbara 280
Star Wars (movie) 88
Stardust (venue) 211
Starland Vocal Band
  (band) 138
Starlight (venue) 293
Starlight Theater (venue)
  220, 232
Starr, Kay 96, 103, 104,
  105, 106, 107, 109, 111,
  112, 145
Starsky and Hutch (TV
  show) 170
Station Inn (venue) 220,
  280, 339, 352
Statman, Andy 369
Sauber, Tom 159
Stauffer, Virginia 63

Stay Hungry (movie) 163,
  164, 165, 166, 167, 168,
  174, 182, 189, 202, 231
Stealing Second (album)
  298
Steamboat Village Inn
  (venue) 186
Steele, Jeff 271
Stegall, Red 252
Stein, Andy 323, 324
Steve Miller Band 150, 151
Stevens, Sally 284
Stevenson, Steve 361
Stewart, Joe 62
Stewart, Rod 174, 213
Stewart, Travis 77, 81
Still Feeling Blue (song) 163
Stills, Stephen 91, 114, 119,
  120, 121, 123, 125, 127,
  132, 151
Stillwater Agriculture
  (event) 359
Sting Ray (movie) 190
Stockdale, G. 302
Stone Mountain Boys
  (band) 44, 64, 66, 71,
  73, 78, 79, 81, 129, 288
Stone Poneys 168
Stone, Cliffie 145, 251, 304
Stone, Sharon 277
Stone, Steve 244
Stone's Rag (song) iv, 241,
  242, 243
Stoneman, Scotty 37
Stoops, Glen 339
Stoops, Rick 339
Stork, Duane 294
Storm Over Oklahoma
  (song) 175
Stover, Don 197
Strad Museum 345
Stradivarius v, 345, 360,
  361, 362, 379
Straight Life, The (song)
  178
Strawberry Festival
  (event) 221, 228, 232,
  237, 262, 294
Strings on Fire (event) 114
Strongbow xiii
Stroud, Don 128
Strueble, Larry 9, 254
Stuart, Chad 99
Stuart, Marty 128, 219

Sugar Hill Records 200, 203, 243, 283, 303, 312
Sugar in The Gourd (song) 243
Sullivan, Ed (TV show) 9
Sullivan, Gene 41
Sulphur Days (event) 335
Sultan, Kenny 252, 275, 357
Summer Breeze Concert (event) 346, 370
Summer Grass Festival 363
Summer Pop Series (event) 271
Summer's Song, A (song) 99
Sumner County Fair 6, 324, 370
Sun Valley Festival (event) 294
Sundance iii, 162, 163, 167, 168, 169, 170, 171, 172, 173, 174, 175, 176, 177, 178, 179, 180, 181, 182, 184, 185, 186, 187, 188, 189, 190, 191, 192, 193, 196, 199, 200, 202, 203, 206, 208, 210, 211, 212, 213, 215, 217, 218, 220, 222, 223, 228, 241, 257, 258, 259, 312
Sundance Saloon (venue) 157, 163, 188, 192, 196
Sunday Sunrise (song) 160
Surreal Thing (album) 176
Sutton, Brian 60, 61
Swallows Inn (venue) 213, 215, 221, 223, 224, 228, 229, 256, 258
Swan, Billy 273, 283
Sweet Adelines (group) 322
Sweet City Woman (song) 135
Sweet Memory Waltz (song) 308
Sweet, Matthew 291, 299
Sweethearts of the Rodeo (band) 174
Sweetwater Café (venue) 174, 301
Swing Low Sweet Chariot (song) 64

Switzer, Barry 343
SXSW (South by Southwest) (event) 277

T

Taffy, Tom 227
Taj Mahal (band) 95
Take a Load Off Annie (song) 369
Take Me in Your Lifeboat (album) 172
Tanaka, Robert 197, 202
Tapia, William 277
Tashian, Barry 128
Tate, Sharon 87
Taupin, Bernie 253
Taylor, Baxter 31
Taylor, Dallas 120, 126, 152, 175, 177
Taylor, James 181
Taylor, Keith 301
Teach Your Children (song) 153
Teeter, Don 33
Tejas Vaqueros (see Texas Trail Ride) (event) 254, 364
Telluride Bluegrass Festival (event) 185, 197, 242, 248, 299
Terry, George 152
Texas Bluegrass Association 316
Texas Cattlemen's Association (event) 340
Texas Music Extravaganza (event) 373
Texas Playboys (band) 250, 318, 351
Texas Shorty v, 19, 35, 372, 374
Texas Trail Ride (event) iv, 251, 253, 254, 271, 301, 321, 331, 357, 364, 366, 370
The Band (band) 170
The Men, (group) 40
The Thing Called Love (movie) 291
Theil, Bruno 346
Theobald, Jack 13, 129
Theobald, Mike 129
Therapeutic Equestrian Academy (venue) 331

These Boots are Made for Walkin' (song) 107
They Don't Play George Jones on MTV (song) 259
Thibodeaux Civic Center (venue) 203
Thiele, Chris 298
Thirtysomething (TV show) 282
Thom, Betty 79, 202
Thom, Harold 79, 202
Thomas, Doug 243
Thomas, Guthrie 170, 171, 176
Thomas, Kit 210, 215, 291
Thomas, Tommy 194, 206
Thomasson, Benny x, 8, 19, 156
Thompson, Bruce 374
Thompson, Hank 23, 252
Thompson, Luke 81
Three on a String (band) 167
Through The Morning, Through The Night, (album) 82, 83
Tickner, Eddie 39, 97, 121, 124, 139, 140, 141, 154, 162
Tidal School Vineyards (venue) 357
Tie a Yellow Ribbon (song) 145
Tillis, Mel 76
Tilton, Linda 331
Time Changes Everything (song) 243
Timex (band) 373
TNN, The Nashville Network 237, 304
To Prove my Love to You (song) 160
Toet, Barend 134
Tom and Jerry (song) 36, 38
Tomlin, Lilly 103
Tomlin, S. 316
Tonight Show, The (TV show) 29, 30
Topanga Skyline (song/album) 142, 145
Tory Pines Golf Course 237

Tower, The (venue) 144,
150, 151
Train of Memory (song) 258
Traitor in our Midst (album) iii, 123, 124, 125,
126, 131, 134, 149, 163
Transatlantic Records 160
Trapezoid (band) 236
Traveler (album) iv, 282,
283
Travolta, John 202
Triggs, Jim xi
Trio Records 160
Troubadour (venue) 40,
92, 93, 112, 113, 115,
139, 155, 176, 180, 181,
182, 184, 244, 293, 361
Truckee Festival (event)
186
Tubb, Ernest 190
Tucker, Don 352, 369
Tucson Community Arts
Center (venue) 233
Tucson Festival 243
Tugboat (song) 243
Tulagi's Club (venue) 116
Tulsa Chili Cook Off
(event) 264, 286, 294,
313
*Tulsa County Blues aka
Tulsa County* (song) 88
Turn of the Century
(venue) 228
Turnbow, Jay 243
Tutt, Ronnie 128
Twentieth Century Fox
128, 133, 188, 207
Twinkle, Twinkle (song) 38
Two Pair (band) 337
Tyler Sports Arena
(venue) 351
Tyner, Dick 218
Tyson, Ian 130

U

UC Irvine Festival (event)
193, 215
UC Riverside Barn
(venue) 250, 168, 174,
176, 187, 193, 213, 248,
250
UCA San Diego (venue)
133

Uncle Charlie and His
Dog Teddy (album)
xii, 95
Uncle Dave Macon 353
Uncle John O'Neal (album) 127
Uncle Pen (song) 61, 201,
202, 203, 283, 313, 356
Union College (venue) 118
United Artists Records iii,
123, 124, 126, 141, 148,
162, 174
Universal 160, 188, 293,
306, 204, 293, 306
Universal Soldier (movie)
284
Universal Soldier (song) 30
University of Evansville
(Indiana) 53
University of Kansas
(KU) 21, 34
University of Oklahoma
(OU) iii, iv, viii, x, 21,
22, 23, 25, 26, 27, 28, 29,
30, 31, 33, 34, 38, 41, 46,
48, 49, 50, 51, 53, 55, 69,
76, 122, 192, 247, 296,
307, 310, 318, 320, 321,
334, 338, 340, 351, 352,
358, 365, 374, 380
University of Maryland
(venue) 120
University of Tulsa Football Stadium (venue)
350
*Until It's Time for You to
Go* (song) 30
Untitled Artspace Gallery
(venue) 368
Urban Cowboy (album)
288, 304
Urban Cowboy (movie)
202
USIS United States
Information Services
225, 260
USOOC Olympic Village
232
Utal, Bobby 287
Utley, Mike 199

V

Valley River Center
(venue) 174
Van Damme, Jean-Claude
284
Van Houten, Leslie 98
Vancouver Folk Music
Festival (event) 236,
249
Vanguard Records 269
Vanilla Fudge (band) 107
Vanishing Point (movie)
104, 110, 278
Variety (paper) 104
Vaudeville Express Melodrama Theater (venue)
279, 293
Vault Records xi, 104
Verch, April 364
Vest, Allan 380
Victorian Walk (event)
328, 380
Villa, Vittorio 345
Village Voice (paper) 146
Villaume 345
Villegas, Joe 179, 187, 200
Vincent, Rhonda 364
Vint, Alan 128
Vinton, Bobby 269, 270,
277
Violin Society of America
322, 340, 344, 347, 355
Virgin Records 271
Virgin River Inn (venue)
272
Virginia Boys (band) 128
Virginia Darlin' (song) xi
Virginia River Inn (venue)
314
Vista Pizza (venue) 231
Voice Stream 327
Vola, Francois 210
Von Netzer, Lieutenant
Garet 76
Voyager Records 35

W

Wabash Cannonball (song)
71, 72, 107
Wagner, Lindsey 100
Wagoner (song) 38
Wagoner, Porter 9
Wakeman, Dusty 303

Walch, Rob 211
Wald, Alan 129, 169, 187
Walden, Dana 291, 294, 295, 316
Waldman, Wendy 126
Walecki, Fred 108, 174, 181, 360, 361, 362
Walecki, Herman 360, 362
Walk in the Irish Rain (song) iv, 256, 260, 283, 311
Walk Right Back (song) 178
Walker House of Lights (TV show) 43, 319
Walker, Ally 284
Walker, Cas 219, 220
Walker, Clint 127
Walker, Ebo 129
Walker, Jerry Jeff 220
Walker, Wiley 41, 42
Wall of Time (song) 47
Wallace, Benny 262, 264
Walnut Valley Festival (event) 128, 129, 130, 179, 213, 228, 233, 238, 243, 249, 254, 264, 272, 284, 294, 302, 313, 321, 325, 336, 339, 342, 346, 350, 353, 364, 366, 370
Waltz to Wesphalia (movie) 287
Wannberg, Ken 128
Wanzer, Lloyd 29
Ward, Bob 25, 26
Ward, Dee Dee 282
Ward, Sam 292
Warner Brothers Records 119, 120, 126, 139, 141, 142, 147, 154, 155, 170, 191, 199, 207, 211, 217, 244, 247, 280, 297, 308
Warner's Center (venue) 293
Warren, Floyd 284
Warren, Johnny 215
Warren, Paul1 28, 215
Washburn University 21
Washburn, Donna 84, 85, 86
Washington Daily News 117
Washington House (dormitory) 23, 49
Washington Park Zoo (venue) 285

Washinton State Festival (event) 301
Wasner, Pete 203, 206, 312
Water Works (event) 358
Watkins, Sara 218, 298
Watkins, Scott 298
Watkins, Sean 218, 298
Watson boys 2
Watson, Chad 262, 272, 299, 308
Watson, Dale 256, 298
Watson, Doc 39, 95, 129, 130, 206, 237, 292
Watson, Merle 129, 237, 292
Watts, Charlie 91
Way Out West (TV show) 237
WE FIVE (band) xi, 100, 104, 162
Wear, John 168
Weary Blues From Waitin' (song) 258
Weather Center Opening (event) 365
Weaver, Dennis 128, 198, 206
Weaver, Robbie 198
Weaver, Smiley 349
Weavers, The (band) 96
Webb, Alan 350, 357
Webb, Bill 269
Webb, Dean 32, 37, 39, 40
Webb, Jimmy 291, 363, 366
Weber, Red Dog 167
Weddington Studios 243
Weed, Joe 287
Weisshaar, Hans 362
Weitzman, Steve 144
Welcome Home Soldier Boys (movie) 125, 128
Wells, Dick 264
Wells, Kitty 9, 62
Were You There? (song) 308
Wernick, Peter 298
Werts, Diane 331
Werts, Kelly 331
Wertz, Kenny 112, 115, 117, 119, 121, 122, 124, 129, 134, 135, 137, 142
West Union High School 53

West, Shelly 221
Western Swing Show (event) v, 348, 349, 357, 363, 365, 363, 373, 375
Western Union (telegram) 21
Westerner Ballroom (venue) 43
Weston, Doug 93, 182
Westphalia Waltz (song) 287
Wewoka Festival (event) 339
Whaley, Don 203, 206, 312
Wheel Hoss (song) 356
Wheel of Fortune (song) 103, 104, 106
When My Blue Moon Turns to Gold Again (song) 41, 64
Whiplash (song) 283
White Rose Studio 320
White, Buck 210
White, Clarence iii, 37, 64, 87, 88, 90, 95, 108, 122, 133, 134, 138, 139, 140, 141, 142, 143, 144, 145, 147, 154, 161, 170, 176, 309, 373
White, Craig 320
White, Eric 138, 139, 141, 153
White, Gary 292
White, Roland 37, 64, 65, 66, 108, 128, 138, 139, 140, 141, 143, 144, 145, 146, 151, 158, 160, 162, 170, 185, 197, 221, 228, 339, 352
White, Susie 145
Whites, The (Buck, Sharon, Cheryl) (band) 203, 326
Whites, The (Roland, Eric, Clarence) (band) 108, 138, 139, 140, 141
Whitten, Bobby 76
WHN 153
WHO (band) 90
Wicher, Gabe 299
Wichita State University 21
Wicked Path of Sin (song) 138

Wilcox Gay 13, 370
Wild Fire (song) 202
Wild Horse Saloon
  (venue) 313
Wild Horses (song) 94
Wild John (song) 38
Wild Life Bar-B-Que
  (event) 330
Wild Oats (band) 97, 192,
  203, 245
Wild West (TV show) 287
Wilders (band) 331
Wildlife Picnic (event)
  335, 351
Wilkins, George 231, 252
Wilkinson, Bud 23, 25, 26,
  27, 28, 33, 34, 49
Wilkinson, Mary 34
Will Rogers Airport
  (venue/event) 344
Will Rogers Park 324
Will the Circle be Unbroken
  (song) 369
Will you be Lonesome Too
  (song) 160
Williams, Andy 192
Williams, Benny 58, 59, 62
Williams, Clayton 340
Williams, Hank 75
Williams, Hank, Jr. 78
Williams, John 88, 89
Williams, Lucinda 270
Williams, Mason xvi, 31,
  138, 160, 172, 173, 174,
  175, 177, 181, 184, 185,
  186, 189, 192, 197, 199,
  202, 203, 204, 207, 208,
  211, 212, 213, 217, 220,
  224, 225, 228, 232, 233,
  235, 242, 249, 253, 254,
  262, 268, 271, 273, 279,
  284, 285, 286, 289, 290,
  292, 293, 307, 308, 310,
  317, 320, 321, 326, 336,
  343, 358, 365, 368, 371
Williams, Phil 35
Williams, Robin and
  Linda (group) 323

Williams, Tex iv, 145, 206,
  209
Williams, Tootie 44, 71,
  72, 79, 81, 129, 288
Williams, Vivien 35
Williamson, Al 17
Williamson, Poly Lewis
  129
Willow Garden (song) 138
Willow Weep for Me (song)
  99
Wills, Bob 5, 201, 250, 318,
  336, 338, 342, 348, 349,
  357
Wilson, Dennis 87
Wilson, Jeff 308
Windmills (album) 126,
  127
Winger, Debra 202
Wingfield, Julie 258, 285
Winkler, Ray 258
Winnipeg Festival (event)
  242
Winter Grass (event) 317,
  362
Winter Park Resort
  (venue) 211
Winterhawk (event) 285
Wise, Chubby 311
Wiseman, Mac 95
Withers, Bill 175
WKRP in Cincinnati (TV
  show) 199
Wolf, Fred 99
Women Executives
  (event) 340
Women's NCAA World
  Series Softball Cham-
  pionship (event) 352
Wood, Bob 44, 310, 313,
  314, 315, 316, 318, 319,
  321, 322, 330, 333, 334,
  339, 341
Woodring, Sonny 41,
  42, 43
Wooley, Sheb 44
World Pacific Studios 39
World Series 1989 302, 303
World War II 260, 261, 316
World's Fair (event) 218

Wright, Betty 152
Wright, Johnny 62
Wronski, Lukas 379
Wyman, Bill 91, 151
Wynette, Tammy 93, 207,
  296
Wyoming Cowboys 11

Y

Yamaha (commercial) 212
Yarrow, Peter 31
Yearwood, Howard 216,
  225, 264
Yesterday's Gone (song) 99
Yo Yo Man (song) 173
Yoakam, Dwight 252, 253
Yohee, Bill 29, 36, 46, 102
York, John 88
York, Paul 133
You are My Sunshine
  (song) 263
You Bet Your Life (TV
  show) iv, 201, 205
*You Were on my Mind (well
  I woke up this mornin')*
  (song) 100
*You're the Reason God
  Made Oklahoma* (song)
  221, 247
Young, Neil 93
Youngblood, Duane 36
Youngblood, Rick 378
Yount, Jay 129
Your Cheatin' Heart (song)
  145
Youtube 93, 118, 215, 251,
  295
Yucaipa Festival (event)
  272
Yukon City Park (event)
  373

Z

Zen Crook Festival (event)
  188
Zoo Grass Series (event)
  284

CPSIA information can be obtained
at www.ICGtesting.com
Printed in the USA
LVHW040017010622
720138LV00010B/1044